Humanism and History

HUMANISM
AND HISTORY

*Origins of Modern
English Historiography*

JOSEPH M. LEVINE

Cornell University Press

Ithaca and London

First published 1987 by Cornell University Press.

International Standard Book Number 0-8014-1885-2
Library of Congress Catalog Card Number 86–16776
Printed in the United States of America
Librarians: Library of Congress cataloging information
appears on the last page of the book.

The paper in this book is acid-free and meets the guidelines for
permanence and durability of the Committee on Production Guidelines
for Book Longevity of the Council on Library Resources.

For DeeDee

Contents

Preface

The following essays might well be allowed to speak for themselves; each was certainly intended for a separate occasion and meant to be self-sufficient. Nevertheless I have brought them together here, despite their apparent diversity, because they share a common preoccupation and help to contribute to a larger story. In order to suggest something of their coherence, I have revised the essays a bit and rearranged them in an order different from the one in which they were first composed. Since the argument may appear new to many and the links are not always explicit, I shall begin by setting it out plainly here, fitting each essay into its larger context and hoping to forestall some of the more obvious objections. If the result continues to show some evident seams, it will, I hope, be sufficient to furnish a reasonably tidy and persuasive account of the subject.

The chief question that I have thought to address in these essays is how and why English historiography found its modern method. And the answer that I propose is that it was principally, though by no means only, due to the influence of Renaissance humanism. To be sure, this is an old idea that would certainly have been endorsed during the period itself, and it is familiar enough to students of continental European scholarship. Why, then, has it failed to find much favor on the English scene? The answer, I suppose, lies partly in the indifference to humanism of many English scholars who have viewed it as an extraneous foreign import grafted onto a pure and indigenous English culture; even more in the open hostility of those formidable critics, from John Ruskin to C. S. Lewis, who have been eager to attack it on aesthetic and sometimes religious grounds; above all, perhaps, in the continuous antipathy of medievalists, who have been naturally resentful of the extravagant claims made during the Renaissance and ever afterward for the novelty and achievement of the new culture and for the darkness and barbarism of the old.

Undoubtedly, there is some justice to each of these contentions, and it would be foolish to claim that humanism was an unmixed blessing either for English culture or for the development of modern historiography; it would certainly be wrong to think of it as an entirely progressive movement. In fact, I have been at pains in these essays to show how humanism acted as both an incentive *and* an inhibition to the development of modern historiography. And since I do not see why the prejudice either for or against humanism should be allowed to exaggerate or to obscure its undoubted influence on the history of English ideas, it will be the chief purpose of these essays to describe something of what happened in that long series of encounters between antiquity and the modern world which began in the sixteenth and culminated in the eighteenth century.[1]

What then was humanism? The term itself is anachronistic, though its roots lie deep in the period, and there has been much controversy as to how it should be used. According to its most influential modern student, Paul Oskar Kristeller, humanism was a cultural and educational program with a special literary preoccupation, a recapitulation of the ancient *studia humanitatis* with its particular cycle of disciplines: grammar, rhetoric, history, poetry, and moral philosophy.[2] According to C. S. Lewis, who takes it more generally, a humanist was "one who taught or at least learned or strongly favored Greek and the new kind of Latin," and humanism was simply the outlook that normally accompanied those studies.[3] Either way, Lewis was undoubtedly right to add that humanism was the first form of classicism, a notion that has sometimes been obscured by the separation of cultural history into arbitrary subdivisions. From that perspective, the years between 1500 and 1800 can be seen as forming a single period, harboring at least one common set of assumptions and habits of mind which acted continuously upon the thought of the time. Those habits and assumptions were deeply rooted in English culture by a nearly uniform education that imposed the Latin and Greek classics on almost every English schoolboy, an education that was devised by the humanists and continued by their successors to meet what were generally (and I think realistically) seen to be the practical needs of the governing classes. The outlook of the age of Burke and Pitt and Fox, of Samuel Johnson and Edward Gibbon, was in some respects the natural culmination of a movement begun three centuries before. But where Lewis was exclusively concerned with the literary manifestations of the new culture, with its insistence upon the imitation of classical language and form, I shall concentrate instead upon the process of recovery, the "revival of antiquity" that accompanied it, and upon the many incidental and sometimes unintended consequences that this process had for historiography.[4]

Unfortunately, explanation in history (like explanation everywhere else) threatens an infinite regress, and it is hard to know just how to make a proper beginning except by plunging *in medias res*. In my first essay, entitled "Caxton's Histories," I have tried to set the scene for the coming of humanism by looking intently at that last medieval generation before the "revival" began. Unhappily, the modern study of late medieval historiography is surprisingly spare, and the particular problem that I wished to solve—that is, what was the method of fifteenth-century historical writing and what therefore was the distinction, if any, that the period made between history and fiction—proved to be very elusive. Apparently neither the idea of history nor the idea of fiction had ever been adequately described for those years, much less the complex and intricate relations between the two. Moreover, it was hard to do justice to the subject and avoid making anachronistic judgments when the principal purpose of the effort was to lay a proper groundwork for subsequent events, to call attention to what the fifteenth century did *not* do as well as to what it did. But how else could one attempt to measure the special humanist contributions of a later time? It was a while before I found a way to come at the problem, to contrive a means of generalizing about a complex set of ideas and materials (much richer than I had anticipated) without either oversimplifying or distorting the situation. It was only by recognizing a unique opportunity in the publications of the first English printer, William Caxton, who had set out deliberately to satisfy his own audience with a representative sample of the best literature of his time, that I found my key.

Caxton was no theorist, but he supplied enough commentary for his printed books to reveal his assumptions—and presumably those of his audience—about their content. By examining all his published works, including some very unlikely "histories," I have been able to confirm the conventional view (often contested and never very well documented) that fifteenth-century writers were usually unwilling and largely unable to make a clear distinction between fact and fiction, either in theory or in practice (though they sometimes attempted it), and that their various methods of reconstructing the past produced a history very different from our own. Caxton and his contemporaries accepted and embroidered an elaborate body of legend, both sacred and secular, and did not seek to differentiate between romance and chronicle or between past and present. The Trojan heroes and Christian saints who helped to populate the first printed books were often entirely imaginary and were almost always portrayed as contemporaries. Caxton understood history primarily as edification, and he did not bother to make distinctions that had no obvious value. This was the view that the English humanists inherited—and gradually transformed.

Not that Caxton and his friends were always indifferent to matters of fact; on one occasion, at least, the printer raised or resumed a question that troubled him and later generations: were the stories about King Arthur and the knights of the Round Table historically true? Since the question persisted for several generations, it is possible to compare Caxton's views with those of the humanists who followed and see just what it was that the new culture had to offer in these matters. In the event, the Arthurian tales, with much else in the traditional history, were soon consigned to legend, as history and fiction began to part company in practice and in theory. Here, then, is a first example of the new scholarship and the new outlook toward the past that it carried with it.

For my next essay, I have retrieved an earlier article in which I reviewed one of the most celebrated events of modern historiography: the unmasking of the *Donation of Constantine* as a forgery. Here again it is possible to compare the different techniques of the two cultures by comparing the efforts of two men who sought almost simultaneously and independently to expose it. The first was another fifteenth-century Englishman, Reginald Pecock, living in a world still largely indifferent to the classics and unaware of the possibilities of humanist criticism, a professional theologian who attempted to use the methods of scholastic logic to make his case. The second was a fifteenth-century Italian, Lorenzo Valla, a humanist who extended the possibilities of the new philological discipline beyond anything known before. Scholastic logic was not the usual instrument of medieval historiography, and the late medieval philosophers (like many of our own) were generally neglectful of, if not altogether hostile to, the pretensions of history. In this exceptional instance, Pecock got the "right" answer by using the "wrong" method, and his effort only serves to confirm the fact that deductive logic had little to offer historiography, then or now. Valla, on the other hand, is usually (and correctly) assumed to have gotten the right answer by a method somewhat akin to our own, although he too was limited by the polemical purposes of his tract and by the preliminary character of his undertaking.[5] However, in the notion of Valla and the humanists that a whole culture had been lost and could be recovered; in their belief that language was the key but like everything else was subject to fundamental change; and, above all, in the methods they devised to effect their purpose—in all this lay the future of modern historiography.[6]

What was required, of course, was to extend this rather narrow beginning from a special problem in ancient history and to continue to improve upon the techniques that had originated in classical grammar so that the entire range of evidence about the past could be exhumed and evaluated—things as well as words, monuments as well as texts, thoughts as well as deeds. In the next two essays I have indicated some of the ways in which this happened. The study of "antiquities" was the Renaissance equivalent of archaeology, the material accompaniment of philology, and in the first of these two chapters I have tried to trace the enormous effort that was made over three centuries to recover the monumental and textual evidence of the English past. I have tried to portray the antiquarian enterprise as a whole (something that I do not think has ever been attempted)[7] in order to show the relationships that existed among scholars working to recover the Roman, Celtic, Norman, and even Greek remains; and to suggest that the methods that they employed and developed throughout the period took continual sustenance from classical scholarship and learning. I have also tried to show what is less obvious, that the same classical inspiration that gave birth to the undertaking proved also to be its limitation, that the modern sense of the past was inhibited from maturing completely in these centuries by the very priority that was always given to classical antiquity. If the humanists first rescued the ancients from obscurity and gave them a genuine historical character, they also tended to idealize them and thus paradoxically to remove them from history and give them a sort of timeless status. Moreover, the humanists, in their reverence for antiquity, continued to write their ordinary history in direct imitation of the classics as a branch of rhetoric, often heedless of the new methodology of the antiquaries and unwilling or unable to incorporate their results. I have explored this peculiar and self-conscious dichotomy among the exponents of classical learning in several places here because it seems so very characteristic of the condition of early modern historiography, poised halfway between old and new.

In my next essay, on the Stonesfield pavement, I have tried to indicate how the classical impulse worked in eighteenth-century England to generate modern archaeology by concentrating on a single forgotten object and subjecting it to careful scrutiny. My intention here, as elsewhere, has been to show a concrete historical question being raised and answered in successive generations, employing the new methods derived from classical scholarship. It would appear that to an appreciable extent this is the way that modern historiography developed, as a cumulative and cooperative enterprise working deliberately to correct error and to improve upon an understanding of past objects and past events. I hope that this assertion will not seem naive in the face of so many forms of modern relativism, but it seems to me that the best answer to any kind of historical skepticism, then and now, lies in just such concrete instances of problem-solving as these. The controversies over Arthur's court and the early history of Britain, or over the *Donation of Constantine* and the Stonesfield pavement, show historical understanding improving dramatically and unmistakably with the exercise of critical scholarship. It is not only the positivists of an earlier time who continue to believe in the possibility of recovering real knowledge about the past.[8]

Humanism thus offered to early modern Europe both a new art and a new science, although they were not in the long run entirely compatible. It offered a new art by insisting on the need for imitation and the employment of classical rhetoric in the composition of narrative. It offered a new science in its pursuit of fact through the new methods of philology and antiquities. Insofar as it aspired to science, it seemed to anticipate or at least parallel the very similar movement of thought that was then transforming the idea of nature. I began by noticing the peculiar confusion (or so it seems to us) between fact and fiction at the end of the Middle Ages, and it is certainly true that Caxton's views of nature were as fanciful as anything in his histories. Eventually, a new method of "observation and experiment" came to be devised for natural science in this period so that it too could attempt to winnow out the errors and marvels that so cluttered the textbooks of antiquity and the Middle Ages, errors caused apparently by false testimony and an unfettered imagination. The result was a new natural history at least as radical in its method and results as anything in the new civil history.

But were these two movements of thought related? Unfortunately, the history of natural history has been even more thoroughly neglected than its human counterpart.[9] Nevertheless, some parallels are obvious, and it is certain that by the seventeenth century the new views were often held and propagated by many of the same men in the same institutions. A key to this connection may lie in the career of Francis Bacon, who was intimately concerned with both movements and whose shadow lies long over the whole period. In my next essay, I have tried to describe the genesis of Bacon's philosophy of nature by looking closely into his early life and thought. And I believe that I have found the key to his mature teaching in the reaction of an ambitious young politician to the rival claims of humanism and scholasticism at Cambridge University. In his attempt to ground his new natural philosophy on a new natural history rather than on Aristotle, Bacon was, I think, consciously imitating those humanists who were also rejecting Aristotle and who believed that moral philosophy could be derived from civil history and put to practical use. Like the humanists, too, Bacon had no patience with the fictions of medieval romance and hagiography; and like Machiavelli, in particular, he thought it wise to distinguish the real world from the make-believe of the idealists. He argued that the first work of the new science was to formulate an accurate description of nature from fresh observations and experiments—a return to the sources. If he was naive in his method and his confidence, so too were the antiquaries; modern science, like modern history, had a long way to go in 1600, not only methodologically but in philosophical sophistication. Theoretical problems were just beginning to appear.

Of course, it was only a matter of time before the new methods, developing in a still traditional culture, caused a crisis of confidence—a crisis reflected in the celebrated quarrel between the ancients and the moderns. Unfortunately, it does not appear that this complicated episode has ever been adequately appreciated, especially in relation to history, and I hope someday to publish a completely new account of that affair.[10] For the moment, I have thought it worthwhile to reprint two essays in which I have shown first how the quarrel was related to historical thought and writing, and next how the greatest historian of the eighteenth century, Edward Gibbon, responded to the issues that had originally been raised to self-consciousness in that struggle; how, in effect, his work summarizes the whole achievement of early modern historiography. In both essays I have attempted to draw a balanced picture and to estimate not only how far modern historiography had advanced by the time of the *Decline and Fall* but how far it still had to go.

For there was undoubtedly still a distance to travel. We read Gibbon and continue to enjoy him, but his method and his viewpoint are not ours. Modern historiography had advanced by his day to the point where it could clearly differentiate the past from the present, not only roughly but in exact detail, and it had established a difference, both practical and theoretical, between fact and fiction. To measure its achievement, one has only to compare Gibbon's view of the past with Caxton's. Yet Gibbon still stands apart from us by an awkward gulf. For one thing, he has not yet seen how to apply the method of the philologists and antiquaries systematically and equally to his whole subject. (He was content, we know, to do his researches in his own library.) For another, he remains confident that the values of his own time and place are still the only standards for all history, that ancient Romans and medieval Christians, Arabs, Turks, and Byzantines must all be held to the same moral, social, and aesthetic standards. As a result, whole cultures were virtually incomprehensible to him. In this he was typical of his age; except that here and there in the eighteenth century a real effort was occasionally made to appreciate and comprehend those alien cultures. Undoubtedly, the most powerful and significant of those attempts in England was the "Gothic revival," with its promise of accomplishing for the later Middle Ages something of what the humanists had done for ancient Rome. In a last essay I have tried to take the measure of that revival historiographically by looking closely at its leading expo-

Preface

nents, the Wartons and their friends, to test again the argument that it was the classical renascence that both impelled and impeded all modern historiography right down to the end of the early modern period.

The implication, then, is that in 1800 something important was still needed to create modern historiography, that it required a climate of thought in which a more relativistic perspective and a more systematic methodology could develop together. The privileged place of classical (and also biblical) antiquity had to be eliminated and the techniques of philological and antiquarian scholarship extended equally to all parts of the past. Something of this had been accomplished in early modern times, and the stage had been well prepared by the humanists and their successors; I have tried to indicate in these essays some of the ways that this was done and how it was retarded. As for the end of the story, I have only been able to hint now and then at its direction. I hope that it will be no anticlimax to pause at the very moment when modern historiography was about ready to turn into its fully recognizable contemporary form; but I am only too conscious of how much more there is to learn about this early period and how much more could still be said to prepare the stage for that final act which is still in progress.

It remains to acknowledge those who have helped me one way or another in the years these studies were collecting, especially to those friends who encouraged me: Donald Kelley, Peter Burke, and James Carley; to Syracuse University for time and support; above all to my family—to DeeDee and to Peter and to Caroline—who helped me at every stage, even to naming the book. Special gratitude goes to John Ackerman at Cornell University Press for helping me to conceive the volume and for his encouragement thereafter. I am grateful also to the original publishers for permission to reprint (in slightly edited versions) the following essays: "Reginald Pecock and Lorenzo Valla on the *Donation of Constantine*," from *Studies in the Renaissance*, 20 (1973), 118–43; "Ancients, Moderns, and History," from *Studies in Change and Revolution*, ed. Paul Korshin (London: Scolar Press, 1972); "The Stonesfield Pavement: Archaeology in Augustan England," from *Eighteenth Century Studies*, 14 (1981), 72–88; "Edward Gibbon and the Quarrel between the Ancients and the Moderns," from *The Eighteenth Century*, 26 (1985), 47–62. Thanks are due as well to the Beinecke Rare Book and Manuscript Library, the Metropolitan Museum of Art, the Worcester Art Museum, and the Yale University Center for British Art for permission to use the illustrations that accompany the text.

JOSEPH M. LEVINE

Syracuse, New York

Humanism and History

CHAPTER *I*

Caxton's Histories: Fact and Fiction
at the Close of the Middle Ages

(1)

It was just three weeks before the battle of Bosworth Field, on July 31, 1485, that William Caxton finished printing his version of Thomas Malory's *Morte Darthur*. It is certainly one of his most impressive efforts, and for the student of historiography it remains his most absorbing. To be sure, it has not always been of much interest to modern historians, whose concern must be with the present value of medieval sources and who have generally found medieval narrative wanting, except perhaps for the contemporary portions of medieval chronicles.[1] If, however, we prefer to know what the Middle Ages made of the past, rather than what we make of past medieval politics, it becomes necessary to cast a wider net. And here Caxton and his publications offer an unusual opportunity. As the first of the English printers, he seems to have set himself deliberately to selecting and editing all that he thought best and most representative in the literature of his time. This included chronicles, of course, but it also embraced some other characteristic representations of the past—romances and saints' lives, for example, which he deliberately placed alongside the more sober narratives. For Caxton, they were all "histories," good stories but also true and useful descriptions of past times.[2]

No doubt this is a little disconcerting to the modern reader—sometimes even to the professional medievalist. For most of us, the distinction between history and fiction is fundamental, although we cannot always make out the precise boundaries; and we insist upon a sharp separation between the novels and the histories that lie on our bookshelves and in our libraries. In the Middle Ages, manuscripts abound in which poems and chronicles, romances and saints' lives, are jumbled together without

19

apparent distinction. Medieval chroniclers invariably, and often deliberately, tell imaginary stories, while medieval storytellers almost always
give sources for their inventions about the past. There is only a little
theory for either history or fiction, and nothing much to keep them
apart, so that the writer of whatever kind promises faithfully to follow
his authority, whether or not he has one and whether or not it is reliable,
and the reader is in no position to tell the difference. If the medieval
historian often appears to be writing fiction, the medieval writer of
fiction invariably pretends to be writing history.[3]

As we shall see, the difficulty was compounded by the relative indifference of the medieval reader to the literal meaning of a narrative,
which he accepted as only one, and that not always the most important,
way to decipher a text—or to read the past. No doubt everyone, then as
now, knew that there was a difference between a lie and the truth,
between a faithful description and a fanciful one, but it was quite another thing to come to value that distinction above any other and to find
out how to establish it in practice. In short, it was necessary to devise
some explicit criteria for recovering the historicity of an event, and a
practical method of proceeding, before it could become possible to define the modern ideas of either history or fiction, much less to defend
their autonomy. It was first necessary to invent a new idea of fact, a
notion that the literal representation of past or present could be interesting in and for itself, or for some present purpose, and that it could and
should be radically distinguished from a spurious or imaginary description. For this, new motives as well as new means were required. But
nothing of this was done, nor was it much attempted, as far as I can see,
until well after Caxton's time. Meanwhile, the modern reader continues
to be baffled by the confusing mixture of history and fiction that he
finds everywhere in medieval narrative and is often at a loss to understand both the intentions and the reassurances of his author.[4]

Take Caxton's first published work, the *Recuyell of the Historyes of Troye*
(1474). Here is a tale that begins with the rivalry of Saturn and Jupiter,
recounts at length the exploits of Hercules, and culminates in the
eventual destruction of Troy by the Greeks. Hercules is introduced as
the flower of medieval knighthood; he displays his chivalry at a great
tournament before a resplendent audience of lords and ladies who look
on from a grandstand. Stranger still, the legendary Callisto takes the veil
and enters a cloister while Jupiter must disguise himself as a nun in
order to take advantage of her. The ancient gods are in this way each
"euhemerized" and brought up to date; as Caxton explains (following
his source), it was the custom in those times to exalt all those who did
great deeds or served the commonwealth and to turn them into gods. So
poetry was turned—or returned—into pseudohistory. Caxton, as al-

ways, follows his authorities and appears to accept their stories without question.[5]

Caxton's immediate source was a recent French romance by Raoul Lefevre, chaplain to the Duke of Burgundy. The influence of the culture of Burgundy upon Caxton (who grew up in it) and upon his English contemporaries was profound.[6] Caxton had originally intended, he says, to stop with a translation of the first part of Lefevre, since he knew that the English poet John Lydgate had already written about the fall of Troy. However, his patroness, the Duchess of Burgundy, persuaded him to complete his story, since Lydgate had written in verse "and also peradventure had translated some other author than this is." Different writers, Caxton explains, have different tastes and tell different stories.[7]

Typically, Caxton did not worry much about the differences. When he had finished his translation, he added an epilogue asking his readers not to be concerned about the subject matter of his book, "though it accord not to the translation of other which have written it." Divers men, he repeats, have made divers books, and they do not all agree about what the ultimate sources—Dares, Dictys, or Homer—report. Nor was this surprising, since Homer favored his Greek countrymen, while Dares supported the Trojans, and everyone was likely to mistake the proper names. What did it matter, since on the main point all agreed? All reported the terrible destruction of Troy and the deaths of many great princes, knights, and common people, "which may be ensample to all men during the world how dreadful and jeopardous it is to begin a war and what harms, losses and deaths followeth." In short, the moral of the tale was unimpeachable, irrespective of its literal veracity, and the moral justified the telling and retelling of the story.[8]

Of course, Caxton was only a printer, at best a translator, and one must be careful not to generalize too easily. Nevertheless, he was an intelligent reader at the least, publishing for a sophisticated audience, and we may be sure that his indifference to fact was not unusual. For us, everything in our history depends upon the sources, and our first instinct (as historians) is to work backward in time through each version of the tale and every recension of the text to the originals, which we then try to evaluate and weigh as evidence. For Caxton, it was enough to find a recent authority and to concentrate on rewriting and translating it into a contemporary prose and setting. This appears to have been the ordinary method of both romance and chronicle. For the first two books, Caxton and Lefevre were content with Boccaccio's *Genealogy of the Gods*, an encyclopedic handbook of classical mythology that had already digested the ancient legends and retailed them as history. They did not know and apparently did not care anything about Boccaccio's sources, which were in fact a mixed bag of ancients and moderns also treated without much discrimination.[9] For the third book, they settled on a long and pedestrian work of the thirteenth century, the *Historia destructionis Troiae* of Guido della Columnis. They did not know, since Guido did not say, that he had relied in his turn largely on a twelfth-century poem by Benoit de Sainte-Maur, the *Roman de Troie*.[10] What they did notice was that Guido's work had been based ultimately on two purported eyewitness accounts by the ancient writers, Dictys Cretensis and Dares Phrygius. Caxton did not realize that Lydgate's poem had also depended on Guido (and so eventually on Benoit) and was thus based ultimately on the same two spurious authorities. Had he known this, he might possibly have worried a little more about their differences, though it is very doubtful that he would have known how to resolve them.

As for Dictys and Dares, we now believe that both were composed early in the Christian period in Greek and translated into Latin, the first probably in the fourth century, the second about two hundred years later.[11] Dictys purports to be a Greek; Dares pretends to be a Trojan. Dares' work is prefaced with a letter in which "Cornelius Nepos" explains to his friend "Sallust" how he had discovered the lost history on a visit to Athens and then translated it. Dares was particularly admired in the Middle Ages as the first of the secular historians (preceding Herodotus) and for his Trojan bias, since all the Western nations, from ancient Rome to modern Burgundy, France and Britain, liked to trace their ancestry back to one or another of the fallen heroes of ancient Troy. It was not an impressive narrative, but it was preferred to Homer, who presumably wrote long after the events, had a Greek bias (so it was thought), and in any case could only be read during the Middle Ages in a meager Latin epitome.[12] It was only after Caxton's time that the two spurious works came under suspicion and only much later that they were decisively exposed as frauds. It was not easy to discard what had been so long accepted as the first beginning and foundation of all Western secular history.[13]

Of course, neither Dares nor Dictys portrayed a medieval Troy. That was left to Benoit and his followers, who visualized it in contemporary chivalric terms. On the whole, the Middle Ages did not share our sense of the past and was untroubled by anachronism; the past was rarely differentiated from the present, however distant.[14] In this respect, Lydgate's *Troy Book* was no better than Lefevre's, though it may have been a superior piece of literature. Like Caxton and Lefevre, Lydgate accepted his authority without question and devoted his own efforts simply to versifying the tale, elaborating its contemporary setting and adding long didactic passages to point the moral.[15] The function of the storyteller, he says, is to enliven the work "with many curious flowers of rhetoric to

Hector and Andromache, a tapestry from the *Trojan War Series* c. 1472–74. The Metropolitan Museum of Art, Fletcher Fund, 1939 (39.74).

Tapestry fragment from the Trojan War Series: Palamedes kill-
ing Deiphobus and killed by Paris; Calchas urging the Greeks,
including Achilles, to fight on. Flemish (Tournai), c. 1475.
Worcester Art Museum, Worcester, Massachusetts.

make us comprehend the truth."[16] Lydgate no doubt thought of himself as a historian, and when his poem was published in the sixteenth century, it was accordingly proclaimed as the *Auncient Historie and onely Trewe and Syncere Cronicle of the Warres betwixte the Grecians and the Trojans* (1555). Guido was applauded then for his faithful digest of Dares and Dictys ("by due conference found wholly to agree") and Lydgate for his Chaucerian verse. Caxton on the other hand was derided for his "long tedious and brainless babbling, tending to no end, nor having any certain beginning." The criticism was not altogether inappropriate, but it had almost no historiographical significance. The only glimmer of something new was the notion in the preface that to print an old text faithfully, like Chaucer or Lydgate, it was first necessary to collate all the manuscripts.[17] Of this neither Caxton nor anyone else in the Middle Ages seems to have had any inkling, though here, if anywhere, lay the future of modern historiography.[18]

Caxton went on publishing romances for the rest of his life, and there is no sign that he ever wavered in his belief that they were historically true.[19] In 1477 he published his *Historie of Jason,* also from Lefevre by way of Dares and Guido, with the story of the Golden Fleece as a pendant to the story of Troy.[20] The opening scene, where Hercules and Jason joust before the court of Thebes, is visualized carefully in a way that sounds just like the modern courts that Caxton knew in Burgundy and Britain. It appears that the more Lefevre or Caxton strove for historical verisimilitude—that is, the more they tried to persuade their audience of the reality of their stories—the more they made their narratives seem contemporary. When Jason is knighted for his prowess, he asks his prince only "that it please you to assign me a place where I may do feats chivalrous and knightly." When Caxton wanted to know about Jason's later career, he turned once again to Boccaccio's *Genealogy of the Gods.*[21]

In 1481, Caxton translated *Godfrey of Bologne* from a French version of William of Tyre's Latin history of the first Crusade. Here was one of the best written and most reliable chronicles of the Middle Ages, though despite William's best efforts its history was soon turned into legend. (For Caxton, the work was "no fable, nor feigned, but all that is therein is true.")[22] In the prologue Caxton remembers the "nine worthies"—the nine greatest heroes in human history—three pagans, three Hebrews, and three Christians: Hector, Alexander, and Julius Caesar; Joshua, David, and Judas Maccabeus; Arthur, Charlemagne, and Godfrey. By the end of the fifteenth century this canon of heroes had long been established and was familiar in chronicle and romance, painting, pageantry, and tapestry.[23] Caxton singles out Hector, whose deeds were described by Ovid, Homer, Virgil, Dares, and Dictys, "each better than other rehearsing his noble works." They made Hector seem "as new and fresh as yet he lived." And he recalls Arthur with the "great and many volumes of Saint Grail, Galahad, and Lancelot de Lake, Gawain, Perceval, Lionel and Tristram." He also picks out Charlemagne for special notice, as though he was already thinking of the two works he was going to print in 1485: the *Morte Darthur* and *Charles the Great*. For the latter he translated another French work, a prose adaptation of a romance that told how the Saracen giant, Fierabras, who was defeated by Oliver, was baptized and sent to heaven. "The works of the ancient and old people," Caxton repeats, "ben for to give us ensample to live in good and virtuous operations."[24] Unfortunately, Caxton does not say anything about the completely fictional love tale *Paris and Vienne* that he also published in 1485, but of the romantic fantasy *Blanchardyn and Eglantine* that he printed a few years later (1489), he recites the now familiar commonplaces: "In my judgment, it is as requisite other while to read in ancient histories of noble feats and valiant acts of arms and war which have been achieved in old time . . . as it is to occupy them and study over much in books of contemplation."[25] As always, the chivalric ideal, timeless and exemplary, meant more to Caxton and his contemporaries than the literal reality of any of the tales they read, and the concrete example, historical or fictional, more than any philosophy.

(2)

The historical fictions of medieval romance had an almost exact counterpart in the historical fictions of medieval hagiography. The lives of the saints offered an alternative array of Christian heroes whose ascetic lives and marvelous deeds were also meant to encourage the reader or listener to emulation. Here also fact and fiction intermingled in subtle and sometimes surprising ways, although the details of Christian narrative, like those of romance, were rarely disputed. Caxton's proudest work may well have been his own version of the *Legenda aurea*, that vast compilation of hagiographical material that so delighted the later Middle Ages. His original was a Latin volume written sometime in the middle of the thirteenth century by an Italian bishop, Jacobus da Varagine.[26] In nearly two hundred chapters, it recounted the festivals and saints of the church calendar, drawing on sources and a tradition that stretched back over a millennium, though characteristically, it reproduced much of its material—often verbatim—from the recent encyclopedia of Vincent of Beauvais. The role of the hagiographer was to compile and rewrite, and Jacobus was industrious and facile. He produced what was undoubtedly one of the most popular of all medieval works, extant still in over a thousand manuscripts and imitated and translated into most of the European languages. Caxton knew the Latin original but relied for the most part (as usual) on a French version as well as on a previous English translation. These he freely altered, adding several new lives and a great deal of fresh historical material drawn from the Bible, turning it into English either on his own or from another unknown source. The result was the most comprehensive version of the *Golden Legend* yet, some four hundred and fifty leaves and six hundred thousand words, an enormous labor that cost him more than a year to print (1482–83) but won him an annual gift from the Earl of Arundel of a buck in summer and a doe in winter.[27]

Caxton hoped that the *Golden Legend* would give "profit to all those that shall read or hear it read and may increase in them virtue and expel vice and sin that by the example of the holy saints amend their living in this short life." His source, Jacobus, was no more concerned than any contemporary romance writer with evaluating the evidence and winnowing truth from fiction. If anything, Caxton was less so, even to the extent of expunging some of the occasional criticism that he found in the original.[28] In this he followed the usual course of medieval hagiography. The modern Jesuit scholar Hippolyte Delehaye, writing from the vantage point of three hundred years of Bollandist scholarship, reminds us that the hagiographer is a poet, not a historian; that he cheerfully disregards facts, prefers general types to real individuals, and is willing to borrow indiscriminately to fill out and color his story in order to sustain interest. His one main concern is to edify. As a result, the saint's life is part biography, part panegyric, part moral lesson. It is true that there is often a historical element which it is the task of modern "scientific" history to detect.[29] But sometimes the whole saint's life is a fiction invented or made up of entirely borrowed elements, like Lydgate's St. Amphibalus, accidentally transformed from the cloak (*amphimallus*) of St. Alban.[30] Caxton knew there was a problem with his life of St. George—discrepancies in the sources about place names and chronology—and for once he, or rather Jacobus, sets them out plainly, but neither he nor the Italian had the faintest notion what to do about it. It never occurred to either of them that there might be no reliable source whatever for the fictional saint who, Caxton points out, was not only the patron saint of England and the cry of men of war, but who had given his name to the Order of the Garter and to the Chapel at Windsor Castle, and whose very heart presently rested there, "which Sigismund the Emperor of Almayn brought and gave for a gift and precious relic to King Harry the fifth."[31]

The parallel between hagiography and romance has often been remarked. From the first appearance of the chivalric tales in the twelfth century, there is evidence that clerics read them and sometimes wrote them. Jongleurs, we know, were often entertained in religious houses. "The figures of romance," we are reminded, "invaded the churches themselves, creeping into the carvings of the portals, along the choir-stalls, and into the historiated margins of the service books."[32] Preachers used them to illustrate their sermons and their manuals of vices and virtues. Chrétien de Troyes, who did more than anyone in the twelfth century to invent and refurbish the Arthurian legends, seems to have been a cleric, as was John Lydgate, the monk of Bury, two hundred years later. (On the other hand, Robert de Boron, who was the first to try to make a coherent scheme of the cycle, and Thomas Malory, who was the last, were probably both knights.) At the same time, saint's life and legendary were directed more and more at the laity and turned into the vernacular, as with the *Golden Legend* or its English counterpart, the *Nova legenda Anglie*.[33] Occasionally, the heroes of romance were transformed into saints, while romance writers and chroniclers drew heavily on hagiography.[34] But the fusion was less than perfect, for the church remained perpetually on guard against the subversive morality of chivalry. The Grail romances that early entered into the Arthurian cycle and were retold by Malory in the *Morte Darthur* were one undoubted response, an attempt to Christianize the knight and turn his military ardor to religious purposes. "There are no knightly deeds so fine," exclaims the author of the *Perlesvaus*, "as those done for the adornment of the law of God."[35] But for some, including Malory himself, it was the combative, adulterous Lancelot who remained the hero, even though it was Galahad who was chosen to win the Grail. Either way, and despite this persistent "clash of ideologies,"[36] it was legend, not history, that mattered, and no one in the Middle Ages seems to have wanted it any other way.

(3)

With annals and chronicles we would seem to be on surer ground. Yet even here in these most sober of medieval narratives, there is ample evidence of the same cast of mind. With his customary business acumen, Caxton chose to print the two most popular and characteristic English chronicles of his time, the *Brut,* a brief version of the national history, and the *Polychronicon,* a grand effort at the history of the world.

For the first, Caxton chose to print an English translation of an anonymous French original, one of many possible versions in several different languages.[37] As a rule the *Bruts* began their story with Brutus, a great grandson of Aeneas who, it seems, wandering far from the fallen Troy, landed one day by chance on an unknown island, which he promptly named for himself. Sometimes this was preceded by a prologue that told how the Syrian king, Diocletian, wed his thirty-three daughters to thirty-three kings whom they later murdered, and how the widows came to England and bred children by the aboriginal giants who lived there. Since the oldest daugher was named Albina, the new land was first called Albion. According to this version, which was the one Caxton used, it was only afterward that Brutus landed with his men and made his conquest. The Albina story seems to have made its first appearance in an Anglo-Norman poem of the thirteenth century that was sometimes bound up with early manuscripts of the *Brut* and other chronicles. With the help of the usual authorities and the evidence of some bones and teeth, the fiction was passed off as history.[38] The chronicle proper resumes with Brutus founding his own "British" dynasty, after which we are treated to a chronological account of his descendants: Bladud (who founded Bath), Belinus and Brennus (who conquered Rome), Lear, Cymbeline, and the rest, until Merlin appears before Uther Pendragon to prophesy the coming of King Arthur. The latter weds Guinevere, founds the Round Table, conquers France, slays a Spanish giant and eventually defeats the Romans, though they are allied with the "Saracens" and other pagans. He is finally betrayed by Mordred and slain, after which the march of the English kings continues down to Caxton's own time, incorporating some additional romantic and hagiographical material along the way. Arthur's memory is not forgotten in the later history, and even the continuators of the chronicle preserve something of his chivalric spirit in their long and sometimes wearisome battle descriptions. Among other improbable things, we learn about St. Ursula and the eleven thousand virgins martyred at Cologne.[39]

The *Polychronicon* was a much more ambitious work, the last great chronicle of the Middle Ages. It was a world history from the Creation until the year 1360, compiled by Ralph Higden, a Chester monk, and translated into English twice afterward (Caxton used the translation by John of Trevisa).[40] It was divided into seven books according to the several ages of human history in order to display the providential plan. Higden's method was the usual method of the medieval chronicler—scissors and paste: "All things excerpt of other men are broken into small numbers but concorporate here lineamentally." Higden's goal was to arrange his disparate materials chronologically, "not only after the order of the times but also after the supputation of every year congruent," so that, as he said, "the order of the process may be observed."[41] An autograph manuscript in the Huntingdon Library shows how he worked, gradually enlarging his chronicle by interpolating new materials into the old under each date as he came upon them. The process could be indefinitely extended, and the *Polychronicon* was later enlarged and continued by others in much the same way.[42] Higden's chief task was to fit his authorities together with as much scruple as he could but without vouching for their truthfulness. "In the writing of this history," he says forthrightly, "I take upon me to affirm for sooth all that I write, but such as I have seen and read in divers books, I gather and write without envy."[43] Equal certitude was not, he admitted, to be found equally in all parts of the work. He leaves many problems deliberately unsolved.

We will not be surprised, therefore, to find in the *Polychronicon* the usual admixture of hagiography and romance, though tempered with a certain amount of caution and restraint.[44] In principle, Higden knows that fables are not history and that fabulous narratives are not the same as true ones, but Higden did not know and probably did not very much care how to distinguish between the original sources and the later ones that he employs with equal confidence. Higden read widely and collected assiduously; he liked a good story, and the *Polychronicon* has lots of good stories to tell, some from the lives of the saints, some from less creditable sources. As a result, Alexander the Great and Charlemagne are seen through the eyes of the pseudo-Callisthenes and the pseudo-Turpin, the fall of Troy through the account of Dares; and the various nations are all shown to have been founded by wandering Trojans.[45] Higden knows more about the classical authors than most of his contemporaries; still, Virgil remains a magician, and the gods are generally retained as the euhemerized heroes of medieval romance. His natural history is as derivative and fabulous as everything else in his work, and even in his geography he prefers to copy his authors indiscriminately rather than looking for himself. The medieval writer usually took his views of nature, as he took his views about the past, from authorities that he made little effort to question, so that a standard reference work like Bartholomaeus Anglicus' *De proprietatibus rerum* (which Trevisa also translated and which Caxton meant to print) unwittingly retells as many fictions about natural history as the ordinary chronicle recounted about human history.[46] In his geography Bartholemew, like Higden, preferred to rely on ancient descriptions before modern observations; griffins and phoenixes are as frequent in his pages as the lengendary heroes in a medieval romance. "The *Polychronicon*," says Beryl Smalley, "like the *De propriatatibus*, is a glorious jumble of fact, legend and marvel."[47]

The trouble was that while Higden accepted a distinction between history and fiction in principle, did not know what to do about it in practice. That he had given some thought to the matter appears from his discussion of early gentile history, where he examines some of the *fabulae* that had come down to him as sources. Higden's task as a chronicler of world history was to reconcile the biblical account of the beginning of history with the pagan sources, and he follows his predecessors, from Eusebius and Bede to Marianus Scotus and Peter Comestor, employing as always his scissors-and-paste technique and often preferring these later authorities even to the Pentateuch itself. The fact that the pagan material was idolatrous caused him some qualms, which he overcame by recalling the Augustinian injunction that it was all right to "spoil the Egyptians." The fact that it also appeared to be "fictional" he tried to get around by finding in his authors traditional devices for discovering some kind of meaning or truth in these unlikely places. In many instances, Higden fell back upon the euhemerist solution: "The gods that pagans worship were men sometime and began to be worshipped after their merits and significance in this life; but through the persuasion of the devil, their successors turned them to be gods . . . which things the poets have helped much." One could try to read these myths back to their historical reality and return the gods to men, and this is Higden's usual tack. In other cases, however, Higden was willing to accept the improbable fables as actually witnessed, as when he read that the companions of the Trojan hero Diomedes were turned into birds, or the followers of Ulysses into beasts, by the demon Circe. This was "truth historical, not fabulous leasing." Sometimes devils or evil men could hoodwink bystanders into believing what they saw: "They may change similitudes through the permission of God, so that the truth of the thing does not appear." (Appearances could change, but God alone could transform nature, as when he changed Lot's wife into a real pillar of salt.) More usually Higden was willing simply to accept a story on authority, as when St. Augustine (citing Aulus Gellius) told of women transformed into men, not as fable but as literal truth. In one case, however, he drew the line; he simply would not accept the tale that Demaenetus (Aesculapius) had been turned into a wolf and back again, though he knew that certain Greek authors had attested to similar tales. "Truly," he concludes with St. Augustine, "there is no leasing, though it be of evident falseness, but it hath some testimony and witness."[48] In the face of this kind of evidence, what was the poor historian to do?

There was another possibility to complicate matters. If some of the gods had once been real people and their deeds real or imagined events, others, he believed, were just personifications, mere figurative expressions for various types of human activity. The poets had invented proper names and shapes for all kinds of reasons, sciences, and powers, like Ceres for tilling the fields and Bacchus for growing vines. Elsewhere in the *Polychronicon*, Trevisa explains that the poets "in their manner of speech feigneth a god of battle and of fighting and clepeth him Mars, a god of riches and merchandise and clepeth him Mercury," and so on.[49]

Neither Trevisa nor Higden seems to have had any difficulty combining to two kinds of explanation. Euhemerism and allegory, like history and fiction, were almost always joined.

From the time of the biblical Isaac, Higden begins to incorporate the events of secular history into his narrative, and so we learn of Ceres, the founder of Crete; Minerva, who invented many arts including cloth; Forneus, who built the Forum, and so on. When Higden comes to Jupiter's ravishing Io and begetting Epaphus, however, he balks; following his source (Isidore of Seville), he prefers to take it as a fable, feigned by the poets, and meant simply to bolster the fame of the two parties. Poets, Higden says, have always assigned offspring to Jupiter in order to establish the nobility of their heroes. He then proceeds to tell of Prometheus, Atlas, Triptolemus, Ceres, Jove, and Saturn, fitting each hero into his chronological place and relying on a motley assortment of writers whom he punctiliously cites. Higden is not always able to reconcile his authorities, as when Marianus Scotus disagrees with St. Augustine about who was the father of Europa, or whether Jupiter gelded Saturn or not, or which Hercules it was who accomplished the twelve great labors. The deeds of Hercules, he thinks, must be histories mixed with fables, though one or two of them were certainly outright fictions with the truth concealed.[50] This raises an obvious problem for the historian, who would like to distinguish them, and for once the chronicler attempts a solution. It is not often that the medieval historian worried publicly about such matters, but Higden pauses in his narrative to consider the problem and he devotes much of the next chapter to the task.

(4)

It was characteristic of Higden to proceed by assembling a string of quotations drawn from his wide reading. As a result, it is a little hard to tell just what Higden himself—or for that matter his translators, Trevisa and Caxton—really thought about the problem. Nevertheless, his quotations make up a little compendium of some of the more obvious things that the Middle Ages had to say about the subject, and if we add to them some other clues provided in Caxton's works, we may hope to get some further idea of what the period thought about fiction and its relation to history.

Higden begins by quoting from a well-known passage of Isidore of Seville. The *Etymologies* was a favorite reference book throughout the Middle Ages, and the discussion of fable there had peculiarly authoritative status. According to Isidore, the poets distinguished fables from histories as things made rather than things done.[51] There were three reasons for poets to invent fictions: first, to please and delight, as in the comedies of Plautus and Terence or the fables of the common people; second, to reveal covertly and indirectly the secrets of nature; and finally, to teach moral lessons, as when Horace writes of the mouse and weasel or Aesop of the fox and the wolf. Unfortunately, Higden saw no reason to quote from Isidore's next chapter, *De Historia*, where he might have found a way to distinguish history from fiction by preferring eyewitness testimony to hearsay; or the later chapter on poetry in which Isidore describes the poet as deliberately changing "what has really taken place." Instead, Higden adds a line from St. Augustine's tract *Against Lying*, in which he allows that although fables are not in themselves true, they may be permitted because of the truths they signify. Here at least was an opening wedge for fiction.[52]

Higden goes on to consider some ancient stories about the descent of heroes from the gods—Aeneas from Venus, and Romulus from Mars— only to dismiss them as patriotic inventions, once again citing Varro. He then resumes his main theme, describing the several different kinds of fiction, relying this time on still another late classical source, Macrobius' commentary on Cicero's *Dream of Scipio* (Higden attributes it to Alexander Neckham, however, who was apparently his intermediary).[53] Once again, he discovers three kinds of fable: those meant simply to amuse, this time Menander and Terence; those meant to instruct through outright fictions like Aesop and Avianus; and those with a substratum of truth like Hesiod and Orpheus. (It is unlikely that Higden knew any of these authors directly.) Still following his source, he declares all three kinds of fable inappropriate to philosophy; only if a fiction concealed a good and decent truth beneath a veil of allegory, like Plato with the myth of Er or Cicero wih the dream of Scipio, was it permissible. In short, among all the different fictions that Macarobius-Neckham could imagine—comedies, beast fables, and allegories—it was only the last, and then only in special circumstances, that could be unequivocally endorsed. Higden seems to agree with this, since he adds on his own authority the example of Boethius, who feigned that philosophy had appeared to him in the guise of a woman—a fiction, undoubtedly, but one that Higden allows as useful for the truth behind the allegory. In this manner only, our monk of Chester concludes, "may a divine use examples mannerly in his telling and speaking."[54]

What Caxton made of this is hard to say; he at least was neither a divine nor a philosopher. The antipathy between philosophy and poetry was of course a very old one, reaching back at least to Plato, and it had been resumed in the Middle Ages by Christian philosophers from Augustine to Aquinas. Caxton had no interest in philosophy or theology and published nothing in this line. He did know Boccaccio's *Genealogy of*

33

the Gods, however, and may well have read the last chapters of that ambitious work, where he would have found another and fuller discussion of the rival claims of philosophy and poetry, this time from the more congenial vantage point of a layman and a poet.[55] Even so, he would have discovered that Boccaccio was still trying to meet the philosophers on their own ground, justifying the truthfulness of pagan poetry in the only way that he knew how, by adapting the method of the theologians and looking behind the surface to detect the underlying meaning. (Dante had done much the same thing, and so too had Boccaccio's friend Petrarch.)[56] By a curious inversion, the medieval defenders of classical mythology were thus borrowing from the theologians the same method of allegorical interpretation that had been originally invented by the classical grammarians to explicate the pagan poets.[57]

An excellent example of this sort of thing by another of Caxton's authors was Christine de Pizan's *Epistle of Othéa.* The work was written about 1400 and eventually found three different English translations: the first by yet another of Caxton's authors, Stephen Scrope; the second by a near contemporary; and the last by Robert Wyer, printed in 1540.[58] The original was brilliantly illuminated and it is only surprising that Caxton overlooked it for his press. What Christine did was to collect a hundred different pieces of classical history and mythology, drawing particularly on two French vernacular works: the *Histoire ancienne jusqu'á Caesar* and the *Ovide moralisé.*[59] For each piece of verse, which either told a story or made a statement, she then supplied a prose *glose* and *allegorie* in which she explicated the moral and spiritual meaning of the text. All was cast in the form of a letter from the goddess of prudence, Othea, to the young Trojan Hector, and was intended to provide a manual of instruction for the youthful knight. The reader was thus meant to get at a single glance the "poetry, philosophy and theology," from what a later publisher called (a little inaccurately) *Les cents histoires de Troye* (1490).[60] Christine, once again uses euhemerism and allegory to establish both the literal meaning and the moral and spiritual lessons that would equip the knight for the struggle against evil on earth and for the journey of his soul to heaven. So, according to the *glose,* Bacchus was the first man to plant vines in Greece, "and when they of the country felt the strength of the wine the which made them drunken, they said Bacchus was a god"; and according to the *allegorie,* "By the god Bacchus we may understand the sin of gluttony."[61] Many of Christine's stories were drawn from the Trojan history, beginning with Jason and the Golden Fleece, moralized and spiritualized exactly as Ovid had been. (So, the story of Helen of Troy teaches us, morally, not to continue in a course foolishly begun and spiritually, that thou shalt not covet thy neighbor's wife.)[62] As always, it is impossible to tell just how historically Christine took her stories in their literal sense, but it is clear that she found the poetry and the history equally to her purpose and that she had little incentive to distinguish between them. She has been unfairly reproached, we are told, for lacking historical perspective and for an inability to distinguish fact from fable.[63] To be sure, this is an anachronistic judgment, but it is perfectly true that she found at least as much history in Ovid as she found fiction in the *Histoire ancienne* and that we who are privileged to view both from the vantage point of modern criticism can find scarcely a line in the whole epistle that may pass for historically true.

That this was Caxton's view also seems likely from the ambitious translation he made from the French of Ovid's *Metamorphoses*. Throughout the Middle Ages but particularly from the twelfth century, Ovid was, next to Virgil, the most appealing classical poet; the *Metamorphoses*—"the *Golden Legend* of Antiquity"[64]—was a text read in the schools, plundered by poets, and explicated and moralized by the theologians, including those "classicizing friars" of the fourteenth century who surrounded Higden and Trevisa.[65] How far Ovid believed in his own mythological and historical stories is still a little obscure, and there was plenty of room for interpretation in the Middle Ages and afterward. Caxton, following his French sources, set out his own views in a prologue to his translation. Whether he ever published it is still uncertain; no printed copy has ever been found. The colophon tells us that the manuscript, which survives in a beautiful scribal hand with illustrations, was completed by Caxton on April 22, 1480. It is perhaps relevant that his old colleague at Bruges, Collard Mansion, published his own magnificent Ovid in French in 1484 and promptly went bankrupt.[66]

Caxton's *proheme* begins with a conventional defense of pagan poetry, relying on the example and precepts of the early Christian teachers Jerome, Justin Martyr, Boethius, and that "great clerk" St. Basil, who had instructed his pupils to select carefully from the poets and chroniclers that which was useful and avoid the rest, like the bee that sips nectar from the flower in order to make honey.[67] Voluptuousness and idolatry should be avoided at all costs. "Let us take but only that which serveth to our purpose and is consonant unto truth. And such things as may hurt and greave, let us leave." But Caxton believed with everyone else that the wisdom of the poets was usually hidden beneath the surface of their stories. The *Metamorphoses* was an admirable poem that had artfully arranged the traditional fables of Greece and Rome in chronological order from the creation of the world to Ovid's own time. Doubtless its matter was part fable and part history and sometimes "tissued and meddled with history and fable together, which is a thing right subtle." No matter. Ovid was not to be reproached for his fictions (which were not his inventions anyway),[68] since under their veil lay hidden the

35

true knowledge of things that had happened or that might yet happen. Indeed, if "chroniclers of histories" had written as well about the deeds of great men and of possible things to come, they too might have been taken for philosophers! All one had to do therefore, to read Ovid aright, was to take away the veil and uncover "sometime poetry, sometime high philosophy," sometimes astronomy and politics, sometimes "gests" or history. And this was what Caxton, following his sources, attempted to do in his own abbreviated commentary on the poem. "Take the fruit and *sens* thereof that lieth covered under the fables."[69] But if this advice of Caxton's was good and helpful to the reader who wished to discover the truth beneath the surface of the text, it could only be distracting for the historian, whose first task and only business was to establish the literal meaning of his sources and to determine the events as they had actually happened.[70] Reading poetry as history, and vice versa, made perfectly good sense to Caxton and his contemporaries, but it necessarily muddled any practical distinction that might be attempted between the two.

(5)

The medieval critic, then, whether Caxton or Boccaccio or Christine de Pizan, all used both euhemerism and allegory to defend and explicate the ancient poets. But where euhemerism was employed as a device to save the historical appearances of classical mythology, allegorical interpretation could only have the effect of undermining its historicity. "Fiction is a form of discourse," Boccaccio repeats, "which, under guise of invention, illustrates or proves an idea, and, as its superficial aspect is removed, the meaning of the author is clear." In his explication of the Dido episode in Virgil's *Aeneid,* Boccaccio allows that the poet, unlike the historian, could take some liberty with both the facts and the order of a narrative to accomplish his purpose. Yet Boccaccio probably did not intend (any more than anyone else) to permit the poet to invent wholecloth—only to modify a received story.[71] From this perspective, the distinction between history and fiction amounted to little more than a choice between reiterating a traditional tale more or less literally, or deliberately modifying it to bring out its underlying meaning.

The medieval theologian, it is true, usually insisted on the importance of the literal historical meaning of the Bible (a meaning established by faith), whatever else he alleged to find in it, while the poetical exegete who wished to salvage some truth in the ancient poetry had, as we have seen, to be circumspect about its obviously pagan surface. Nevertheless, both exhibited the same habit of mind, a reflex which (whether one

36

accepted the literal level of the text or not) sought always to uncover a hidden meaning, and this was an outlook that was bound to distract from any need to establish the simple facts about the past.[72] For quite different reasons, then, neither medieval theologians nor medieval poets had any incentive to meddle with their very different texts or the historical reality behind them, and it was a shock to both when, only a few years after Caxton, Erasmus, and his friends began to do exactly that.[73] To the extent that medieval theologians remained hostile to the pretensions of secular poetry—and history—except to allow for an underlying providential or exemplary meaning, medieval poets were left with little recourse but to pretend that their fictions were something else, either moralizing histories or philosophy. Most writers of romance took the first course; Boccaccio valiantly attempted the second; Christine de Pizan, as we have seen, tried both.

Whatever Caxton may have made of all this, he was really not much interested in theory. He printed romances as history and beast fables as fiction without much worrying about the difference. When he published a collection of Aesop (in 1484), it was borrowed from a Latin-German original by way of the French, stripped for the most part of its scholarly apparatus. The German editor, Heinrich Steinhowel, had employed Isidore's definitions for his preface and emphasized the moral lessons in the fictional tales of the Aesopic corpus. No doubt Caxton approved. He did not use Steinhowel's preface, but in a later passage he wrote, "Every fable is invented to show men what they ought to follow and what they ought to flee. For fables mean as much in poetry as words in theology. And so I shall write fables to show the ways of good men."[74] The epilogue to *Reynart the Foxe* (1481) makes much the same point. Whether a fable was to be believed or not was essentially irrelevant (though Caxton argues Reynard's truth): "There be many figures, plays founden that never were done nor happened, but as for example to the people. . . . Who that will read this matter, though it be of japes and bourdes, yet he may find therein many a good wisdom and learnings."[75] The idea of a useful fiction was a commonplace and was often defended (by Boccaccio among others) by recourse to the parables in scripture itself. The author of the *Ovidius moralizatus* writes, "Some men shall turn away their ears from the truth and shall be turned unto fables, as saith St. Paul (2 Tim. iv 4). . . . Which may be thus expounded, that we must oftentime make use of fables and enigmas and poems, that some moral sense may be extracted therefrom, so that even falsehood may be turned into truth."[76] Caxton's near contemporary Stephen Hawes devoted a whole section of *The Pastime of Pleasure* to developing this theme.[77] That histories or romances or saints' lives were all pretending to do the same thing—that is, teach morality by example—was bound to breed confusion among them, something that Caxton himself eventually noticed, though by and large neither he nor anybody else seems to have paid it much attention.

It might be thought that Isidore's injunction that history depended on eyewitness testimony, which was preferable to hearsay, would be helpful, and it was in fact repeated endlessly throughout the Middle Ages—by Caxton, for example, in the epilogue to *Reynart*.[78] But this emphasis on direct testimony could have only limited practicability in a society still largely committed to listening rather than reading, to oral testimony before documentation. What was one to do with events long past, beyond the memory of living people? And even after literacy began to grow with the growth of record-keeping and bureaucracy, there still remained many problems of application.[79] For it was one thing to learn to use eyewitness testimony that could be heard directly in a court of law or through the efforts of an ambitious chronicler; it was quite another to try to ferret it out and examine it in a written document or account. (The ancient world had in this respect done little better.)[80] Medieval chroniclers like William of Tyre could do remarkably well interviewing contemporaries, but they faltered invariably before the written sources. "I do not wish that credence should be given to everything that I have written in this work," writes Giraldus Cambrensis, "since I do not myself give credence to anything except what I have actually seen or might have observed. As for the rest, I forbear to pronounce on them one way or the other. I leave the rest to the readers' judgment."[81]

As we have seen, this was exactly Higden's view. Dares and Dictys had both claimed to be eyewitnesses and were on that account expressly preferred to Homer, who had written later, by nearly every chronicler and romance writer who attempted the history of Troy. Common sense is not the same as critical historiography; the Middle Ages had common sense enough to understand that there was a basic difference in principle between historical truth and fiction and to make occasional discriminations for practical purposes. In contemporary matters, in law and in chronicle, it could sometimes approach modern critical standards, though even here the evaluation of testimony was more likely to rest on moral than on circumstantial grounds.[82] The forged charters that clogged the chanceries and filled the chronicles were almost impossible to detect. What was missing was a way to handle the evidence of documents from a distant time beyond the memory of men—and a motive to do so.

For Higden and for Caxton the overriding purpose of history, just as for fiction, was edification. That this was bound to create difficulty is evident from the blunt words of Higden's contemporary, the preacher John Bromyard: "It does not matter whether it is the truth of history or fiction because the example is supplied not for its own sake, but for its signification."[83] Caxton sets out his own notion of history in his prologue to the *Polychronicon*, borrowing this time from a French version of a Latin translation from the original Greek of Diodorus Siculus—a tribute, if one were needed, to the long and continuous life of his ideas.[84] History, he writes, is a "perpetual conservatrice of those things that have been done before this present time and also a quotidian witness of good and bad deeds, great acts, and triumphal victories of all manner of people." Its chief use was to spur virtue and deter vice by offering a fund of vicarious experience.[85] Like Higden, Caxton saw that fiction could accomplish something of the same thing, but on this occasion at least he prefers history. "If the terrible feigned fables of poets have much stirred and moved men to pity and conserving of justice, how much more is it to be supposed that history, assertrice of virtue, reformeth and reconcileth." He acknowledged that there were some who preferred to stir men's morals by means of fiction, some even who "sothly teacheth to lie," but it was a risky business, he thought, to mix the undoubted benefit of a good story with suspicion of untruth or, as Caxton puts it, "to mix utility with harm." Better a genuine history, "representing the things like unto the words," where utility was unsullied. But how was it possible to tell— how much did it really matter—whether a good story was literally true? Once again, Caxton does not say. Instead, he returns us to those dubious heroes of old like Hercules, who had been transformed into gods. And he goes on to couple the *Polychronicon* with the *Legenda aurea* as histories equally true, precious, and profitable. In the preface to his new edition of the *Canterbury Tales,* written about the same time, he thanks the clerks, poets, and "historiographs" together for having composed so many notable books of wisdom.[86] Caxton, like Higden, understood that a true story was not an invention, that history was not fiction, but neither they nor any of their contemporaries seem to have had any idea how practically to distinguish between the two—nor, when all is said and done, any strong motive to do so.

(6)

In all this Caxton was entirely representative. Perhaps one more contemporary example will do. John Bourchier, second Lord Berners, was also a translator from the French. Like Caxton, he chose to translate both chronicle and romance, and as in Caxton, it is often hard to distinguish between the two. His most ambitious work was an English version of Jean Froissart's famous fourteenth-century chronicle, which he printed (1523–25) with a preface that sounds exactly like Caxton's introduction to the *Polychronicon:* "The most profitable thing in this world for the institution of human life is history."[87] In recounting the events of the Hundred Years War, Froissart had traveled widely, talked to eyewitnesses, and even used documents from time to time. Nevertheless, his history often reads like fiction. He made no effort to cross-examine his sources or penetrate their stories for the truth, and he was typically helpless when (in the earlier portions) he had to use the work of a predecessor. As a result, modern historians find him thoroughly unreliable, even though they still must use him.[88] Froissart writes, says Huizinga, with "the fiction that chivalry ruled the world," a point of view not surprising for a poet who also wrote a good deal of romance. (Thirty thousand lines of the Arthurian *Meliador* had preceded the chronicles.) "Froissart", we are assured, "was not a modern man. . . . In his writing he passes back and forth between the worlds of reality and fantasy; perhaps they never were in fact for him entirely separated from each other."[89] Nevertheless, it is certain that Lord Berners took everything he found in the chronicles for true, and Caxton agreed. If his readers wanted to know about the virtuous and noble acts that had once inspired chivalry, Caxton could think of no better advice than to "read Froissart."[90]

It may be that Berners and Caxton would have taken Froissart's *Meliador* for history too. Certainly, Berners' next translations were outright romances with almost no historical foundation whatever, yet he looked at them in much the same way as he did the chronicles. Berners recommends *Huon of Bordeux* for its value in exemplifying and encouraging virtue by describing "high and adventurous actions." And he expressly defends the historical veracity of *Arthur of Little Britain,* even though he found it full of "hard and strange adventures" that "to human reason should seem to be incredible." It seemed like folly to translate "such a feigned matter wherein seemeth to be so many unpossibilities." Fortunately, he recalled that he had read many a volume of history containing knightly deeds with "many a strange and wonderful adventure, the which by plain letter was to our understanding should seem in a manner to be supernatural. Wherefore I thought that the present treatise might as well be reputed for truth as some of those, and also I doubted not that the first author of this book devised it not without some manner of truth or virtuous intent."[91]

No wonder, then, that Caxton thought of printing the *Morte Darthur* as history when he was urged to do so one day by a distinguished company of visitors. His choice of this most famous of romance stories was almost inevitable, and he had evidently been thinking about it for some time. The *Morte Darthur* was, of course, a retelling of the familiar "matter of Britain," the history of King Arthur and his court, extracted from the popular French romances of the previous century. One of Malory's sources, however, and perhaps an early inspiration for his work, was the chronicle of John Hardyng, in which he also found many of Arthur's exploits recounted and a full enumeration of the knights of the Round Table.[92] Caxton's work was completed, he tells us, in the year 1469–70 by a knight "seeking deliverance" named Sir Thomas Malory, an author who has otherwise contrived to remain obscure.[93] That Malory, like his predecessors, accepted the essential truthfulness of his story and thought that he was rewriting history seems unmistakable. Toward the end of his work, he describes a scene at Camelot when the knight Sir Bors is reunited with King Arthur: "And when they had eaten, the King made great clerks to come before him, for cause they should chronicle of the high adventures of the good knights." And when Bors recounts the story of the Holy Grail, Malory tells us that "all this was made in great books and put in almeries in Salisbury."[94] (Lydgate had earlier described much the same scene, with clerks recording on the spot the adventures of the Arthurian company.)[95] Malory continuously refers to his sources—or lack of them[96]—and it is as the latest in a long and authoritative sequence that he must have imagined himself. Whether he intended a unified history of the *Morte Darthur* or a number of separate works has been much debated, but almost all his modern commentators are agreed about the essentially historical character of his enterprise. Like nearly everyone else, Malory accepted his romance sources as true, as they in turn had accepted theirs, and he confined himself to rewriting and reinterpreting them. His chief concern was to extol the culture of chivalry as he believed it once had been and to encourage its revival.[97] In the process, he seems typically to have assimilated the events of the distant past to those of recent times.[98]

Caxton says that he took up the work as a result of a visit from some noblemen and gentry who came to ask why it was that he had neglected to publish anything about the most famous and only Englishman among the nine heroes; to which the printer replied that while he had often thought about it, some people had been arguing that there was no such Arthur and that "all such books as been made of him be but feigned and fables because (as they said) some chronicles make of him no mention nor remember him nothing, nor any of his knights." To this startling suggestion there was fortunately an answer, which Caxton then reports, an answer sufficient to reassure him about the historicity of his hero and to undertake the work. Unfortunately, Caxton does not identify the skeptics, which has led at least one modern reader to wonder whether Caxton's reminiscence was not itself a bit of historical fiction![99]

Certainly, the skepticism was unexpected and peculiar. To raise a question of fact and examine it in close detail as though it mattered was not, as we have seen, the ordinary impulse of the Middle Ages. Why then did the unnamed skeptics suddenly raise the question? One can only

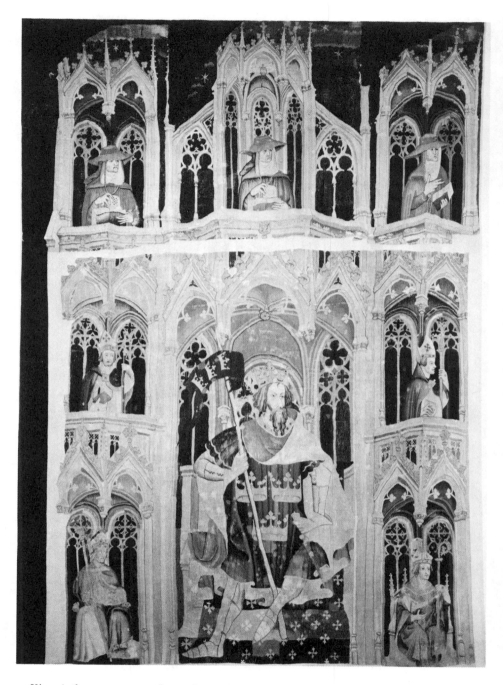

King Arthur, a tapestry from the series The Nine Heroes, end fourteenth century. The Metropolitan Museum of Art, The Cloisters Collection, Mensey Fund, 1932.

speculate, but it looks as though it must have been because of the very special circumstances that had from the first attended the history of King Arthur.

Fortunately, there is no need to rehearse here the long and complicated story of how Arthur and the Round Table were described and developed in chronicle and romance over many centuries, except to say that the Arthur of medieval history was, like Brutus and his successors, pretty much the invention of the twelfth century, and especially of the Latin chronicler Geoffrey of Monmouth, who says he took his matter from an "old British book."[100] Perhaps because the tale appeared so suddenly, it was immediately suspect to some, particularly to William of Newburgh, who took the trouble to refute it by noticing the strange silence of earlier writers, who apparently knew nothing of Arthur's fabulous exploits. Nevertheless, William's skepticism was quickly submerged by a host of chroniclers and romance writers who took up the tale, enlarged and embellished it, and thus made it increasingly difficult to dispute.[101] It was only with Ralph Higden and the *Polychronicon* that skepticism surfaced once again.

Now, Higden is, in this respect, the exception that proves the rule. As a compiler of a fresh world chronicle, he took the trouble to start out anew and gather up the authorities, ancient and modern, for the early history, trying—as we have seen—to stitch them together into a consecutive account. His scissors and paste method, like William's (whose work he does not mention), was sufficient to turn up some of the same problems. Comparing authorities and attending to chronology revealed some peculiar omissions and discrepancies in Geoffrey's story. How was it that Geoffrey alone among the chronicles described Arthur's conquest of thirty kingdoms, including France and Rome? Geoffrey has Arthur conquer Frollo, King of France, and Lucius, procurator of Rome. But no Frollo appears in any other work, and the only Lucius that Higden could find lived many generations later. It seemed to Higden that it was only another case of a nation magnifying its heroes and exaggerating its deeds, as the Greeks had done with Alexander and the Romans with Augustus. He accepts a bit of the story that he finds elsewhere and hurries on.[102]

Higden's doubts, like William's, were provocative but not very complete or consistent. He was not only eager to employ most of Geoffrey's legendary history from Brutus until the time of Arthur; he even preferred it at one point to the more judicious William of Malmesbury, accepting the fictional Bladud over Julius Caesar as the founder of Gloucester. William did not, he explains, have the advantage of Geoffrey's old British book, and was probably just guessing![103] Even so, Higden's first translator and Caxton's immediate source, John of Trevisa, went out of his way to answer Higden point by point and defend the legendary Arthur. First of all, he argues that the silence of the chroniclers and the discrepancies in their accounts could be disregarded, since as we know, even the gospels varied in their accounts of the life of Christ. If John reports things not to be found in Matthew, Mark or Luke, must he be ignored? Besides, some writers of histories were undoubtedly enemies of Arthur. As for "Frollo" and "Lucius," it was well to remember that names varied then in different places; Trevisa reminds us again that William did not have the benefit of Geoffrey's old British book. Finally, it was a fact that Arthur's reputation was well known throughout Christendom. Perhaps Arthur had been overpraised; Trevisa is himself dubious about the story that Arthur would one day return to rule Britain, and he recognizes that other magical tales had been told about him.[104] But he defends Geoffrey's story generally and with conviction. That his was the common opinion we need have no doubt; chroniclers and romance writers continued to celebrate the lengendary history—John Hardyng (c. 1460) and John Rous (1486) equally with Malory's *Morte Darthur*.[105]

As we have seen, it was Trevisa's translation of the *Polychronicon* that Caxton employed for his own in 1483, and so he was well aware of the medieval argument even before he sat down to edit the *Morte Darthur*.[106] It was quite possibly the inspiration for the discussion he reports, but the reply to the skeptics that he says he heard then goes far beyond anything that Caxton could have found there. His interlocutor, possibly his old patron Earl Rivers,[107] supplied him with a long and remarkable catalog of evidence for the historical Arthur. First, there was the sepulchre at Glastonbury Abbey where Arthur and Guinevere had been exhumed.[108] Then there was the impressive account in Boccaccio's *Fall of Princes*, known to Caxton in Lydgate's version. And of course there was Geoffrey's British book. Besides those testimonies, there were many memorials of the great prince and his knights scattered throughout England, like the seal that could still be seen at Westminster Abbey on which was written, *Patricius Arthurus, Britannie, Gallie, Germanie, Dacie, Imperator*. There were other objects: at Dover Castle, Gawain's skull and Craddock's mantle; at Winchester, the Round Table itself; at Camelot in Wales, among other things, the royal vaults, "which divers now living hath seen." Elsewhere, there was Lancelot's sword and still other reminders of the glorious company. How could anyone doubt the existence of this foremost of the nine heroes whose fame extended even beyond the seas to the Dutch, Italians, Spanish, Greeks, and French?

Caxton was easily convinced. Had he not himself seen many fine volumes in French about Arthur when he was still living abroad? He thought it best simply to take Malory's book, which had brought the story together from all these sources, and print it, "to the intent that noble men may see and learn the noble acts of chivalry." When Caxton closed his preface, he urged his audience, "all noble lords and ladies and all other estates," to read the *Morte Darthur* through and take example. "For herein may be seen noble chivalry, courtesy, humanity, friend-liness, hardiness, love, friendship, cowardice, murder, hate, virtues and sin. Do after the good and leave the evil and it shall bring you to good fame and renown." He hoped his readers would profit from it and enjoy it, whether they believed everything in the story or not. In the end, Caxton left his readers at liberty to accept the *Morte* as history or fiction or both, as long as they recognized that it was written to encourage virtue. A good parable for example, as he puts it in the epilogue to *Charles the Great,* was more likely to remain in the memory than any other kind of instruction.[109]

This unexpected conclusion may seem a little disappointing after so spirited a defense of the history, but it was no doubt characteristic of its time. Caxton had stumbled onto a question of fact and had done what he could to fathom the issue. The criticism of Arthur was most unusual in raising the question; the defense was even more unusual in attempting to meet the challenge by systematically assembling the evidence. It failed, of course, because the evidence was counted, not weighed. But what else could Caxton do? There was nothing in his training, nothing in all his culture, that could help him to evaluate the motley assortment of objects and testimonies, words and things, that had accumulated over the centuries. Perhaps, if the issue had mattered more to Caxton and his friends, they might have done better. But here, as elsewhere, the distinc-tion between history and fiction did not really make much difference. For that, a whole new culture was required—a culture, as it happened, that was just then waiting in the wings and that was, among other things, about to begin to make a profound transformation of English histori-ography.

(7)

Renaissance humanism came to England belatedly and in a sluggish and irregular manner still not wholly understood. Certainly there was not much of it to be seen in Caxton's day. It is true that throughout the fifteenth century there were sporadic contacts between England and Renaissance Italy, but they bore only modest fruit, and it was only after Caxton's time that the generation of Linacre and Grocyn, Colet, More, and Erasmus began to display the possibilities of ancient Latin and Greek culture. When the Italian humanist Poggio Bracciolini visited

England early in the century, he was appalled at the backward state of English letters.[110] "There was a noble clerk named Poggius of Florence," Caxton recalls, "which had in the city of Florence a noble and well stuffed library which all noble strangers . . . desired to see, and therein they found many noble and rare books." But Caxton seems to have known nothing of the wonderful discoveries that Poggio had made of lost classical authors and very little of work by Poggio himself.[111] It was only long after Caxton's time, long after the practice of classical imitation began to take root in the schools, that humanist scholarship—that is, the philological and antiquarian techniques that fifteenth-century Italians were inventing as a means of recovering the past—began to be appreciated in England. Caxton did print one or two works by Italian humanists, though they seem to have been at the request and under the direction of the authors; and he published a couple of brief pieces by Cicero, though they were translated by others, one at least from the French. Apart from this (and from Caxton's Ovid) there is hardly a trace of anything classical in the whole corpus of his works.[112] To later times it looked like a strange and unforgivable omission. "To comply with the vicious taste of his readers," Edward Gibbon complained characteristically, Caxton had thoroughly ignored the Greek and Latin authors and "amused the popular credulity with romances of fabulous saints."[113]

It is not altogether surprising then that when Caxton decided to translate the *Aeneid* in 1490, it was from a French romance version of the poem rather than the original. Though he recommended it to all clerks and gentlemen who understood "gentleness and science," he was a little embarrassed about his rendering, which he hoped that the young poet John Skelton might revise. Skelton knew something directly of the classical authors, several of whom (according to Caxton) he had read and translated—poets and orators, as the printer admits, "to me unknown."[114] For Caxton, Virgil was still a magician and the *Aeneid* a chivalric tale of adventure.[115] The French version that he employed had thoroughly reorganized the tale, preferring a "natural" chronological order and supplying some of the missing events of Trojan and Roman history before and after Virgil's story. But the translator also left out much, including the whole sixth book that recounts the descent of Aeneas into hell. In Caxton's words, "This matter I leave, for it is to be feigned and not to be believed."[116] The Dido episode troubled him in another way, for he found that Virgil's story was contradicted by Boccaccio's *Fall of Princes*, which he read in Lydgate's poetic version. How Boccaccio could have done this, he was at a loss to say; his only recourse was to print both versions and (presumably) leave it to the reader to judge.[117] That Caxton and his predecessor thought they were writing history and (as the Frenchman says in his prologue) teaching useful lessons by the examples of the past is unmistakable.

It was not long before Caxton's *Eneydos* began to look ridiculous. Just one generation later, the Renaissance Scot Gavin Douglas compared Caxton's work with the original and complained that "the two are no more alike than the Devil and St. Austin" or the owl and the popinjay.[118] When Douglas attempted the *Aeneid* himself, it was from the Latin original with the help of other ancient works and some recent humanist commentaries. He was thus able to see Virgil as a Roman poet in his own Roman setting, deliberately exalting his hero, Aeneas, for the practical advantage of his patron, the Emperor Augustus.[119] Douglas even began a commentary of his own where he meant to explain to his readers many of the historical allusions—the names, places, and customs—that had been mangled or obscured in Caxton's version. His translation has often been praised as the best in the language.[120] If Douglas still commits some anachronisms and continues to show a "medieval" ambivalence to the classical deities, he is nevertheless miles away from Caxton's *Eneydos*.

Still, Douglas was precocious, and it is hard to see what else Caxton could have done. The English were not ready, or only barely so, to discover in the ancient works something of use. The culture of chivalry was still very much intact, though the feudal institutions that had attended its birth and long since begun to fade.[121] It may even be that as the bonds of traditional feudalism loosened and the military ascendency of the aristocracy was undermined, there was an increasing nostalgia for an imagined golden age, not merely in literature but at court and among all classes. It has often been noticed that even as knightly armor and costly tournaments were losing their practical importance in actual warfare, they grew ever more popular and sumptuous, until they turned into something like pure pageantry—into a kind of playful make-believe. Yet throughout the lives of Malory and Caxton, knights-errant like Richard Beauchamp, Earl of Warwick (who might have been Malory's lord) or Earl Rivers (who fought a memorable duel with the Bastard of Burgundy in 1467 and was Caxton's best patron) pursued their chivalrous adventures and stirred the popular imagination. The greatest court pageants of the day accompanied the wedding of Margaret of Burgundy and Charles the Bold in 1468, with Caxton attending.[122] And it was Henry VII who urged Caxton to translate Christine de Pizan's *Fayttes of Armes and Chivalrye* (1489), who named his first son Arthur, and who continued to hold tournaments on important ceremonial occasions. If chivalry was having less and less effect on the real politics and war of its time, the illusion at least remained formidable.[123]

Nevertheless, it was generally agreed that the great days were gone.

47

This was the view of Malory, certainly, and of Caxton, among others. In 1484, Caxton translated Raymon Lull's *Book of the Order of Chivalry* and complains in the prologue that the rules were no longer being followed as once they were when English arms had ruled the world and set the example. He longs only to return to the days of Arthur and the Round Table, and he advises the king, Richard III, to hold jousts with prizes and to revive, if possible, "the noble order of chivalry as it hath in late days passed."[124] Caxton seems blissfully unaware that the conditions of war and politics had changed irrevocably and that the passage of time had made the chivalric aspiration less and less plausible as an ideal way of life. In much the same way, the ascetic ideal of monastic hagiography seems also to have been fading on the eve of the Reformation, though again hardly anyone seems to have noticed.

No doubt the appeal of Renaissance humanism was at first only to those few in England who were shrewd enough to see or to sense the disparity between the ideals of chivalry and the cloister and the new world that had come in almost unobserved to transform the old. Needless to say, this apprehension was limited at first to a handful and was very slow to take root. It was the generation of humanists who followed immediately after Caxton—More, Erasmus, and the rest—who first deliberately turned their backs upon romance and hagiography and denied both their values and their premises. For Juan Luis Vives, the Erasmian who spent the 1520s largely in England tutoring the princess Mary, Dares and Dictys were frauds, Brutus and his followers transparent fictions, and the lives of the saints—especially the *Golden Legend*—"polluted with fabrications." As for the romances, how could anyone find enjoyment in their immoral lies? "One killeth twenty himself alone, another thirty, another wounded with an hundred wounds and left dead, riseth up again and on the next day made whole and strong, overcometh two giants." Vives admitted that he sometimes read romances himself but had never found an iota of goodness or wit in any of them; his own preference, naturally, was for Cicero and Seneca, St. Jerome and Holy Scripture.[125] In the next generation Roger Ascham continued the onslaught against medieval fiction, and by the end of the century, the prejudice had become commonplace though still far from universal.[126]

For Caxton, as we have seen, ancient history was derived entirely at second hand from romance and chronicle, where it had long before been transformed into the familiar terms of medieval chivalry. The stories of Brutus and Arthur or Hercules and the Trojan heroes were all as plausible in this setting as those of Alexander the Great and Julius Caesar. For the humanists who read the ancient authors directly in the ancient languages and who were laying the foundations of modern critical scholarship, it was different. They *began* with the notion that ancient and medieval culture could be sharply differentiated, and as a result they developed a keen sense of anachronism. As we shall see, the new historiographical sciences that they invented under the name of philology and antiquities were all predicated on the conviction that truth could be winnowed from error and that the effort was worth making. It hardly needed argument to persuade someone like Polydore Vergil, who was both a humanist and a foreigner, that the British history was all legend, though he was too polite—or too intimidated—to say so directly. However, when Gavin Douglas asked him his opinion of the story that Scota (Pharoah's daughter) had founded the Scottish kingdom, Vergil responded with his usual skepticism, and Douglas was persuaded, "so easily is truth always discovered from feigned fancies!"[127]

Fortunately, there is no need to trace here the way the legendary history was attacked and defended throughout the sixteenth century until the new method triumphed and the time-honored tales were declared a fiction. It was John of Wethamstede in the fifteenth century, a proto-humanist in the circle around Humphrey, Duke of Gloucester, who resumed suspicion of the story; it was the Erasmians and their followers, Vives, George Lily, John Twyne, and Thomas Elyot, who were soon ready to discard it; and it was William Camden, finally, who set out all the evidence and politely disposed of it once and for all in the *Britannia*.[128] As a contribution to the debate, Vergil had edited and printed an early medieval text, the first of its kind but a harbinger of many to come.[129] The movement back to the sources had begun. To be sure, it was another humanist, John Leland, who tried to defend the Arthurian story early in the century, but he failed in the long run precisely because he agreed to play the same historiographical game: to collect all the original sources archaeological and literary, and to date and sift and compare them. "If these witnesses of some credit make not sufficient for most apparent knowledge of the truth," he insisted correctly, "surely there can nothing at any time availably serve."[130] Put to the test, it became gradually clear that all the evidence for the historicity of the British story—not only Geoffrey of Monmouth and the medieval romances but Arthur's seal, floating traditions, gravestones at Glastonbury, even the Round Table itself—were equally untenable.[131] The whole business would have to be done again.

(8)

So, history and fiction began to part company in practice, at least as far as the new method would allow; and romance and hagiography were gradually banished from sober chronicle. The contrast between Caxton's *Brut* and the works of John Speed and Samuel Daniel a century later may help to measure the gap: both abandoned the legendary British history for the relative security of ancient Rome.[132] At the same time the idea that history and fiction were different and autonomous activities, each with its own justification, began to grow and become commonplace, not only among historians who insisted on proclaiming their superiority but among the poets also, who were proud now to defend their own work in and for itself and only too happy to enjoy their new freedom from authority. The Italians, as usual, led the way, drawing inspiration from the newly discovered *Poetics* of Aristotle, where they could find a spare but suggestive treatment of the difference between history and poetry.[133] Now, however, the ever more insistent voice of humanist historiography, with its exclusivist pretensions to knowing the truth about the past, led some critics to speculate beyond anything they found in the Greek philosopher. On one proposition, however, all seem to have agreed: history and poetry could and should be distinguished by the historian's special ability to know the past. "Whereas the historian ought to write only the facts and actions as they are," writes Giraldo Cinthio *On Romance* (1554), "the poet shows not things as they are but as they ought to be for the ameliorizing of life." Here at last was a frank admission that the poet was free to invent his fictions, and a proud claim that the result was better, if not "truer," for teaching the moral life. "The poet," Cinthio reflected later, "does not deal in things as they are but as they ought to be and so changes history and makes it become a fabulous creation, of greater worth indeed than if he had treated the matter factually."[134] More radical than this was the view of Ludovico Castelvetro in 1570 that poetry should abandon all pretense of teaching and address itself simply to pleasing and entertaining the reader. For Castelvetro, history was the prior art; good fiction was possible only if one first knew how to establish the truth about the past and thereby free the inventive faculty. Castelvetro's views alarmed some of his contemporaries, but they honestly reflected one of the central problems in Renaissance critical thought: in the words of Baxter Hathaway, "how to make the distinction between historical factuality and fiction."[135] And at least one Englishman, Sir Philip Sidney, drew something from him.

It is not surprising, therefore, to find the Renaissance critics rallying around their cause in a slew of *artes poeticae* aimed (at least in part) against the humanist historians and their new *artes historiae*, attempting to defend the autonomy of fiction and the imagination.[136] As always, theory rallied to practice, and in England, Sidney and Puttenham took up the cause and domesticated the Italian message. Both defended "feigned history" as an improvement over literal history, and Puttenham at least was prepared to defend the completely fictional tale as best of all, "because the Poet hath the handling of them to fashion at his pleasure," while the historian "must go according to their veritie."[137] It was left to Francis Bacon to try to redefine the distinction between the two in terms of the new philosophy. In the *Advancement of Learning* (1605), he attaches history to memory (and memory to the recovery of testimony) and assigns poetry to the imagination, "which, being not tied to the laws of matter, may at pleasure join that which nature hath served, and sever that which nature hath joined, and to make unlawful matches and divorces of things."[138]

Bacon preferred the facts, but by Bacon's time the poets were exulting openly in their new-found freedom and autonomy. "The poet's eye, in a fine frenzy rolling / Doth glance from Heaven to earth, from earth to Heaven / And as imagination bodies forth / The forms of things unknown, the poet's pen / Turns them to shapes and gives to airy nothing / A local habitation and a name."[139] John Marston announces in 1606, "Know, that I have not labored in this poem to tie myself to relate anything as an historian, but to enlarge everything as a poet." The last thing he intends is "to transcribe authors, quote authorities and translate Latin prose."[140] And Thomas Dekker boldly declares in 1607, "And whereas I may . . . be critically taxed that I falsify the account of time and set down not occurrents according to the true succession, let such (that are so nice of stomach) know that I write as a poet, not as an historian, and that the two do not live under one law."[141] The allegorical mode continued, it is true, in Spenser and Harington and with new commentaries on Ovid, but its energy was flagging, and it may be questioned whether the literal level was any longer required to have a plausible historical meaning. Thomas Lodge, we are told, in his *Scillaes Metamorphosis* (1589), was the "first to come out into the open with an epyllion pretending to no hidden meaning."[142] Francis Bacon wondered whether the ancient poets had written first and the allegories had been attached only afterward.[143] Much earlier, Rabelais had already poked fun at the genre in his prologue to *Gargantua*, and it looks as if medieval allegory had begun its long slow decline. Meanwhile, the old romances began to lose their appeal to the upper classes and, like the chivalry they celebrated and the knighthood they admired, slipped gradually into oblivion.[144] The new Spanish romances that temporarily replaced them were treated frankly as fictions.[145] When Ben Jonson finally noticed their disappearance after so long a decline, he was, like Cervantes and like Francis Beaumont in the *Knight of the Burning Pestle*, honestly amused.[146] We have come a long way from the deeply felt regrets of Malory and Caxton.

51

(9)

I close with a last example of this mutual declaration of independence. The poet Michael Drayton had what he called a "natural inclination to love antiquity," and he made his first reputation with a number of historical poems before turning to the great subject that was to occupy him for the rest of his life.[147] By 1598, he had already begun the *Polyolbion*, but it was only after many years and much discouragement that in 1612 he was able to publish the first part of his long poem. By then he was afraid he had lost his audience, and in truth the poem was not a great success. Still, he labored to finish it, and a second part finally appeared a decade later. It was a "chorographical" poem, part history, part topography, describing all England and Wales county by county; a kind of versified William Camden, "the first of its kind," he boasted—and apparently the last.[148]

Drayton knew many of the antiquaries of his generation, including Camden himself and his translator, Philemon Holland, and he admired their work.[149] At the same time, he loved the old stories that had come under criticism, and he preferred deliberately to write as a poet. That he knew and appreciated the difference is perfectly plain, for when it came time to publish his work, he turned to the brightest and most learned of Camden's disciples, John Selden, to annotate it. Selden had already declared himself about the fabulous matter in a Latin treatise of 1610, translated later as *The Reverse or Backface of the English Janus*.[150] There, he devoted two whole chapters to exposing the story of Brutus as a fiction; it was, he pointed out, just the kind of thing that poets like to invent. It was, however, Drayton's idea to take this freedom of the poet upon himself and in the course of his work retail the whole legendary history of Britain, while at the same time attaching a learned critical commentary in order to make clear that nothing of this was to be mistaken for historical truth. "Thou hast the Illustrations of this learned gentleman, my friend, to explain every hard matter of history, that, lying far from the common reading, may . . . seem difficult to thee." The young Selden, who understood the new historiography probably better than anyone else in England, could not have been a better choice.[151]

Selden took his job to be that of the ordinary humanist commentator: to explain the poetical allusions and to recover the truth behind the fiction. "After explanation," he warned, "I oft adventure on examinaton and censure." If Drayton had drawn upon Geoffrey of Monmouth, the *Polychronicon*, and the *Morte Darthur*, among other unreliable sources, it was Selden's task to expose them at every point for their "intollerable antichronisms, incredible reports, and bardish impostures." His method was the new critical historiography that had been developing in England for a century, "weighing the reporter's credit, comparison with more persuading authority, and synchronism (the best touch-stone in this kind of trial)." "My thirst compelled me always to seek the fountains and by that, if means grant it, judge the river's nature." Everyone who understood the message of the new learning knew what errors resulted from "trusting authorities at second-hand and rash collecting (as it were) from visual beams refracted through another's eye."[152] Selden's commentary picked up each of Drayton's allusions to the legendary history and turned them into "truthpassing reports of poetical bards." Brutus, Albina, Belinus and Brennus, Arthur, Merlin, the Round Table, St. Ursula and the eleven thousand virgins—all fell before his critical pen. Caxton's Malory, like Dares the Phrygian, was for Selden pure fiction. "Poetical liberty" might be allowed to Drayton; "historical liberty" was permitted to no one, and the two must never be confused.[153]

Would Caxton have been persuaded? It is hard to say. Undoubtedly, he would have shared Drayton's nostalgia for medieval culture and enjoyed the retelling of so many familiar tales. "The capricious faction," Selden had well understood, "will, I know, never acquit their belief . . . although some Elias or Delian diver should make open what is so inquired after."[154] But Caxton was a successful businessman in tune with his times, not an independent thinker. I have an uneasy feeling that he would have seen the shrinking market for medieval fiction in Drayton's day and thrown in with the historians—or at least with the newer forms of fiction that were coming to replace romance. I can see him printing Spenser and Holinshead, Camden certainly (in translation), and his admirer Ben Jonson; but as for poor Drayton, who wanted to have it both ways—old fiction and new history—I rather think that Caxton, like the printers of Drayton's own day, would have given him short shrift.[155] As for us, despite and whatever our twentieth-century misgivings about the objectivity of history and the hardness of fact, we shall have to concede the victory in this matter, at least, to the humanists and go on reading the medieval writers (to the extent that we do so at all) as fictions, whatever it was that they and their first printer may have intended.

CHAPTER 2

Reginald Pecock and Lorenzo Valla
on the *Donation of Constantine*

The story of the exposure of the *Donation of Constantine* is a familiar one. In the middle of the fifteenth century, it will be recalled, two different men, writing independently of each other in England and in Italy, demonstrated conclusively that the document was a forgery. Others had long suspected it and, on one occasion at least, carefully examined and rejected it.[1] But it was left to Reginald Pecock and Lorenzo Valla to complete the criticism. When they were finished, it was difficult, if not impossible, to continue to believe in either the document or the event. In this way, European historiography took a major step forward, and the Renaissance relieved itself of one of the many legends that cluttered its understanding of the past.

Unfortunately, the tale, in this version, is too simple. For one thing, conviction in the *Donation* survived the assault.[2] For another, the coincidence of the criticism of Pecock and Valla was merely fortuitous.[3] In neither purpose nor method, background nor influence, did the effort of the two men have very much in common. Finally, their achievement was not at all unambiguously progressive; their anticipation of a modern conclusion (for the *Donation* is indeed a forgery) conceals the fact that their historiographical techniques were rooted solidly in their own time and remain quite remote from the present. It is the purpose of this essay to try to dispel some of these confusions. In so doing, I shall not advance anything very startling; I shall simply try to show that the two contemporary critics of the *Donation* inhabited essentially different intellectual worlds, and that each employed the characteristic devices of his training for the solution of a practical problem: scholastic logic in Pecock's case, humanist grammar and rhetoric in the case of Valla. That the different elements of the trivium were often opposed during the Renaissance is well known; that they were antithetical in their relationship to historiography, perhaps less so. In any case the comparison between Pecock and Valla affords a rare opportunity to compare in detail the different approaches of a scholastic logician and a Renaissance philologist to a common historical problem and thus to illuminate each. Incidentally, it allows us also to place the episode in relation to the evolution of modern historiography. In the end, as we shall see, it is Pecock with his syllogistic logic who proves the more alien to modernity, while Valla, with his new philological method, though promising much for the future, only begins to point the way.[4]

(1)

Of Pecock's career not much need be said. Indeed most of it, including the dates and circumstances of both birth and death, remain obscure.[5] We do know that he attended Oxford University from about 1409 to 1424 and that he received a Doctor of Divinity degree there, some twenty years later. Unfortunately, the university had passed its great days; Grosseteste and Roger Bacon, Scotus and Ockham, even Wyclif, were long gone, although their works lived on in different ways after them. Students were scarce, and outstanding teachers even more so. But the curriculum remained intact: the familiar scholastic education of the medieval university designed to train clerics in theology and law, and built almost exclusively upon the instruments of logic and dialectic. Rhetoric and grammar, the other kindred disciplines of the trivium, were either ignored or subordinated. The chief aim, as the statutes of 1431 made plain, was to train the student "to analyze and subdivide, to know the pros and cons of every argument, to be alert in disputation, in posing questions, and in suggesting replies."[6] There was no need here for literature in general, or for the classical authors more specifically.[7] And there was no place whatever for the study of history, ancient or modern. It is clear that Pecock thoroughly mastered the Oxford curriculum: his works display the same preoccupation with logic and dialectic, the same ignorance of Latin and Greek literature.

Pecock's career was less typical than his course of study. Upon leaving the university, he became rector of a Gloucester church and then, in succession, Master of Whittington College, London (1431), Bishop of St. Asaph (1444), and finally Bishop of Chichester (1450) and member of the Privy Council (1454). Unfortunately, his preferment was advanced by the Lancastrian party, and with the accession of the Yorkists, his downfall was even more precipitous than his rise. But his failure was more than simply the result of politics; for some years a large clerical party had been leveling allegations of heresy at him, and the combined pressures of temporal and religious opposition resulted ultimately (1457–58) in a public recantation, the burning of his books, resignation from office, and incarceration in an abbey for his remaining days.

It was an ironic end. Pecock saw himself throughout his life as the self-appointed champion of orthodoxy against the challenge of Wyclif and Lollardy. He was familiar with the heresy from his days at the university, where it lingered despite vigorous measures to eradicate it, and more especially from his life in London. In twenty years, he wrote perhaps fifty apologetic works (although only five survive) meant to vindicate the church exactly as he found it with all its imperfections. It is in this context, as we shall see, that he wrote the work known as the *Repressor of Over Much Blaming the Clergy,* in the course of which he exposed the *Donation.* But his accusers found that "the damnable doctrine and pestiferous sect of Reginald Pecock exceedeth in malice and horribility all the other heresies and sects of heretics heretofore known." The defense of orthodoxy had somehow led the bishop into heresy.[8]

The paradox of Pecock's career was rooted in his attitude to what he calls the "doom of reason." The Lollards had argued that man's reason was "a thing which in his dooms and judgments oft faileth." For every truth, they insisted upon a scriptural citation; on any point, they asked but one thing: "Where groundest thou it in Holy Scripture?"[9] Pecock's reply was to defend and to exalt reason as a separate and legitimate avenue to knowledge about sacred things. But in doing so he appeared to elevate reason above scripture, as well as above the Church fathers and tradition, and there were the charges laid against him which he afterwards recanted.[10]

In fact, Pecock's teaching was more complicated. But it is undoubtedly worth some attention here because it provides the only appropriate context in which to understand his attack upon the *Donation.* To determine his position it is helpful to draw upon all the surviving works, along with the *Repressor.* Indeed, Pecock himself urges this upon us with an elaborate system of cross-references to his own writings. He clearly meant them to be taken as a whole, a kind of *Summa Theologiae* in which everything found its logical place.[11] He even says that he worked upon several treatises at one time, and his continuous rewriting makes them impossible to date exactly. His teaching is therefore very much the same, whether in the *Repressor* or in the *Book of Faith,* which seems to have been written just before his downfall, or in the *Reule of Crysten Religioun,* which was apparently the first of his works.

What did Pecock understand to be the relation between reason and faith? It was a problem familiar enough in scholastic literature. Pecock resolved it by radically separating the two; reason and faith (philosophy and divinity) are, he writes, "two diverse faculties each of them having his proper to him bounds and marks . . . truths and conclusions."[12] Neither may be used to prove the truths of the other. At the same time, Pecock limits the conclusions of faith while he extols the range and competence of the rational faculty. Each is legitimate and valuable, but "doom of reason" is more extensive, more reliable, and in a sense more valuable than knowledge of scripture. Pecock, it seems, is hard to fit into any convenient scholastic category; his conclusions are equally removed from St. Thomas and from Scotus (both of whose works he knew and cites) and from most other medieval thinkers.[13] It is his confidence in reason that sets him apart and that has given him (for some at least) a thoroughly modern air.

By reason, Pecock meant the logic of the syllogism. He never tires of extolling its value as a means to truth. Give him two premises that are reliable, and he will deduce a third that is also true, "though all the angels in heaven would say and hold that conclusion were not true."[14] The reasoning of a syllogism is as true and compulsive to a Moslem or Jew as to a Christian. Indeed, when full and formal, logic "faileth never, neither in any time [doth] err." Men are only deceived in reasoning when they are too impatient to reduce an argument to syllogisms or when the premises are not sufficiently grounded. The twenty types of syllogism, Pecock is confident, cover all the possibilities of argument, although he has not the time to illustrate them. Still, he hopes that even the common people may be taught logic—so universal is its value—and expects some day to write a vernacular handbook for the purpose.[15] It is not the least of Pecock's claims to originality that he wrote most of his works in English. It was obviously not easy, nor was there any precedent for turning a systematic scholastic philosophy (with its complex technical vocabulary) into a readable fifteenth-century English.

But the syllogism depends for its value on its premises, and these may be either certain or probable. A premise is certain when it is self-evident. Here perhaps, Pecock is less helpful than he might be. Certainty is defined simply as that situation when "experience of sensitive wit or at full plain in reason" is so "openly true" that no man can err.[16] A premise is only probable, on the other hand, when the arguments on one side cannot be overborne by arguments on the other, when it is "so likely true that it is rather to be hold for true than for untrue." Dialectic, the *sic et non,* is thus the instrument which is used here and at each stage of argument to establish a probable truth.[17] Together, dialectic and the syllogism provide a method sufficient to combat any heresy. Pecock is so optimistic of the power of reason that he is even led to advocate toleration. Let all opinion, he urges, be so secure that anyone "come and go and speak and argue and answer without bodily harm and without any loss of his riches or fame."[18] We are reminded again of the irony of Pecock's career.

But not all truth is known by reason; there are also truths of faith. These are known "by the assertion or the witnessing of a person, which is not likely therein to make leasing and to beguile."[19] Pecock is concerned, of course, primarily with vindicating scripture. Even so, he finds it useful to justify the knowledge of faith by an appeal to reason. Such knowledge is not derived from reason, but it is determined to be knowledge by reason. After all, how does one know whether scripture is reliable in the first place? How can one determine the extent of scriptural truth? The meaning of a scriptural passage? For Pecock, unlike the Lollards, these things are not immediately apparent, nor are they the result of the goodness of the believer. They are problems resolvable only by the intellect, by the doom of reason. Thus, "if any seeming discord be betwixt the words written in the outward book of Holy Scripture and the doom of reason . . . the words so written withoutforth ought be expounded and interpreted and brought for to accord with the doom of reason in that matter." But never the reverse.[20] It was this conviction that eventually led the bishop into charges of heresy.

Pecock develops his idea of scriptural exegesis at some length. It is interesting to us both because it helps to define Pecock's idea of history and because it allows a useful contrast with Valla. Scripture, he writes, contains three kinds of matter. In the first place there is supernatural information, beyond the reach of reason, like knowledge of the Trinity. All that reason can do here is to show that scripture is not likely to have lied.[21] In the second place there is matter that is agreeable to reason. Finally, there is history, that is to say, "fetes, works, and deeds of creatures—as is, that such a king did such a victory and that such a person came of such a father and had such a progeny." Knowledge here depends on the "credence giving to the revelator and to the teller thereof which must be such as we ought always know and trust for his truth." In the case of scripture, this means applying two tests: first, comparing it with other scriptural testimony to see that there is no contradiction; second, seeing that it does not conflict with reason. In the case of human testimony, "in storying or chronicling, or by speech of himself or of his messenger without writing," knowledge is also an act of faith dependent on reason.[22] But here Pecock is less explicit; he is, after all, not really concerned with secular history. Still, one can infer his method readily enough; he would no doubt compare authorities, examine their "credibility" by the integrity of their characters, and then measure the result against the doom of reason. It is in fact the very method that he employs with the *Donation of Constantine*.

A more concrete example of his approach to history is his explanation of Genesis. The problem here occurs in a dialogue between father and son known as the *Book of Faith*.[23] The son is troubled over the fact that no scripture existed before Moses. That means to him that before Moses oral tradition had been sufficient. Why, he wants to know, is it no longer? Why did Moses need to receive it by inspiration and prophecy?

The father replies by setting up the problem as a dialectical question. If one could prove that it was more likely than not that no writing on the faith existed before Moses, then we might indeed wonder why we would need a written Scripture. But the probability of the contrary is in fact much stronger. For when we read the Master of the Stories (that is, the twelfth-century writer Peter Comestor), we discover that learning in the seven sciences was invented shortly after Noah's time. Likely enough, then, there was writing of the faith soon after the Flood, since writing existed and there were men of faith. But there is evidence that even before the Flood, Enoch had found letters (the authority is again Peter Comestor). Since the Bible says Enoch was a holy man who lived in the days of Adam, it is likely again that he wrote of holy matters even then. Moreover, it is probable that Noah, himself a holy man, would have protected these writings on his ship. His preaching against sin would clearly have profited from such "great cunning of full ghostly things." Another likelihood is that Enoch would have given his writing to his son Methuselah, from whom it could again have come to Noah. Noah would surely have passed it on to his sons and they to Abraham, Isaac, Jacob, and so on, each no doubt adding an account of his own. "And so at the last, Moses gathered all this together, and made a book thereof which is called Genesis."[24]

This chain of probabilities seems to Pecock altogether more likely than the story of divine inspiration, depending as it does upon a miracle. Indeed, belief in miracles is for him a last resort only, since we ought not to "feign, forge, allege, put, trow, or hold any miracle to be done, save when need compelleth us thereto." The haste to explain by means of a miracle makes nonsense of any resort to evidence.[25] In this case at least, there is a plausible alternative. The evidence we have suggests that a written scripture did exist before Moses and grew gradually over the generations until its final redaction by him.

It is startling to see Pecock anticipating the conclusions of the modern higher criticism in so curious a fashion. It is very like what he does with the *Donation*. His chain of deductions from a twelfth-century source leads him to a viewpoint about the composition of Genesis somewhat similar to that derived by modern textual criticism but utterly without its foundation. Needless to say, the coincidence in conclusions tells us nothing about Pecock's modernity or his understanding of historical criticism.

The notion that he possessed "a historical sense, unequalled in England for more than a century, and a capacity for the scientific view-point" begins to seem unlikely.[26] The bishop simply did not understand the modern preoccupation with original sources or their criticism.

But Pecock has a second and more general argument against the oral tradition. Take heed, the father cautions the son, how "a tale of a tiding, by the time that it hath run through four or five men's mouths, taketh patches and clouts and is changed in divers parts, and turned into leasings, and all for default of, thereof the writing."[27] It is impossible to imagine transmitting the long tale of the scriptures truly, through centuries of oral repetition. Especially is this unimaginable when we realize that language itself changes through time and place until it becomes impossible to understand a man of another country and century. Pecock is obviously sensitive to the limits of oral testimony; in another place he suggests its failings for contemporary affairs.[28] But he is apparently quite unaware that the same alterations and inaccuracies are possible in the transmission of a written text. There was apparently nothing in the logician's training to suggest the problem. This, despite the fact that he understands that the Bible is in one sense just like any other document. "Holy Writ," he notices, "may be taken for the outward letters written and shaped under divers figures in parchment or in vellum." Taken in this sense, he continues, it "is not holier neither better than any other writing in which hath like good ink, and is like craftily figured."[29] But this is not the sense that interests him; he is concerned with the inner meaning where reason, not textual criticism rules, and so he passes on to other things. For the humanist, by contrast, the textual problem was at once obvious and to the point. Valla saw immediately that the corruption of the New Testament had occurred through the passage of time and that the errors of scribes and translators had obscured its meaning; he also, as we shall see, tried to remedy it.

The example of the *Donation* is even more revealing, however, of both the extent and the limits of Pecock's historiographical technique. The Lollards had attacked the Church for many abuses, among them its great wealth and endowments. They had urged many arguments against them and Pecock was at pains to refute them all. The Lollards had charged, among other things, that as "the Church waxed in dignities it decreased in virtues," and they found in the *Donation of Constantine* one ultimate cause. That document purported to describe the gift by the Emperor Constantine to the Pope of great temporal possessions. The Lollards repeated the story that at the time of the endowment the voice of an angel was heard to cry, "In this day venom is hilded into the church of God!"[30] In other words the endowment of the clergy with great territory was "unvirtuous and evil." To refute the charge, Pecock felt that he must refute the story of the angel's voice, and this he does by first refuting the *Donation*. The larger question depends for him on the resolution of the subordinate *quaestio;* the refutation of the *Donation* is to take the form of a scholastic disputation.

It was a strange thing for Pecock to do. The *Donation* had been used for centuries, had indeed been invented in the first place in order to justify the papal claims to her endowments. Criticism of it, both earlier and later, depended for its motives largely upon the attack on those papal privileges. Yet Pecock meant to refute the *Donation* for the same purpose for which it had been invented: that is, to justify the papal claims. Only a logician with a supreme confidence in reason could have imagined such an undertaking.

Pecock begins with the story of the angel's voice. He argues first that the tale originated with Giraldus Cambrensis, the twelfth-century Welsh chronicler. However, he finds that Gerald told it not of a good angel but rather of the devil. Obviously, one may give little credence to the voice of a "fiend." Not content, he next assails Gerald's reliability. It is hard to believe the tale when "none elder story or chronicle can be found written before the said storying of Gerald."[31] Having cast suspicion on the angel's voice, Pecock next assails its foundation. He now challenges the story of Constantine's endowment, the alleged provocation of the angel.

The story Pecock inherited and which was generally believed in his day may be briefly told. Constantine, the Emperor of the West, had begun to persecute the Christians once again and forced Sylvester, Bishop of Rome, to take refuge. The emperor was afflicted with leprosy, however, and sought a cure. He rejected the solution of pagan priests (a bath in the blood of infants) and was rewarded by a dream in which two figures appeared promising relief if he would but seek out Sylvester and obey him. This Constantine did. Sylvester showed him likenesses of Peter and Paul, whom Constantine identified as the visionary figures. The pope then directed Constantine to submit to fasting and to baptism, upon which event Constantine was at once miraculously and, in a blaze of light, healed. In return, the emperor at once directed Christianity to be adopted throughout the empire and heavily endowed the Church. He built the Lateran Palace for the bishop as well as various places of worship, furnished them liberally, and supplied the pope with his ceremonial garments, scepter, etc. Finally, and most munificently, he bestowed upon Sylvester the city of Rome and all the provinces of the West, transferring his own seat to Byzantium. Thus the miraculous cure of Constantine by Sylvester and the consequent donation of Constantine are the two main elements in the story Pecock received, each with a separate source. But though each had a different origin, they had long been interdependent.[32] Pecock believed neither, and urged refutation of each as proof against the reliability of the other. His arguments are not easy to follow, especially in their scholastic form and fifteenth-century English; nevertheless, they are worth restatement, if only because they have been so frequently misunderstood.

Pecock begins by examining the story of Constantine's baptism and cure. Immediately, he insists upon the need for testimony. In general we ought not to believe such tales unless some "storier or chronicler had written" of them. It is a virtue of Pecock's method in general that he is continuously insistent on the need for evidence. "Our reason," he argues, "may not know any truth and consent thereto without this, that our reason have evidences for to so consent."[33] It is the historian's task to discover the "fundamental undoubted evidences," the testimony for each incident. In this case, as it happens, there are witnesses on both sides. But if it can be shown conclusively that Constantine was *not* baptized in Rome, then the witnesses affirming it cannot be believed (and the story of the angel's voice must also fail). In short, we cannot believe both that Constantine was and that he was not baptized in Rome; we must choose the more probable story by examining the evidence on either side. As with the case of the Mosaic testimony, Pecock sets up the problem as a dialectical question. But his criteria for evidence and for probability are not in the end more persuasive here than they were for establishing his view of Genesis.

What evidence does Pecock have? Telling the miraculous tale he finds two sources, an anonymous life of Sylvester and the narrative in the *Liber Pontificalis*. From these, he is sure, the other histories and chronicles have derived their accounts. On the other side, he discovers an alternative story in the writings of Eusebius of Caesarea and in the *Tripartite History*. There, Constantine is said to have been baptized only at the end of his life, by an ordinary bishop in a city called Nicomedia. Obviously, one may not believe both.

For Pecock the choice is clear: Eusebius is a reliable authority. No one would know better than he the circumstances of Constantine's baptism, for he was "living and conversant with the same Constantine and was privy with Constantine in the councils of his heart and of his conscience." Furthermore, Eusebius' *Ecclesiastical History* had been praised and celebrated by St. Jerome and the authors of the *Tripartite History*. Next to the Bible, Pecock declares, it was the most famous and credible story known to Christians. And Eusebius' *Life of Constantine* was also the natural result of his having been so "privey and so homely" with the emperor. That work was thus the most reliable authority by the best informed of men and deserves full credence.[34] It was certainly worthier of belief than the sources of the alternative story. Of the *Life of Sylvester*, "no man can tell who wrote it, neither whence it came, or whither it will." Pecock re-affirms his suspicions of the miracles of saints' lives in general: "In legends be found many full untrue fables." As for the account in the *Liber Pontificalis*, that was written long after the events by Pope Damasus and is not entirely reliable anyway.[35]

Pecock adds two further arguments against the legendary story of Sylvester. First, he notices that both Ambrose and Jerome believed the alternative in Eusebius. But surely they would not have followed him against Damasus without sufficient evidence. Furthermore, the chroni-cles "most credible next" to Eusebius, the *Tripartite* authors, also witness that Constantine was baptized just before his death at Nicomedia. These witnesses together surely outweigh the others and tell a story more credi-ble than the contrary, which must therefore be "an apocrif."

The ground is now clear for Pecock's assault on the *Donation* itself. The last prop for the tale of the angel's voice has to be removed. Con-stantine is shown to have made no endowment such as that usually attributed to him. Pecock's next argument, therefore, suggests that the first endowments of the Church had occurred much before Constantine. He cites two instances, the endowments made a hundred years earlier as recorded in Pope Urban's *Decrees* and those made earlier still by Pope Eleutherius to the British king, Lucius. Of both these endowments, "old stories and chronicles (being famous and worthy and credible and not being apocrifs) make mention." He then argues against the abundancy of Constantine's endowments. The large donations attributed to him were only made much later by Pepin, Charles the Great, Ludovic, and Matilda. Here again, unnamed chronicles and stories are brought to bear witness.[36]

But how to dispose of the detailed enumeration of gifts in the received story? Again Pecock marshals a number of arguments. First there is the argument from silence. If the donation had occurred, surely there would have been "some mention . . . in some fundamental and credible story or chronicle." But in fact there is none except for the *Life of Syl-vester* and the stories and chronicles that are based upon it. We have seen how little value they possess. Then, again, there are the alternative ac-counts of more reliable authorities. For example, the *Tripartite History* says that Constantine left his empire to his three sons, including the western part, with the eldest son inheriting Rome. Again, Constantine's quick determination to move to the East to build Byzantium is contra-dicted by the story in the *Tripartite History*, which tells how Constantine meant to build his capital in another place altogether and even had some of it built when a warning in his sleep turned him aside from his program.

But most elaborate are his proofs drawn from the later history of

Rome, all contradicting the story of the *Donation*. For example, about two hundred and fifty years afterward, Pope Boniface IV wished to convert the Pantheon in Rome to a church. But he had to ask the eastern Emperor Phocas "leave for to so do." Why should he have had to do this if Rome and the surrounding country were already his? Again, the chronicles show that from Constantine to Charlemagne there was an unbroken succession of emperors who reigned over both East and West. It was only in Charlemagne's day that the empire was divided and probably only then that the popes gained lordship over Rome (and that at the behest of Charles and later Ludovic). Finally, Pecock asserts that for hundreds of years after Sylvester's death the elections of popes had to be confirmed by the emperors, "as can be proved by sufficient credible chronicles and stories, and in special for to see in the chronicle of Martyn, where he speaketh of Pope Vitalian."[37] Pecock does not deny the possibility of small endowments by Constantine; he is confident that his arguments refute the main point that Constantine had bestowed great lands and territorial sovereignty upon the pope. If that was not done, there was no need for an angel to denounce it. Pecock's argument is complete.

How may we assess Pecock's performance? Certainly, his main conclusions are correct by the standards of modern scholarship. Neither angel's voice nor miraculous conversion nor *Donation of Constantine* is historically authentic. That is how Pecock won his reputation for modernity. But this is surely to obscure the main issue: Pecock's method of arriving at his conclusions. Essentially, what he did was to compare authorities and choose among them. As R. G. Collingwood has reminded us, however, the mere comparison of authorities to determine which is right and which is wrong is a kind of scissors-and-paste historiography that the modern historian no longer finds adequate. (This, is of course, a special temptation to the logician who has no other means but to affirm or deny the consistency of a series of statements.) What we want to know of our sources now is what they meant, not simply whether they were right or wrong. We need not either reject or accept them wholly. If we know their purpose and intention, we can then interpret their usefulness to the question at hand. But Pecock has not asked these questions, not even of his favorite, Eusebius, and still less of the alternative accounts. What is the *Life of Sylvester* or the *Donation of Constantine* if they are not what they seem? Why were they written, and what was their intention?

But even in its own terms, Pecock's method is not completely successful. The number of his authorities is, for one thing, much too small.[38] Scholastic logic finished little incentive and no technique for historical research. It *was* possible, for example, to find the story of the angel's voice long before Giraldus. It was also possible to find a wealth of information about Constantine's reign and the condition of the Church both before and after, all relevant to his argument. Ignorance of well-known Latin authorities and inability to read any Greek at all were, in the end, insurmountable handicaps to his position. Here the contemporary humanist Valla shows his great advantage. Yet examination of Pecock's own evidence is not more satisfactory. The chronicler "Martyn," Martinus Polonus, for example, is a thirteenth-century writer thought to be notoriously unreliable today; his value is exactly like Peter Comestor's for biblical events. Why is he "sufficient credible" for Pecock? The gifts to the Church by Popes Urban and Eleutherius are as mythical as those of Constantine, and dependent upon authorities at least as untrustworthy. Nor was it Charlemagne who vested the Church with its Italian lands. The attack on the alternative authorities will not do either. What reason, besides the contradictions of allegedly more certain authorities, is there to suppose that the *Life of Sylvester,* the *Liber Pontificalis,*[39] or the *Donation* itself—not to mention the many corroborative chronicle accounts—are false? It is true that miraculous stories are to be received with caution. But does not Eusebius also tell us of a miracle by which Constantine was converted to the faith? Why then prefer the *Vita Constantini* to the *Vita Sylvestri?*[40] Indeed, if one simply reverses Pecock's skepticism, his arguments will work almost as well against Eusebius as they do against the *Donation.* It is true that the story of Pope Damasus is late, but so too was the *Tripartite History* on which Pecock relies so heavily—especially in the only version known to him, the Latin abbreviation by Cassiodorus. How late were they? What was their point or purpose? In the end, Pecock's ideas of historical evidence and of historical probability were determined—like those of his Lollard opponents—more by his prejudices than by his methodological sophistication. His arguments may have afforded the fifteenth century an ingenious logical exercise, but they left the meaning and reliability of the documents, and therefore the history of his subject, pretty much where Pecock had found them. Thus the course of medieval historiography remained unaffected by his efforts.

In short, Pecock was not a modern critical historian. But his achievement was not for that reason negligible. The comparison of authorities is indeed a critical step, although a first step only. If Pecock invented no new method, it is fair to say that he at least invented a problem, one difficult to avoid thereafter. And within the limits of his method he showed great ingenuity in solving it—how great we may see at once simply by comparing him with his fifteenth-century critics. Without exception (in England at any rate) they remained content with the traditional story. In one case, at least, Pecock was directly answered. The Abbot John of Wethamstede, in his *Granarium* (a work contemporary with the *Repressor*), tried to rebut the skeptical arguments against the *Donation* altogether but entirely missed their force.[41] Thus, he meets Pecock's argument from silence not with fresh evidence—something that might well have impressed the bishop—but by analogy with the Gospels. The fall of the idols when Christ entered Egypt, he suggests, is not in Matthew or Mark, yet St. Jerome tells it and not as mere gossip. Nor does lack of notice in the synoptic Gospels discredit the stories about St. John. Silence is thus no argument. As for the tale of Constantine's conversion, authorities abound, and Wethamstede supplies a long list of writers to confirm it—all obviously late, however. For the abbot, comparison of authorities may yield any result, since he recognizes no criterion of authenticity whatsoever. That a lie might be repeated—obvious enough to Pecock—never enters his head, and he seems to have felt that a miraculous story need have no contemporary source whatever to authenticate it. In this context Pecock appears sophisticated and critical indeed. But this was not the only context that the fifteenth century offered.

(2)

Lorenzo Valla's career and achievement are altogether more familiar than Pecock's. It may be enough, then, simply to recall some of its chief incidents.[42] Curiously, even in its external character, Valla's life furnishes a running contrast to the Englishman's. Both attacked more than one traditional opinion; both stirred opposition by their arrogance as well as their ideas; both were accused of heresy. But where the one was ruined, the other was saved by political alliance. And where one was forced to recant what he would surely have defended as orthodoxy, the other, Valla, was confirmed by papal appointment in opinions that were more overtly heterodox—or at least reformist in intention.

Valla was the younger man by about ten years. His education at once set him apart from men like Pecock. He was taught entirely outside the scholastic curriculum by two of the leading humanists of his generation, Giovanni Aurispa and Leonardo Bruni. This meant an education in the Latin and Greek classical authors and languages, essentially, that is, in grammar and rhetoric—an education impossible to obtain in fifteenth-century England.[43] From the first and throughout his career, Valla fought against the Aristotelian logic of the schoolmen, and when he came at last to teach in the universities, he taught the new subject of "eloquence."[44] Like many other Italian humanists he found his vocation as a tutor and Latin secretary; although he had taken orders, this meant an essentially secular career—even perhaps after being appointed to the papal court. But if Valla was neither a philosopher nor a theologian in Pecock's sense, he was interested in the problems of each. His interest, however, was not so much logical as it was philological. He thought that the problems of moral philosophy and Christian metaphysics were more likely of solution by a critical examination of their sources and their language than by dialectic or syllogism. He worked, says Garin, "to grasp the precise original meaning of words, a meaning that lies beyond any meaning that can be established by traditional logical discussions. In going back to the oldest meaning of a word he aimed at determining its connotations and denotations. And thus he hoped to advance to the sources of the thought that is enshrined in words."[45]

Valla was thus, first of all, a grammarian. And his greatest achievement was probably the grammatical work known as *On the Elegancies of the Latin Language*. He wrote, he said, to restore the language of Rome to the Romans, to return it to its glory and purity before the barbarian corruption. That this was desirable no humanist could doubt; the ancients were the models for imitation, and close imitation depended upon exact knowledge. Valla aimed to supply it and succeeded as no one before. He showed correct Latin to be determined not by rules—certainly not by reason, as the scholastics had occasionally argued—but by the actual usage of the classical authors. Grammatical study was thus freed from logic; it became in Valla's hands a historical discipline. He was clever enough to see that Latin had been a changing language from its origins—as we have seen, there was a hint of that in Pecock—but even more clever to be able to demonstrate differences in style among the classical authors as well as the "barbarous" medieval writers. He could correct, from the evidence of usage, not only medieval grammarians but even classical authors like Priscian as well.[46]

The *Elegancies* taught all Europe the meaning of classical style. But Valla's work as grammarian was much more various. In characteristic humanist fashion he edited, translated, and commented upon the classical authors, Greek as well as Latin. The historians especially interested him—Herodotus, Thucydides, Livy. Most characteristic and most unusual was his work on the New Testament. The contrast with Pecock could not be more precise. Both were aware of the document as a piece of "parchment and vellum," as the work of fallible human scribes. But where for Pecock this was unimportant, for Valla it was a fact of great significance. How was one to know the meaning of Scripture if one could not rely on the language before one's eyes? Pecock would no doubt have replied, "by doom of reason"; indeed, he expressly denies the value of grammar to theology at one point in his discussion. "Grammar and divinity," he wrote, "be two faculties atwine and asunder departed, and therefore they have their proper to them bounds and marks that none of them enter into the other."[47] Valla might well have been answering the Englishman when he announced his own intentions: "Some people deny that theology is subject to the rules of grammar but I say that theologians ought to obey the rules of language, whether written or spoken." Intelligibility itself, he argued, was at stake. Before anything else could be done to recover the true meaning of scripture, the text itself had to be established, and the corruptions and errors of scribes and translators removed. Valla began the task; he collated three Latin and three Greek codices, showing, where he could, the grammatical misunderstandings and unhappy translations—not excepting from his criticism even Jerome. His emendation of the passage in Romans 1.17 from "The just live by faith" to "The just shall live by faith" shows how much was at stake. His notes were retrieved by Erasmus and published in 1505; they helped to inspire the next great humanist grammarian to tackle the problem.[48]

Valla was thus, before anything else, a grammatical critic in search of error. His sense of the historicity of language made him exceptionally attuned to anachronisms. Was it any surprise, then, that he discovered them at once in various startling places? Like Pecock he questioned the authorship of the Apostles' Creed;[49] unlike Pecock he also disputed the apostolic authority of the work of Dionysius the Areopagite. Nor was he satisfied with the authenticity of the letter of Jesus to King Abgarus. To a man of his sensibilities the *Donation of Constantine* was at once and obviously a forgery, and it is his detailed refutation of that document that is his critical masterpiece. But unlike Pecock's work, which was embedded in a complex and difficult philosophical treatise, Valla's tract was an independent work in the new classical idiom. It soon struck a responsive chord and became widely known and influential—particularly, as one might expect, among the Protestants of the next century.

Yet the *Declamation on the Donation of Constantine* is more than an example of grammar. It is a masterpiece of humanist invective as well, a concrete example of the value of eloquence.[50] Pecock had dismissed rhetoric, in much the way he had disposed of grammar, in a brief passage in the *Repressor*.[51] His own work makes no effort to persuade by anything but its appeal to logic. Valla, on the other hand, would have found Pecock—as he found the scholastic writers generally—barbarous and nonsensical. An appeal to the will and to the emotions was as necessary for him as an appeal to reason. It is eloquence, particularly eloquence informed by the study of history, that rises superior to any philosophy. "In my view," he wrote in the preface to his own history of Ferdinand of Aragon, "historians show a greater seriousness in their speeches, greater insight and civic wisdom than the philosophers with their general maxims."[52] His *Declamation* is therefore both a rhetorical and a grammatical work, with the methods of both disciplines applied to a specific historical problem.[53]

The tract begins with a flourish in which truth is proclaimed over death and the papacy; at once the humanist outlines his argument. It falls into several fairly distinct parts. The first concerns the inherent plausibility of the *Donation*. This is followed by a discussion of the historical evidence. Then comes a close philological reading, revealing many errors and inconsistencies in the text. And finally there are legal and moral arguments that conclude the work. What Valla says is this: look at the *Donation* and you will see that even on the face of it, it is highly improbable. If you take the trouble, you will find it completely unsubstantiated by evidence. Moreover, it is riddled with clumsy errors that show it to be a forgery. But if all this fails, still you must agree that even had the *Donation* existed historically, its illegality and immorality make it entirely unacceptable.

As the arguments unfold, it is clear that most of them depend upon a broad reading of classical history. Even the argument over probability, a favorite weapon of the rhetoricians, depends upon putting oneself in Constantine's or Sylvester's place and considering what the likelihood of certain actions and their consequences would have been. Valla invents a series of orations for each of the parties showing what their reactions would have been to such an act. In each case, he argues, the *Donation* would have been rejected by them. More convincingly, he then imagines what would have concretely transpired from the gift, had there been such an event, and asks for evidence of it. For example, if the Church had indeed secured possession of it, certain things ought to have followed: an imperial ceremony, the traditional tour of the provinces, and the like. What governors and rulers, Valla asks, did the pope select for the provinces and cities? Were the old magistrates relieved and new ones appointed? What battles were fought and under whose leadership? But there is no evidence, unless "all these things were done in the night time and therefore no man could see them." If Sylvester was in possession, then who dispossessed him? for none of his successors held Rome. "O marvelous and wonderful chance that the empire of Rome which was gotten and won with so great labors with so much blood-shed should so peaceably, so quietly, either be gotten or lost of the Christian priests . . .- that no man knoweth or can tell by whom this thing was done."[54] Who is there, Valla asks, who does not know ("if he be any thing acquainted with histories") the least details of the Empire, so well has its story been recorded, its consuls, tribunes, censors, and so on? In exasperation he demands of the author of the *Donation*, "What records or what authors can you bring forth of those things?" Obviously none, for the *Donation* is thoroughly implausible even on the face of it.

In place of the missing evidence, Valla supplies his own for the more convincing story of Constantine's continued rule. There is Eutropius, "which saw Constantine and his sons"; there are the gold coins of Constantine minted after his conversion with inscriptions in Latin (not Greek) of all the emperors in succession. Where are the coins for the popes? Moreover, every history deserving the name speaks of Constantine as a Christian from boyhood, long before Sylvester. Both Eusebius and Rufinus, "well near in Constantine's time," attest to that, as well as Sylvester's own successor, Pope Melchiades.[55] Valla dismisses the evidence of Gratian and the *Life of Sylvester*, the one as a later interpolation of no credence, the other as spurious altogether. When later he returns to consider the *Life*, he reveals, like Pecock, a general but not complete skepticism of hagiography. Not everything in the lives of the saints is false, "but I can not suffer that they be mingled with fables and lies." True Christianity does not need the support of false miracles. Yet even casual examination of the *Life of Sylvester* suggests that it is a bad example of its genre. For instance, it tells the story of an enormous serpent consuming Rome with its poisonous breath, and only pacified by devouring young maidens, until bound in its cave by Sylvester. Is this credible? Valla summons all his knowledge of dragons, classical and biblical, to deny its plausibility. But that story is only one of the incredible tales of the *Life;* such a document surely can carry no conviction.

Valla is now ready to analyze the text itself, and he begins a massive philological assault upon the document. Page upon page of criticism exposes the *Donation* as riddled with linguistic errors and anachronisms. A few examples will show his method. The very title of the gift, "the page of the privilege" (*paginam privilegii*), is peculiar. "Callest thou the donation of the world a privilege?"[56] Could it possibly be written so in such a document? But if the title is ridiculous, what are we to imagine of the rest? At once we hear of imperial "satraps." Whoever heard them mentioned in the councils of the Romans? Valla can remember neither Roman nor provincial "satraps" in any of his reading. Yet here they may be found more important even than the Senate. Then there are the "nobles" (*optimates*) spoken of in a way hardly consonant with the customs of the Empire, and there is the phrase "the people subject to the Roman Church" (*Romanae ecclesiae subiacens*), rather than "the Roman people." Passage by passage, Valla exposes the faulty language of the document.

His concern for style reveals the bad and inappropriate Latin of the work. Thus, we are told that Constantine chose the apostles "to be [*esse*] his intercessors," instead of "as his intercessors." Valla wonders, "Did the scribes of the emperors (because I will not say the horsekeepers) speak after this manner and fashion in thy time?" The scribe must have put in the infinitive (*esse*) to make the words fit more trimly together! There is the phrase "our imperial power" (*nostra terrena imperialis potestas*), "where he joineth two adjectives without a conjunction copulative." And "clemency of our imperial serenity" instead of "grandeur and majesty"; "chief over the priest" instead of "chief of the priests," and so on.[57]

There are still other kinds of faulty usage that Valla's superior knowledge of Roman affairs helps to reveal. Thus, the diadem is made of gold but ought to have been of cloth. The *Donation* speaks of a tiara (*phrygium*): "How great barbarousness is there in these words: who ever heard this word Phrigium used in the Latin tongue?" Thus, not only is the document shown to be spurious, but it is revealed to be a later forgery. For, Valla asks, "doth not the very barbarousness of the manner of speaking witness openly: that this carol hath been feigned not in the time of Constantine but in a time more late?"[58] There is still more to Valla's argument, but he is ready at last to add his conclusive point: even if true, the *Donation* would be illegal and immoral and hence invalid anyway.

The *Declamation*, it should be said, was written by Valla to support the King of Naples in a territorial dispute with the pope. He was very proud of its rhetoric. But although it is a polemical and rhetorical production, it is obviously a first-rate piece of historical criticism as well. Valla has not the mastery of the sources of a modern historian, but his range is very much wider than Pecock's. To a broader knowledge of the literary authorities, Greek as well as Latin, he adds, besides, information derived from coins and inscriptions. His familiarity with the customs, legal forms, and language of the fourth century is extensive enough to declare the *Donation* at once anachronistic. For the humanist, no aspect of antiquity was uninteresting; all sources of information had become possible. The modern idea of research was born of the classical philologist's concern to illuminate his texts, to understand them again as they had been written. Thus Valla turns upon the *Donation* the full equipment of his craft. The existence of a historical problem impels him to examine the full range of relevant sources, not simply to compare those conveniently at hand. His scorn for the anonymous forger is partly due to his rhetorical posture; it is also the genuine response of a humanist to the apparent ignorance and clumsy Latin of the author. The arguments from silence and from the contradictions of later events are more convincing than Pecock's because Valla's knowledge is greater and more authoritative. His comparison of the sources is also sounder, although he too takes some of the argument for granted and makes some important errors. But it is Valla's "grammatical" argument that is in the end the most significant and persuasive and provides the *coup de grâce* to the *Donation*. He has gone back to the texts and subjected them to a systematic philological criticism. By considering the language of his sources and by setting them into their contemporary context, he has recaptured their meaning and intention—at least sufficiently to declare the *Donation* conclusively anachronistic. Renaissance grammar, it turns out, is more efficacious for the solution of a historical problem than scholastic logic, and the humanist much the superior historian to his rival the professional theologian.[59]

Yet once again there was more to be done, and Valla does not do it. The modern historian is not satisfied merely with the destructive argument. The *Donation* is not what it purports to be; what is it, then? When was it written and why?[60] It is easy to see why Valla stops short. He is not writing history; he is writing polemic. He has satisfied the needs of his patron and of the rhetorical declamation.[61] To tell the story of Constantine's reign, or of the accretion of papal temporalities, in a thorough and critical fashion remained a work for the future. In fact, it was a task beyond the powers or at least the interests of Valla and his contemporaries. The demands of eloquence set limits to the employment of scholarly technique; rhetoric remained for a long time in conflict with grammar in the writing of history. It was a very long time before historians would use the techniques of humanist philology systematically to reconstruct the past. Furthermore, the humanists for the most part had no interest in and only little sympathy for the Middle Ages. Their very sensitivity to the changes in culture, from ancient to medieval to Renaissance, awoke a historical sensibility but then limited it. For the classical revival involved not only an apprehension of change but a judgment upon it—a judgment that had the effect of limiting interest and understanding for the whole long period after antiquity.[62]

But we should not be too eager to judge the past by the standards of the present. If Pecock and Valla in different ways and in different degrees fail to meet the historiographical standards of the present, we should no more condemn them than more superficial critics have praised them for their modernity. At the same time, we must not confuse their different techniques or their different attitudes toward history that were at bottom very unlike. Of the two, it is clear that we stand closer to Valla; and it is to Renaissance philology, rather then to medieval logic, that the future of historical method belonged. But how it came to pass that Valla's technique was transformed from philology and polemic into a systematic and constructive historiographical method is another and still not very well known story. In any case, and of this we may be sure, it did not occur until long after the exposure of the *Donation of Constantine*.

CHAPTER 3

The Antiquarian Enterprise,
1500–1800

(1)

When at last, after twenty years and half a dozen quarto volumes, Edward Gibbon thought to bring the *Decline and Fall* to a conclusion, he remembered the Italian humanist Poggio Bracciolini, sitting on the Capitoline amid the ruins of ancient Rome, reflecting on the vicissitudes of fortune. "The hill of the Capitol," Poggio had written, "was formerly the head of the Roman Empire, the citadel of the earth, the terror of kings. . . . This spectacle of the world, how it is fallen! how changed! how defaced!" Poggio's reaction, Gibbon remembered, had been to take an immediate inventory of the visible remains, as though he could somehow reverse that terrible decline of fortune and restore some part of the original grandeur of the awful scene: to recreate in his imagination the bridges, arches, temples, baths, theaters, columns, sepulchers, walls, and gates of ancient Rome.[1] When, some three hundred years later, the young Englishman came to rest on that very spot, he was naturally moved by almost the same reflections, and there of course it was that he conceived the idea for his great work. If Poggio was not the first nor Gibbon the last to take inspiration from those somber ruins, their dates (c. 1447–1764) mark almost the exact interval during which the study of antiquities came to flourish and began to decline in western Europe.[2]

The antiquarian impulse was born of the revival of antiquity; it was from first to last a by-product of the admiration for the classics that first awoke during the Italian Renaissance and that flourished for generations as the bedrock of European education and culture.[3] It was humanism that created it, nourished it, and also, as we shall see, paradoxically, limited it. Much has been written about the beginning of the classical revival; much less about its endurance in many different situations over

73

several hundred years. If it is still not easy to say just why it was that Europeans should have thought it necessary to admire and imitate the classical authors after a lapse of fifteen hundred years and more, it is even harder to know why it was that they should have remained the models of humanistic culture for so long a time. But it is clear that from Poggio's careful training in Renaissance Florence to Gibbon's irregular schooling in Georgian England, it was classical Latin and Greek alone that really mattered; and it was natural enough that both the fifteenth-century Italian and the eighteenth-century Englishman should come to share the same ambition, to acquire literary fame by deliberately following the example of the ancients, although one wrote directly in Latin and the other in a latinized English and French.

In short, the continuity of classical culture in early modern times has not, I think, been sufficiently stressed. The bond between Gibbon and Poggio was not at all imaginary, and the eighteenth century usually remembered its indebtedness to the Renaissance. Even the "moderns" in the battle of the books, who wanted to free English culture from the bondage of an overdependence upon antiquity, applauded the neo-classical reformation of language and culture that had begun in the days of Thomas More and Erasmus, and they continued to despise the Middle Ages, which (like Gibbon) they found barbarous because they thought that no one in the period understood or appreciated good Latin. And if the moderns had more confidence in present and future than the "ancients," they still hesitated to disparage antiquity and continued to take most of their cues—in the humanities, anyway—from the examples of the classical authors.[4]

No doubt it was education above all that forged the link; for once the schools had altered their curriculum in the sixteenth century to an exclusive dependence upon the Latin and Greek authors, there was little further change, and every cultivated European began life with the two classical languages and a common stock of antique learning. If Lyly's Latin grammar had been compiled by the founders of St. Paul's School at the beginning of the sixteenth century, it was still in use as the royal grammar in the eighteenth century; if Roger Ascham's *Schoolmaster* had expounded the theory and practice of classical imitation for the Elizabethans, it was still thought worth republishing two centuries later with a life and approving preface by Samuel Johnson.[5] The ideal of the classically educated gentleman was indeed almost perfectly continuous from Thomas Elyot under Henry VIII to Horace Walpole and the Earl of Chesterfield under George III and probably found its finest realization only in the golden age of Burke and Pitt and Charles James Fox. Despite an occasional equivocation (largely from religious dissidents) and some oscillation in the choice of authors (from Cicero to Seneca, Homer to Virgil, and back again), the succession of generations showed a gradual but definite deepening of knowledge, an increasing mastery of classical idiom, and a persistent commitment to one classical ideal or another.

No doubt one of the things that sustained this commitment to antiquity was the belief, almost universal throughout the period, in the practical value of the classics to the life and work of the governing classes. The Renaissance humanists taught that the best training of the statesman lay in a mastery of ancient rhetoric and political example, in the literature and history of antiquity; and the practical politicians of the period accepted this advice without equivocation, from Henry VIII and Thomas Cromwell, each of whom saw to the education of his own children, to the great parliamentary orators of the Augustan age. They cheerfully paid the price of the new learning (though never quite to the satisfaction of their teachers), and they identified themselves with the ruling classes of antiquity, who furnished the models not only for their prose styles but for their life styles, for their practical politics, and for the great houses and churches they built wherever they ruled. If the English were belated in their return to antiquity compared with Italy and continental Europe, they nevertheless made amends and eventually caught up. From this vantage point, eighteenth-century English neoclassicism must be seen not simply as the name of a particular style but as the natural ripening of tendencies that had begun many generations earlier.

Now it was this long-term commitment to the classics, to the educative value of ancient literature, that was the matrix for antiquarian thought and activity throughout the centuries. Even upon its first appearance in Italy, the admiration for classical letters provoked an interest in antiquities. It was almost inevitable that Petrarch should scribble into the margins of his copies of Livy and Eusebius notes on the ancient topography of Italy and Rome, moved already—like Poggio and Gibbon later— by the sight of the crumbling walls, arches, baths, and amphitheaters.[6] Upon his first visit to Rome in 1337, he wrote a memorable letter describing his tour of the city and his attempts to identify some of the places where the great historical events had occurred.[7] If he often mistook what he saw, he had no ready guide, and his attempt to reconceive republican Rome in his epic poem *Africa* was bound to be inadequate, though it certainly anticipates one of the great antiquarian activities of the future. His interest in ancient coins and inscriptions, which he used to illustrate and explain the references in his reading, also forecast the direction humanists were bound to take once they had become infatuated with the classical authors. It was Petrarch's friend Cola di Rienzi who first saw the political use of Roman antiquities which, like the literature of republican Rome, came to life in his imagination, though they had been almost unintelligible a generation earlier.[8]

By Poggio's time, humanism was no longer isolated in a few individuals but had become a vigorous movement of thought and a formal system of education with powerful patronage. The effort to restore the classical authors was advancing on all fronts, not least through Poggio's own memorable discoveries of lost works by Cicero, Quintilian, Plautus, and so on. As these manuscripts were read and imitated, the problems of their exact meaning and interpretation became more pressing, and Renaissance philology was born. Each text had to be recovered, deciphered, collated, edited, and interpreted. It was at once understood that the material remains of antiquity could be useful in this effort to throw light on the classical authors, as well as vice versa: that words could be illustrated by things, and the ruins of the ancient world by its literature. Poggio was not satisfied with mere description; he set about cross-examining the old remains in conjunction with the written sources. His discovery of a rare manuscript of Frontinus at Montecassino was of obvious value in viewing the Roman aqueducts, and he even managed to turn the Greek authors, now suddenly open to Renaissance Florentines, to good account. His archaeology remained unsystematic, and he continued to make errors, but he understood clearly the many possibilities of antiquarian study.

What were they? In the first place, as we have seen, the monuments could be used to restore the setting for ancient events, literary and historical. "Each memorable spot," Gibbon recalled, as he climbed the steps of the Capitol, "where Romulus stood, or Tully spoke, or Caesar fell, was at once present to my eye, and several days of intoxication were lost or enjoyed before I could descend to a cool and minute investigation."[9] But what held for the Capitol could be extended to all the ancient world—to the Campagna, for example, where Poggio and Gibbon tried to find the old villas of Cicero;[10] and to all the provinces of the Empire, including Roman Britain; even to Greece and the East when travel became easier. The visual imagination of early modern times was not only stirred by the sight of these ancient things; it was, as we know, redirected among artists and architects (and their patrons) by the same desire to imitate antiquity that governed the humanists. Once again, the story is more or less continuous from the generation of Poggio, when Brunelleschi and Donatello were said to have visited Rome to copy monuments, and a little later of Mantegna, who most certainly made an antiquarian tour of Lake Garda,[11] to the high Renaissance and beyond, until every artist who could find a way and every gentleman who could afford to went to Rome and brought home a portfolio of Piranesi prints, or the like, to keep in his studio or library and remind him of the scenes of his youthful reading.

It was Poggio's contemporary Flavio Biondo who made the first systematic survey of the monuments of ancient Rome (the *Roma instaurata* of 1453) and the first for all Italy (the *Italia restaurata*, 1457–59), whereupon each new generation added its own contribution and made revisions. The ancient geographers Strabo and Pausanias furnished a kind of rough model of how to combine topographical description and antiquities, while Ptolemy and the *Antonine Itineraries* supplied tantalizing hints as to the whereabouts of the ancient cities and roads. In the eighteenth century, Gibbon relied heavily on the "elaborate treatises" of Nardini for Rome, which took him sixteen days to read and which he admired for their learning and accuracy, and Cluverius for Italy, "a learned native who had measured on foot every spot, and digested every passage of the ancient writers." (For a brief moment he even considered writing his own description of Italy, following the example of Strabo and improving Cluverius.)[12] If, at the beginning of the revival, Petrarch could only lament the destruction of the ancient monuments,[13] Biondo and his successors believed that they could at least restore an exact memory of them. And if the antiquaries rarely aspired to literary elegance themselves, they never forgot the direct relationship that existed between the revival of letters and the new scholarship. "Since the present century," wrote Biondo, "has seen the rise of the arts, notably the arts of eloquence and literature, and as these studies have created in us an ardent desire to understand the past, I have determined to make an attempt . . . to restore to life the names of the ancient places and peoples, to rediscover the origins of cities still standing and give to those now ruined that life which remembrance can bestow, in other words, to shed light on what is obscure in the history of Italy."[14]

In the second place, the material remains of antiquity could be used to provide specific information about the past, to illustrate the activities of ordinary life (manners, customs, dress, and so on), to recover events and people otherwise lost, and to clear up the meaning of obscure passages in the literary texts. Here the ancient model was Varro, whose work on antiquities was known only partially and indirectly.[15] In particular, it was seen that the inscriptions and coins of the ancient world, so copious in Greek as well as Latin, could be made to yield their due. Poggio collected what he could of both kinds, and Gibbon prepared himself for his visit to Rome by surveying the whole existing state of knowledge on the subject.[16] It was Poggio's friend Ciriaco of Ancona (1391–1453) who virtually invented the new science, traveling the Mediterranean both east and west, collecting and recording in his manuscript commentaries every scrap of epigraphic evidence he could discover for the whole life of antiquity.[17] In

1421, we are told, while he was contemplating an inscription on an arch of Trajan, he resolved to undertake his life work. His commentaries are a kind of travel diary (a forecast of many to come), in which he recorded descriptions of ancient sites, passages from classical authors, sketches of ruins, and most copiously, perhaps, copies of inscriptions, many taken directly from the monuments themselves. His aim, he said, like Biondo's, was "to wake the dead," to restore the ancients to life among the living. And though his own Latin was clumsy and his Greek belated, he too took his inspiration from the classical authors whom he carried with him, and one would like to believe (though the episode is apocryphal) that he read Livy to the Sultan himself before the walls of Byzantium in 1452. Like Biondo's, his efforts became the foundation for others who desired to add to his work and refine his methods.[18]

Finally, the material remains exercised a fascination in their own right as *objets d'art,* as ornaments to the houses and libraries of the classically educated. Here as everywhere else, there was ancient precedent. "Even the most learned of the ancients," Poggio has Lorenzo de' Medici say in his dialogue *On Nobility,* "spent time and energy in the acquisition of sculptures and paintings. Cicero for one and Varro and Aristotle, as well as other Greeks and Romans . . . adorned their libraries and gardens with art in order to ennoble those places and to show their own good taste and well-spent efforts. For they believed that images of men who had excelled in the pursuit of glory and wisdom, if placed before the eyes, would help ennoble and stir up the soul."[19] Poggio made a great effort to find antique statues for his own garden and helped to set a fashion that would last for centuries. If the English were a little backward in this, too, by the seventeenth century they were beginning to make up lost ground, and it is no accident that when Sir Robert Cotton decided to separate the parts of his great library, it was with the busts of the Roman emperors (a practice that was later to become commonplace),[20] and that the Earl of Arundel had to compete with the Duke of Buckingham and the King himself to secure the marbles from the East that still bear his name.

The consequence of all this activity was that by 1500 the Italian humanists had invented many of the problems and developed most of the skills that were to preoccupy European antiquaries for the next two centuries. When Poggio visited England between 1418 and 1422, he found a society still medieval, still largely indifferent to classical authors and unaware of classical remains.[21] When William Caxton set up his printing press at Westminster fifty years later, he still had little direct access to antiquity (though there had been some fitful activity in between); and he thought of the Romans as the chivalrous knights of romance, undifferentiated in any substantial way from his own time. The best guide to Rome was *Ye Solace of Pilgrimes* by the Augustinian

friar John Capgrave.[22] It was only after that, with the first real generation of English humanists, that the story of English antiquarianism may
be properly said to begin. The reading of the classical authors and the
schooling of the governors in classical eloquence, as always, awoke an
interest in the ancient monuments.

(2)

The first English antiquary of any consequence was John Leland. It is
true that upon occasion in the fifteenth century and sometimes before,
an interest had been displayed in early remains, but it was always haphazard and indiscriminate, apparently without method and lacking that
Renaissance sense of the differentiation of past from present culture; it
was also without direct influence.[23] Leland proudly took upon himself
the title *antiquarius*, and with a single great stride, carried England into
the Renaissance in this regard, just as a few years before, Erasmus,
More, and their circle, had taught the nation the value of the classical
authors.[24] Leland had been brought up by these earlier humanists, beginning at St. Paul's School—which had just been newly refounded by
John Colet with a set of statutes that expressly barred the medieval
authors—and later at the two universities. Leland wrote their history
and applauded their teachings in his Latin epigrams,[25] and he acknowledged his special debt to William Lyly, the first headmaster of St. Paul's,
who (like most of the others) had been to Italy, but (beyond any of the
rest) had ventured as far as Greece itself to complete his education. For a
time Leland lived in Paris (1526–29), then the center of northern humanism, meeting and learning from a host of great men, including the
formidable Guillaume Budé, the leading Greek scholar and numismatist
of the day.[26] He never made it to Italy, though he seems to have considered a visit. But perhaps it did not matter; like Erasmus before him, he
found all that he needed for classical Latin and Greek in the impressive
roster of scholars that he met in London and Paris, and he returned to
England an accomplished classicist who believed he was a poet. It was in
Paris that he got his first taste of antiquities and began to pursue the old
manuscripts. There he discovered, among others, the medieval Latin
poet Joseph of Exeter, and this whetted his appetite for more.
On his return to England, Leland won preferment in the church and
eventually entered the service of Henry VIII. Thereafter, he drew
steady patronage from the crown and assisted critically in the building
up of the Royal Library. All the while he continued to write and publish
Latin poetry, expertly, if without great distinction.[27] With the dissolution of the monasteries, he undertook his first serious antiquarian task:

canvassing the old libraries for their ancient manuscripts, selecting some for the king and some for himself, and listing many of the rest.[28] He welcomed the change but lamented the loss; the abbeys began to look to him and to subsequent generations a little like the classical ruins: that is to say, like monuments to a lost time.[29] If the medieval period was not a golden age and had been marred by barbarism and superstition (a Renaissance commonplace that Gibbon inherited), it made up nevertheless the bulk of English history, and the kingdom could not afford to be deprived of its past. National feeling was growing fast in the sixteenth century and furnished a powerful motive for antiquarian interest; religious politics added its bit. Leland saw how history could be employed to defend the Henrician break with Rome. About 1540 he wrote a Latin treatise to that effect in favor of the Reformation, the *Antiphilarchia*, which, however, remained in manuscript.

A classical education combined with patriotic and religious motivation was an excellent prescription for studying English antiquities. The humanists had once and for all shattered the medieval view that the past was continuous and undifferentiated, and called attention to the evidence for change in the manuscripts and monuments.[30] Already in Italy, Biondo had seen the value of inspecting the Middle Ages, as well as antiquity, from an antiquarian perspective; the very title of his most ambitious work, *Historiarum ab inclinatio Romanorum imperii decades*, seems to anticipate Gibbon's *Decline and Fall*.[31] In the north of Europe, where the ancient monuments were less obvious and less directly linked to the present, the preclassical and postclassical remains beckoned, and in France and Germany the work of examining them had already begun. How much Leland knew of all this activity is still uncertain, but in one telling epigram he describes himself as doing for England what Beatus Rhenanus was doing for Germany,[32] and a friend compared him to Conrad Celtis and Annius of Viterbo, as well as the ancient geographers.[33] Sometime after his return to England, Leland conceived of the heroic scheme of taking an inventory of all the English antiquities, Roman, Celtic, Saxon, and later. And he seems to have won the king's support and set about seriously undertaking the task. Of course, his overmighty ambition was doomed to frustration and his enemies laughed when he went mad and had to give it up altogether about 1548. Nevertheless, he left his scheme behind and a wonderful set of manuscript collections to inspire later work. "Leland," it was said without exaggeration in the eighteenth century, "hath been a Fund for whatever hath been attempted about our Antiquities since the Reformation."[34]

Leland's scheme was announced in a New Year's Gift to Henry VIII in 1546 and published with a commentary a few years later by John Bale.[35] Bale admitted Leland's "vaingloriousness" but applauded his ambition.

Had he been able to finish his work, Bale insisted, Leland would "have fully and worthily painted, described, or set forth this our realm and all things therein, with all the dominions thereof, and with all such things as have from time to time been done in them." First, however, it was necessary to master the languages and literature of the past, and so Leland "not only applied him self to the knowledge of the Greek and Latin tongues, wherein he was (I might say) exclusively learned; but also to the study of the British, Saxonike, and Welsh tongues."[36] Philology, as always, was primary, and Leland left behind some preliminary word lists that confirm his interest and are the proper beginning for the massive efforts of later generations to retrieve the languages and cultures of Saxons and Celts.[37]

For the moment it was more than a single scholar could hope to do. Meanwhile, Leland promised Henry to continue his search through all the libraries of the realm in order to retrieve the ancient literature of the nation. English history was obscure because English antiquities were obscure, buried in forgotten manuscripts and unnoticed monuments, but the English past would be seen as equal to any other, once it was recovered. Leland also promised Henry four books, *De viri illustribus*, describing and ennumerating the lives and works of all who had ever written anything worthwhile in England.[38] In attempting thus to furnish a guide to the manuscript sources of English history, in supplying biographies, bibliographies, and word lists, Leland was indeed laying a foundation for all later work, though his unfinished manuscripts were not published until the eighteenth century.

Yet there was still more to Leland's ambition. He explained how, in reading about the past, he had become "inflamed" to visit all parts of the kingdom and so had traveled widely for many years, recording in his itineraries an account of everything he saw. "You shall find him," Bale forecast correctly, "no less profitable to us, in his description of this particular nation, than were Strabo, Pliny, Ptolemy, and other Geographers to their perusers,"[39] and Leland's descriptive notes were again read and copied for generations until they too were printed in the eighteenth century. In his *Itineraries*, Leland combined geographical and topographical description with an inventory of antiquities from all periods. He meant to write a *Liber de topographia Britanniae primae*, a book "concerning the description of the first Britain," and a *Liber de antiquitate Britannica*, with as many books as there were shires, "showing the beginning, increase and acts of all the chief towns and castles in the realm."[40] And even this did not exhaust his plans. Unfortunately, he left behind only notes; but they were enough to get the antiquarian enterprise going.

Leland's accomplishment is hard to gauge, and he has never really received his due, though generations of antiquaries admitted or concealed their indebtedness to him. Everyone agreed that he was "the first to have turned the eyes of the kingdom upon that kind of learning,"[41] and he does appear to have been the first in England to grasp what needed to be done and the methods to be employed. As he wandered about Britain, he looked at everything with a curious eye, remembering the value of coins and inscriptions as well as old buildings and monumental remains. With his friend Robert Talbot, whose work is even more obscure at this distance, he saw the possibility of determining the Roman places from the literary evidence (for example, the *Antonine Itineraries*) and the actual remains. (Talbot was among the first English antiquaries to collect Anglo-Saxon manuscripts, some of which he lent to Leland.)[42] Leland understood thoroughly the interrelationship of word and object, and he believed that the study of Celtic and Saxon antiquities could be modeled upon the Roman precedent; it was his particular genius to discover how the techniques of classical scholarship could be extended to the Middle Ages. In short, he understood clearly and before anyone else in England that the many new devices of Italian humanism could be employed not only to resuscitate classical antiquity but to recover the whole of the British past. When he needed an assistant, he asked for a young man like himself, "learned in the Latin tongue and versifying, and that beside can in the Greek tongue *sine cortice natare.*"[43]

(3)

What happened after Leland? I have been suggesting that it was the classical impulse that first generated and then nurtured the antiquarian enterprise. As the classical authors fastened their hold on the curriculum and came into common currency, the enthusiasm for classical antiquities became more and more apparent. The schools themselves helped by introducing antiquities into the curriculum as essential background for the reading of the ancient authors. Among the first and most popular manuals of Roman antiquities was the one written originally for the Abingdon School (1622) by the master, Thomas Godwin, and expressly intended "for the better study of Classical Authors."[44] It described the life and layout of ancient Rome under several headings that dealt with topography, religious and political institutions, and warfare—in effect the old topical headings of Varro. This little work was usually bound up with two others by Oxford dons: one for ancient Israel, meant to illustrate the Bible; the other for the ancient Greeks, meant to help schoolmasters "who undertake to read the Greek Orators to raw Scholars."[45] All were digests, *hautes vulgarizations,* of more ambitious scholarly works,

like the imposing volume of Johannes Rosinus, *Antiquitatum Romanorum,*
which lay behind the Abingdon book, a thousand double-columned
pages in its later versions. Each passed through many editions until
superseded by fuller and better efforts, some illustrated, like Basil Kennett's *Romae antiquae notitia* (1696) and John Potter's *Archaeologia Graeca*
(1696–97). These new texts were also continuously reissued, even into
the nineteenth century, though they had much competition.

Classical antiquities were thus introduced into the life of the gentleman. When Sir Thomas Hoby visited Italy in 1548–49, he deliberately
sought out the monuments and kept a journal of his discoveries, copying
out the inscriptions at length. Rome was inevitably the high point, and
Hoby was rapturous about the statues, stones, and inscriptions that he
saw in the Belvedere; about the Pantheon, "which is the fairest and
perfectest antiquitiy in Rome"; and about the triumphal arches, the
Colosseum, and so on, too many to enumerate: "I leave the searchers out
of them to the instructions of Lucius Faunus, Martian and Biondo."[46]
One of his companions, William Barkar (the translator of Xenophon),
published a small collection of Latin inscriptions on his return, to com-
memorate their visit.[47] Another English traveler who returned to England about this time to tutor the young King Edward VI, William
Thomas, published an original *History of Italy* in 1549, in which he too
combined antiquities with topography, personal observations, and (for
Rome) the works of the ancients (such as Frontinus and Pliny) and the
moderns (e.g. Biondo and Andrea Fulvio). Like Poggio and Gibbon, he
was moved to tears and to moral reflections at the sight of the ancient
ruins. "Imagining withal what majesty the city might be of when all those
things, flourished, then did it grieve me to see the only jewel, mirror,
mistress, and beauty of the world, that never was like, nor (can I think)
never shall be, lie so desolate and disfigured."[48] Thomas did not fail to
supply his own catalog of the monuments, with copious reference to
ancient events and personalities—nothing very original, but replacing
once and for all such medieval guidebooks as Capgrave's *Solace of
Pilgrimes.*

For the moment, however, travel to the Continent was interrupted by
the Counter-Reformation and the great struggle with Spain and the
papacy. A license to go had to be obtained from the Privy Council and it
was almost impossible to receive permission to visit Rome, then the very
center of Catholic conspiracy. The grand tour as the capstone to the
education of a gentleman had, therefore, to be postponed, although the
appetite was already there. The example of the Earl of Arundel, the first
great aristocrat to accomplish the visit in the seventeenth century, was all
the more significant, for it set a fashion that was to be adopted wholesale
when travel became frequent again after the Restoration.[49]

Arundel was the scion of an old Catholic family, the Howards, and already the heir to a great library and collection of paintings when as a young man he began to collect for himself. He seems to have attended Westminster School under William Camden, who later became a friend, and it is just possible that the great English antiquary transmitted something of his own interest to the brilliant young nobleman. In 1612, Arundel had to go abroad for his health, and in the following year he returned to Italy with a large retinue that included the architect Inigo Jones. He spent eighteen months visiting the sights in Italy as far as Naples and forbidden Rome, collecting everything he could lay his hands on, including some statues that had to be dug out of the ground— though someone seems to have planted them there for that very purpose! On his return to England, he set them up at Arundel House in London, in the first real Italianate long-gallery of its kind, the precursor of many to come. A friend, Lord Roos, who had also been to Italy, perhaps with Inigo Jones, turned over his collection of statues to Arundel, and "at one clap" the earl found himself with one of the great museums in Europe.[50]

By now Arundel was soliciting help from everyone, particularly from the English ambassadors at the several European courts, and receiving regular shipments of antique statues. On one occasion he purchased the entire cabinet of Daniel Nys—gems, coins, and medals—for the immense sum of ten thousand pounds. When opportunity opened in the East with the embassy of Sir Thomas Roe to the Porte, Arundel immediately saw his chance.[51] For the next several years he was preoccupied by one ambitious effort after another to procure the antiquities of ancient Greece for his collection. His special agent, William Petty, was eventually successful enough to supply a boatload of statues and inscriptions, to the great excitement of the antiquaries. When the cargo arrived in London, Sir Robert Cotton immediately awoke his friend John Selden and begged him to set about deciphering the Greek inscriptions. Selden, who had by then gained a reputation as the most learned man in England in his generation and a master of European humanist learning, set to work at once with the help of two scholar friends, Patrick Young and Richard James. The result was the *Marmora Arundeliana* (1628), a transcription and commentary on twenty-nine Greek and ten Latin inscriptions, one of them the famous Parian Marble, an ancient Greek chronological work that became the favorite recreation of generations of later scholars.[52]

Arundel's ambition knew no bounds, and had Roe and Petty had a little better luck, they might have walked off with the best reliefs on an entire triumphal arch in Constantinople—the so-called Porta Aurea, which had originally been erected for Theodosius I—and thereby anticipated Lord Elgin and the marbles of the Parthenon two hundred years later. On another occasion, Arundel was thwarted in an effort to carry off a fifty-foot granite obelisk from Rome. But his collection was impressive enough. When Francis Bacon visited Arundel House in 1626, "coming to the Earl of Arundel's Garden, where there was a great number of Ancient Statues of naked Men and Women, [he] made a stand, and as astonish'd cry'd out, the Resurrection!"[53] A few years later, Arundel could count thirty-seven statues, one hundred and twenty-eight busts, two hundred and fifty inscribed stones, and many sarcophagi, altars, and fragments—not to mention old manuscripts, coins and medals. Unfortunately, the collection was divided by his heirs and neglected until John Evelyn persuaded Oxford University to retrieve some of them for the museum, where they came to the renewed attention of the antiquaries who produced a new *Marmora Oxoniensia* to describe them, and where they may still be seen today.[54]

Arundel's tour of Italy and his collections made a powerful impression on his contemporaries. He seems to have inspired both the Duke of Buckingham and the young Charles I to rivalry, and for a time poor Sir Thomas Roe found himself caught between the demands of the two great aristocrats for antiquarian treasure. Meanwhile, his friend and advisor Inigo Jones was making his own use of the Roman opportunity. While there, he purchased a copy of Palladio's treatise on architecture, the fourth book of which was entirely devoted to describing the ancient Roman buildings, and took it with him to the actual sites, checking the engravings against the monuments. He was probably the first Englishman to take such an exact interest in these remains and make use of them in his own architectural work, thereby inaugurating a new style.[55] Perhaps Jones's startling transformation of Stonehenge into a classical Roman monument (in a posthumous publication) even better illustrates the impact of classical antiquities on the English imagination.[56]

Another of Arundel's admirers was the tutor and miscellaneous writer Henry Peacham, who commemorated the earl's activities in a new chapter especially prepared for the third edition of his *Complete Gentleman* (1634). The original work (1622) had been written for young William Howard, the earl's son, and was intended to instruct the gentleman in the good life, a familiar Renaissance genre going back in England at least to Leland's friend Thomas Elyot.[57] The new chapter, "Of Antiquities," was an attempt to make the study and collection of statues, inscriptions, and coins part of the ordinary recreation of the gentleman: "For next men and manners, there is nothing more delightful, nothing worthier observation, than these copies and memorials of men and matters of elder times, whose lively presence is able to persuade a man that he now seeth two thousand years ago."[58] Peacham did not fail to describe the great new collections of his time, nor to supply a bibliography for his readers.

In short, a smattering of classical antiquities was becoming *de rigeur* for the English gentleman, who was gradually turning into a *virtuoso*. With travel easier and social circumstances more favorable after the Restoration, the type was soon perfected. And for his edification, a whole popular literature was conjured into being to instruct him and guide him through the massive scholarly tomes that were also rapidly accumulating: elegant works like Evelyn and Addison on coins, Dr. Arbuthnot on ancient weights and measures, and Joseph Spence on statues.[59] New guidebooks for foreign travel also made their appearance, full of antiquarian information, like the English translation of François Schott's *Itinerario d'Italia*, called *Italy in its Original Glory, Ruine and Revival* (1660).[60] As the flood of visitors turned into a torrent, tour guides began to make a profession of showing foreigners around the ancient ruins, like the Italian Francesco Ficoroni, who shepherded Addison around Rome, or the Scotsman James Byers, who looked after Gibbon a generation later.[61] The learned gentleman was eventually to become something of a contradiction in terms, as we shall see, and so the model proposed in Pierre Gassendi's life of Nicholas Peiresc, *The Mirrour of True Nobility* (1657), was beyond practical realization, but a modest appreciation of antiquities was soon thought necessary to complete the education of the gentleman and fashion his taste.[62] In the next generations, great noblemen like the Earls of Pembroke at Wilton and Leicester at Holkham continued to lead the way in collecting and patronizing antiquarian activities, though of the many famous "cabinets" of later times the most ambitious may well have been that of Arundel's direct descendent, Charles Townley, whose vast assemblage of classical antiques (now in the British Museum) was said to duplicate Pliny's villa.[63] Indeed, by the later eighteenth century, these activities had become so characteristic that the *Gentleman's Magazine* had some difficulty in defining an "antiquary"; it found the term commonly used more for a "man who is fond of collecting and commenting on antiquities, than one who aspires to the more important task of illustrating history, laws or poetry."[64]

Now all this was just the popular side of a scholarly enterprise that was also advancing year by year all over Europe and should be seen as offering the audience and the patronage and the favorable intellectual climate that was essential to sustain it. Inevitably, the English were as laggard as classical scholars as they were as collectors, but here too they caught up eventually with the rest of Europe. Cuthbert Tunstall, whom Leland coupled with Guillaume Budé in a Latin epigram, was hardly in the same class as the Continental humanist, though he knew his work and was interested in some of the same things.[65] It is only toward the end of the sixteenth century that we can find anything like a serious effort to elucidate a classical author, when Sir Henry Savile translated Tacitus with notes, and added "A View of Certain Military Matters or Commentaries concerning Roman Warfare" (1591). Even so, he was probably not up to his Continental counterpart Justus Lipsius. The appearance in England of Isaac Casaubon at James's court, and Gerard and Isaac Vossius later, helped to bridge the gap; for the rest of the new century, Englishmen did make some modest contributions to the stock of antiquarian learning that was collecting all over Europe, to such recondite matters as chronology, ancient weights and measures, Egyptology, and so on.[66]

On the whole, however, English scholars were drawn to other things, above all to ecclesiastical history and controversy and to the national antiquities, though many of them continued to keep abreast of Continental work, and Englishmen bought the Dutch variorums and Delphin classics by the boatful, until eventually the English presses (and editors) began to catch up. In the early eighteenth century it was still the great compilations of the Dutchmen Graevius and Gronovius—one series for the Romans, another for the Greeks—and the dozen volumes of Montfaucon's *Antiquitée expliquée* that lined the bookshelves of the great private libraries and summarized the state of classical antiquarian scholarship after three centuries. But by then the greatest classical scholar in Europe was an Englishman, Richard Bentley, and the "neoclassical age" was at hand.

(4)

Even though Englishmen preferred to work at the national antiquities, they always began with Roman Britain. Leland himself had tried to take account of what he saw, describing the Roman remains where they were obvious, as at Bath, and the finds of coins and inscriptions as they turned up along the way.[67] One of his manuscripts contains a series of extracts from the classical authors about Roman Britain, including some notes on the recently edited geography of Ptolemy, a collection that led John Bale to think that he had intended a separate work, *Antiquitates Britanniae*.[68] "Almost no man," Leland had complained, "can well guess at the shadow of the ancient names" that had been used by the classical historians—Caesar, Strabo, Tacitus, Ptolemy, and the rest. "I trust so to open this window, that the light shall be seen . . . [and] the old glory of your renowned Britain reflourish through the world."[69] His friend Robert Talbot actually began to make headway with the difficult task of locating the ancient Roman roads and cities in Britain. For that purpose, he procured a copy of the *Antonine Itineraries*—like Ptolemy, newly retrieved and edited—and began to annotate it, leaving behind still another manuscript for later antiquaries to pore over and try to perfect.[70]

The use of the ancient geographers was, of course, part of a European campaign to map the classical world, and after a few years Talbot's notes were sent abroad to help the Dutchman Abraham Ortelius, who employed them in his own *Synonyma geographica* as well as his famous atlas, and who returned the favor by encouraging several Elizabethan antiquaries to the same task—notably, Humphrey Lhuyd, Daniel Rogers, and above all, William Camden.[71] Lhuyd had set out to do the job for Wales and had shown the value of using Welsh for the ancient place names.[72] Rogers was a Latin poet and diplomat who mixed with the best humanist scholars of his time and who seems to have intended to trace out the whole dominion of Roman Britain.[73] He knew the value of coins and inscriptions, as well as the literary authorities, and left another helpful collection of notes to his successors. Still other Englishmen, such as William Harrison and William Lambarde, made similar efforts to identify the place names and understood the need for the Celtic and Saxon languages, but it was left to William Camden in 1586 to complete the *Britannia,* for which all this had been useful preparation.

Meanwhile, however, medieval antiquities were not being ignored. Between Leland and Camden, a coterie of scholars (all of them good classicists) were gathered around the new Archbishop of Canterbury, Matthew Parker, and began to retrieve the Anglo-Saxon remains for the principal purpose of illuminating the early church and defending the Anglican settlement. Parker himself, with his secretary John Joscelyn, led the way, resuming the original task of Leland and Bale of trying to collect and preserve all the ancient manuscripts of value in Latin and English that might serve his purpose. One assistant alone claimed to have brought him six thousand seven hundred volumes in four years' time![74] Parker's correspondence is full of begging letters and grateful replies which show that he was not alone in his new enthusiasm. (One friend who shared it was William Cecil.)[75] Moreover, Parker was able to realize Bale's hope (and Polydore Vergil's example) and actually see a fair number of these works in print, among them the first ever in Anglo-Saxon type and several of the most famous Latin chronicles.[76] From this time on, the printing of the narrative sources of medieval history became a continuing exercise of antiquarian scholarship. If editorial methods lagged far behind the best humanist versions of the ancient historians, there was nevertheless some effort to replicate humanist philological method, to collate the manuscripts and emend them, and to try to understand the meaning of obscure passages. Unfortunately, attitudes toward the Middle Ages remained ambiguous at best, and the Saxons were rarely idealized to the extent of the Romans or treated with the same reverence or respect. The work of recovering medieval antiquity was therefore conducted without the same attention to detail, and by fits and starts.[77]

One of the first among Parker's friends to understand what was required was the somewhat shadowy Lawrence Nowell, who has only lately been resuscitated. Like Leland, whom he may have known, he published nothing about antiquities and aborted all his schemes. Like Leland, he was an accomplished classical scholar with a good command of Latin and Greek. In the 1560s he got a copy of Leland's topographical poem, the *Cygnea Cantio,* to which Leland had appended some notes on the appropriate places, and joined to it some more notes from Leland and some of his own. He was determined to resume where Leland and Talbot had left off and add to the Latin gleanings whatever could be learned from the Anglo-Saxon and Welsh about the ancient geography of Britain. This meant acquiring the two languages, and Nowell set earnestly to work on an Anglo-Saxon dictionary, which he left in manuscript for others to build on. It meant also combing the medieval chronicles, many of which he transcribed and annotated, and some of which were printed afterward by his successors Lambarde and Camden.[78] He also transmitted Leland's idea of a topographical-antiquarian description of England to the new generation, where it developed into William Lambarde's *Topographical Dictionary.*[79] He even drafted a map of Anglo-Saxon England with the medieval places determined, which wound up in the Cotton collection and was noticed by George Hickes a century later. He took a modest (and exceptional) interest in Anglo-Saxon poetry and owned the manuscript of *Beowulf.* In 1586 he stopped work abruptly and went off to France; his work had to be finished by others.

The story of subsequent Anglo-Saxon scholarship has been well told elsewhere.[80] Suffice it to say that interest was sustained by religious and political controversies throughout the seventeenth century,[81] even though the disparagement of all things medieval remained a commonplace of humanist teaching. Progress from the Parker circle to the Hickes circle was not smooth, but each generation had the advantage at least of building on the one before. When in 1638 Sir Henry Spelman set up a first Anglo-Saxon lectureship at Cambridge for the study of "domestique Antiquities touching our Church and reviving the Saxon tongue,"[82] it was a milestone, but it did not last long. Nevertheless, its funds were diverted to the publication of William Somner's *Dictionarium Saxonico-Latino-Anglicum* (1659) and so helped prepare the way directly for the efflorescence of medieval studies at the end of the century. Spelman himself left behind a variety of influential antiquarian works, including a glossary and commentary on medieval legal and ecclesiastical terms, the *Archaeologus* (1624–64).[83] He was in close touch with the most advanced continental scholarship and has been credited with the "discovery" of English feudalism as an integral system of laws and customs akin to those elsewhere in Europe and occupying a specific chronological chapter in medieval English history. It was a notion that bore much fruit and led to much controversy among the later Stuart antiquaries.[84] Like others in his time who combined law with antiquities—and like the heralds, who were busy in their own right—Spelman discovered the value of charters, rolls, and other early documents behind the narrative sources; he sought out these new materials in the Tower of London, in the parish and parochial records, and elsewhere, so that they became characteristic resources for seventeenth-century historical scholarship.[85]

William Somner was among the first English antiquaries to receive a contemporary biography.[86] (Spelman and Selden got theirs soon afterward.) Somner was educated first at the King's School, Canterbury, where, like everyone else, he was "initiated in the elements of Rome and Grece." He got some employment nearby which led him to the study of local antiquities and his first publication, *The Antiquities of Canterbury* (1640). Within the city, he sought out "the genealogy of houses and walls and dust"; outside, he walked for recreation but also "to survey the British bricks, the Roman ways, the Danish hills and works, the Saxon monasteries, and the Norman churches. At the digging up foundations, and other descents into the bowels of the earth, he came after to survey the Workmen, and to purchase from them the treasure of Coins, Medals and other buried reliques."[87] He was a true disciple of his countryman William Lambarde, whose edition of the Saxon Laws he translated and whose county history of Kent he tried to elaborate. He left behind a manuscript for it, only part of which was printed as *A Treatise on the Roman Ports and Forts in Kent* (1693). "His most constant delight," we are told, "was in classic Histories, in old Manuscripts, Ledger-Books, Rolls, and Records."[88] Above all, he understood the view of Lambarde and Spelman about the importance of the Saxon language, "as without it the Antiquities of England be either not discovered, or at the least imperfectly known," and so he compiled and published his famous dictionary.[89] Renowned in old age, he became the recourse of all contemporary medievalists and contributed to many of their works. To his friends and to his biographer, he was the very model and exemplar of the English antiquary.

It is clear, then, that all these men had learned the first lesson of classical scholarship: that a proper understanding of the past depended upon a mastery of the languages of the past, and that language was itself historical and could only be understood in its setting. As a result, they studied Anglo-Saxon and edited the manuscripts, trying to improve the texts by fresh collations after the fashion of the humanists. (Typically, it was the young editor of Quintilian, Edmund Gibson, who tried his hand at the *Anglo-Saxon Chronicle*.)[90] And eventually, they discovered also the usefulness of examining the monuments, inscriptions, and coins of the same period. George Hickes's vast collaborative work, the *Linguarum veterum septentrionalis Thesaurus* (1703–5), was before anything else a set of grammars and vocabularies for all the northern languages,[91] as well as a valuable anthology of Anglo-Saxon literature. But it was also a repository of antiquarian information of every kind about the whole life and culture of the early medieval period, a true Varronian enterprise. In it, there was a whole book devoted to Saxon coins by the virtuoso Sir Andrew Fountaine, as well as a still more impressive volume cataloging the Saxon manuscripts by the brilliant paleographer and bibliographer Humfrey Wanley; elsewhere in the work, Runic inscriptions and Saxon crosses were depicted, and Anglo-Saxon charters deciphered and explicated. Hickes's skill at evaluating medieval documents, at detecting anachronisms and exposing forgeries, was the wonder of the age, an exact analog to the humanist criticism of Latin texts that had arisen during the Renaissance and that is exemplified in Lorenzo Valla's exposure of the *Donation of Constantine*.[92] The great French scholar Mabillon, codifier of the science of diplomatics, praised Hickes's work when it appeared, even though he had been criticized in it.

So the Saxonists deliberately emulated the classicists and joined the study of words and things in an effort to recreate the whole life of the past. The Welsh attempted the very same thing for their own ancient culture, and from the Elizabethan Humphrey Lhuyd, to the Augustan Edward Lhwyd, Celtic studies traversed almost the same path as Roman and Saxon studies, from dictionary to thesaurus of antiquities.[93] The model and common ground was always classical scholarship. But this affiliation was by no means always helpful. Throughout the early modern period, interest in the language and literature of the Middle Ages—whether Latin, Anglo-Saxon or Welsh—invariably suffered by comparison with the classics, and nearly every medieval scholar felt under obligation to defend his interest against the prevailing humanist (and Protestant) prejudice that everything in the Middle Ages must have been barbarous, superstitious, or worse.[94] The same monastic culture that had moved Leland and his friends also repelled them, and they greeted the dissolution with praise, even while they tried to conserve the old libraries. As serious study proceeded, the old humanist and Protestant inhibitions remained. " 'Tis well known," wrote Thomas Tanner late in the seventeenth century, how "Mr. Camden and Mr. Weever were forced to apologize for barely mentioning the Monasteries, and what outcries were made upon the Publication of that glorious work the *Monasticon*."[95] It may even be that old feelings hardened after the Restoration.

As a consequence of this perennial prejudice against the Middle Ages, Saxonists like Hickes, who found intrinsic merit in their subject, were forced into an unhappy comparison of Saxon literature and poetry with the Latin and Greek classics, and of the Saxon language with the classical tongues, in which the standards were invariably set by the classicists. Despite an occasional disclaimer, it was usually thought that Greek or Latin was the supreme language and Latin the best model for modern English, and it was natural for Jonathan Swift to disparage Anglo-Saxon in his effort to reform and standardize the tongue. One of Hickes's students, Elizabeth Elstob, tried to meet Swift's arguments, "to show the polite Men of our Age, that the Language of their Forefathers is neither so barren nor barbarous as they affirm." But despite her best efforts, this was not an easy thing to do. Polite men required a polite language. If Swift found Anglo-Saxon primitive and monosyllabic, then Mrs. Elstob must prove it, "for aptness of compounding and well sounding words, and variety of Numbers . . . scarce inferior to the Greek itself." She would probably have done better to defend the strength and simplicity of the monosyllable, as she does with a few telling examples. But classical propriety was stacked against her and against medieval scholarship in general. As a result, when religious and political conflict subsided at last in the eighteenth century, the impulse to pursue medieval antiquities was seriously diminished, and neoclassical prejudice was left almost alone. Now, when gentlemen traveled abroad, they returned "captivated with the Medals, Statues, Pictures and Antiquities of Greece and Italy [but] they seldom have any relish for the ruder products of Great Britain."[96] It was a hundred years before Anglo-Saxon scholarship regained its impetus and the work of Hickes and his friends was resumed.

(5)

But I have gotten ahead of my story. Long before the medieval part of the antiquarian enterprise reached its climax and petered out, each of the different strata of the English past was gradually differentiated and described, beginning with the Romans and proceeding to the Saxons, Celts, Danes, and Normans. Nor was Leland's grand scheme of combining them into a whole forgotten. Both Lawrence Nowell and William Lambarde made efforts in that direction, but it was a younger man and a greater scholar, William Camden, who finally turned the trick and realized Leland's ambition.[97]

Camden was educated at St. Paul's School and then at Magdalen College under the humanist Thomas Cooper, the author (or editor) of a new Latin dictionary (1573) which, among other things, tried to identify many of the ancient Roman places. At Oxford, Camden was already taking an interest in antiquities, encouraged perhaps by his friends Philip Sidney and the brothers George and Richard Carew. From 1571 to 1575 he traveled far and wide to look for himself. Eventually, he became master at his old school, a professional classicist who wrote some occasional Latin verse and a schoolboy grammar of Greek that took its place as standard beside Lyly's Latin text. It may have been John Dee, himself a great collector of manuscripts,[98] or perhaps Daniel Rogers, who put him in touch with the continental humanists, and he met Ortelius in London in 1577. Camden's correspondence is full of Latin letters that kept him abreast of the latest foreign scholarship. It was Ortelius, he recalled, "that excellent reviver of ancient geography," who urged him to put his notes in order and write the *Britannia* so that he might, in Camden's words, "restore antiquity to Britain and Britain to its antiquity."[99] Camden appreciated the work of the Parker circle and saw the necessity of learning some Anglo-Saxon and Welsh; he discovered Leland's collections and looked at the notes of Talbot, Rogers, and Lhuyd.[100] He continued to travel and consult the learned; he read every Greek and Roman writer who had mentioned Britain and many of the medieval authors also (later, he edited a batch of chronicles). He consulted "public records, ecclesiastical registers, many libraries, the archives of cities and churches, monuments and old deeds." No one could have been better prepared; the *Britannia* was a triumph.[101]

There was indeed something for everyone in the pages of the *Britannia,* but perhaps the humanists appreciated it most, and Camden was at once compared with Varro, Strabo, and Pausanias.[102] It was written in Latin, although there was really no direct classical model for a compilation of this kind, and Camden was apologetic for its style. He had not attempted eloquence, he said, since Cicero himself had pointed out that the subject was not suitable for rhetoric. He was uncomfortable at having to quote the medieval writers in their "barbarous" language but felt that truth demanded it. Camden had written some Latin poetry, including an encomium for Roger Ascham, who was the best advocate of classical imitation in his time. Camden thought that the taste of the "middle age" was generally, "so overcast with dark clouds, or rather thick fogs of ignorance, that every little spark of liberal learning seemed wonderful."[103] The *Britannia* was, therefore, first and principally a commemoration of Roman Britain; Elizabethans were to be reminded of their direct and immediate descent not from the apochryphal Trojan-Celtic history beloved of the Middle Ages but from classical antiquity, as a

93

province of the Roman Empire, the equal of any other. Camden, it need hardly be said, knew his Biondo and Beatus Rhenanus.[104] We have come a long way indeed from Caxton's *Polychronicon*.

It is, then, as a sort of commentary on Roman Britain, transformed by time and subsequent invasions, that the *Britannia* should be read. Camden's fundamental text remained the *Antonine Itineraries*. "It is worthy observation," wrote Thomas Fuller, "with what diligence he inquired after the ancient places, making hue and cry after many a city which was run away, and by certain marks and tokens pursuing to find it; as by situation on the Roman high-ways, by just distance from other ancient cities, by some affinity of name, by tradition of inhabitants, by Roman coins digged up, and by some appearance of old ruins."[105] In a first draft (1579–80), the description of the Roman province preponderates, but Camden never stopped adding Roman materials throughout the long life of the *Britannia* and its many editions; in this, as in everything else, he was helped by a host of friends and well-wishers at home and abroad.[106] Eventually, there were plates of coins and a veritable *corpus inscriptionum* (these were among the first archaeological illustrations to be printed in England).[107] It was into this framework that Camden stuffed the antiquities of later Britain, using the geographical design and much information from Leland's itineraries. And, like his predecessor, he continued to travel to see for himself.[108]

Leland's design was thus fulfilled—almost too well, it turned out, since Camden was accused (unfairly) of plagiarism.[109] When William Lambarde read the manuscript, he immediately deferred to the younger man and gave up his own attempt, confining himself thereafter to the county of Kent and thereby inventing a new antiquarian genre, the county or local history.[110] It was clear to everyone that Camden was the master of the new antiquarian discipline, that he understood both its critical and constructive possibilities better than anyone in England, and he at once became the center of a newly founded Society of Antiquaries and the informal instructor of a whole generation of like-minded men.[111] His criticisms of Geoffrey of Monmouth and the legendary Trojan history and his suspicions of some early Christian history were so effectively argued in terms of appeal to the evidence that he was able to secure and extend the new critical historiography of Renaissance humanism to whole new areas of the past. The *Britannia* passed through five editions in Camden's lifetime, each improved over the last, plus an English translation. It was renewed in 1695 by another team of scholars under the direction of Edmund Gibson, enlarged, amended, and retranslated. And it was renewed yet again at the end of the eighteenth century and for the last time by Richard Gough, the best antiquary of his generation, to close out and provide continuity to our period. From

John Leland's scheme to Gough's four folio volumes, for nearly three centuries, the idea of the *Britannia* had acted to give form and momentum to the English antiquarian enterprise.

It is possible, therefore, to think of all this labor as belonging to a single great collective activity in which the various layers of the English past were gradually exposed and differentiated, and then reintegrated into a new configuration along the lines laid out in the remarkable essay that Camden prefixed to the *Britannia*. Classical philology and antiquities had furnished the first insight, as well as the model and underpinning for the rest, and so it continued throughout the whole period. An excellent example is the work of John Weever, one of the many who took inspiration from Camden. Weever had been able to travel abroad and visit Rome. Upon his return, he set himself to antiquities and traveled widely in England in search of inscriptions for his work on the *Ancient Funerall Monuments* (1631). The inspiration for his collection, he says, came from "the Epitaphs of Italy, France, Germany and other Nations" as he found them in the works of Continental humanists. Camden had encouraged him to scour the cathedrals and parochial churches; he borrowed books and manuscripts from Cotton, that "worthy repairer of eating-times ruines," and he received help from Spelman and Selden, "the most learned Antiquaries now living."[112] The result was a nine-hundred-page magazine of medieval inscriptions— many now lost—copied carefully in the original orthography, a typical antiquarian collaboration and a worthy analog to the massive compilations of classical inscriptions that were continuing to grow abroad from generation to generation.

Unfortunately, the great collective enterprise began to collapse even before the eighteenth century was well under way, long before Gough's version of Camden or Gibbon's *Decline and Fall*. It was, inevitably, the medieval antiquities that began to falter first, and the reasons are not hard to seek. We have seen that the principal motives for medieval scholarship were a result of religious and political quarrels that turned Englishmen of all parties back upon the past for justification. So Hickes agreed exactly with Parker that the study of Saxon antiquities would "show the faith and other chief doctrines of the Anglo-Saxon Church to be the same with ours and perfectly answer that never ending question: what was your church before Luther?"[113] In much the same way, the legal antiquaries had turned back to the Middle Ages to settle their disputes and even forced James I to close down the Society of Antiquaries and Charles I to sequester the Cotton Library out of suspicion of their political motives.[114] It was John Selden who wrote to his friend Cotton to apologize for his *History of Tythes* and to regret (in others) that "too studious affectation of bare and sterile antiquity, which is nothing else but to be exceeding busy about nothing." For himself, he desired that "fruitful and precious part of it, which gives necessary light to the present." Selden's antiquarian treatise was neither the first nor the last to provoke bitter controversy.[115] When, however, sectarian conflict finally subsided the motive of mere "curiosity" was left alone to face a general and increasing classical contempt. The fact is that it was not only hard to read the barbarous authors and defaced remains of the Middle Ages; it was, for the "polite" gentleman, positively distasteful.[116] Nor was it only the Saxonists who were discouraged; even the Welsh found it hard to sustain their enthusiasm for the past in the homogenizing climate of the Augustan world.[117]

So it was classical antiquities alone that continued to prosper in the eighteenth century. On the whole, the primacy of classical scholarship was taken for granted. No one, Thomas Hearne wrote, could hope to be a "complete antiquary" without following that method: "In short all our Learning in Antiquities hath such an entire Dependence upon the Greeks and the Latins, that none of our British Antiquaries ever proved complete without joyning all these together, as may be instanced in Mr. Leland, Sir H. Savile, Sir Robert Cotton, Mr. Camden . . . and in a great number besides."[118] Those who, like John Stow or John Bagford, could not claim such accomplishments were generally derided. Hearne had himself served a long apprenticeship, first editing Cicero and Livy and cataloging the ancient coins in the Bodleian Library before undertaking the medieval chronicles for which he is best remembered. As a result, new Roman discoveries, accidental or otherwise—like those that appeared in digging up London, or the tesselated pavements that were unearthed from time to time in the countryside, or the once famous shield of Dr. Woodward that turned up in an ironmonger's shop—all received prompt attention and study, either in the renewed eighteenth-century Society of Antiquaries or outside.[119] The topography of Roman Britain, the location of ancient roads and cities, remained a particular preoccupation.[120]

It was in these circumstances, therefore, that John Horsley produced the greatest antiquarian work of the new century.[121] In the three large books of the *Britannia Romana,* each a whole treatise in itself and lavishly illustrated, Horsley brought together with his own exemplary fieldwork everything that had so far been discovered about Roman Britain: its transactions and monuments, coins and inscriptions, place names and ancient geography. His preface raised the perennial question: "What signifies that knowledge . . . which brings no real advantage to mankind?" What did it matter which way the Roman Wall ran or what an inscription said? Horsley had no difficulty showing that "a minute inquiry into circumstances of time and place" was a necessary underpinning for history, and even less trouble affirming the value of ancient history, when "the youth of every polite nation are generally employed in acquiring some skill in the Roman language, antiquities and customs; and an acquaintance with these is supposed to be essentially necessary to a learned education."[122] So long and assiduously did he labor at his task that his work remained standard even until recently, and modern students still find it useful. Indeed, it is hard to see how it could have been done better except by the systematic excavations of modern archaeology, a method of investigation still largely unknown to the antiquaries of early modern Europe.

For a while, however, taking stock of the monuments above the ground was absorbing and difficult enough, and it was only when the discoveries of Herculaneum and Pompeii were announced in the middle of the century that the possibilities of wholesale excavation became widely apparent (though work on those sites remained sluggish and haphazard). Those discoveries were quickly reported in England, not least by the English ambassador to Naples, Sir William Hamilton, who was himself a serious student of classical antiquities and a great patron of the arts.[123] They made a wonderful impression, and for the first time, perhaps, it became fully apparent how extensive and illuminating were the treasures still beneath the earth. ("There is nothing of this kind known in the world," exclaimed Horace Walpole about Herculaneum in 1740. "I mean a Roman city entire of that age, and that has not been corrupted with modern repairs.")[124] Hamilton published his own magnificent collection of Greek vases, and Josiah Wedgwood (who was elected to the Society of Antiquaries in 1780) began to imitate them in his factory. Toward the end of the century, the search for Roman Britain took a new turn with the first systematic excavations of Samuel Lysons; the antiquary was giving way at last before the modern archaeologist.[125]

Meanwhile, opportunity had begun to open at last in the East. George Wheler, who had toured Europe with his tutor, George Hickes, decided to attempt Greece itself, then still largely unexplored, and set off with a French companion, Jacob Spon, in 1675. On their return, each published an account of the voyage, describing the monuments they had seen and whetting appetites throughout Europe: they also brought back some marbles and inscriptions.[126] For a time, the Levant Company remained the best English link with Asia Minor; its commerce with the eastern Mediterranean furnished a regular conduit through which books, manuscripts, and Greek antiquities could travel. Residents like John Covel, who was at Constantinople, 1670–76, and Edmund Chishull at Smyrna, 1698–1702, sought out the monuments and described what they had found. Chishull published a Latin commentary on one of the earliest Greek inscriptions in 1721.[127] But it was not until the end of the

1740s that interest and opportunity coincided to produce a spasm of activity that stirred all Europe and prepared the way for the "Greek revival."

In 1748 two young British artists, then at work in Rome, drafted some proposals for a voyage to Greece and sought patronage. James Stuart and Nicholas Revett addressed themselves to a world that had long accepted the precedence of antiquity in the arts, but they noticed that Athens, the nourisher of Rome, had been strangely neglected. Why? The answer was plain: "Greece, since the revival of the Arts, has been in the possession of Barbarians, and Artists capable of such a Work, have [not] been able to satisfy their passion, whether it was for Fame or Profit, without risking themselves among such professed Enemies to the Arts as the Turks are. The ignorance and jealousy of that uncultivated people, perhaps render an undertaking of this sort, still somewhat dangerous."[128]

Stuart and Revett gained their patronage in a newly founded aristocratic club, the Society of Dilettanti. "In the year 1734," a contemporary account recalled, "some Gentlemen who had travelled in Italy, desirous of encouraging *at home*, a Taste for those objects which had contributed so much to their entertainment *abroad*," joined together to encourage the pursuit of antiquity.[129] As always, Rome was the point of departure and the model for antiquarian study. Stuart had picked up his classical education while living there and even published a small Latin tract on an obelisk that was found in the Campus Martius.[130] By 1751 he was in Athens, drawing—while Revett measured—all the visible monuments of the ancient city with a precision and detail unknown before.[131] At almost the same time, Robert Wood and James Dawkins were embarked on a similar expedition to Greece and on one remarkable occasion actually ran into Stuart and Revett in Athens. Wood had started out as a tutor and was known as a good classical scholar. On his return to England, encouraged by the Dilettenti, he published two beautifully illustrated volumes that entranced the young Edward Gibbon among many others: the *Ruins of Palmyra* (1753) and the *Ruins of Balbec* (1757). He also helped get the society to underwrite Stuart and Revett's *Antiquities of Athens* (1762), a work that profoundly influenced European taste.[132] And he wrote the prospectus for still another expedition by Revett and Richard Chandler, this time to make plans and measurements of the monuments of Smyrna, draw the bas-reliefs and ornaments, and keep "minute diaries."

Meanwhile, Wood himself determined to go still farther east, to read "the *Iliad* and *Odyssey* in the countries where Achilles fought and Ulysses travelled and where Homer sung—a reminder, if one were necessary, of the continuous inspiration of classical literature behind the search for classical antiquities. (When the Montagus were returning from Constantinople in 1718, Lady Elizabeth Wortley Montagu wrote an ecstatic letter describing how moved she had been "to see the place where Achilles was buried . . . the valley where I imagined the famous duel of Menelaus and Paris had been fought. . . . While I viewed these celebrated fields and rivers, I admired the exact geography of Homer, whom I had in my hand.") In 1767, Wood brought out *A Comparative View of the Antient and Present State of the Troade*, with an *Essay on the Original Genius of Homer* and started two controversies among European scholars.[133] Richard Chandler had edited a version of the Greek elegiac poets as a young man and reedited the *Marmora Oxoniensia* after the university obtained some more of the Arundel marbles. On his return from the East, he published the results in several new works: the *Ionian Antiquities* (1769); the *Inscriptiones Atticae* (1774); and two books of travels (1775–76). By then, in England, everyone seemed to be building in the new classical Greek style.

(6)

So, even while the search for medieval antiquities was faltering, the revival of classical culture continued and took new forms. The search for Greek antiquities and neoclassical Greek imitation were, in effect, the natural conclusion of the same revival of antiquity that had begun long before in the Italian Renaissance.[134] In scholarship, as in literature and the arts, the neoclassical age was continuous with humanist erudition. If the English had been content for most of the time to follow Europe, by the eighteenth century they were more than holding their own. Yet there is something of a paradox hidden in all this activity; the fact is that the self-same neoclassical impulse that had given rise to antiquarian study in the first place, and sustained it for most of its life, came in the end to set some limits to it and even at times to inhibit it altogether.

I have tried to show how almost all antiquarian study was ancillary to some other purpose: either to classical imitation or to religion and politics. We have seen how a concern for "polite" culture limited the pursuit of medieval antiquities; unexpectedly, it also impeded (though not to the same extent) the pursuit of classical antiquities. The trouble was that mere curiosity, the love of exact detail in and for itself, was rarely appreciated and often derided by the classical teachers who dominated the polite world. Here is what the educator Guarino da Verona wrote about Poggio's friend Niccolo Niccoli at the beginning of the Italian Renaissance:

> Who could help bursting with laughter when this man in order to appear also to expound the laws of architecture, bares his arms and probes ancient

buildings, surveys the walls, diligently explains the ruins and half-collapsed vaults of destroyed cities, how many steps there were in the ruined theater, how many columns . . . how many feet the basis is wide, how high the point of the obelisk rises. In truth mortals are smitten by blindness. He thinks he will please the people while they everywhere make fun of him.[135]

Humanism was an essentially literary and practical education, meant to appea. to the man of the world; it did not encourage scholarship beyond its immediate present use. In this respect it left a legacy that continued to bedevil English historians right up to our own time.[136] In the seventeenth century, just as Henry Peacham was recognizing the value of a smattering of antiquarian knowledge for the gentleman, his contemporary John Earle—who was also a gentleman and as good a classicist—was doing his best to make sure that that knowledge would remain only a smattering, by turning it to satire. The antiquary was becoming a laughing stock:

> Hee is one that hath that unnaturall disease to bee enamour'd of old age and wrinkles, that loves old things (as Dutchmen doe Cheese) the better for being mouldy and worme-eaten. . . . A great admirer he is of the rust of old Monuments and reads, onely those Characters where time has eaten out the letters. . . . His estate consists much in shekels, and Roman Coynes, and he has more pictures of Caesar than James or Elizabeth. . . . He would give all the Bookes in his Study (which are rarities all) for one of the old Romane binding, or sixe lines of Tully in his owne hand.[137]

A play in 1641, called *The Antiquary* picked up the same theme, which was to be developed and reiterated ad infinitum in the next century; the joke about antiquarian rust was repeated endlessly.[138]

"Some there are," Camden complained, "who cry down the whole study of antiquities."[139] And more there were, perhaps, with every passing year, as the antiquaries became more erudite and the English gentlemen more polite. As the gulf grew more apparent, criticism and the edge of satire grew more bitter. Of course, the study of antiquities could be fun and was often pursued for recreation, even though it was usually justified by its ancillary value to something or other: "No study was more pleasant than Antiquities," Richard Graves told Thomas Hearne, even while he noticed at the same time that it was a great help to the study of law.[140] The conjunction was not unusual, though not everyone agreed about either the pleasures or the uses of erudition.

If there was anyone in the period who appreciated antiquities in and for themselves, it was probably Hearne, who came to represent the type for his time and who was flayed mercilessly—and not altogether undeservedly—for his peccadilloes as a scholar, by the polite "wits" of his generation. No one worked harder than this very self-conscious heir of Leland and Camden who once wrote in his diary, "Antiquity . . . indeed is the only true Learning, so that if any one were to ask me *what is Learning?* I would reply *Antiquity*. And if, *what is Antiquity?* I should as readily answer *Learning*."[141] His friend and fellow worker, Thomas Baker thought that he died from overwork, "a martyr to Antiquities."[142] But Alexander Pope found it all amusing and put Hearne in the *Dunciad* where he remained undefended for the rest of the century. Even Gibbon, who knew better, was ambivalent and tried to balance judgment halfway between laughter and gratitude. It was much as Hearne had said of Anthony Wood, "Indeed he was a meer Scholar, and consequently must expect from the greatest number of men, disrespect."[143] The antiquary, who had begun his career proudly as a virtuoso, was somehow turning into a useless pedant.

With this in mind, it is easy to see how classical scholarship became a central issue in the "battle of the books."[144] Both sides were beholden to the classics, but when the "modern" William Wotton proclaimed the progressive achievement of modern philology in understanding the past, the "ancient" William Temple was astounded. He was willing to allow a modicum of critical learning to those first humanists who had edited the classics, but he was sure that their work had long been done and was now complete; he preferred for himself a simple unadorned text (like the Oxford editions of Fell and Aldrich) to the cluttered erudition of a Dutch variorum. He could not see how the massive learning of the scholars that surrounded and dwarfed the originals, or was heaped together in unreadable tomes, could in any way be helpful in reading or writing polite literature; that is, in putting the classics to use. To Temple and to many in the eighteenth century, too much learning was a dangerous thing, more likely to obscure the originals or (worse yet) to make them appear irrelevant to modern life. When Temple wrote his own elegant history of England, he did not much bother with research or exactness of facts; he put all attention, like his admired ancient models, on style and political lessons. Though his work covered the early history of England, he looked at no antiquities and learned no Anglo-Saxon. Wotton was delighted to catch him in some appalling errors, but the world applauded. We shall find that Wotton's own contribution to history (a history of Rome in decline that anticipates Gibbon), with its copious antiquarian learning, was generally overlooked and soon forgotten.[145]

To be fair, Temple's predecessors had not done much better—certainly not Samuel Daniel or John Milton, both of whom had written on the same subject. The fact is that antiquities and histories were largely different things and separate activities throughout the early modern period. Francis Bacon had seen in theory how the one might be used to underpin the other, but this was an unusual idea, and when he himself decided to write a history of the reign of Henry VII, he typically avoided documentary research and simply rewrote—like any good narrative historian of the time—the works of his predecessors.[146] On the whole, historians did not use or compile antiquities, nor did antiquaries write histories. When, exceptionally, they did attempt both things—as when Camden composed a narrative account of the reign of Queen Elizabeth, or Wotton his history of the later Roman emperors—they were very conscious of the different demands of each genre and eager to avoid confusion. Camden certainly employed documents to an unusual extent, but he did not mean to spoil his narrative with any of the apparatus of the new scholarship, the footnote citations, critical dissertations, or explanatory digressions of antiquarian history—the kind of thing he had done so well in the *Britannia*.[147] In any case, a work of contemporary scholarship was not the best test of antiquarian method. Wotton's Roman history is more interesting than Camden in this respect, with its elaborate critical notes and systematic use of epigraphic and numismatic evidence, but it failed to meet the contemporary standard of elegant narrative, as Wotton himself seems to have realized. It seemed impossible to marry the two with any kind of success.[148]

Indeed it was only the chroniclers who tried with any consistency to incorporate antiquarian findings in their annalistic compilations—but again at the cost of further alienating their polite readers by their obvious inattention to the demands of style and narrative technique. Although chronicles continued to be written, like Richard Baker's popular narrative which passed through a dozen editions between 1643 and 1733, or the more ambitious works of Robert Brady, James Tyrrell, and Lawrence Echard, they were always considered a little vulgar and beneath the dignity of proper history. Until Hume finished his work in the middle of the eighteenth century, it was generally agreed that England had not yet received the polished narrative that was her due, like those for ancient Rome or (modeled upon them) modern France and Spain.[149]

Of course, it was the ancient Greek and Roman historians who had emphasized rhetoric to the exclusion of scholarship and so set the fashion for early modern Europe. Reverence for those authors was so profound that until the eighteenth century hardly anyone dared to rewrite the history of the ancient world, despite the enormous advances in learning that had been won by the new scholarship.[150] And the most learned English scholars, such as Selden and Spelman, or Dodwell and Bentley, remained reluctant to write "histories" either ancient or modern. "What a world of historical matter," Selden had complained, "both of our church and state, lies hid in the records kept in the several offices of the exchequer, in the tower, in the chapel of the rolls, in the paper chamber . . . in the journals of parliament, in the registers of the Archbishop of Canterbury, Winchester, Lincoln and obscurer places, whereof there is not so much as any memory in our common histories." To write a history without these materials was "but to spend time and cost in plastering only, or painting of a weak or poor building, which should be employed in provision of timber and store for the strengthening and enlarging of it."[151] Yet Selden, "that unmatched Antiquary,"[152] who spent most of his life publishing the documents and pillaging them for his own voluminous works, never wrote a narrative. Nor did he ever make any effort to polish or clarify his style, so that only his table talk remains readable today. Richard Bentley was undoubtedly the most learned classicist in England between 1500 and 1800. His work displays a mastery of the ancient sources—coins and inscriptions, languages and manuscripts—and a critical technique that very few have ever commanded. He probably knew more about the history of the ancient world than anyone in his time. But all his learning was cast in the form of a commentary on classical authors, even the celebrated *Dissertation on the Epistles of Phalaris* (1699), in which it was possible to learn so much about the culture of ancient Greece. Bentley never wrote history or pretended to write for the polite world, except to defend himself when he thought he had been unfairly attacked. But for two generations, he was pilloried for his learning and his manners by the Augustan "wits."

The classical scholar and the classical gentleman thus drifted apart. When William Camden decided toward the end of his life to establish a first chair of history at Oxford, he left directions that it be devoted to reading and explicating a classical historian, Lucius Florus.[153] (A second chair at Cambridge went to a Dutch humanist, Isaac Dorislaus, who chose Tacitus.)[154] The first incumbent, Degory Wheare, took eight years to cover only the first book, drawing comparisons between ancient and modern events as he plodded along, but when he put his thoughts together about the method of history, he simply repeated the commonplaces of the familiar Renaissance *ars historia* and confined himself to narrative.[155] A later incumbent (1688–89), Henry Dodwell, became one of the most erudite men in an age of erudition, but he so crowded his endless pages with detail that he was remembered afterward (by Gibbon, among others) more for the clutter and confusion of his mind than for the very real contributions that he made to classical and Christian antiquities.[156] No wonder, perhaps, that a reaction set in and the wits won the upper hand. Erudition began to look suspect to the eighteenth century, and narrative history never did learn how to profit from the accumulations of the antiquaries.[157]

It would be hard to find a better example of this ambivalence than Horace Walpole. Walpole was, of course, a very great gentlemen, a dilettante and virtuoso who had been to Rome with Thomas Gray and returned a connoisseur and arbiter of taste. He was also an antiquary, at least in common parlance (and sometimes in his own estimation), and he was elected to the society in 1753. He collected antiquities, made antiquarian tours around the countryside, remodeled his famous house at Strawberry Hill in the "Gothic" manner, wrote and printed some popular antiquarian works: the *Catalogue of Royal and Noble Authors* (1758), the *Anecdotes of Painting* (1762–71), and so on.[158] Admittedly, he did little hard labor, relying on others for his information, and took a rather casual stance toward the new standards of exactness and detail that the antiquaries had introduced. As he explained to his lifelong friend William Cole, "I have a wicked quality in an antiquary, one that annihilates the essence; that is, I cannot bring myself to the habit of minute accuracy about very indifferent points."[159] Once he boasted that he was "the first that ever endeavored to introduce a little taste into English antiquities, and had persuaded the world not to laugh at our Hearnes and Holingsheads." "I love antiquities," he admitted, "but I scarce ever knew an antiquary who knew how to write about them. Their understandings seem as much in ruins as the things they describe."[160] He was furious when his work on Richard III was criticized by his fellow antiquaries in the society; he resigned at once and began to satirize the members and their new journal, the *Archaeologia,* with all the old humor of the wits. Nevertheless, he promptly accepted the invitation of the new Scottish Society of Antiquaries when it was tendered a few years later. "Tom Hearnality" simply would not die.[161]

The trouble was that Walpole's neoclassical prejudices kept interfering with his antiquarian inclinations, just as to some extent they circumscribed his Gothic ambitions. "I know nothing of barrows and Danish entrenchments, and Saxon barbarisms and Phoenician characters—in short I know nothing of those ages that knew nothing." Saxon and Danish discoveries were worth no more to him than the Hottentots.[162] "Bishop Lyttleton used to plague me to death with barrows and tumuli and Roman camps, and all those things in the ground . . . but in good truth I am content with all the arts when perfected . . . and I care less for remains of art that retain no vestiges of art."[163] Typically, the neoclassical Walpole was even hesitant about the Roman antiquities in Britain. In 1780 he wrote to his long-suffering antiquarian friend Cole to describe his reading of William Hutchinson's *View of Northumberland:*

> I do not devour it fast, for the author's predilection is to Roman antiquities, which, such as are found on this island, are very indifferent, and inspire me with little curiosity. A barbarous country, so remote from the seat of empire, and occupied with a few legions that very rarely decided any great

events, is not very interesting, though one's own country—nor do I care a straw for the stone that preserves the name of a standard bearer of a cohort, or of a colonel's daughter. Then, I have no patience to read the tiresome disputes of antiquaries to settle forgotten names of vanished towns, and to prove that such a village was called something else in Antonine's *Itinerary*. I do not say that the Gothic antiquities that I like are of more importance, but at least they exist. The site of a Roman camp, of which nothing remains but a bank, gives me not the smallest pleasure.[164]

(7)

This then, or something like it, was the situation when Gibbon mounted the steps of the Capitol and pondered the ruins of ancient Rome. Like Walpole, Gibbon was a gentleman with literary ambitions and a private income, and he shared the prevailing admiration for classical style and rhetoric. But unlike Walpole and most of his contemporaries, he had a profound knowledge and unwavering appreciation of the antiquarian enterprise of three centuries. He had himself tried a youthful hand at some recondite problems in philology and chronology, and he defended learning against the contempt of the wits and philosophers in his first published work.[165] Now, as he prepared himself for that fateful moment on the Capitol, he read everything he could find in the works of European erudition about ancient and medieval Rome. The ruins themselves inspired him to his extraordinary undertaking; he meant nothing less than to put back together what had been torn asunder, to marry literature to erudition, history to antiquities. The *Decline and Fall*, therefore, is a work that can only be appreciated as the culmination of three hundred years of classical imitation combined with three hundred years of classical scholarship, a work almost unique in its time.[166]

Yet even as the *Decline and Fall* was appearing, doubts were being expressed in Germany, where a new historical method and a new historical profession were coming into being. Modern "scientific" history and archaeology were about to be conceived, to take over and transform this rich legacy of early modern times. In the process, the chief victim was destined to be classical narrative and the neoclassical contempt for specialized research and exact detail; the chief beneficiary was a new method and an unrestricted subject matter.[167] When that happened, the antiquarian enterprise was freed at last from some of the persistent restraints that had retarded it throughout its long life. With new motives and fresh incentives to recover the past, it turned somehow into modern academic history. Just how and why that happened is, of course, beyond our present compass, but one thing is certainly clear: without the long preparation first laid by the great collaborative enterprise of the anti-quaries, without their stubborn insistence upon getting back to the sources and seeing for themselves, and without the cumulative learning they piled up in their massive tomes, modern historiography as we know it today would never have come to pass.

CHAPTER 4

The Stonesfield Pavement:
Archaeology in Augustan England

The history of archaeology has hardly been attempted—its early years are especially obscure. That it began in the Italian Renaissance and developed thereafter to the enormously wider fields and more systematic techniques of modern scientific investigation is generally conceded. But what was it that happened during those long centuries of gestation after the first efforts of the Italians to recover the material evidence of ancient Rome but before the revelations of such familiar moderns as Schliemann, Layard, or Sir Arthur Evans? How did the search for antiquities turn into the science of archaeology? To answer this we need to recover the intermediate period, not merely the climactic events like the discoveries of Pompeii or Herculaneum but the more deliberate and continuous efforts of scholars and antiquaries who were trying throughout those years to retrieve and classify all the nonliterary remains of antiquity so that they might realize their ancient goal of comprehending the whole life of the past. To this the Augustans made their contribution, forging a crucial link in the chain that led to the modern science, and I should like to illustrate something of this by following in detail one characteristic but utterly forgotten instance of antiquarian enterprise in eighteenth-century England. I do not suggest for a moment that the discovery of the Stonesfield pavement in 1712 can be compared to the unearthing of Pompeii or Herculaneum, nor even to those other contemporary neoclassical events, Addison's *Cato,* Bentley's *Horace,* or Pope's *Homer,* but it raised nearly as much clamor, and it too left behind a legacy worth attending.[1]

My story begins one winter day in 1712, when a farmer plowing a field happened upon some large stones beneath the earth.[2] Turning them over, he came upon an ancient urn and then—with growing excitement—what appeared to be a great tiled pavement. Such things had

Part of the central panel of the Stonesfield pavement, from George Vertue's engraving for the Society of Antiquaries, c. 1725. From a copy in the possession of the author.

happened before, but now a tremor ran swiftly through the world of learning. As soon as the news got abroad, the rush began. Crowds poured in upon the vacant field; the post carried the tidings everywhere in England, and even overseas. Scholars began to squabble over the discovery, and artists vied to do justice to the splendid work. A new Roman tesselated pavement—for such it proved to be—was no ordinary event. It was after all some thirty-five feet long, twenty feet wide, colored, and with an elaborate design. It offered the most vivid and immediate evidence of the Romans in Britain, surpassing those other more plentiful but less dramatic remains—the coins and inscriptions, the busts and reliefs—that filled the antiquaries' cabinets. Apart from another pavement or two there was hardly anything on this scale to be seen in England; one had to travel abroad for the like. No wonder the Augustans were excited.

The pavement was discovered on Friday, January 25, 1712, on a farm called Chesthill Acre near the village of Stonesfield, about two miles from Woodstock. In a few days news reached Oxford that a great parcel of Roman coins had been unearthed there and on February 1 a fragment of the pavement was given to a young antiquary at St. Edmund Hall, Thomas Hearne. The very next day he walked over to see for himself and (as was his custom) jotted down his observations in his ever-present notebook. He noticed that the spot was very near the old Roman road known as the Ikenield Way or Akemanstreet, which went on to Bath. The pavement had a picture, he was told, with "A Dragon or Serpent and Apollo on it, several Ornamental Figures, as a Cock, a Hen Pheasant, and several Flower Pots." The tiles were variously colored and the paving bricks exactly nine inches square. It was said that several small pieces of Roman money had been planted there to impress the tourists. Indeed, Hearne's skepticism grew as he was shown about. He was doubtful about the urn, which he was told had disintegrated and was nowhere to be seen. He looked in vain for Roman bricks and at length decided he was being fooled; here was no Roman monument, "only the ornament of some Person of Quality," perhaps a manor house as was commonly reported. As for Apollo, he was barbarously done, and Hearne preferred to think him Saint Michael running a dragon through. "His spear is in his left hand and his Shoes without Heels are of the post Normannic Form." Nevertheless, he kept his opinion to himself.[3]

Meanwhile, Oxford was all astir. A few days after Hearne's visit, Dr. Gardiner, the warden of All Souls, showed him a sketch of the pavement that he had made himself. Gardiner took the work to be Roman and the figure to be Bacchus with a thyrsus, "but as for the Beast he knew not what to call it." Later that day Mr. John Urry, an antiquary then at work on a new edition of Chaucer, brought with him another sketch by one

Mr. Ford, a chaplain at Christ Church. He too believed that it was Bacchus with a thyrsus, and he was confident that the animal was a tiger. "There are various Opinions besides about the Matter," Hearne confided to his diary, "which makes great mirth in the University and elsewhere; but for my own Pt, I have not as yet declar'd my Opinion to any one."[4] By the end of the month a great delegation came from Oxford to view the monument, led by the astronomer and professor of geometry Edmund Halley, and including the vice-chancellor and several heads of houses.

News spread fast in wider and wider circles. Among the first to learn about the discovery was the great statesman and bibliophile Robert Harley, Earl of Oxford. Twice within a week he received letters describing it, the first from the botanist Tilleman Bobart, the second from Urry, who sent along his sketch.[5] Bobart's description was especially full, as might be expected from a man accustomed to scientific observation. He told how the pavement had been found, set down its measurements, and noticed the design. "Near the South end of the floor," he wrote, "is represented in a pretty large Circle a humane figure with a Cup in one hand and a spear in the other and riding a Dragon or some such Animall with two Cocks and two Henns . . . resembling pheasaunts." Like Hearne, he was suspicious of the coins. "There are many Spectators daily to see it and very different in their opinions as to its former use. Some suppose it to have been a Roman Temple, others a Generall's Tent, and some (perhaps with more reason) a place to burn their dead bodies, there having been found some remains of humane bones and burnt wheat." Hearne confirmed that the pavement had been covered with rubbish, pieces of stones and slate, great broad bricks, coal, and corn.[6]

Urry's letter included Ford's sketch, but he cautioned Harley that the owner of the field would not let Ford do it on the spot "unless he would pay him five pounds," so that it had had to be drafted from memory. Indeed, the "owner" was making the best he could of his find. He was an obscure man named Handes, and Hearne discovered that he was in fact only the tenant. Apparently he had found the pavement some time earlier but kept the news to himself until he could renegotiate his lease, cunningly introducing a new proviso that he could "dig the Ground." When the lease was sealed, "Handes discover'd the Treasure he had found and said he would not take 500 lbs. for it."[7] The real owner threatened to invoke the law, but it is unclear whether or not he succeeded. Urry does not seem to have paid any fee on his return; his new sketch was probably surreptitious, as it was certainly unsatisfactory. He wished that a better artist than himself might copy the pavement, "for it seems to me (but I never saw any such thing before) very beautiful." While he was there, he reported seeing a picture-dealer from London stealing still another sketch of it, which he promised Harley he would try to obtain.[8]

Who can say how many different avenues carried the news of the Stonesfield pavement? Hearne's friend the nonjuror scholar Hilkiah Bedford wrote him in March to say that he had already seen two letters about it "and had an imperfect account of it from one that was there." He begged Hearne to tell more.[9] One of the heads of houses, the indefatigable gossip Arthur Charlett, sent the news of that "noble Piece of Antiquity" to his friend Bishop William Lloyd even before visiting it himself.[10] Halley, we know, informed the whole of the Royal Society but not before news had reached that august body from a variety of sources, including its own secretary, Sir Hans Sloane.[11] By the end of February, surely everyone who cared about such things must have known about the new discovery.

It was in the Royal Society that enthusiasm was keenest. The secretary, whose business it was to know such things, was able to report the find on February 14, but his information was still imperfect; he got the dimensions right but the figure remained puzzling. In the discussion that followed, "it was the Opinion of some present that it was the Pavement of a Roman Praetorium, only the Bones and the wheat do not seem to argue with [that] supposition."[12] It may seem strange that a scientific society should concern itself with such matters, but the members were almost all virtuosi pledged equally to the recovery of physical and human nature. Their "curiosity" (it was a favorite word) knew no bounds, and there were few in that assembly who did not possess at least a few Roman coins and great appetite for Roman things. The Royal Society was still the only learned body in England with a journal and a museum; it was the natural forum for learned discussion of every kind.

In this respect Halley was typical; together with astronomy and mathematics, he kept a lifelong interest in ancient history, contributing papers on both subjects to the *Transactions* of the society. His appetite for the pavement seems to have been whetted by someone named Dewe, who sent him a vivid account on February 20.[13] "It is indeed a Sight worth seeing," Dewe wrote, "the Mosaick work intire and the Colours as fresh as I believe at the first laying." Once again, however, the design remained a little obscure; the figure looked to Dewe like "a Briton with a spear doubly barb'd mounted upon a dragon with a long taile and webb'd feet." In an accompanying sketch he labeled it "Image of a Man sitting on a Leopard (as a woman on a horse) but on the wrong side; a Thyrsus in his left hand, a Cup or flower pott in his right (the Leopard has no wings but feet)." He found the antiquaries disputing whether it was Roman or Saxon, and like the other visitors he could get no sight of the coins alleged to have been found there.

Dewe's letter was read to the society along with several others on February 28, and there was a lively discussion. "They all agree to the Dimensions and Descriptions of the Pavement," Sloane recorded, "only some take the Birds Represented to be Pheasants, others call them Cocks and Hens."[14] Halley, who had by then seen the pavement himself, believed them to be "two Pheasant Cocks and Hens alternate." He thought that the figure was a Bacchus and the animal a tiger; he noticed also that the wheat found there was "very soft and friable." Dr. John Harwood, who took a special interest in such matters, showed the members a piece of the wall that had been built around it ("of a Rude Stone and about a foot high.")[15] A week later, a Mr. Edward Loving showed the society, "a very curious draught" in proper colors, which he proposed to have engraved on a copper plate: "It seems to have been a Work of Great Labour and Cost." When at last it was printed (in May), the Society ordered a copy to be framed and hung in the precincts.[16]

So the Stonesfield pavement became known throughout the land. And yet with all the excitement, no one was quite sure just what had been discovered. Was it Roman or British; was it Saxon or Norman? What was its purpose? And what did the strange figures that made up part of the design represent? The confusion was natural enough. As Urry confessed, the pavement was the first he had ever seen, and without comparison, identification and interpretation were difficult. But not everyone was stumped. As the discussion proceeded, it became clear that there were a few possibilities of comparison after all. Other pavements— or pieces, anyway—had been unearthed elsewhere in England, and there was considerable description and illustration in the voluminous antiquarian literature of the period. By consulting these it was soon possible to demonstrate conclusively that the pavement was Roman, even if the other problems remained less tractable. So Hearne, for example, was won over easily enough: "Upon a more mature Consideration," he wrote beside his early doubts, "I am persuaded 'twas a Roman Praetorium, and can answer all Objections."[17]

In fact, there were more pavements discovered in Britain than one might think. They had a way of turning up wherever serious digging was done. Unfortunately, a new discovery was more often than not only casually reported; and the monuments themselves, accidentally discovered, were as often accidentally demolished or deliberately restored to the earth so that work might go on. Occasionally, attempts were made to preserve them; in Monmouthshire an owner tried to save what his servants had not destroyed by removing a portion piece by piece to his garden. Although interest was growing, it does not seem to have occurred to anyone yet to take an inventory of these discoveries. The nearest attempt perhaps was Camden's *Britannia*, that massive repository of all things ancient which had been newly updated in 1695, and where among the "additions," one might find, mixed with countless reports of other monuments, some terse descriptions of recent finds and on one occasion even a small illustration.[18]

But if no one had yet thought to take a close inventory of these remains, there are indications that interest was quickening in the years just before 1712, when several new pavements became prominent. At Roxby in Lincolnshire a farmer stumbled upon one while repairing a fence, and a neighboring antiquary, Abraham De la Pryme, rushed at once to the scene.[19] Before the local schoolboys could damage the find, he and his friends fell to work to clear it. It turned out to be six or seven yards square, with a geometrical design decorated with urns, flowers, and knots, "exceeding beautiful and pretty." He reported the discovery at once to his learned friend the dean of York, Thomas Gale, who in turn passed the news on to the Royal Society, where it appeared eventually in the *Philosophical Transactions*. De la Pryme was frustrated in his efforts to obtain the pavement for his own collection. He had hoped either to "begg it or buy it and contrive some way to take it up whole and so set it in a table frame at my house at Hatfield whither I send all the Antiquitys and Raritys that I can procure." In the event, he had to leave it where he found it, covered up again beneath the earth.

Closer still to Stonesfield was the publicity that attended a pavement at Leicester. This had come to light apparently about 1675 and gradually won a modest reputation as a curiosity worth visiting. Early in 1694, Richard Richardson wrote to Edward Lhwyd about it: "There is now in Leicester city nigh the market place in a sellar, an entire Roman pavement, perhaps the finest in England, upon which is the portraiture of a stag in full proportion and a boy standing at his head with a bow and quiver." He thought it must represent the fable of Actaeon.[20] The new *Britannia* agreed. "It is a very rare piece and (as is conjectur'd by most) of Roman Antiquity . . . and Few travellers of curiosity pass by that way without sight of it."[21] Even so unsympathetic an observer as Jonathan Swift, who on the whole despised the antiquaries and scholars as foolish pedants, could not forbear having a look. He wrote to the Earl of Pembroke in 1709 that he had sent to their mutual friend Sir Andrew Fountaine (along with Pembroke, one of the great collectors of the age) a "very learned Description" of the pavement, "which is to be sold a Pennyworth." He found only two objections to buying it, "First that it cannot be taken up without breaking, and secondly, that it will be too heavy for Carriage."[22] Here indeed was one of the principal obstacles to the progress of this sort of learning which by comparison with the study of coins or inscriptions was so laggard. The pavement was further publicized the following year when it was described in full and illustrated in the *Philo-*

sophical Transactions by the Reverend Samuel Carte, who repeated the traditional view that it represented the fable of Actaeon.[23]

One way or another, then, it was increasingly possible to get information about the pavements, even those discovered abroad, though the obstacles to close inspection remained. Descriptions and pictures began to appear in the compilations of foreign antiquaries[24] and even in those inventories of natural curiosities at home like Robert Plot's *Natural History of Oxfordshire* (1677 and 1705) and John Morton's similar work on Northamptonshire (1712).[25] A foundation for critical study was being laid, if only one could get at it. For someone like Thomas Hearne the antiquarian puzzle was immensely intriguing, and at hand were all the means of solving it. He was within easy walking distance of the pavement itself, which he visited repeatedly in the following months. His job at the Bodleian, where he was underkeeper, gave him convenient access to the most recondite scholarly books. He also knew the ancient coins there, which he had in fact catalogued. His passion was the past, and he divided his time equally between two great interests: the history of Rome and the history of England. What could be more to the point than an object from Roman Britain? Hearne had already won a modest reputation for his editions of various historical works, especially his Livy, and he had written a popular introductory handbook, the *Ductor Historicus*. He was about to begin that great series of edited medieval chronicles by which he is still known. In 1712, however, he was still at work on two major projects: a new Cicero, which was unhappily floundering, and a new edition of John Leland (the sixteenth-century English antiquary), which was in process of becoming a great success.

Thus, everything conspired to set the young scholar to writing a discourse on the new discovery. His notes rapidly accumulated and his convictions hardened. "The Barbarous Form of the Figures upon the Pavement at Stonesfield plainly shew that 'tis not of the more early Roman times. The tesselae are but course, yet well laid, and far better than could have been done in the Saxon or Danish times, or indeed since." He thought that the work must be later Roman and the floor from some general's villa. Perhaps it could even be dated to the year 369, the year the Emperor Theodosius visited Britain. The figure on it he now believed was Apollo Sagittarius. This set him in opposition to most of the spectators, who continued to prefer Bacchus. But he found much to support his view in a wide sweep through the authorities. Hearne realized that he needed an illustration for his little tract, but the owner insisted on his fee. And the Oxford painter Webb, who had also drawn the pavement, wanted what Hearne thought was an exorbitant price for his copy. The discourse was finished by the end of March, but with some frustration Hearne set it momentarily aside.[26]

How Hearne overcame the problem of payment does not appear, but on April 21 he paid his sixth visit to Stonesfield, this time bringing along with him the university engraver, Michael Burghers, with the object of drawing the pavement exactly. He intended to include an engraving in the eighth (and last) volume of his Leland, together with his discourse. It took several visits before the work was done, but Burghers was finished at the end of June, and Hearne was pleased to think that his engraving would correct all previous renderings, especially that of the egregious Webb. "A great many People go still to see this Curiosity," he noted with satisfaction in his journal. Burghers' plate, he wrote to Urry, was mightily approved—so much so that it would be sold separately, as well as with Hearne's discourse. Hearne might find himself differing from the "generality of Spectators," but at least no one could accuse him of taking his task lightly.[27]

The *Discourse concerning the Stonesfield Tesselated Pavement* was a small tract set in a large and miscellaneous work.[28] Hearne admitted honestly that he had first attempted to establish a post-Roman provenance for the pavement but that he had been won over by the discovery that there was no evidence whatever for such work ever having been practiced in the Middle Ages. The architects then, he observed with a characteristic Augustan sneer, "were illiterate, and understood nothing of curious Workmanship much less could they pretend to the *opera musiva*."[29] If the workmanship showed signs of barbarousness, that was because the pavement was late Roman; Hearne repeated his guess for the year 369. Most of his essay was descriptive (with some characteristic digression), but Hearne attempted also to solve the two main interpretative problems. The *use* of the pavement he had for a time believed was as the floor of a large private dwelling, "in all Probability . . . of a Dining Room, done by some curious and rich Gentleman, and not (as I had once conjectur'd) a Roman General's tent."[30] Upon further consideration he had returned to his first surmise: that it was made for some general, probably serving under Theodosius. He argued also against those who thought that the room was a bath and explained that the passages outside the pavement were not used to draw off water but to supply heat. He thought that the house must have lasted until the end of the Roman occupation, when it was burned to the ground. As for the *iconography*, Hearne reaffirmed his conviction that it was Apollo who was represented astride a feigned beast with a dart or javelin (and not a thyrsus) in hand. All was proposed modestly, "as nothing more than the uncertain Conjectures of a mean and obscure Person."[31]

The discourse, along with Burghers' plate, was received enthusiastically. Apparently, Hearne sent the original drawing to the Royal Society, for which he was warmly thanked.[32] The London virtuoso Dr.

Woodward was won over by Hearne's arguments and gave up his belief in Bacchus. And the Yorkshire antiquary Ralph Thoresby wrote, "Some here run mightily upon the Deity in the Tesselated pavement being Bacchus rather than Apollo but I am mightily pleased with your curious Dissertation thereupon."[33] Characteristically, Hearne continued to amass the evidence for his conclusions, growing ever more confident.[34] But whether one accepted his arguments or not, it was hard to disagree with Samuel Gale, who applauded him for publicizing the new discovery. "The Learned World is indebted to you for your Sedulous Preservation of so many antient Monuments which otherwise in a little Time must have utterly perished."[35]

Not everyone was happy, however. John Pointer was a chaplain at Merton College who was so far undistinguished in any way except perhaps for his growing collection of "curiosities."[36] For a man who loved Roman coins, the pavement was of natural interest, though just when Pointer decided to publish about it is not clear. His opportunity came because Hearne continued to insist, against the majority, that the pavement represented Apollo rather than Bacchus. In most respects Hearne was the superior scholar, more learned by far, more industrious, more serious. He knew how the work should be tackled; he understood that the image upon the pavement must be systematically compared with other authenticated images drawn from classical mythology—on coins, reliefs, and elsewhere—and with the descriptive literature, both the ancient sources and the modern antiquaries. But Hearne lacked critical judgment and here, as elsewhere, let an idea that he wanted to believe determine what in fact he found. Moreover, he depended more upon his knowledge of books, which was vast, than upon his knowledge of things, which was limited, especially as he rarely ventured far from Oxford. The difficulty was that the simplified drawing of the mosaic did admit of various possibilities; for example, it was not immediately obvious just what sort of animal was represented or what implements the figure held in his hand. As Hearne explained to Dr. Woodward, the artists, like the antiquaries, tended to see only what they wished or expected to find: "The London Draught is all Fiction. The Engraver was told 'twas a Bacchus and a Tyger and accordingly he put a jolly big Fellow upon a Tiger."[37] Unfortunately, Hearne was wrong, and the majority, including John Pointer, was right; the more assiduously the comparison was pursued, the plainer it became that it was indeed Bacchus who was depicted there.

Pointer's tract was ready in 1713. It was a useful piece of work and had the advantage of drawing upon Hearne as well as criticizing him. Pointer's description of the discovery and the pavement was full and clear, and he relied on his rival to prove that the work was Roman, although he added a long and impressive list of ancient and modern authorities to describe the Roman practice. He treated Hearne respectfully but disagreed on several points, including the date and origin of the work, which he thought might better be assigned to the entourage of the Emperor Allectus—who had actually been in Oxfordshire in A.D. 287—than to Theodosius. He thought the work, far from being barbarous, "the most Elaborate Piece of Roman Workmanship of this sort and One of the Finest of the Tesselated Pavements that has been hitherto found in all Britain."[38] He was dubious about Hearne's notion that the artist was a soldier; above all he disputed with Hearne about Apollo. He used William King's *Historical Account of the Heathen Gods* for its descriptions of Apollo and contrasted them with the image in the pavement. Where was the harp, the shield, the bow and arrows, the graceful long hair, the long robe and sandal with gold? "Never was the great God . . . so degraded, disarm'd and disrob'd, etc."[39] Nor was Hearne's wavering account of the mysterious animal any more satisfactory. On the other hand, all authorities agreed that Bacchus was youthful, beardless, and naked, crowned with ivy, had a cantherus or cup in one hand and a thyrsus in the other, and carried a spear adorned with vine branches and ivy. (Pointer's long list of authorities began with Ovid and Macrobius and concluded with Spanheim's great modern treatise on ancient coins.) The evidence appeared to Pointer conclusive.

And so it did to most of his contemporaries. Hearne reacted, as he usually did, with vituperation rained down upon Pointer in the safety of his private diary. There was something acutely exasperating at being corrected by a man of obviously limited talent, and Hearne was right in condemning Pointer's subsequent productions as lightweight and the Stonefield essay a "silly, illiterate, mean Account."[40] He defended himself to his friends, at least a few of whom took his side, and eventually in the preface to his edition of Leland's *Collectanea* (1715).[41] But this only caused Pointer to reply in a public advertisement; there he printed a number of testimonials that had accumulated after the publication of his own book, including two that must especially have hurt, from John Morton and Dr. William Musgrave.[42] In the end Pointer's work carried the day with the virtuosi.[43] The only solace for Hearne was that many years later his rival got into trouble at Merton and was forced into premature (though apparently temporary) retirement.[44]

There is nothing so stimulating as controversy, and the quarrel had the effect, if no other, of drawing further attention to the monument and to the problem of interpreting it. It even became known abroad; the Dutch scholar Hadrianus Relandus got hold of the engraving and passed it along to Samuel Pitiscus, who printed it in his *Lexicon antiquitatum Romanarum* (1713) as the frontispiece. From there it found its way into Bernard de Montfaucon's authoritative work, *Antiquity Explain'd,* where it was brought to European attention.[45] The Stonesfield pavement had won for itself an international reputation.

It is a little strange, then, that it should have fallen so swiftly into neglect. But who was there to take care of such a monument? The pavement could be protected *in situ* only at great cost, and the owner or tenant must have found it beyond his means and his interest to do so.[46] Moving it would have been even more difficult and expensive. As for institutions, there were hardly any yet in sight to participate. Archaeology was still outside the university curriculum and even history had barely been admitted. The Ashmolean Museum and the Bodleian Library found it hard enough to keep track of their coins. The Royal Society was virtually the only other learned body in England, but however interested its members became, it could only take a marginal interest, since its real business lay elsewhere. In a few years, it is true, the Society of Antiquaries was founded, but its efforts were naturally limited at first. Not until much later did it become possible to imagine institutional support. Until then and indeed for a long time afterward it was easier for visitors simply to walk off with a few tiles that could be added conveniently to their own personal collections. Thus the genuine archaeological interest of an individual like Ralph Thoresby or even of an institution like the Royal Society—each of which received gifts of pieces of pavement—contributed paradoxically both to the study of the monument and to its disintegration. Frost and contention between owner and tenant seem to have done the rest.

Less than a year after its exposure, the great mosaic had begun to suffer. "The last time I saw it twas much damaged," Hearne wrote to his friend Richard Richardson, "and yet this was before Winter; so that I fear it hath suffered much more."[47] Much later the antiquary Richard Gough reported, "On its demolition by the mob, who refused to pay for seeing it, or by the farmer, whose rent had been raised on that account, large fragments were carried off, and dispersed about the neighboring villages."[48] Yet interest did not disappear. Sometime after 1725 the pavement was reengraved for the Society of Antiquaries (which had earlier received some pieces of the original) by George Vertue.[49] And in 1735 the old virtuoso William Brome told a correspondent how a lady friend, who had been much taken by his copy of the pavement, borrowed his Hearne for a model and embroidered a nine-foot carpet with all the colors of the original.[50]

So, although the memory of the Stonesfield pavement began to fade, it was not entirely forgotten. Meanwhile, as the years passed, other pavements were discovered, reported on, and lost to view, while evidence about their nature, composition, use, and iconography gradually accumulated in the writings of the antiquaries. In every case, Augustan fascination with the Roman past provoked a broad general interest, though somehow the result was always a little unsatisfactory. As at Stonesfield, there was never an effort at a complete excavation; nor was anyone able, although the Society of Antiquaries on one occasion gave it a try, to take a systematic inventory of the surviving remains, so that a thorough comparison of the pavements remained impossible.[51] Failing that, errors like Thomas Hearne's were inevitable.[52] In short, modern "scientific" archaeology had yet to be invented, although much of the motive and something of the technique had begun to prepare the way.

The Stonesfield pavement is thus an early example of archaeological enthusiasm. Although it was an opportunity only half realized, its importance lay in the contribution that it made to the quickening of interest and the accumulation of knowledge that led in the end to the more systematic modern discipline. It is a mistake, I think, to imagine that such a transformation, when at last it came, arrived suddenly, or that it was brought into being through any single event or even a specific succession of events. What we know as modern archaeology developed, like all other branches of historiography, as a result of a confluence of many circumstances but especially of the long and persistent fascination with antiquity that began with the Renaissance and culminated in the Augustan age and (as a result) the slow and deliberate accretion of techniques and experience in the collective labor of antiquaries throughout Europe. When the Stonesfield pavement was rediscovered in 1779, something of that advance was apparent.

Once again, accident—so often the occasion for archaeological discovery—took a hand. Some laborers digging on the Stonesfield common seem to have stumbled again upon the remains of the pavement and reawakened interest in it. In the next few years, possibly under the patronage of the Duke of Marlborough, whose Blenheim estates lay nearby, an ambitious series of excavations took place which were reported to the Society of Antiquaries. The vice-president, Daines Barrington, examined the site in 1780 and kept the members informed. He was surprised to discover "that the Room and Pavement engraved by Hearne, continued in tolerable Preservation." Not far away the laborers had excavated another room with a tesselated pavement: "'Tis true the Size is not great, yet it equals that of the several Rooms at Herculaneum."[53] (By 1780 the Italian excavations had become well known in England.)[54] Next to the room was a complete bath, and "at a small distance from these Remains were evident Marks of their continuing." Barrington hoped they would be exhumed and properly cleaned; he thought it would not be expensive, "if the whole was surrounded with a Pale, to prevent the Deprivations of those who may visit these Antiquities." Meanwhile, he was able to show the society some of the bricks, glass, pottery, and cement found at the site.[55] The figure on the main pavement he described unhesitatingly as Apollo.

The work proceeded slowly, whoever was responsible. When the local rector, Thomas Warton, drew up his brief history of Oxfordshire in 1782, he described the new discoveries and speculated, against Hearne, that the building must have been "a mansion-house of some Roman person of distinction." For four hundred years, he recalled, the Romans had occupied Britain and brought peace and tranquillity. He thought it likely that this house had been built by a wealthy family, perhaps even a British one, since the Celts must eventually have built in the Roman style. Warton reported that many of the new discoveries at Stonesfield were being removed, though "carefully preserved." One Mr. Walker of Woodstock, auditor to the Duke of Marlborough, had large pieces of the pavements, and he was making careful drawings of the tesselations.[56]

In 1784 the results of the excavations were at length fully reported to the Society of Antiquaries by one of its members, Sir Henry Englefield.[57] He laid before the assembly a half-dozen colored drawings of the site. They were designed by William Lethington and cost the society twenty guineas. Today they may be seen still in Burlington House in a large red portfolio, impressive testimony to the expanded archaeological taste of the time. They reveal that three more large pavements had been uncovered besides the original, as well as a sudatory and cistern. There was also "a paved entrance or door-way walled in each side, from the Floor mention'd by Mr. Hearne."[58] It was now possible to trace the flues beneath the pavement and see exactly how the building was heated. Everything was precisely drawn and measured. For the first time the whole layout of the ancient building could be seen and the place and function of the Stonesfield pavement of 1712 understood.

But the Stonesfield excavations were not an isolated case. Almost at the same time, the Society of Antiquaries resumed interest in the Leicester pavement which, as we have seen, had been known for over a hundred years. A Mr. Blackburn of Southwark presented the society with a sketch he had made in the Leicester cellar by first tracing out the original and then copying it.[59] Although the general opinion was that it was Actaeon surprising Diana bathing, there were other ideas—for example, that it represented the youthful Hercules.[60] The society got another drawing later, still more accurate, and reviewed the whole subject at a separate meeting. It was noticed among other things that Carte's old engraving of 1715 had reversed the subject without mentioning it. At least it could be reported now that the fragment was carefully preserved and that the owner "with great Readiness and Civility permits it to be shown to any person desirous of seeing it." Today the pavement is in the

Leicester Museum, and it is thought that the subject is the story of Cyparissus and the stag.[61]

Perhaps it was only at Woodchester at the very end of the century that the gradual development in archaeological enthusiasm and technique that we have been tracing reached its fulfillment. Hearne had already known about a pavement there, and it was reported to the Society of Antiquaries first in 1724 and then again, this time with a colored drawing, in 1730.[62] It was said to be one hundred and sixty feet long and sixteen feet wide and was obviously the most important pavement and one of the most impressive Roman monuments that had yet come to light in England. Even so, it was many years before it could be properly examined and studied, in part because of its inconvenient situation beneath a graveyard. The society looked at a drawing in 1783, but it was left to Samuel Lysons in 1797 to report on it exactly and completely to the satisfaction even of the modern archaeologist.[63] Excavations that began in 1793 enabled Lysons to measure the pavement precisely for the first time. Observing it directly and using the evidence of previous drawings and descriptions, he was able to reconstruct it and identify the central figure as Orpheus playing on his lyre; he was helped here by comparison with several other pavements discovered since Stonesfield. At Woodchester for the first time, the excavations themselves were described, as well as everything recovered. Special trenches were dug to establish the relationship of the various rooms to one another. Lysons received plenty of help, even some from the royal family. "I had a *grand encampment,*" he wrote happily to Sir Joseph Banks, "three tents, an artillery Wagon, and two-and-twenty mules."[64] "The ground was opened afterwards in every place where any reasonable expectation could be entertained of finding a construction of the building."[65] The classical authors, of course, were mined for every scrap of information about the Roman buildings, but comparison could now be made directly with a newly uncovered villa at Pompeii. Best of all were the forty splendid color plates that delineated the site, its environs, building plans, strata, etc. The king himself, George III, who came to visit the excavation, was impressed with the results.[66]

Lysons went on to even more important archaeological achievements, some of them involving other ancient pavements, but we must leave that story for another occasion. In the new century the Stonesfield work was not forgotten. Unfortunately an enclosure divided the property among three different owners in 1801 "so that," it was feared, "not a vestige of the Roman remain will soon be left."[67] The self-taught draftsman and antiquary, William Fowler, an old rival of Lysons, set out to engrave the pavement again and had the ground opened in 1802. He found part of the pavement still in good preservation, and with the help of a drawing in the Ashmolean Museum and some fragments there, he published an impressive new plate of the work.[68] By 1813, it was again thought to have been pretty much destroyed by the country people, although about that time a new attempt at excavation was made. The idea was to get a more complete view of "the form and extent of the building and . . . an accurate ground plan which would still further illustrate the domestic habits of its original inhabitants." The excavation did not get very far—although the investigators were able to define the whole area of the site, for the first time, as one hundred and ninety by one hundred fifty-two feet—but they were led on to the discovery nearby of a new villa site at North Leigh.[69] Perhaps it is not surprising that Thomas Hearne had known of this pavement, too, though he confused it naturally enough with Stonesfield.[70] But progress in archaeology was (and is) slow, and it is only recently that Northleigh has really become known. In 1933 it was noticed that of thirty Roman sites identified in Oxfordshire, only two had been completely opened and only one "scientifically" explained.[71]

As for Stonesfield, it had quite vanished again by the middle of the nineteenth century and it is hard now to know even where it originally lay. The fields that had been plowed over the pavement for more than a thousand years, had returned to cover the site. We may be thankful, however, that although the original has long since disappeared, it can still be seen in the pages of Hearne and Pointer, in the plates of Burghers and Vertue and Fowler, and in the copious correspondence of generations of antiquaries, a reminder of its importance once to the intellectual life of the Augustans and to the progress of modern archaeology.

CHAPTER 5

Natural History and the New Philosophy:
Bacon, Harvey, and the Two Cultures

For a long while, no one stood higher in the estimation of later times than Francis Bacon. In the seventeenth century he was the immediate inspiration for almost everyone who wrote about politics or thought about nature. For the men of the Enlightenment he was "the greatest, the most universal, and the most eloquent of the philosophers."[1] In the nineteenth century he was still revered as the first of the moderns, though the worm had begun to turn. Now, finally, by a strange twist of fortune, the reputation of the great man seems to have slipped altogether, though no doubt he must still be reckoned with in the history of English prose style. As a statesman, Bacon has been judged a failure; as a scientist, he is generally derided; as a philosopher, he has almost dropped out of the curriculum. How did this happen?

At first glance, it looks like the familiar problem of historical anachronism. If Bacon's admirers were too ready to assimilate him to their views and see him as a prophet, his recent critics would seem to be at least as hasty in discrediting him because he does not suit their predilections about the nature of science or philosophy. Both sides appear to have erred in the same way, by comparing and conflating Bacon's ideas too directly and immediately with their own. The first villain in this "whig interpretation of history" may well have been that archwhig himself, Thomas Babington Macaulay, who willfully mistreated the political Bacon in a famous essay that his biographer, James Spedding, tried to answer in two large but largely unsuccessful volumes. The most recent villains may be those historians of science who have been treating the intellectual Bacon with the same kind of unappreciative and dismissive contempt as did Macaulay.[2] They like to look upon modern science much as Macaulay viewed the triumph of Parliament, as progressive, necessary, and inevitable, and they choose up sides accordingly. What would seem to be required to understand Bacon's thought fairly and to appreciate his lost reputation is a proper dose of intellectual history, an effort to restore Bacon to his original situation and concerns. Then and then only might it become possible to criticize his ideas justly and place them in an appropriate continuum.

In short, the first task of the historian (here, as always) is to discover, if possible, just what Bacon was getting at, just what the problems were that he was attempting to solve when he first set pen to paper and became a philosopher not of science (for of course even the term is anachronistic) but of nature. Unfortunately, this is not an easy task. It is complicated by the fact that Bacon's works are extraordinarily diverse and voluminous; that they are often fragmentary and incomplete; that there is little information about his early years; and (in part as a result of all this) that there is still no decent modern biography. The collected works in twelve volumes and the letters in seven, the life work of James Spedding, are a monument to nineteenth-century industry, but they are over a hundred years old and were never integrated. If little new information by or about Bacon has turned up since, knowledge of his world and times has been multiplied many times over. And there have been some notable modern studies on many of Bacon's separate activities: as a lawyer and politician, orator and rhetorician, essayist and visionary.[3] Nevertheless, we are left still with the central question: what was Bacon up to when he conceived his philosophical vocation? The problem remains to find a key to the multifarious activities of a man who took nothing less than all knowledge for his province by recovering his purpose. The hope is that in so doing we can not only come to terms with Bacon but throw some light on his times, in particular, on the peculiar relationship that seems to have existed between philosophy and history in his day.

(1)

Sometime, probably in the winter of 1580–81, a new Latin comedy called *Pedantius* was produced at Trinity College, Cambridge. The hall was crowded with undergraduates, who seem to have found the satire uproarious. One auditor, Sir John Harington, still remembered being present, along with the young Earl of Essex, ten years later.[4] The plot was simple enough, although the models were plainly classical. The satire was directed at the hero Pedantius, a rhetorician who can hardly make himself intelligible, and his friend the philosopher Dromodotus, who is equally obscure though in his own fashion. As the story unfolds, Pedantius woos the uncomprehending Lydia, who has her heart set on another. With her boyfriend, she has no difficulty duping Pedantius and

Engraving for the frontispiece of the first printing of *Pedantius*, 1631, showing the protagonist beneath a shelf of humanist texts. The Beinecke Rare Book and Manuscript Library, Yale University.

defrauding him of his love, money, and dignity. Along the way, the author makes great fun of the impractical and unworldly mannerisms of both the humanist and his scholastic colleague—in effect, of the two cultures that then ruled at Cambridge University.[5]

The story of the interaction of the two cultures at Cambridge is by now a familiar one, at least in outline.[6] At the beginning of the sixteenth century, the medieval university was still intact; in the curriculum, logic and Aristotelian philosophy still held sway, and theology ruled as queen of the sciences. The main purpose of higher education remained the training of clerics. It was not long, however, before humanism began to make inroads. Erasmus and Richard Croke introduced Greek; lectures in "humanity" and rhetoric began to appear.[7] The idea, as the statutes of Corpus Christi College put it quaintly, was "to extirpate all barbarism from our bee-hive."[8] With the Reformation, the study of canon law was banished; the friars disappeared; and Scotus and his fellows were routed from lectures and libraries and (as they said at Oxford) banished to Bocardo.[9] More important, perhaps, the universities began to open their doors to a new kind of student, the fee-paying gentleman or aristocrat who did not want or need professional training and could not tarry for a degree but who only desired a little more of what he had already received, an introduction to "polite learning": i.e., the literature of the classics; poetry, history, and oratory. The demand was met not so much through the old instruments of university lecture and dialectical contest as through new means gradually improvised in the colleges, chiefly through tutorials. In time, the center of gravity of the university altered, though much of the old remained intact and was even restored, and humanism took its place side by side with scholasticism in an uneasy and perhaps unnatural partnership that was nevertheless destined for a long coexistence.

That the two forms of culture were uneasy companions is suggested by the contests that broke out between them at the introduction of humanism in England early in the century. So, for example, the new chancellor of Oxford, Thomas More, had to intervene in 1518 on behalf of the Greeks against the "Trojans" with a plea for the new learning;[10] while at Cambridge, Erasmus fought a long series of skirmishes against his hostile scholastic colleagues.[11] In the *Praise of Folly*, everything is grist for his mill but he takes a special pleasure in prosecuting the logicians and philosophers for their fooleries. He mocks their jargon, poking fun at their interminable quiddities, hecceities, formalities, and the rest, as mere "strifes of words"; and he finds their subject matter and their hopeless questions absurd and irrelevant. In his aversion to contemporary philosophy, as in other respects, Erasmus was a true disciple of the Italian humanists—of Petrarch, for example, or Lorenzo Valla—and there is throughout the immense corpus of his work hardly a trace of interest in logic or metaphysics, mathematics, or natural philosophy.[12] Nor did he care much more for formal theology, preferring, as he told Luther, to put aside all metaphysical disputes (like the problem of freedom of the will) for the simple imitation of the life of Christ. Like Petrarch before him, he preferred ignorance to dogmatic assertion, correct living to correct belief. One can perhaps exaggerate the antipathy of the two cultures in sixteenth-century England, but at bottom it was real enough and always latent.

Of course, even in this, ancient precedent had its effect. The quarrel between philosophy and eloquence, natural science and literature, was after all as old as Western civilization itself. The Renaissance knew it on the one side through the works of Plato and Aristotle, where the sophists were given short shrift for confusing convention and opinion with knowledge, for sacrificing truth to expediency, for subverting morality, and for elevating the practical and ephemeral over the theoretical and timeless. The Renaissance knew it on the other side through the works of Isocrates, who was among the first to defend himself effectively against these charges, and through his spiritual descendants Cicero and Quintilian. Through these authors the Renaissance learned of the inadequacy and pretentiousness of any philosophy that claimed dogmatic certainty. From this perspective, the natural sciences and philosophy appeared to be essentially irrelevant to the practices of the real world and effectively useless to the statesman. Through these writers, the Renaissance learned of the value of the ancient alternatives to logic and dialectic and rediscovered rhetoric and poetic and (not least) history, each of which had been despised by the ancient philosophers and subordinated or ignored altogether in the curriculum of the medieval schools.

Fortunately, there is no need to rehearse here either the prehistory of this ancient rivalry or its renewal during the Italian Renaissance and then again in England and elsewhere during the sixteenth century. It has been described more than adequately for antiquity by Jaeger and Marrou (and others), who have laid the classical arguments bare.[13] The fact is that there *was* indeed something incompatible about the alternative ideals of philosophical wisdom and practical eloquence which made them, despite the best efforts of both ancients and moderns, impossible to reconcile easily. Perhaps this is regrettable, but it has never been easy to think of a remedy, although there have always been some who have hankered after one. When, not long ago, Lord Snow wistfully renewed the appeal for some bridge between the two cultures, lamenting the fact that there was hardly anyone nowadays who could expound both the second law of thermodynamics and a novel by Charles Dickens, he was startled by the savage reply of an unrepentent F. R. Leavis, who showed not the slightest intent toward either reconciliation or synthesis. At Cambridge in the sixteenth century no more than at Cambridge in the twentieth century was there an easy conjuncture, but at least a *modus vivendi* was improvised; the two cultures were permitted to live side by side, each to furnish its own skills and values to a mixed body of students who were left to choose among them for their own purposes. Thus was worked out, in the words of Samuel Eliot Morison, "an unwilling compromise between gentility and learning."[14] If this seems to have satisfied most of the students and fellows, then as now, there were a few among them who chafed and, as we shall see, at least one among them who wanted to take up the whole matter from scratch and think it through for himself.

It must be emphasized that though the problem of reconcilation became academic when humanism entered the university, its roots were in conditions outside. In particular, the new culture was encouraged by new social and political circumstances that only lately have begun to be explored. Suffice it to say that the "rise of the gentry" and the Tudor "revolution in government," however problematical, were realities sufficient in the sixteenth century to create a demand for the skills and training appropriate to a new style of life. Chivalry died a lingering death, but to humanists like Roger Ascham the culture of the feudal aristocracy seemed no longer relevant to practical life and had to be replaced.[15] Humanism in England was thus a cultural movement created to serve the leaders of a new society who were self-conscious about their needs,[16] and it won success by gaining their patronage. The Tudor court from Henry VII to Queen Elizabeth took the lead in educating its own, and the aristocracy and gentry followed swiftly afterward. When Thomas Elyot set down his ideal of the governor in 1531, it was a fair reflection of the cultural aspirations of the new classes in their new situation, and its popularity was uncontested for two generations. *The Book of the Governor* exalted the orator-statesman as the new humanist ideal and it resuscitated the classical goal of eloquence to the complete exclusion of medieval philosophy and theology, which it never even thought to mention. Only moral philosophy, by which Elyot meant the practical guidance to life that Cicero and Xenophon offered equally with Plato, was included. For the rest, it was the imitation of good letters, of classical poetry, oratory, and history, that offered the basic training for public life. For all practical purposes the world of nature might not exist, and both science and divinity were entirely excluded.

It was something like this cultural ideal, then, that swiftly captured the grammar schools and entered the universities in the years after Erasmus came and went. With only some Latin and less Greek, the Tudor schoolboy who was ambitious needed (or so it was generally thought) more of the same thing. At the age of fourteen he was hardly ready to play a role on the world's stage. If the story of the transformation of grammar school teaching in Tudor England has been thoroughly told, it has perhaps not yet been completely appreciated. What is clear from the school statutes and timetables, the textbooks and teacher's manuals, and the reminiscences of schoolboys is the triumph of humanism and the eclipse of scholasticism, the endorsement of classical grammar and rhetoric at the expense of medieval logic, the restoration of the Isocratean-Ciceronian ideal and the practical disdain for natural science and philosophy. It was as if the whole of secular society, or at least that part of it that mattered, had made a unanimous collective decision to choose one side over the other in the ancient quarrel and give the victory to eloquence. And yet theology, with its underpinnings in Aristotle and the Middle Ages, refused to disappear altogether; and Protestant divines, locked in combat with papists as well as their own, continued to find their weapons in the reason and dialectic of the Middle Ages. If the first Protestant reformers despised systematic theology, there is no doubt that the next resurrected it and that scholasticism made a comeback as the century advanced.[17] So medieval logic and Aristotelian philosophy could not be banished altogether from the universities, however much it might be discouraged in the schools, and even Scotus and the rest returned to the bookshelves of the students of divinity.[18] Nor, finally, could laymen remain indifferent in a world rent by theological controversy. The elementary school curriculum might be heedless of all this; the universities could not.

It was at Cambridge in the 1540s that classical humanism gained its first academic triumphs. The university had already been tainted by both Renaissance and Reformation, by the Greek of Erasmus and the Luther of Tyndale, Barnes, and the White Horse Tavern,[19] and its progressive reputation seems to have appealed on both counts to a generation of ambitious men who wanted to change the world, or at least to enjoy its benefits. In 1545, Roger Ascham protested to the Archbishop of Canterbury that the new students "were for the most part only the sons of rich men, and such as never intended to pursue their studies to that degree as to arrive at any eminent proficiency and perfection in learning, but only the better to qualify themselves for some places in the state." The same complaint was echoed by William Latimer (1549) and Thomas Lever (1551), and still later by William Harrison (1587).[20] Yet it was Ascham himself who had boasted proudly in 1542 that "Sophocles and Euripides are more familiar to us than Plautus was in your day. Herodotus, Thucydides and Xenophon are read and discussed more than Livy was then. What Cicero once was Demosthenes is now and students have more copies of Isocrates in hand than they used to have of

Terence. Nor do we overlook the Latin authors but study ardently the best writers of the golden age."[21] Philosophy was not entirely absent from Ascham's purview, since Plato was read along with Aristotle, both now in the original Greek. But it was Aristotle's *Ethics, Politics* and *Rhetoric*, not the *Physics* and *Metaphysics*, much less the other scientific works, that interested him.[22]

Ascham credited his old college, St. John's, and his old tutor, Sir John Cheke, with the innovation; it was Cheke's work and example, he insisted, that encouraged a whole generation, and that is how it was remembered for a long time afterward.[23] Apparently Cheke read the Greek classics in his own rooms in the college, "privately in his chamber," running through many of the poets and historians, all of Homer, Sophocles and Euripides, Herodotus, Thucydides, Xenophon, Isocrates, and Plato. He was about to tackle Demosthenes and Aristotle, according to Ascham, when he was summoned to court to tutor the young Prince Edward. When at last Cheke was forced into exile under Mary, he set up shop in Padua to the same effect, hosting the English community there and reading through Demosthenes at last.[24] Certainly the idea of the tutorial was catching on ever more strongly. John Beret remembered that when he taught at Cambridge about 1555 and had "pupils studious of the Latin tongue, I used then often to write epistles and themes together, and daily to translate some piece of English into Latin for the more speedy, and easy attaining of the same." He wrote a dictionary afterward to facilitate the exercises and named it the *Alvearie;* apparently the beehive still needed to be purged of its barbarism.[25]

Thus the men of Cheke's generation were agreed to concentrate their attention on polite learning, although they had to improvise the means to attain it. As we have seen, the Greek reading and the Latin composition that they managed were expected to prepare young men for public life, and it is no accident that many of them—beginning with Cheke himself—left the university for public careers. Cheke's colleague Sir Thomas Smith is a perfect example of the type, a Greek scholar second only to Cheke himself, who was successively public orator (1538), regius professor of civil law (1544), and vice-chancellor of the university (1544)—all before the age of thirty. His biographer divides his life into four parts: "(1) At the University where his learning made him famed; (2) Under King Edward when he became a courtier; (3) Under Queen Mary when he concealed himself, and lived in a private capacity; (4) Under Queen Elizabeth, when after she had much employed him in her service, both in his own and foreign courts, he piously concluded his useful life."[26] He was, among other things, civilian, ambassador, and secretary of state, and he produced some of the best political prose of the whole period. "You only," Ascham wrote to him in 1551, "and Mr.

Cheke have pulled forward by the example of your diligence, learning, conscience, counsel, good order, not only of studying but of living, all such as in Cambridge have since sprung up."[27] The conjunction of literature and life, of the classics and politics, was never forgotten. The roll call of those who were colleagues of Cheke and Smith and who made successful political careers is long and impressive: William Cecil, Francis Walsingham, Walter Haddon, Thomas Wilson, Walter Mildmay, Thomas Hoby, and many others—not least, Sir Nicholas Bacon, the father of our philosopher.[28]

It is doubtful whether there was anyone in this long list of scholars-turned-statesmen who took the scholastic side of the curriculum very seriously.[29] Yet logic and Aristotle lumbered on, and it would not be difficult to supply another whole list of clerics trained in the university, this time Anglicans and puritans, who did take degrees and for whom theology was a serious professional business.[30] Degree requirements were not relaxed in these years, nor is there much sign that the formal curriculum was much influenced by all this "humanity."[31] It is not surprising, then, to find that the normal routine at Corpus Christi College, to take an example, in the years under Robert Norgate (1578–87), was to split the day more or less into halves, one for each of the two cultures. Three daily lectures were prescribed, beginning at 6:00 A.M. with Aristotle's natural philosophy, the *Organon,* and the logic of John Seton; resuming at noon with Greek and Latin instruction via Homer, Demosthenes, Hesiod or Cicero; and concluding at 3:00 P.M. with a rhetoric lecture on some further part of Cicero. Various exercises of a dialectical kind were also enjoined on the undergraduates, while the fellows were to wrestle on Friday afternoons with "problems in divinity."[32]

To judge by the elaborate instructions of Richard Holdsworth, sometime later, much the same thing seems to have happened on the tutorial level. The date of this Cambridge tutor's *Directions* is still conjectural, but it is likely that he was already using them (or something like) when he taught Simonds D'Ewes at St. John's College in 1618–20.[33] The *Directions* were meant to show the undergraduate just what to do, "what books to read, and how and when, and what time may be allowed to each, briefly; how every month in the whole four years before you come to be a Bachelor is to be employed."[34] Once again, the synopsis that follows divides each day of the course of study into mornings and afternoons, the first being devoted exclusively to logic, physics, metaphysics, and natural philosophy; the second "to the Greek and Latin tongues, history, oratory and poetry, studies not less necessary than the first, if not more useful, especially Latin oratory, without which all the other learning, though never so eminent, is in a manner void and useless."[35] This matchup of two kinds of instruction, book by book and day by day for four years, kept apart only by lunch, is a perfect example of the separation and coexistence of the two cultures that was characteristic of the Cambridge curriculum in Francis Bacon's day. D'Ewes, very like Bacon, was typical in his puritan earnestness, diligently pursuing his studies both in the mornings and the afternoons, picking up a good deal of logic and some natural philosophy, some classical rhetoric and history, and lots of Greek through the public lectures of Mr. Downes—but leaving without a degree after about two years.[36]

Under the circumstances, then, it seems natural enough that the students at Trinity College were amused to find both kinds of instruction characterized separately and satirized equally in *Pedantius*. The logician and the rhetorician were familiar types indeed, and there must have been plenty of times when the adolescent student wondered what it was all about, how either scholastic disputation or classical declamation could ever be of any use, and what in the world they were doing lodged uncomfortably together in the curriculum after so many centuries.

(2)

It is still uncertain who wrote *Pedantius*. Of all the candidates who have been proposed, I suppose that Francis Bacon is the least likely, though he once inspired a whole book on the subject.[37] Of course, Bacon has also been assigned the rest of the Elizabethan theater at one time or another and with about as much plausibility. But the suggestion is interesting because it calls attention in this case to a real similarity of perspective, between the anonymous satirist and the author of the *Advancement of Learning*. Bacon had only recently left Cambridge when the play was performed; it is very likely that he knew the author. Like everyone else, he must certainly have recognized the satirical victims, for it was plain to all that Pedantius, at least, was none other than the notorious university lecturer Gabriel Harvey, and Dromodotus very likely Harvey's friend John Duffield, praelector in philosophy.[38]

Now, Harvey is worth remembering here because his career almost exactly spans the years when Bacon was involved with Cambridge, and because his response to the intellectual situation there and to the two rival cultures is so amply documented. Harvey provides the context in which the philosophical thought of Bacon was first conceived, and which is missing from Bacon's own biography. On the whole, the internal life of the university, the intellectual scene behind the statutes and regulations, is not easy to penetrate in the sixteenth century, but Harvey was a scribbler, very much self-absorbed and reflective, and he never tired of writing down his opinions and reactions in his notebooks and in the margins of his reading. As a result, we have the example of one man anyway, "for some fifteen years, one of the most noteworthy and most widely known of the members of the university," deeply engaged in many of the same issues that concerned Bacon.[39]

Harvey went up to Cambridge in 1566, took a degree, and became a fellow of Pembroke Hall in 1570. He was joined by two brothers soon afterward. Harvey's patrons were two of the leading humanist politicians of the day, Walter Mildmay and Thomas Smith, and he seems to have accepted their basic point of view, even to modeling his career after their examples.[40] Like Simth in particular, for whom he had a special affection, Harvey set out first to win fame in the university community as a scholar, then to attempt a life in public service through the medium of the civil law. Unlike Smith, he was thwarted in both ambitions, though for a time he won some respect as a teacher. His political career never really got off the ground. Perhaps he came the closest about 1579–80, when it looked as though the Earl of Leicester was ready to employ him. But something failed him then as always—his personality, perhaps, which was eccentric and irascible, or his learning, which may have seemed a little too academic for public life. As his enemy Thomas Nashe put it later, sarcastically, "He that most patronized him . . . told him that he was fitter for the University than for the Court or his turn, and so bade God prosper his studies, and sent for another Secretary to Oxford."[41]

In 1573, just about the time the young Bacon was arriving at Cambridge, Harvey seems to have encountered his first academic obstacle. He had hoped to obtain his M.A. at Pembroke in the usual way when he found several of the fellows of his college arrayed against him. Apparently, the difficulty was both personal and intellectual, and since all we have is Harvey's account in a letter to the master of the college, it is a little hard to evaluate or separate the two. On the one hand, Harvey was accused of being unsociable and taking the fellowship lightly. On the other hand, and perhaps more significantly, he was accused of opposing the authority of Aristotle: it was alleged that Harvey, "was a great and continued patron of paradoxes and a main defender of strange opinions, and that commonly against Aristotle too." Apparently, his opponents seemed to think "that this singularity in philosophy is like to grow to a shrode matter, if I once convert my study to divinity."[42]

Harvey did not entirely deny the charge; he was ready to admit that he had posed some new ideas, though he claimed to have drawn them from such modern writers as Melancthon and Peter Ramus. As for Aristotle, Harvey insisted that he had always spoken the philosopher's praise, in private talk as well as public disputation, but that he could not accept his absolute and unquestioned authority: "Marry not so, that I can straight way take it for scripture what soever he hath given his word for." In particular, he singled out a number of propositions that he was willing to urge against Aristotle, such notions as that the world is not eternal, that the heavens do not consist of a fifth element, and so on. One, he attributed to Ramus alone ("Nihil est Physikos infinitum potentia"), but he was confident that the Frenchman could satisfy "any reasonable natural philosopher in that point."[43] Anyway, what was to be done? Eliminate all controversial propositions, and what point was there to philosophy? One would be left only with such outworn conventional themes as *de nobilitate, de amore, de gloria,* and *de liberalitate,* "more fit for scholars' declamations to discuss upon than seemly for masters' problems to dispute upon." Such matters, Harvey complained, had been thoroughly canvassed long ago, "and every one that can do any thing is able to write whole volumes of them, and make glorious shows with them." That, surely, was no way to the advancement of learning. Yet to be politic, Harvey was willing, if need be, to "lock Melancthon and Ramus up in my study, and bring Osorius and Omphalius in to the chapel."[44] Since Harvey had no intention of studying divinity any further, this was hardly a deprivation; perhaps the rhetoricians could be made to suffice after all.

The master, Dr. John Young, took Harvey's side; the young man got his fellowship, was appointed Greek lecturer in the college, and started on the best part of his career. Scholastic disputation was put aside; humanist declamation became his chief concern. In 1574 he was chosen university praelector, or professor of rhetoric, and was reappointed twice in the next few years. With the advice of Thomas Smith, he began now to study the civil law and to think of possibilities beyond the university. As Nashe put it later, sarcastically, "Divinity (the Heaven of all the Arts) for a while drew his thoughts unto it, but shortly after, the world, the flesh, and the devil with-drew him from that, and needs he would be of a more Gentleman like lusty cut; whereupon he fell to moral epistling and poetry." Some of Harvey's pieces in Latin and English were later printed and drew him into friendship with another Cambridge poet, Edmund Spenser.[45] Meanwhile, in the ordinary course of his duties, he delivered lectures on Greek and rhetoric, which were now printed.[46] It is possible that Bacon was among his auditors, or at least among his readers. Harvey had claimed modernity for his philosophical interests; as a rhetorician he was no less unorthodox. The time was ripe for fresh ideas; Harvey was certainly up to date, and it appears that he was momentarily very popular.

As praelector, it was Harvey's responsibility to address the undergraduates four times a week on the classical rhetoricians. In 1577 he revised and published two sets of these orations: the *Rhetor,* which he seems to have delivered in 1575, and the *Ciceronianus,* probably the next year.[47] (Bacon left Cambridge sometime between the two.) In the first,

Harvey sets out for his students a method that relies expressly on the recent rhetoric of Ramus's colleague Omar Talon; in the second, he considers some of the broader issues of classical imitation that were raised also by Ramus. The autobiographical passages in the latter, which chronicle his conversion from a narrow Ciceronian to a liberated Ramist, are particularly interesting.[48] Not long before, it seems (having shelved dialectic as fruitless), Harvey had thrown in his lot with that special brand of humanists—Bembo, Longoliuis, Sadoleto, and the rest—who had insisted that Cicero alone among the ancients and moderns should be imitated. At the same time, he took a dislike to those critics, chiefly Erasmus, who had derided the Ciceronians as narrow pedants. Harvey mocks his own rigidity here with some comical examples, remembering how very pure his own style had become in its literal dependence on the Roman model. (His use of such Ciceronian *clausulae* as "esse posse videatur," which he recalls here, was not forgotten by Nashe a dozen years later.) Unfortunately, Harvey remembers, "I valued words more than content, language more than thought, the one art of speaking more than a thousand subjects of knowledge. I preferred the mere style of Marcus Tully to all the postulates of the philosophers and mathematicians; I believed that the bone and sinew of imitation lay in my ability to choose as many brilliant and elegant words as possible, to reduce them into order, and to connect them together in a rhythmical period."[49]

"Ciceronianism" was of course a familiar controversy after a century of debate. (Even the ancients had once argued the question.)[50] Harvey rehearses much of the story here and must certainly have impressed his auditors, as he still impresses us, with his erudition. His own conversion, he says, was a result of reading the *Ciceronianus* of Peter Ramus, probably in 1569.[51] "I began forthwith to ponder how dangerous it is for one enslaved to prejudicial opinions to take shelter in authority."[52] From Ramus, Harvey learned that Cicero had faults and that others of the ancients had virtues, and that both were worth attending. It looks as though the revolt against Aristotle had been followed in Harvey's case (as with Ramus) by a revolt against Cicero. His young audience must have enjoyed his surprising effrontery.

Yet Harvey's Ramist revolt was not perhaps very profound. For one thing, the anti-Ciceronians from Erasmus to Ramus had meant only to qualify their endorsement of Cicero, not to eliminate it. (Harvey's main objection to the Ciceronians was only that they had exaggerated the importance of Ciceronian language over Ciceronian wisdom.)[53] Eloquence was still the goal and imitation of the classical authors the means, though not in the narrow and exclusive sense of the pedantic Ciceronians.[54] In this respect all were indeed humanists. Nor, apparently, did

Harvey have any intention of reaffirming an interest in scholastic philosophy, despite the fact that he was attracted by the Ramist claim to have reconciled the two rival cultures: "You taught me from Plato and Aristotle what I might have learned long ago from Marcus Tully, that all the learning of the liberal and humane arts is bound together with a single bond of fellowship. . . . You united eloquence and philosophy in a most amiable knot of friendship."[55] Whether Ramus really succeeded in this is an open question; he certainly taught both logic *and* rhetoric, literature *and* the quadrivium, all in the same curriculum. He claimed, moreover, to have rescued Aristotle from the scholastics and Cicero from the rhetoricians, and joined them in such a way that their lessons might reinforce each other.[56] For Ramus, the antipathy of oratory and philosophy was unnecessary, since all expression depended upon reason and adornment. There was really only one art of arts.[57] Nevertheless, it is hard to see how Ramist method could be of much help to the philosopher except in popularizing his wisdom, or to the orator except in introducing him to the classical authors.

Among those who doubted Ramus was Roger Ascham. As early as 1550–52 he had expressed some reservations to his close friend Johannes Sturm, the famous Strassburg school teacher with whom he shared so many ideas.[58] Ascham agreed with Ramus that Aristotle's style was too obscure and his doctrine too difficult to be taught without examples,[59] but he disagreed with the rest of Ramus's pedagogical reform. Apparently, a problem arose because of Ramus's peculiar view that the best way to teach logic and rhetoric was to redefine and separate them in the curriculum in a new and unconventional fashion.[60] So far, we have seen that the humanists either ignored or underplayed logic vis-à-vis rhetoric, but there was another possibility and that was to reform it in such a way as to make it compatible with the aims of the new education. And so, from Agricola and Melancthon to Sturm and Ramus, the effort was made, one way or another, to define a humanist logic that might go along with a humanist grammar and rhetoric. In this way it was hoped that the gap between the two cultures could be narrowed.

It is perhaps unnecessary to enter into details.[61] Suffice it to say that most of the proposed reforms appeared shallow to Bacon (as to some modern commentators); they amounted at best to a simplification of the traditional curriculum rather than anything new.[62] Ramus believed that logic should be identified with dialectical reasoning and that it was required for *every* subject. The Aristotelians had confined dialectic to probable matters and reserved the syllogism for science and certainty.[63] Ramus insisted that every exposition, philosophical or not, depended upon finding arguments and arranging them properly and that therefore invention and judgment—which were usually assigned to rhetoric—should be thought of as the principal parts of logic; and he believed that it was the topics (the seats or general places of argument) rather than the syllogism that was fundamental. Ramist logic therefore offered no new means for discovering or evaluating truth but only for expounding what was already known. Since it was a convenient instrument for theological dogmatics it appealed immensely to the English puritans, but for anyone with an inquiring spirit, like the young Bacon, who confronted it early, it seemed hopeless.[64] On the other hand, Ramus had left rhetoric to deal with the adornment and delivery that he thought were also useful to a persuasive exposition, and here Bacon was more sympathetic. Meanwhile, there was enough in all this to scandalize both the Aristotelians and the Ciceronians—though the humanists, at least, had they looked more closely, might have taken solace from the fact that Ramus had left the whole of classical imitation intact and even meant to teach logic with examples drawn from classical poetry, oratory, and history.

Ascham remained unpersuaded despite a friendly letter from Ramus himself and despite the Frenchman's conversion to Protestantism. Ascham continued to criticize Ramus's unorthodox views and to affirm his own Ciceronianism in his *Scholemaster* (published posthumously in 1570).[65] For Ascham and for Sturm, the trick was to try to steer between the two shoals of a pedantic imitation that "caught at words to the neglect of matter," and the even more contemptible barbarism of the schoolmen.[66] As for Harvey, he accepted Ramus wholeheartedly and without reservation and was indeed among the first in England to teach him publicly.[67] Nor, naturally, was he entirely satisfied with Ascham's work, despite its formidable Cambridge reputation. "Mr. Ascham," he wrote in his copy of Quintilian, "in his fine discourse of Imitation, is somewhat too precise and scrupulous for Tully only, in all points."[68] To Harvey, it is clear, the differences between the old and the new humanism were real enough, though only a matter of degree. (Ascham remained for him *noster Isocrates*.)[69] So also it appears to have looked to the other side—to Harvey's old tutor, for example, William Lewin, who had been a personal friend of both Ascham and Sturm. When Harvey asked him for a letter of recommendation, Lewin provided it cheerfully and praised his eloquence, but he also took care to defend his own orthodox Ciceronianism and the views of his two old friends against Ramus. Sturm, in particular, he thought, had said the last word on the subject.[70] That Harvey chose to print the letter before his *Ciceronianus* suggests that the gulf between the two viewpoints can easily be exaggerated. It looks rather as though it was the logicians more than the rhetoricians, the Aristotelians more than the Ciceronians, who were offended by Ramus and his new pedagogy. Harvey had to face some wicked satire, it

is true, but his dialectical successors—William Temple, for example—
had to cope with a more serious and sustained invective when open
warfare broke out at Cambridge between the two philosophical camps in
the 1580s. Bacon certainly looked on with interest (though with eventual
disgust), but by then Harvey had turned to other things.[71]

(3)

For the student of Francis Bacon, Harvey's interest is not exhausted by
his Ramism or his Ciceronianism, though that was the Harvey Bacon was
most likely to know. There was also the Harvey who admired Bacon's
father and nursed his own political ambitions, oddly anticipating the
same sort of frustration that young Francis was to endure. And there
was the Harvey who dabbled in science and managed thereby also to
anticipate many of Bacon's interests. The parallel is not exact, but it is
instructive.

Of course, Harvey's political ambition was commonplace. All around
him at Cambridge, young men were preparing to launch themselves on
the world. "Yourself are not ignorant," he wrote to the master of his
college, "that scholars in our age are rather more Aristippi than Di-
ogenes and rather active than contemplative philosophers." The date
they most celebrated was "when Duns and Thomas of Aquine with a
whole rabblement of schoolmen were abandoned our schools and ex-
pelled the university." The philosophers had been routed, Harvey insisted, by the latest writers on political life and conduct—especially by the
Italians della Casa, Castiglione, Guazzo, and Guicciardini, and the
French Bodin and Le Roy; Harvey himself was infatuated with Machiavelli.[72] "Aristotle's Organon is as little read as Dunses Quodlibet. His
economics and politics every one hath by rote." But even this was not
enough for him; it was apparent to Harvey that political instruction,
matters of council and policy and court, were more effectively taught
outside the university by practical men of the world who were "better
trained and more lively experienced therein then we university men are
or possibly can be."[73]

Ah, there was the rub! Try as he would, Harvey could not make it
outside the cloister. If he had become an amusing figure within the
university, he had also become something of an embarrassment outside.
The anti-Ciceronian who derided academic pedantry was yet too academic to cope successfully with practical life, or so it appears.[74] Yet
Harvey did not give up easily. Characteristically, he turned to the Roman law as a possible avenue to success, although if he had looked
around, he would have noticed that it was the Inns of Court and the
common law that really beckoned.[75] Harvey lamented his bookishness,

but he could not alter it. "Who would not rather be one of the Nine Worthies than one of the seven wise masters?" "Experience is a man and a perfect creature; theory is but a child or a monster."[76] Great men, he wrote, were all either great doers or great speakers and usually both. Audacity, he thought, was required besides eloquence. Wolsey, More, Gardiner, and Cromwell were his heroes under Henry VIII. He found a "Roman Disposition" in Cromwell, like Marius or Sulla: "Small Learning but nobly minded and Industrious with sufficiency of common wit, utterance, and experience." Cromwell "overshadowed and obscured even our greatest clerks." Harvey compared his Elizabethan heroes also to the ancients: Smith to Aeneas, Cecil to Nestor, Essex to Achilles, and Nicholas Bacon to Scaevola.[77] When Sir Nicholas died in 1579, Harvey wrote his epitaph in Latin.[78] "When you have no certain present object to think upon," he reminded himself, "bethink you of some one or two most notable, and egregious examples, either of profit, of pleasure, or of honour. Some memorable act, and brave practice, either very profitable, very pleasurable, or very honourable."[79] He was obsessed with the popular proverb "The greatest clerks are not the wisest men."[80] There was simply no school philosophy of any kind to furnish the wisdom that was needed to join with eloquence.

And so the years slipped by. Thwarted in politics, Harvey indulged himself in science, not the natural philosophy of the schools but the more practical kind of applied science that was so fascinating to the Elizabethans. There is one indication, it is true, that Harvey kept alive some interest in Aristotelian physics: in a letter to Spenser on earthquakes, which he published in 1580, he argued for a naturalistic rather than a providential explanation.[81] But it looks as though even here Harvey felt the insufficiency of mere book learning and the empty speculations of the schools. For a man who desired action, the claims of some of the new sciences and pseudosciences of the Renaissance must have been particularly intriguing. "Scholars have the books," he wrote in one of these practical texts, John Blagrave's *Mathematical Jewel* (1585), "and practitioners the learning." Blagrave's work was a manual that dealt with instruments used in navigation. "An youth," Harvey noted, "and no university-man, the more shame for some doctors of universities, that may learn of him."[82] Once again, he thought that it was direct experience of the world that was denied the schools. In a Latin passage very suggestive of Francis Bacon, he wrote that all the sciences were founded upon perception and reason. Experience was necessary for demonstration, and it alone was irrefutable. He insisted upon eyewitness testimony for every principle, experiment, or instrument.[83]

Harvey's appetite for practical science was certainly extensive; he appears to have bought almost every book on the subject as it appeared and read them all with his usual care.[84] He also came to know and respect many of the men who were promoting it—Blagrave, for example, and Thomas Digges, as well as many of the artisans and instrument-makers who were working in and around London.[85] It was mathematics, mensuration, and astronomy that particularly caught his attention, and at a time when all were thriving. But it does not appear that he ever did any science himself (unlike Bacon), and his understanding of its methods and achievements remained perhaps a little superficial. Harvey seems to have thought of himself primarily as a poet; he took an interest in science partly because he believed that the description of nature was necessary for good poetry: "It is not sufficient for poets to be superficial humanists: but they must be exquisite artists and curious universal scholars."[86] It seems that Harvey would have liked to reconcile the two cultures even on this ground and so was prepared to praise Chaucer and criticize Spenser for their understanding of the sciences or lack of it.

Of course, Harvey saw more in the new sciences than their service to literature; certainly the men he knew and admired, like Blagrave and Digges, had other and more practical concerns. For the student of Bacon, one of the striking things about all this mathematics and applied science is how its practitioners invariably set themselves against the authority of Aristotle and insisted upon the value of fresh observations and experiments, as well as upon the practical consequences of theoretical knowledge. One of Harvey's heroes was Robert Recorde, who set about developing a pedagogy for the sciences quite outside the formal curriculum. (In 1572, the new Cambridge statutes had quietly dropped mathematics altogether from the undergraduate program.)[87] Recorde's revolt against Aristotle was a revolt against the authority of books in general. "It is commonly seen," he wrote as early as 1543, "that when men will receive things from elder writers, and will not examine things, they seem rather willing to err with their ancients for company, than to be bold to examine their works or writings." Such "scrupulosity," he goes on to say, "hath engendered infinite errors in all kinds of knowledge, and in all civil administration, and in every kind of art."[88] Thomas Digges, who was one of the first English Copernicans and who had as one of his patrons Bacon's father,[89] argued that the ancients had gone astray precisely because they had reversed true scientific method and used theories to explain parallaxes instead of vice versa. Observation should always precede speculation. In a work dedicated to Leicester (1579), Digges boasted of having spent many years "in reducing the sciences mathematical, from demonstrative contemplations to experimental actions, for the service of prince and country." The practical and experimental nature of Elizabethan science, it has well been said, cannot be too strongly emphasized.[90]

Just how far Harvey understood all this is hard to say; for the most part his thoughts were confined to incidental comments and marginalia. There is, however, a fine appreciation of the practical Elizabethan achievement in his attack on Nashe known as *Pierces Supererogation* (1593).

> He that remembereth Humphrey Cole, a Mathematical Mechanician, Matthew Baker a ship-wright, John Shute an architect, Robert Norman a Navigator, William Bourne a Gunner, John Hester a Chemist, or any like cunning and subtle Empirique (Cole, Baker, Shute, Norman, Bourne, Hester, will be remembered when greater clerks shall be forgotten) is a proud man, if he contemn expert artisans, or any sensible industrious practitioners, howsoever unlectured in Schools or unlettered in books. . . . What profound mathematicians, like Digges, Hariot, or Dee, esteemeth not the pregnant Mechanician?[91]

Perhaps Harvey's appreciation for mathematics was whetted also by the fact that Ramus in old age had written a number of textbooks on the quadrivium, some of which began to find their way into English late in the sixteenth century. There is a report of an encounter between Ramus and the astronomer Tycho Brahe that suggests how far the Frenchman's anti-Aristotelianism could become a call for empiricism, an "astronomy without hypothesis."[92] Harvey couples Recorde and Ramus as the two best writers on arithmetic.[93]

Harvey's concern for science extended beyond even this, however. Like Francis Bacon, he took an interest also in those other practical Elizabethan preoccupations, astrology and medicine. While the evidence is scanty and ambiguous, it appears that he was drawn to the first by his two brothers, somewhat against his will, and to the second by his persistent need to make a living. An elegy written toward the end of his life (about 1630, now lost) seems to have reported that Harvey "practised physic and was a pretender to astrology."[94] His brothers had followed him up to Cambridge and, perhaps under his tutelage, taken up the anti-Aristotelian and Ramist cause. Richard Harvey in particular seems to have become notorious "for abusing Aristotle" while still an undergraduate and, if we can believe Nashe, "setting him up on the school gates painted with 'Asses ears on his head."[95] In 1583 he wrote a praise of Ramist dialectic, which he dedicated to the young Earl of Essex.[96] In that same year, he collaborated with his brother John on a work of judicial astrology in which they predicted that the conjuncture of Saturn and Jupiter would bring about dire events in the following year. They dedicated their work fondly to their older brother, dissociating him, however, from their enterprise.[97] But when nothing happened in the appointed year, laughter again descended upon the Harvey family and it did not help Gabriel's reputation. (He did win his law degree about this time, after some difficulty, but seems never to have gotten a case.) Harvey read a lot about astrology and may even have come over to its tenets, but it looks as though his enthusiasm remained tempered by a measure of skepticism, carried over perhaps from his early reading of Pico della Mirandola.[98] That did not stop Nashe from heaping more satire on his victim.

As for medicine, it seems that Harvey began to practice about 1583 and to read widely, after his usual fashion, in the latest literature on the subject. This brought him into direct contact with the world of magic and the occult, whose practitioners were then making their own large claims to knowledge of the natural world and to the field of medicine. Once again, it is not clear how much Harvey concerned himself directly with these matters—apart from listing (and no doubt reading) the works of Paracelsus, della Porta, and the rest, and copying out medical recipes—or how far he subscribed to the claims of magic and alchemy to control nature.[99] Perhaps he found the antischolastic attitude of these writers appealing; there is no reason to suggest that he took their more extravagant claims too seriously except that his old patron and admired friend, Thomas Smith, certainly had. Unfortunately, the quarrel with Nashe seems to have confirmed his view that writing and publishing were useless, and even before the new century began, Gabriel Harvey, all his ambition discouraged, fell into a long and unrelieved silence, from which it is now impossible to salvage anything.

Just before he disappeared, however, into final obscurity, Harvey wrote a last appeal to Robert Cecil. It was 1598, and the mastership of his old college was once again vacant. He turned now to Cecil, as he had turned before to his father, to describe his qualifications. "I can say for myself that I have spent so great a part of my age either in reading the best authors extant, as well in Law as in other employable faculties, or in writing some discourses of private use or public importance . . . I had ever an earnest and curious care of sound knowledge and esteemed no reading or writing without matter of effectual use." If Cecil or his father would only command, Harvey was ready to publish from his ample store in prose and verse something in "Humanity, History, Policy, Law" or else in "Mathematics, Cosmography, the Art of Navigation, the Art of War, the true Chymique without imposture (which I learned of Sir Thomas Smith not to contemn) and other effectual practicable knowledge." "For I can," he boasted, "in one year publish more than any Englishman hath hitherto done."[100] It may have been true, but the moment passed, and all was silence.

(4)

It was just about this time that Francis Bacon was directing his own appeals to the Cecils, and with something of the same results. In 1592 he wrote a famous letter (not the first) to Lord Burghley asking for help. "I wax somewhat ancient," he began—he was thirty-one years old and still unemployed. He hoped now to get a position with the queen, both for patriotic and for personal reasons: to serve the state and to mend his own mean fortunes. Like Harvey, he boasted of his learning: "I confess that I have as vast contemplative ends as I have moderate civil ends: for I have taken all knowledge to be my province." Unlike Harvey, he could not offer to rewrite the bits and pieces of a lifetime; he proposed instead a grand design for the future, nothing less than a complete reform of scientific learning. "If I could purge it of two sorts of rovers, whereof the one with frivolous disputations, confutations and verbosities, the other with blind experiments and auricular traditions and impostures, hath committed so many spoils, I hope I should bring in industrious observations, grounded conclusions, and profitable inventions and discoveries."[101] Bacon sought political power, so he said, in order to advance the cause of learning, and he offered a scheme. He was prepared to replace both the old scholastic science and the new magic with something better and more useful.

According to his chaplain, William Rawley, Bacon remembered taking up his characteristic philosophical stance when he was still at the university. Then it was, at the age of sixteen, that "he first fell into the dislike of the philosophy of Aristotle, not for the worthlessness of the author, to whom he would ever ascribe all high attributes, but for the unfruitfulness of the way; being a philosophy (as his lordship used to say) only strong for disputations and contentions, but barren of the production of works for the benefit of the life of man; in which mind he continued to his dying day."[102] It is not, I think, hard to see how he arrived at this conclusion. At Cambridge, Bacon confronted the same collision of cultures that Ascham and Harvey, Cecil and his own father, had faced before him. But while he was prepared to adopt their critical vantage point and accept the values of a humanistic political culture, he was unwilling to abandon philosophy altogether. Indeed, what he seems to have set out to do upon leaving the university was to reconstruct philosophy in such a way that it could be made to answer all the humanist objections and appeal to the practical men who governed the world.

The key to Bacon's natural philosophy is therefore his political education. From the cradle he grew up in an atmosphere of politics and classics. We know nothing about his early education except the name of his tutor, but we can guess the rest.[103] His father was the chief judicial officer of the kingdom and a member of the privy council and held decided views about the bringing up of children. Nicholas Bacon had won his own way to fame and position through the law and his eloquence, which was universally praised.[104] He was on close terms with his Cambridge contemporaries Cheke, Ascham, Cecil, Parker, and the rest. Throughout his life he remained interested in education, drafting proposals and statutes, endowing public schools and his old university, and befriending scholars. It is not surprising to discover him in the pages of Puttenham's *Arte of English Poesie* as the exemplary statesman-orator: "I have come upon the Lord Keeper Sir Nicholas Bacon," the author remembered, "and found him sitting in his gallery alone with the works of Quintilian before him; indeed he was a most eloquent man, and of rare learning and wisdom, as ever I knew England to breed, and one that joyed as much in learned men and men of good wits."[105]

Apparently, the child Francis was often brought to court, where he entertained the queen with his wit; she liked to call him "the young Lord-keeper."[106] At home, in the great house that Nicholas built at Gorhambury, Francis could improve himself by studying the classical *sententiae* that his father set out on the walls of the long-gallery, and admire the busts of the "Greek and Roman Emperors and Heroes" on the ceiling. (The banqueting room was adorned with portraits of Cicero, Isocrates, Demosthenes, and Quintilian, illustrating "Rhetoric.")[107] Perhaps the best evidence of Nicholas' views on education are the reform schemes he drew up for Henry VIII about 1538–40, proposing a London college for law and statesmanship and another for the Court of Wards, which he first suggested under Mary and sent to Cecil in 1561. He had, needless to say, no use for the "barbarous authors, very enemies to good learning," and was all in favor of the revival of that classical knowledge which had for so long a time been "almost trodden under foot."[108] Greek and Latin letters and civil law, along with military exercises, modern languages, and music were designed for the young wards. There was, it is hardly necessary to add, nothing at all of philosophy or science. Most interesting in this regard is a speech he delivered as Lord Keeper to the first Parliament of Elizabeth. "You will," he pleaded with the members, "in your assembly and conference clearly forebear, and as a great enemy to good council, fly from all manner of contentions, reasonings and disputations, and all sophistical captions and frivolous arguments and quiddities, more meet for ostentation of wit, than consolation of weighty matters, comelier for scholars than councillors, more beseeming for schools, than for parliament houses."[109]

If anything, Francis Bacon's mother was even more formidable in her own way than his father. Lady Ann Cooke was the most accomplished of the five extraordinary daughters of Sir Anthony Cooke, all famous for their Latin and Greek—an unusual feminine accomplishment in the sixteenth century and one which had the advantage for them of being unencumbered by any scholastic training. Cooke himself was still another of that extraordinary Cambridge generation of humanist politicians, an intimate of Cheke and Smith and one of the many who had contributed to King Edward's education.[110] Though he never held high office, he won unusual respect and for a time exerted considerable influence. He educated his daughters and married them all well and into politics—one of them, Mildred, to William Cecil, who thus became an uncle to Francis Bacon; another to Sir Thomas Hoby, the diplomat and translator of Castiglione's *Courtier*. Lady Ann was not only a good classicist but a staunch puritan, and she looked closely after the fortunes of her two sons, Francis and Anthony. She translated Bishop Jewel's famous *Apology* and some sermons by Bernadino Ochino, the first into and the second out of Latin, and peppered her letters to her sons with advice and classical quotation. When her husband took ill, she nursed him back to health, reading to him from *her* Cicero and *his* Seneca.[111] Bacon was not flattering her when he wrote apologetically in 1580, "I am not yet greatly perfect in ceremonies of court wherof, I know, your ladyship knoweth both the right use and true value."[112]

It is, therefore, no coincidence that Bacon followed exactly in his father's footsteps. Nicholas, it is true, did not particularly favor him—Francis was, after all, the youngest son of his second wife—and the lord keeper died in 1579, before he could really be much help.[113] Nevertheless, it is clear that Bacon was determined to repeat his father's success. Like Nicholas, Francis followed Cambridge with a stint at Gray's Inn, a trip to Paris, and a tilt at the law. He had a habit of recalling his father on public occasions, sometimes to the annoyance of his audience. In the Parliament of 1584–85, he spoke of the queen's generosity and said that "his father had received by her, ability to leave a fifth son to live upon, but that is nothing to the matter." Fleetwood, the recorder, interrupted rudely, "Then you should have left it alone."[114] When at last he did rise to Nicholas' station many years later in the reign of King James I, he once again gratuitously invoked his father's name, much to the annoyance of at least one onlooker.[115]

Even at Cambridge, it is likely that Bacon reinforced his political education. That, we have seen, was the job of the tutor: to instill more of the Latin and Greek that was thought useful for political eloquence. Bacon and his older brother Anthony arrived at Cambridge in 1573 and were enrolled together in Trinity College. They stayed for about two and a half years, with one long interruption for the plague. Their master was John Whitgift, a protégé of the elder Bacon, a fine theologian and stern

145

disciplinarian. He had just recently seen to the revision of the university statutes and had been rewarded by being chosen vice-chancellor. Unfortunately, he found the college embroiled in controversy, thanks to the efforts of the Puritan Thomas Cartwright. All the while the Bacons were in residence, the master fought the enemy within the gates. But he was not too busy to look after his students. According to his biographer, "He had divers Earls and Noblemen's sons to his pupils, as namely the Earls of Worcester and Cumberland, the Lord Zouch and Lord Dunboy of Ireland, Sir Nicholas and Sir Francis Bacon. . . . All which together with the rest of his scholars of that house, he held to their public disputations, and exercises, and progress . . . always severely punishing . . . omissions and negligences."[116] Five future bishops were among his students, as was Anthony Wingfield, the most likely author of *Pedantius,* whose term overlapped the Bacons'.[117] Whitgift even dined with his students so that he could keep an eye on them, and of course he kept their accounts. His careful records reveal something of what was taught, as well as the parental concerns of the master, who had to look after the young men's clothing and equipment, servants and transportation, fees and books.[118]

For the Bacons, Whitgift's first purchase was some standard classical texts: Livy, a Ciceronian rhetoric, Demosthenes, Homer (in Greek), and Caesar's *Commentaries.* Later, among such typical disbursements for shoes, bows and arrows, paper and ink, and "oyle for Frances neck," there is another batch of books—this time Cicero's works, two Aristotles and two Platos, a commentary on Cicero's orations, a Xenophon in Greek and Latin, and a Sallust. Still later appears a Hermogenes, two maps, and a Latin Bible for Anthony. There is, of course, no reason to suppose that this was the whole reading of the two brothers during their Cambridge stay, but if one compares it with Whitgift's accounts for his other students, it appears that the two Bacons entered the college with a particularly good classical education that was not neglected. It is doubtful that they read any natural science with their master.

Yet Bacon remembered long afterward, that it was at this time that he first took offense against the Aristotelians. It is too bad that we don't know more about how he spent his days at Cambridge. Did he attend the philosophical lectures and listen to the public disputations? Did he hear Gabriel Harvey? Did he perhaps poke fun at his masters with the author of *Pedantius?* One thing at least seems clear: Bacon could not have avoided witnessing the two cultures in rivalry and hearing something of the contempt that each had for the other. Although he went on to Gray's Inn and politics, he kept contact with Cambridge and the humanistic and philosophical interests that he had encountered there.[119] And he began to think for himself.

(5)

Bacon set out his first philosophical conclusions about 1584 in a tract, since lost, called *Tempus partus maximus*. How much this anticipated his later philosophy, we have no way of knowing, but a title very like it was used again for a manuscript draft of 1603 which does point the way to the *Great Instauration*.[120] In 1597, Bacon finally published his first literary work, the slim book of essays that brought him to contemporary notice. It was only after that, in the years beginning the new reign of James I, that he began seriously to write out his philosophy. Even so, he left many drafts incomplete, and the *Advancement of Learning* itself shows signs of haste. Apparently, Bacon was finished with the first book in 1603 but had to hurry the second into print in 1605 to try to win the patronage of the king at the outset of his reign.[121] The opportunity seemed too good to be lost. Bacon was forty-five years old; he was a leader in Parliament and by all accounts a brilliant orator; but he had not yet held an important public post.[122]

Bacon's first task, as he understood it, was to take stock of existing knowledge, to see what was wrong or inadequate about traditional learning and so to prepare the way for a new philosophy.[123] In this undertaking it is clear that Bacon used the quarrel between the two cultures as a point of departure, taking advantage of the humanist criticism of philosophy and the philosophical criticism of humanism as the groundwork for his own reconstruction. The world that he looked out upon was the world of Gabriel Harvey: the world of Ciceronians, Ramists, and Aristotelians, of alchemists and astrologers, artisans and mechanics, all competing for attention, all claiming to know something important. Bacon's first reaction was undoubtedly skeptical, a little like that of the author of *Pedantius* or of that popular Elizabethan manual, *De incertitudine et vanitate scientiarum* by Henry Cornelius Agrippa, or even of Cicero in the *Academica*. The difference was that Bacon resolved to do something about his skepticism, to build something constructive out of the competition for knowledge and the resulting uncertainty.[124]

From this perspective, Bacon's contribution to contemporary thinking may be seen as an attempt to reconcile the different cultures, to weed out the errors but also to reintegrate what was best in each; more specifically, to use the insights of his own political-classical training to address the problems of natural philosophy. If the result could not possibly satisfy either Lord Snow or F. R. Leavis, it did have immense possibilities for its own time. It was precisely because Bacon's audience shared his vantage point and many of his assumptions that they were won over (eventually) to his revolutionary philosophy. Throughout history, Bacon remarks, politic men have heaped scorn on the *pedantes,* but history itself only proves how valuable learned men have been to politics.[125] Bacon meant to show how very much more valuable learning could be if properly reformed. If, incidentally, doing so would also help his own career, so much the better; self-advancement was for Bacon the most reliable way he knew to promote his cause.

So, Bacon's rebuff to the politicians, to their traditional disdain for knowledge, was a necessary first step in the advancement of learning, and that explains the considerable space that he gives to answering their complaints in the first book of his published work. They had argued, in effect, that learning was impractical, distracting from the business of life and subversive of government. In fact, Bacon returns, learning has always been as necessary for government as government was necessary for learning; all history proves that one cannot flourish without the other. He accepts the customary humanist view that the Romans reached the height both of empire and culture at exactly the same moment, "for in the time of the first two Caesars, which had the art of government in perfection, there lived the best poet, Virgilius Maro; the best historiographer, Titus Livius; the best antiquary, Marcus Varro; and the best, or second orator, Marcus Cicero, that to the memory of man are known."[126] Nor was this mere coincidence; learning teaches good politics both by example and precept, so that it "cannot be but a matter of doubtful consequence if states be managed by empiric statesmen, not well mingled with men grounded in learning."[127]

The point is worth developing. The humanists, we have seen (like Thomas Elyot), and their ancient teachers (above all, Cicero) had insisted on the special value of the humanities to public life, in particular on the use of examples drawn from classical history and poetry to furnish the stock of political wisdom needed to join with eloquence to make the perfect statesman. Bacon accepted this view, though he insisted on history to the practical exclusion of poetry. When he was asked to furnish some advice for the young Earl of Rutland in 1595, he told him flatly, "Above all other books, be conversant in Histories, for they will best instruct you in matters moral, military and politic."[128] And when he was asked, a few years later, to do the same thing for the poet Fulke Greville, who was bound to Cambridge to do some research, he enlarged upon the same point. Bacon advised Greville first of all to make his own selection of books, since he would find little of value in the university in "humanity." (He here drops some characteristic antischolastic and anti-Ciceronian reservations that might well have come from Gabriel Harvey.) As for the field of study, Bacon again recommends history above all other subjects. His list of authors now includes Tacitus, Livy, and Thucidides, with even the worst of the ancients to be preferred above any of the moderns. He directs his friend to take notes under several headings—moral, political and military—rather than to make epitomes, suggesting such topics as "war" or "revolutions of states."[129] In this way, Bacon imagines building a collection of examples that could be put to use in practical life as a kind of empirical foundation for moral and civil knowledge and action. "I hold collections under heads and common places of . . . profit and use, because they have in them a kind of observation, without which neither long life breeds experience, nor great reading great knowledge." (Unlike Ramus, Bacon believed that the topics that furnished this preliminary store belonged more properly to rhetoric than to logic; he also believed that they might be used to direct inquiry, not simply to win arguments.)[130] In these matters, Bacon agreed exactly with Harvey that the greatest clerks were not the wisest men, a proverb that he too repeats again and again.[131]

When, in the *Advancement,* Bacon turns to consider the various claims to learning in his time, he takes them in order, beginning with the least pernicious, which he calls "fantastic" learning and which we have called humanism. He describes the revival of the ancient languages and literature, beginning in the time of Luther, and suggests that it was moved in part by opposition to the schoolmen, "who were generally of the contrary part, and whose writings were altogether differing in style and form." The quarrel we have been tracing was thus real enough to Bacon, though he tells the story a little differently. Eloquence, he goes on to say, and variety of discourse came to be especially prized. So far, Bacon approves.[132] But after a while, he says, this grew to excess, "for men began to hunt more after words than matter," more for the sound of the phrase than the soundness of the judgment. He particularly singles out Osorius and Sturm as culprits and, at Cambridge, Carr and Ascham, who had almost deified Cicero and Demosthenes and had begun to allure all the young men to that "delicate and polished kind of learning."[133] "Then grew the learning of the schoolmen to be utterly despised as barbarous." With these recollections of his student days, Bacon might well have been remembering Harvey; instead, he invokes Erasmus poking fun at the Ciceronians. "In sum," he concludes, "the whole inclination of the time was rather towards copie than weight."[134]

For Bacon it was, of course, the old objection of philosophy to rhetoric. Yet he qualifies his criticism: it is too bad "when men study words and not matter," but one should not for that reason condemn rhetoric out of hand. Indeed, rhetoric is the essential cloak for all knowledge, for philosophy itself (witness Xenophon, Cicero, Seneca, Plutarch, and Plato, "in some degree") but especially for knowledge of civil occasions, "of conference, counsel, persuasion, discourse or the like." Bacon was not prepared to give up the genuine eloquence of political life—not even the rhetorical garnish that all serious expression deserved—but merely its excess. It was in any case not nearly as wicked as the next "distemper," the one that Bacon calls "contentious" learning and that we have called scholasticism.

Now it is vain matter that Bacon objects to, not vain words.[135] The learning of the schoolmen was degenerate because it was shut up in the authority of a few authors, chiefly Aristotle. Since they were ignorant of history, "either of nature or time," they had no matter for their speculations and were reduced, like spiders, to spinning cobwebs for their learning—subtle and intricate, but void of all substance or profit. Bacon objects also to their method of argument, which rested not at all upon evidence but only on "monstrous altercations and barking questions." He thus accepts the humanist and Ramist objections to the schoolmen without much qualification, except to say that if they had only joined their "thirst of truth and unwearied travail of wit" to some real knowledge of the world, they might well have been able to aid in the advancement of learning.[136]

For the third and worst of the vanities of learning, Bacon has even less to say in extenuation. He lumps together all those who have accepted "deceit, imposture, and credulity" in their reports about the natural world, both in the pseudosciences of astrology, natural magic, and alchemy and in the popular compendia of natural facts, from Pliny and Aristotle to the Arabs, "fraught with much fabulous matter, a great part not only untried but notoriously untrue." (Bacon classed these reports with the fictions of medieval romance rather than history; they were, like poetry, more the result of imagination than observation.)[137] On the other hand, like Harvey and his father and like most prominent Elizabethans, Bacon was fascinated by the applied science of his time. Nevertheless, to the extent that it lacked system and theory, he would not allow it as science or admit that its results were much better than accidental. "Empiric" science was no better for Bacon than "empiric" politics, though there was something perhaps to be learned from each.[138]

There is much more in the *Advancement* about the errors of traditional learning, but undoubtedly the worst of these for Bacon was its mistaking its true purpose. Some men, he observed, pursued knowledge out of curiosity and others to quarrel, most for "lucre and profession," but hardly anyone ever set out to serve society and discover the kinds of learning that could be useful to men.[139] "Knowledge," Bacon said later in a famous aphorism, "is power." Here, he insisted that knowledge must have as its main purpose the improvement of life. If so, it was no mere contemplative activity, after the traditional view. Bacon (like Harvey)[140] was prepared to resolve the famous Renaissance debate about the relative value of the active and the contemplative life—a topic that he could have found debated both ways in Castiglione's *Courtier,* for example. At one point he had wondered whether a "mixture of contemplative with an active life, or retiring wholly to contemplations, do disable and hinder the mind more."[141] But in the end, he resolved that the two should be joined together. Like Socrates, he was prepared to call philosophy down from heaven to converse upon earth; unlike Socrates, or the humanists, he did not mean to abandon science altogether for morality and politics. No ancient philosopher, certainly not Aristotle, had gotten it right, and only James I among worldly princes had properly combined the two![142] "But as both heaven and earth do conspire and contribute to the use and benefit of man, so the end ought to be, from both philosophies to separate and reject vain speculations and whatsoever is empty and void . . . that knowledge may be . . . but as a spouse for generation, fruit and comfort." Natural philosophy, like moral philosophy, must be vindicated by works.[143] So political conquest must take second place to conquest of the works of nature.[144] The two cultures must be advanced together for the improvement of life,[145] though the one was already mature while the other had hardly begun.

There is not space here to describe the way that Bacon worked out all the implications of this new vantage point—in his manuscripts, in the second book of the *Advancement,* and in the rest of his large corpus. We set out to discover the genesis of his philosophy and the basic problem that he was determined to solve, and they were already visible by 1603. Politics was Bacon's life and philosophy his recreation, though he liked to put it the other way around. He could hardly help looking out at the world of nature with the eyes of a humanistically trained statesman. In 1603 he sent to the new king a characteristic political memorandum, "touching the happy union of the Kingdom of England and Scotland."[146] "There is," he begins, "a great affinity and consent between the rules of nature and the true rules of policy, the one being nothing else but an order in government of the world, and the other an order in the government of an estate." Bacon did not think it strange that Heraclitus had written a book (now lost) that some took for a discourse of nature and others for a treatise on policy. Indeed, a contemporary of Bacon's who has been proposed as the author of *Pedantius,* Edward Forsett, wrote a whole book about the correspondence between the two.[147] But if there was, as Bacon insisted, a "congruity between the principles of Nature and Policy," what better plan was there than to take the knowledge and method of the one and apply it to the other? It is clear from the second book of the *Advancement* that Bacon was pretty well satisfied with the achievements of the humanities, including moral and political philosophy, though he had many specific recommendations for their improvement. It was inevitable that he should borrow the success of the one to remedy the inadequacy of the other.

In what did that success consist? Moral and political philosophy had achieved a genuine and practical knowledge because they had built upon the foundation of civil history. There were, Bacon agreed, "two exemplar states in the world for arms, learning, moral virtue, policy and laws"; these were ancient Greece and Rome, and the historians that recounted their fortunes were "extant in good perfection."[148] Machiavelli appealed to Bacon even more than he had to Harvey, because he understood how to generalize the particulars of that ancient history, how to turn examples into rules.[149] Bacon saw that particular instances both illustrated and constituted the precepts. It was just as Roger Ascham had said, echoing the conventional humanist wisdom: no argument could be persuasive without copious illustration drawn from history and oratory.[150]

But examples could also be viewed as giving rise to precepts. So, for example, for the anonymous Cambridge logician (echoing Aristotle), only probable arguments can be built upon examples, though they can be very persuasive. "Induction and example," the student agrees, "look rather to the orators than the philosophers. These arguments, though they conclude less cogently, more easily sway the popular mind. He who uses induction and example often will confound his adversary no less than he who battles with syllogisms and enthymemes." "Induction," he continues, "is argument which is formed by enumerating single instances so as to form a universal conclusion. For example, as the tyrant Dionysius came to a bad end, as Phalaris to a bad end, as the bloody Nero to a bad end, as Caligula similarly, so all tyrants perish miserably."[151] With all this Bacon agreed but he thought that inductive logic could be improved by the use of negative and "prerogative" instances and thus approach certainly.[152] What was needed was a *novum organum*, a new logic. Only then could induction become truly scientific.

Beneath this conviction was another presupposition that Bacon shared with the humanists: namely, that there were regularities in human behavior that could be extrapolated from human experience, that the future could be anticipated by the past. As Bacon put it, "there is such a concordance between the time to come and the time past, as there will be no reforming the one without informing the other."[153] In exactly the same way, Bacon believed in the regularity of nature and in the priority of natural history for natural philosophy, and he never tired of insisting on the need to gather a "great storehouse of facts" as a preliminary to any speculation.[154] "For knowledges are as pyramids, whereof history is the basis: so of natural Philosophy, the basis is Natural History."[155]

Aristotle's chief fault (worse still in his followers) was to speculate without sufficient knowledge of things, to desert experience, and thus to produce something closer to logic than to physics or metaphysics.[156] Bacon seems to have thought that this notion about the priority of history was the most novel and fundamental in his philosophy, for as he wrote in 1621, not all the wits in all the ages and all the universities together could make any progress in philosophy and science without a proper natural and experimental history.[157] It was so important to him that he left the *Novum organum*, his most polished philosophical performance, unfinished in order to see whether he could make a beginning at least and gather up some facts as an inspiration to others.

Needless to say, not everyone was convinced. According to John Aubrey, who knew him well, the physician William Harvey certainly had his doubts. William had also been to Cambridge (1593–99) but had taken a degree and followed it with a doctorate at Padua. When he returned to England, he became famous as a physician and attended James I at court. He was an untiring observer of nature, an anatomist of genius, and, of course, the discoverer (among other things) of the circulation of the blood. Nevertheless, he remained something of an Aristotelian and was as close to a professional scientist as the age was to produce. According to Aubrey, "he had been a physician to the Lord Chancellor Bacon, whom he esteemed much for his wit and style." But Harvey would not allow that Bacon was much of a philosopher: "Said he to me," Aubrey remembered, "He writes Philosophy like a Lord Chancellor."[158] Of course, Harvey was right, but where he and many other philosophers since have been disturbed by the thought, I cannot see that Bacon would have been at all embarrassed by it. Harvey understood perfectly what Bacon had set out to do (but disapproved), that is to say, to combine the two cultures, to tackle philosophy from the vantage point of a Renaissance statesman and call it to practical account. For most of Bacon's contemporaries, and especially for the virtuosi who later took over the Royal Society, that seemed a perfectly plausible thing to do.

Undoubtedly, much more could be said about Bacon's use of the humanities to reconstruct the sciences. (I pass over what Bacon had to say about the humanities in and for themselves.) He argued, for example, against the private character of traditional philosophy and the secretive practices of the alchemists and astrologers, and for a public, collective, and collaborative enterprise—a proposal that helped eventually to produce the Royal Society and its *Philosophical Transactions*. He saw the use of the arts of discourse in presenting the conclusions of science and employed them brilliantly in his own philosophical writing.[159] He even built upon the traditional logic and rhetoric to create the inductive method of the *Novum organum*. In the words of Neal Gilbert,

"Bacon transformed the debating procedures of the *Topics* into a transaction in which Nature replaced the respondent and the challenger became the scientist."[160]

Whether Bacon succeeded thus in reconciling the two cultures is another matter. There is something suspicious about his denigration of thw works of the imagination, particularly of poetry.[161] And he overlooked the importance of mathematics to the new philosophy. But in his advocacy of history as the foundation of all humanistic and scientific learning, he did hold out a promise, if not for reconciliation, for at least a bridge between the two cultures. Moreover, here as elsewhere he began to show the way concretely, resuscitating the pre-Socratic philosophers, for example, in a fine piece of historical detection, and calling for a history not only of philosophy but of culture and technology.[162] By example and by precept, Bacon thus anticipated something of what we have been attempting in this essay, although his own attention, as usual, was fixed entirely on the problems of his own time. If he did make some contribution to bridging the two cultures, it was by opening up some new possibilities of connection between them. Reconciliation and comprehension were his basic position in religion and politics,[163] as they were also his hope for literature and science. If both today are still elusive, there may be something yet to learn from his teaching.

CHAPTER 6

Ancients, Moderns, and History

(1)

Whatever claims for change may be alleged about the later seventeenth century, it is clear that historical writing and thinking were largely unaffected. In its forms and methods, in its purposes and aspirations, English historiography remained continuous with a much earlier time. It is true that there were some alterations in subject matter, a shifting of emphasis, and a steady refinement of technique. But (as I have tried to show earlier) the overriding characteristic of the large historical literature of these years was its essential identity with the intentions and the achievements of Renaissance humanism. Some recent claims to the contrary, there was no "historical revolution," neither then nor at any time in the whole long period after the early Tudors. Once the problems and techniques of a new historiography had been announced by the first humanist generation after 1500, they changed hardly at all for two or three centuries.[1]

Unfortunately, it is harder to describe continuity in a brief compass than revolution, especially for so long a span of years. But it is possible at least to describe the conception that the period had of itself and of its relationship to the past. And while this may not prove conclusive, it is certainly suggestive to discover that in all the diversity of late seventeenth-century opinion, there was agreement over this much anyway, that the years from about 1500 to about 1700 marked an integral period in European culture and especially in the history of history. And this opinion was more than simply theoretical; in some of the most significant and representative historical works of the day, there was a deliberate and concerted effort made to collect and to summarize the achievement of the past two centuries.

This agreement is the more interesting perhaps because it may be discovered in that noisiest of disagreements, the great quarrel that marked the closing years of the seventeenth century, the battle between the so-called "ancients" and "moderns." Although some attention has been paid to that episode in recent years, the quarrel has, in fact, not been entirely appreciated in the history of ideas. It was certainly not the mean and trivial performance that Macaulay described; nor should it be viewed simply as background for *A Tale of a Tub*. On the other hand, neither was it exclusively a quarrel between science and the classics, although that was an important ingredient in the squabble.[2] In fact, it was more than any of these things; it was at bottom a dispute over the uses of the past, a quarrel about history. And it holds its interest both for the argument itself, which was strident and amusing and involved most of literary London, and for the less obvious underlying agreement between the rivals, which was so much more extensive than they realized.

The quarrel, it will be recalled, had its French and its English episodes.[3] Essentially, it was about the relationship of ancient—that is, classical—learning and letters to modern life. Were the ancients the supreme standards in all matters, to be admired and emulated but never to be surpassed, or had the moderns in fact already left them behind? Was progress possible, or were men destined indefinitely to fall short of the classical models and to continue sighing for the Golden Age? In France the battle, already begun, had centered on literature; in England the inclination had been, since the days of Francis Bacon, to match the rivals over the whole field of natural philosophy. Now, beginning in 1690, the battle was renewed, and for the next two decades it excited and amused the English world of letters.

The first protagonists in the field were oddly matched. Sir William Temple was an elderly country gentleman enjoying a retirement from an active political and diplomatic career, a friend of the king and a man of the world, endowed with wealth, taste, a remarkable wife (Dorothy Osborne), and an even more remarkable secretary (Jonathan Swift). From his home at Moor Park, he launched the great controversy with a typically polished and graceful performance in favor of the ancients. Although he had been provoked to his reflections by two recent tracts, he was merely reiterating opinions that he, like so many men of his generation, had held from childhood. Indeed, so evident did his defense of the ancients appear to him that he was truly astonished at the clamor it raised and which rang in his ears until his death. William Wotton, on the other hand, was a very young man, one of the great prodigies of the age. His father, rather like James Mill later, had determined to give his son a precocious education in Latin and Greek, as well as Hebrew, beginning at the age of four years and six weeks. He kept careful testimonials thereafter to his son's progress and later described it in a book that was meant to broadcast his new pedagogy. So successful was he that young William was able to enter Oxford before he was ten, and it was not long after that he became a Fellow of the Royal Society. Wotton was thus raised a scholar from his earliest years, and so he remained, never setting foot into the larger world but dabbling capably in almost every scholarly achievement of his time. If he did not know the king or the world of affairs, he did know Isaac Newton and the world of nature and scholarship as very few men in his time. His reply to Temple was ready in 1694.[4]

However different their careers and attainments, the two men had at least one thing in common: they had each received a classical education. It was, of course, inevitable in their day. It is true that Temple's Greek had, to his regret, lapsed and it is true also that Wotton had added to a mastery of the classical languages an astonishing array of modern learning. There is at first sight something paradoxical in the fact that the more accomplished classicist, young Wotton, should be the modern, while the man with the imperfect Greek should be the impassioned ancient, but there was a reason for this, as we shall see.

What is at once apparent is that beneath the quarrel, which ranged over the whole map of learning, there was a broad area of agreement. As each man reflected on the culture of past and present, he drew in one respect a surprisingly similar picture. Temple, for example, began his review of Western culture with that notable age when Greek and Latin had reached their "height and purity." He marked the time precisely: from Lucretius to Paterculus, from the Jugurthine War to the rule of Tiberius. This golden period had been followed by the fall of Rome and the decline of all learning and letters. In the next age, Greek was wholly lost and Latin was debased. In a word, all culture became barbarous. Then, as a result of the downfall of Constantinople, Greek refugees were thrust into the West to begin the revival of antique civilization. "Thus began the Restoration of Learning in these Parts with that of the Greek tongue; and soon after, Reuclyn and Erasmus began that of the purer and ancient Latin." It had been, therefore, just two hundred years since that "dawn of a new day" when the ancient languages and learning had begun to be restored. And to that revival, Temple at least was confident, all recent European achievement was due. The modern age, Temple's own time, was thus the period inaugurated in Italy and introduced into the North by such men as Erasmus and Reuchlin. It was not, however—for here Temple took his stand with the ancients—in any way the equal of that great period which had served as its model.[5]

When Wotton responded, he largely reiterated what Temple had said. It was the circle of Erasmus that had renewed classical style and learning and thereby ushered in the modern age. "Soon after Learning was restored," he wrote, "when Copies of Books by Printing were pretty well multiplied, Criticism began, which first was exercised in setting out Correct Editions of Ancient Books. . . . It soon became the fashionable Learning; after [that] Erasmus, Budeaus, Beatus Rhenanus and Turnebus dispersed that sort of Knowledge . . . which had been kept together amongst the Italians." Even more specifically than his rival, Wotton pinpointed the revival in England to the time of Henry VIII. More, Pole, Linacre, Colet, Cheke, and Ascham, he declared, "wrote Latin with a Purity no Italian needed then to have been ashamed of."[6] The present age was thus the age of renewal; if neither man used the word "renaissance," they both agreed to a periodization of Western history exactly like that of the classical humanists who divided the past into an ancient, a medieval (or "barbarous"), and a modern culture. And they both agreed that modern learning had been launched as a result of the classical revival. It remained only to estimate its success.

I shall not try to summarize the general argument further here. Temple had thrown down the gauntlet and announced the superiority of the ancients in everything. Wotton was compelled to pick it up by reviewing the whole field of knowledge; Temple's essay was greeted, therefore, with a full-sized book. Wotton attempted to be judicious; he was not an inflexible modern, and he was prepared to concede much. What he would insist upon was the principle; unless men believed in the possibility of progress, there would surely be none. (On the other hand, he was prepared to admit that contempt for antiquity would equally frustrate learning.) About some things Temple was clearly wrong: the moderns excelled the ancients in technology, for example, and in natural philosophy. In other things, especially in literature, he was more nearly correct. In eloquence and poetry particularly, Wotton was willing to allow the classical superiority; the best of the moderns were those who had most carefully imitated the ancient models. "The Masters of Writing, in all their several Ways, to this Day, appeal to the Ancients, as their Guides; and still fetch Rules for them, for the Art of Writing." Wotton was even willing to explain the classical superiority here in the advantages of language and politics that the classical world possessed. Thus the superiority of Greek (its native "smoothness") and the priority of Latin over the modern languages assured the classical writers of an advantage, while the free political constitutions of the ancient world fostered the development of eloquence. (Modern public business, even the pulpit, he thought was not very helpful to true eloquence.) Certainly the ancients cultivated the art of rhetoric with far more enthusiasm and care than any today. It was incontestable, therefore, "that former Ages made greater Orators and nobler Poets than those later Ages have done." Still, with the same circumstances and advantages, it might yet be possible to produce again a Cicero or a Virgil; Wotton was careful to leave the door to progress ajar.

In this first exchange, history was not overlooked. Temple's method was to pair the ancients and moderns in each of the various branches of learning, always to the disadvantage of the latter, and when it came to history, he set the recent works of Davila and Strada beside those of Herodotus and Livy, and Sleidan next to Caesar. The choice was evidently not difficult. Although all histories were useful, "how indifferently soever the Tale is told," the ancients alone combined style with content to furnish perfect works of instruction and entertainment.[7] The moderns might be read anyway for their "relations of matter of fact," and Temple obviously indulged himself as much as any man, but the ancients' superiority was clear; it was a result both of their eloquence and their political experience. As most men agreed in his day, and as Temple had written elsewhere, history was read primarily to inform the citizen or the statesman how best to comport himself in public life. Classical histories embodied the sum of political wisdom and experience and furnished the perfect models of government, laws, and men. The best modern histories could merely attempt to imitate them.[8]

To much of this, Wotton agreed. Since he too had awarded the palm of eloquence to the ancients, and since eloquence included "all those Writers in Prose who took pains to beautifie and adorn their Stile," the ancients were necessarily superior here also. But Wotton entered a reservation; history was less a matter of rhetoric to him than it had been for Temple. Indeed, his own favorite among the ancients was Polybius, who took pains to neglect "all that Artful Eloquence which was before so much in fashion." And he was willing to match the Polybian virtues with two modern works, the *Memoirs* of Philippe de Commines and *The History of the Council of Trent* by Paolo Sarpi. Their merit lay in their matter, in their impartiality and instruction. Of Davila and Strada, however, he was less sure; he might defend them more vigorously "if there was as much Reason to believe their Narrative as there is to commend their Skill in Writing." He let the comparison with the ancients pass.[9]

There was, however, another contention that divided the two men more profoundly. It was raised by Wotton independently of Temple and concerns philology. He devoted an entire chapter to it in the *Reflections*, and it is apparent that more was at stake than the claims of "modern" linguistic study. For it was Wotton's idea that the Renaissance revival of the classical tongues had led modern scholars to know more about antiquity than, "any of the Ancients Themselves ever had, or indeed could have." "To compare the Moderns to the Ancients may seem a Paradox," he was fully aware, "when the subject matter is entirely ancient," but there was no gainsaying that moderns like Scaliger, Casaubon, and Selden (to name only a few) were without doubt superior in their knowledge of ancient things to the ancients themselves. How was it possible? Of course, the modern scholar did not know Plato and Aristotle better than they knew themselves. But the ancients had, after all, not lived together at one time, though our great distance from them sometimes made it appear so. Consequently, they often knew less about their predecessors than a modern scholar, with the instruments of modern scholarship, could attain. The invention of printing alone ensured that the ancient books could now be compared, examined, and canvassed with an ease unknown to previous times. But it was the discipline of philology itself, barely known to past ages (and the invention of the Renaissance humanists) that gave the moderns their ultimate advantage.[10]

It is clear that Wotton knew much about this new discipline. Among his associates—fatefully, as it turned out—was the greatest philologist of the age, Dr. Bentley. "To pore in old Manuscripts," Wotton wrote, "to compare various Readings; to turn over Glossaries, and old Scholia upon Ancient Historians, Orators and Poets; to be minutely critical in all the little Fashions of the Greeks and Romans," all this was new and fascinating. New too, he noticed, and scarcely less important for history, was the modern science of chronology and the modern competence in geography. All this together—philology, chronology, antiquarian study of every kind—could recall the memory of things either quite unknown to antiquity or lost sometimes within fifty or a hundred years of its use. It even seemed to Wotton that the thousands of corrections and annotations of modern scholarship had required "more Fineness of thought and Happiness of Invention" than the originals upon which the corrections were made. After all, Wotton wrote, "he that discerns another Man's thoughts, is therein greater than he that thinks."[11]

It was an extravagant claim and not calculated to persuade Temple. In fact, Temple resisted replying for a time, though obviously stung by Wotton's criticism. He left an essay begun about 1695–96 incomplete, but it was published at last after his death by his secretary and literary executor, young Jonathan Swift.[12] For the most part it merely recapitulated the earlier argument; on the main point Temple was recalcitrant. The attacks of the moderns reminded him simply of the "young barbarous Goths or Vandals breaking or defacing the admirable Statues of those ancient heroes of Greece or Rome." He took satisfaction at least that many had rallied to the ancients, at home and in France. Of the special claims for history, Temple had more to say. He chose the stronger ground of eloquence first. To rival Sarpi and Commines with Herodotus and Livy (Wotton in fact had not) could only be a jest. Everyone agreed that the first prerequisite of a historian was the choice of a "noble and great subject"; that alone was enough to exclude Sarpi, while Commines' work was at best a memoir. As for philology, "I know not what to make of it; and less, how it came into the number of the sciences." That it had once been useful in editing, correcting, and translating the old authors Temple was bound to admit. But "he must be a conjurer that can make these moderns, with their comments, and glossaries, and annotations, more learned than the authors themselves." To Temple it was pedantry; he could dispense with those "vain niceties" about words and syllables, hours and days, about the ancient names of persons or places. Who cared? In any case it was not history, at least not in any way that the defender of the ancients could possibly recognize.

Temple died in 1699, and Wotton was able to have the last word. Two years before, he had printed a second enlarged version of the *Reflections* and in 1705 (stung by the anonymous *Tale of a Tub*) a third and final one. The second edition was notable for the contributions of Wotton's friends and especially for an essay appended by Dr. Bentley and entitled "Dissertation upon the Epistles of Phalaris." The third included Wotton's direct reply to Temple's last thoughts. Bentley attended to the attack on philology; Wotton to the criticism of his defense of modern narrative.

The latter problem was the simpler. Wotton at once corrected Temple's misapprehension that he had exalted the eloquence of Commines and Sarpi. On the contrary, he had chosen Polybius among the ancients "as an Instance that a History may be incomparable, that has not Rhetorical Ornaments to set it off." "The question between us was not," he continues, "whether the Modern Historian absolutely taken exceeded the Ancients" (presumably Wotton conceded the issue here), "but whether some Moderns have not (considering the Subjects they wrote upon) Composed as Instructing Histories as any of the Ancients." Wotton was sure they had, just as he was sure that the subject of the Council of Trent was a worthy one. True, there was no fighting, no burning of towns, "no knocking out of Mens Brains"—all of which Wotton agreed (somewhat ironically) were necessary for a "great and noble subject." But there was a "Depth of Contrivance and such a Train of Refined Politics" in the modern event, and such insight into motive in the modern historian, that in his own way Father Paul (Sarpi) stood alone.[13] But still better, indeed superior to all but the greatest of the ancients, was the very latest history to be published, the Earl of Clarendon's *History of the Rebellion and Civil Wars* (1702–04). It was, Wotton thought, and he was sure that Temple would have agreed, in all respects an admirable work. In fact, its virtues were exactly those that Temple (with all the conventional wisdom of Renaissance humanism) had assigned to the works of antiquity. The subject, Wotton declared, was as great, the events as surprising, and the conclusions as miraculous as any Temple could have desired. There was fighting enough, and negotiations, great examples of virtue and fortitude, and characters of good and evil men vividly described. All this was accomplished "with so much Strength of Stile, and such a rich Copia of Words" that posterity was bound to recognize it, for both "Matter and Elocution," the equal of the most celebrated of classical histories.[14]

Would Temple have been persuaded? What is clear is that the two men were not so very far apart, after all, in their conceptions of narrative history. Both thought that its primary function was the education of the statesman. Both considered it, at its best, a branch of literature. Both believed that the most perfect examples of history lay in the past. And both agreed that the moderns would have to be evaluated according to classical standards as to subject, style, and composition. Both even agreed to admit the modern historians, despite their rhetorical imperfections, for their subject matter. No doubt they disagreed on the emphasis to place on the various qualities of the ideal history. And no doubt they differed in their evaluations of particular works as well as their views of future prospects. But beneath their quarrel there remained enough agreement to identify them securely as part of a single—humanistic—culture.

It was another matter with philology. Wotton understood that the humanists had not been content simply to imitate the classics but that in the process they had also learned to criticize them: that is, to recover their precise meaning. Even Temple saw the use of editing them correctly, but he failed altogether to understand how humanistic scholarship, beginning with the criticism of authors, was necessarily a cumulative process, that it gradually built a stock of knowledge through the mastery of small details and that it could gradually transform an understanding of the past. He failed also to recognize that the philological activity of the early humanists had sprung free from mere textual commentary and had become an end in itself, a kind of history with no resemblance to traditional narrative but with new possibilities of historical understanding quite unknown to the ancients.[15]

If the first skirmish between ancients and moderns thus failed to settle anything, at least it clarified the issue with respect to history. For Temple and Wotton both, the modern period was characterized essentially by the revival of antiquity, which they thoroughly approved as dispersing medieval darkness. To that extent, they were both in the "humanist" tradition of the earlier Renaissance. Both recognized also that the virtues of modern historical narrative depended on a reiteration of the forms and techniques of classical history (they only quarreled about how successfully it had been or might be accomplished). And finally, they both agreed that the modern period had seen the beginning of something new, the philological and antiquarian activity of the humanists—although the one, Temple, thought the world "surfeited," while the other, Wotton, could not have enough of it.

That Wotton had the better of this part of the argument was made devastatingly clear by his friend Bentley. Unfortunately, Temple had chosen among his classical models Aesop's *Fables* and Phalaris's *Epistles*, crediting them as not only the first ancient works of prose but the best. The *Epistles*, he thought, had "more Race, more Spirit, more Force of Wit and Genius, than any others I have ever seen, either ancient or modern."[16] Although he was aware that some of the early humanists had suspected them, he was perfectly certain of their authenticity. No matter that Temple knew them only in translation, while their critics had read them in the original Greek; having dismissed philology as menial, Temple could ignore its doubts and put all faith in his literary evaluation. The letters were authentic because they read like a statesman's; who would know better than a man with Temple's experience?

Needless to say, Bentley did. Fortunately, there is no need to retell the familiar story of that next episode in the battle of the books. It is enough to say that Bentley communicated his doubts to Wotton in a casual conversation and was pressed into service in time for a second edition of the *Reflections*. The ancients, represented by the "wits" of Christ Church, then joined forces to defend Temple and concocted a brilliant satire on Bentley that provoked him at length to produce his masterpiece of philological criticism, the *Dissertations upon Phalaris* (1699). Beginning as an appendix to Wotton, the work grew into a book, a series of learned essays on the culture of ancient Greece joined to show that the *Letters of Phalaris* were, as Politian and Erasmus had long before known, the forgery of a late Greek sophist. But at the same time the work served another purpose: it furnished a wealth of information about the whole culture of early Greece, about its chronology, its literature, its institutions, its religion, its money, and so on. And the evidence was drawn—with all the assurance of the now established antiquarian learning—from coins, inscriptions, and monumental remains, as well as from literary documents and especially from an understanding of the evolution of the Greek language. In short, Bentley demonstrated the techniques of humanist philology at their most sophisticated, the result of two centuries and more of development, and he showed at once their possibilities for solving a historical problem. If he was not a historian in seventeenth-century terms but rather a "critic," he showed others like Wotton how critical learning could be put to the service of historical scholarship. But already there were many in the field (as there had been since the revival of learning) doing just that, defining another kind of history to set beside the classical narratives.[17]

163

(2)

It is tempting to pursue the quarrel further, especially since it had only just begun. A barrage of pamphlets, tracts, and satirical pieces soon delighted literary London. But it would only confirm the basic positions of the original rivals and their views of historical writing. Suffice it to say that neither side won; the wits and men of the world were satisfied, particularly after the contributions of Swift, that the ancients had been vindicated, and were able casually to brush aside Bentley's erudition. On the other hand, there were few scholars after 1699 to defend them, at least in the unqualified fashion of Temple or the Christ Church company that had rallied to his cause.[18] The division between the two attitudes toward classical culture, with their corresponding views of history, became, if anything, increasingly impassable, at least until Gibbon tried to bridge them. But the discussion was not simply theoretical; history was in fact being written by both ancients and moderns, and even a quick review of it suggests also the continuity of this double-sided historiographical tradition. In fashioning their new historical works, both the writers of narrative and the compilers of antiquities looked back self-consciously to their humanist forerunners.

Temple, for example, about 1694, conceived of a great scheme for the revision of English history. It was natural enough for a man with such strong convictions about the subject and so much practical experience. It seemed plain to him that what was most required, and what was most lacking in his day, was a single narrative history of England written according to the classical canons of form and style. It was an idea, and a complaint, that had been reiterated for more than a century. Since it appeared somewhat unlikely, however, that any one man could rewrite the whole, he could think of nothing better than to piece together a composite work from such appropriate examples as did exist. The variety of styles that this would entail might, he believed, even be an advantage in so long a work. Temple himself had ready a piece or two of his own that could be used, and there were a number of other obvious choices, all written since the revival of letters. He did not, however, relish the job of editing, altering, and correcting that would be necessary; "he must be excused, being not of an age or a humor at present to engage in such a trouble."

Temple's scheme was outlined to the bookseller John Dunton by his chaplain, Thomas Swift (cousin to Jonathan and rector of the nearby church of Puttenham) in 1694.[19] Dunton was an eccentric but very successful publisher—at least in these years—the author eventually of a famous autobiography, who prided himself on devising and promoting ambitious literary projects.[20] Just previously, for example, he had successfully launched his *Athenian Gazette,* a collaborative literary newsletter, and won some contributions for it from Temple and Temple's young secretary, Jonathan Swift. Perhaps it was he who first thought of a "General History of England"; in any event, he had soon solicited Temple's aid for the project. The latter was willing enough, but the scheme failed when Dunton and his friends found themselves unable to gain the rights to reprint the suggested works.

But now Temple was very interested. He had already on hand a work of his own which he thought would make a perfect introduction to the proposed history. And he had taken the trouble to set down the proposal in detail. Early in 1695, therefore, he sent the scheme (again through his chaplain) to a new set of publishers. But once again, this time without further explanation, the project foundered. There was nothing left to do but to publish the introduction separately; later that year Temple's contribution appeared by itself. For the time being, the larger scheme disappeared from view.

It was a most interesting proposal, however, especially in the light of our theme. The "General History" that Temple intended was not to be simply another chronicle like, for example, the popular work of Sir Richard Baker. On the other hand, Temple realized that his project could not be accomplished in the new humanist style without a delay of many years—if, indeed, at all. Under the circumstances, the best that could be done would be to collect all those smaller pieces of English history, such "Parcels or short Periods of our History" as had already been written "by approved and esteemed authors," and string them together into a single complete work. He imagined it something like this: the compilation would begin with an introduction and account of William the Conqueror's reign—Temple's own. It would then be followed by the history of Samuel Daniel from William Rufus to the reign of Edward III. Daniel was "an author of good judgment and no ill style." For the reign of Richard II, Temple vaguely remembered having seen an anonymous work, but he left it to the publisher to try to recover it. From Henry IV to Henry VI, "the noblest part of the history of England," he could think of no suitable history; it would have to be newly collected. For the next two reigns, however, there was the old work of Sir Thomas More, if it could be found. The Tudors were easier; here a complete set of histories existed, each of which was ideal for the purpose: Bacon on Henry VII, Lord Herbert of Cherbury on Henry VIII, John Hayward on Edward VI, and William Camden on Elizabeth. All these works had, of course, appeared during the period of revival; all possessed at least some of the virtues of classical narrative.[21] Some abridgment would probably be necessary, and Mary would have to be filled in from Holinshed's *Chronicles,* but otherwise the compilation could be simply done. That was as far as Temple's directions went, but if the new publisher, Bentley, would undertake it, Swift promised many subsciptions and a satisfactory sale.

By 1695, Temple despaired of his project; his own *Introduction to the History of England* does not allude to it. In the preface, however, he repeated his objections to the sorry condition in which he found his country's story. It seemed to Temple disgraceful that a nation as noble as England, with writers as excellent, should not yet have produced "one good or approved general history of England." France, Spain, the Empire could all boast examples distinguished by their writing, but the English past had been written "by such mean and vulgar Authors, so tedious in their Relations, or rather Collections, so injudicious in the Choice of what was fit to be told or to be let alone, with so little Order and so wretched a Style," that Temple thought it "hardly worth the Time and Pains to be informed." The only exceptions were the short pieces that he had earlier suggested to Bentley, and that were now enumerated again—with the one exception of Daniel.[22] From these and from other writers Temple thought that a history could, after all, be freshly written, one that would be acceptable "if collected with Pains and Care, and digested with good Order." Apparently, he had once thought of doing it himself, after the model of the Frenchman, Mézeray, whose history he noticed was so popular, but he had been diverted by other things.[23] He had also tried to persuade friends to the task but had been refused by their "modesty." He was left with the *Introduction* only, which he now thought to publish with the one hope that it might encourage someone else to resume the task.

Thus Temple, at one time or another, seems to have had in mind at least two different ideas for the rewriting of English history: a collection of discrete pieces strung together, on the one hand; a fresh abridgment of the whole along the lines of Mézeray, on the other. The *Introduction* was meant for either the one or the other. In either case, he was defining what he thought a good history was and at the same time delineating a tradition of historical writing in which to place himself. He wanted to write a history along the lines of those who, from the days of Thomas More, had deliberately shaped their works along classical lines. His list is not exhaustive, but it certainly includes the principal examples still read in his own day. In compiling it he scrupulously avoided the chronicles that were plentiful throughout the whole period. These he dismissed for their triviality and irrelevance: "Strange events, inclemencies of seasons, raging diseases," and the like, "neither argue the Virtues or Vices of Princes, nor serve for Example or Instruction to Posterity, which are the great ends of History and ought to be the chief Care of all Historians," at least historians with a classical intention. He was also disturbed by their formlessness and careless style. Similarly, the numerous antiquarian disputes, even those over the origins of the English races and institutions, were to be avoided.[24] History was the story of politics and war, and the first duty of the historian was to seek out the causes of great events and to narrate them clearly, vigorously, and elegantly.

His own *Introduction* is a successful example of the type. It is divided into two unequal parts, not very skillfully joined together and possibly written separately. The first, and very much the shorter, takes the story from pre-Roman Britain to the Norman Conquest. The second resumes with the Conquest, repeating some of the details, and then elaborately recounts the history of William's reign. Inevitably, it seemed to contemporaries that the work must harbor a political motive; narrative history was expected to inform politics (had not More and Hayward and Bacon so designed their works?), and the choice of William I could not be idle when another William (and another conqueror) occupied the throne. "It was the general Opinion," wrote Temple's contemporary biographer, that the historian, "who continued to the last a true Friend to the Prince of Orange," had published the *Introduction* "both to compliment that Prince under the character of the Norman Conqueror, which he draws and sets off to great Advantage; and to assert the late Revolution, by shewing, that Edgar Atheling, who had [like James II] an undoubted Right of Succession to the Crown, was twice laid aside."[25] In any case, the work was well and persuasively written, and herein lay its distinction and Temple's intention. Of historical research—in the sense that the philologists and antiquaries understood it—Temple knew nothing and cared less. Like his models in classical antiquity, he thought that the writing of history meant essentially the rewriting of histories. His task was thus to choose the best narrative and to recast it with the help of other convenient works, adding his own gifts of style, organization, and political insight. And this is precisely what Temple accomplished in the *Introduction,* using Samuel Daniel's earlier work (republished with a continuation in 1685), paraphrasing and echoing whole passages of it, but without any acknowledgment. His history was at once commended on its publication—even by the moderns—for the very virtues that he intended and that he had discovered in the classical tradition, the virtues essentially of form and style and political good sense.

Among Temple's admirers was his secretary, Jonathan Swift. Of course, there was every reason that he should be; he had very likely helped in the composition of Temple's history, as he certainly did in preparing it for publication. He was in these years writing directly for Temple at Moor Park, and he seems to have shared completely the older man's view of politics and the world—and English history.[26] The *Tale of a Tub* and the *Battle of the Books* are express apologies for Temple and attacks on Wotton and Bentley. And it seems likely that Swift was among those too "modest" to write the abridgment Temple had in mind. But he did start to compose one—we have the fragment—though he put it aside and never completed it.[27] And it picks up the story immediately after Temple's *Introduction,* with the reign of William II, continuing until it breaks off abruptly in the middle of the reign of Henry II. Since Swift himself did not think it worth completing, it probably does not merit close inspection. But even on a casual view, it reflects the same intentions and the same virtues and defects as the work of the older man. One can see in it, anyway, the outlines of a larger ambition: to fulfill Temple's dream and to rewrite English history according to the classical standard. But as Temple had forecast, the task was not easy for a single author to accomplish, and by 1703, Swift had discovered other talents and ambitions more uniquely his own; his lifelong ambition to be a historian was never fulfilled.[28]

Still, Temple's idea would not die. It was too obvious and too attractive to disappear.[29] It was the booksellers who remained interested—not the original parties, but a new syndicate. The "undertakers," Swalle and Churchill, had to rally an unexpectedly large company of booksellers to join in the event. But the project too was unexpectedly large—three enormous volumes in the end. Indeed, the whole undertaking was prodigious; eventually, about seven hundred and eighty subscribers had to lend their support. The result was the *Complete History of England,* published first in 1706, reprinted several times, and revised in 1719. It was a fitting monument to the taste of the age and a climax to two centuries of historical writing in the new manner. There can be no doubt that Temple would have enjoyed the result.

But of course Temple was dead, and Swift engaged in other things; it was necessary to find a new editor. Other hands were needed as well: someone to write the missing portions of the narrative, someone else to annotate and correct the older works, and perhaps most critically, someone to bring the account down to the present. The work was meant to be a complete history; it would have to start at the beginning and finish with contemporary events. The poet and miscellaneous writer John Hughes was selected as editor; the antiquary John Strype and some others were to contribute to the text; and Bishop White Kennett was chosen for the contemporary portion. The whole was managed with considerable skill; the sheer logistics of the undertaking must have been very demanding.[30]

Hughes was well equipped for the job. He was a young man still when he was commissioned for the history, and indeed he died young without ever reaching that literary distinction which he seemed at times close to attaining. He wrote a good deal of verse that was generally well received, many essays, some translations from Latin and French, and one very popular play; he also contributed to the *Spectator* and knew most of the literary personalities of the day. In addition, he was a musician and librettist of some renown. At his death Steele spoke for many when he said that "all men who have a Taste of good Arts, will lament the loss of this Gentleman." His works were reprinted for some time, and he received a "life" by Dr. Johnson. Somehow, though, most of his writing remained second rate; perhaps it was because his ideas were so commonplace.[31]

Originality, however, is not a special virtue in an editor. Hughes was industrious and facile, and his ideas were exactly suited to his time. At the age of twenty-two (in 1698) he had written a little tract, "Of Style," which describes well enough his view of letters. Polite learning, he wrote, "files off the Rust of the Academy. . . . In a Word, it adds the Gentleman to the Scholar." Hughes himself was no academician but very much a gentleman scholar after the fashion of Temple and the Christ Church wits who had attacked Bentley. The two chief branches of polite learning, he thought, were history and poetry. But like the men of taste for whom he wrote, he infinitely preferred "good sense and polite learning" to any form of scholarship: "A plain unletter'd Man is always more agreeable Company than a Fool in several Languages." Was he referring perhaps to Wotton or Bentley? His remarks were followed, in any case, by lavish praise for Temple.[32]

When Hughes undertook the *Complete History*, he was thus prepared to accept the standards of his model and predecessor. His lengthy introduction to the new work describes his plan and the problems in pursuing it. He begins with some brief commonplace remarks on the value of history in entertaining and instructing men, in furnishing the material for political and personal reflections, and in improving morals, "for what we admire we are easily dispos'd to imitate." He resumes Temple's criticism of the existing state of English history, "the mean and imperfect Performances of our most common Historians." It is the form and style to which he objects; that is "the Reason why Many are more negligent in reading our story than they would perhaps have been, if they had met with it better related. For tho' the Matter of History is the first thing to recommend it, the Form, which depends wholly on the Writer, is almost of equal Consequence." Of course, "to record great Actions in the finest manner" is as difficult as to perform them. His summary of the virtues of the perfect history is a perfect description of what the humanist rhetorician desired, "a judicious Proportion of all the Parts of his Story; a beautiful Simplicity of Narration; a noble, yet unaffected Stile; few and significant Epithets; Descriptions lively, but not Poetical; Reflections short and proper; and lastly . . . a good Conduct thro' the whole, and an animating Spirit that may engage the Reader in every Action as if personally concern'd." He is plain about the sources of his idea here; he recommends his reader to the standard contemporary texts on the art of history.

To write a perfect history was not therefore an easy task; to write the history of a whole nation perfectly was well-nigh impossible. Hughes thought that only Livy and Mariana, one ancient and one modern, had been completely successful.[33] In England there was no one at all. Some national history had been attempted, but either in the form of a chronicle or antiquarian compilation, and neither would do. The first was tedious, filled with "a World of frivolous Matter and minute Circumstances"; the second was but "a laborious Plunder of Libraries, Manuscripts, publick Rolls and Records." No amount of labor could overcome a "cold and barren Stile." English history remained to be written. In the meantime there was nothing to do but follow Temple's suggestion, to put a single narrative together from those pieces that were acceptable. Here England was fortunate, for over the past two hundred years, many short histories had been written to the humanist measure: "These are the standing Authorities and Guides to which all Attempters in this Way must have Recourse."

Hughes's plan was more ambitious than Temple's, although the design was exactly the same. Securing the appropriate works had been very difficult; some were scarce and expensive, others corrupt through many and late editions. There were more histories to obtain than Temple had known, and the scale of the narrative was grander. No abridgments were to be made, but additions were another matter. Besides those recommended by Temple, Hughes added Edward Habington's Edward IV, Francis Godwin for Mary, and Arthur Wilson for James I.[34] Ironically, he substituted John Milton's account of pre-Conquest Britain and Daniel's William I for Temple's *Introduction.* Undoubtedly, the slight scale of Temple's work had something to do with the change; certainly the first part of his history was inadequate, and if one were to use Daniel anyway for the many reigns after William Rufus, one might as well start from the beginning of his work. Finally, a whole volume of the three was devoted to seventeenth-century England and freshly written by Bishop Kennett. There were other additions, some notes and documents, and much fresh translation.

As derivative as was the result, there was something majestic and definitive about it. The Augustans were accustomed to large folios and learned works, but where else was one to find a combination of large scale and literary perfection to match this history? If it was something of a pastiche, its variety alone, Hughes thought (with Temple), would relieve it from tedium. And what excellence in its parts! Hughes's description of each of the works is elaborate and helpful in defining his literary standards. Again, the terms are exactly like Temple's but fuller. The standard remains classical: Milton carries "the Majestick Air of old Greece or Rome"; Bacon is compared to Tacitus. All are commended precisely (and almost exclusively) for their form and style: Daniel for his smooth and clear narrative, his good sense and just eloquence; More for his "Masterly Command of the Delicacies" of the Latin language (here translated, however); Bacon for all "the Ornament of a descreet Orator"; and so on. There could be no doubt about the purpose; the *Complete History* intended a complete anthology of humanist historical narrative from the beginning of the English Renaissance. Nor did it omit entirely the most admired of all those works, the Earl of Clarendon's *History of the Rebellion.* It was impossible to include it whole (it came to three large volumes by itself), but White Kennett deliberately incorporated as much as he could into his own volume, particularly the "characters" that had given it special fame.[35]

The *Complete History* was thus the fulfillment of Temple's idea and realization of one main Renaissance aspiration: the rewriting of the whole of English history according to the classical standard. How far it succeeded depended, of course, upon its parts, an analysis of which would be far beyond the means of this essay. But Temple and the editors of the *Complete History* were not alone in their estimation of what constituted the classical tradition in English historical writing. Here again the ancients and the moderns were agreed. Thus the very works employed in the *Complete History,* from More to Clarendon, were almost identically described and praised, their virtues proclaimed and endorsed, by other writers on both sides.[36] And the classical theory of narrative history was reiterated in Temple's day, as it had been for two centuries, *ad infinitum ad nauseam,* in a host of works too numerous to recount.

(3)

Inevitably, one of Temple's readers was William Wotton. He was less impressed by the *Introduction* than most of those who read it. It contained too many "strange Mistakes," like the double error where Temple attributed the mission of St. Augustine to Pope Boniface and set Athelbert on the South Saxon throne, "tho' every body knows that Athelbert was only King of Kent, and that it was Gregory the Great who sent Augustine into England." Exactness in detail was admittedly not one of Temple's strengths.[37] What Wotton thought of his style, he does not say—an inadvertent admission of its excellence, perhaps—but style, after all, meant less to him than substance. Humanist scholars, unlike humanist gentlemen, were willing to bear with the most awkward and difficult works as long as they contributed to knowledge. Much later, Wotton wrote an apology for the great antiquary John Selden: his "Way of Writing is obscure and intricate, and his Digressions many and long," he agreed, "but the uncommon Variety of things worth knowing compensates for the Trouble." The relish for detail in any form was characteristic.

Like Temple, Wotton not only held strong views about the nature of history; he wrote some as well. And, just as with the older man (though largely in the opposite direction), his history reflected the preconceptions that underlay his part in the quarrel between the ancients and the moderns. It was Wotton's task to illustrate the philological and antiquarian traditions of the humanist, much as Temple had described the parallel humanist tradition of rhetoric. In 1701 appeared *The History of Rome from the Death of Antoninus Pius to the Death of Severus Alexander*. It had been written initially at the instigation of his old patron Bishop Burnet, who for a time had charge of the education of the king's son. For the instruction of the prince, Wotton drew up some papers consisting of two pairs of lives of the Roman emperors, Marcus Aurelius and Commodus, Elagabalus and Alexander Severus. Burnet had chosen them expressly "as the properest Examples in the whole Roman History, to Instruct a Prince how much more Glorious and Safe it is and Happier both for Himself and for his People to govern well than ill."[38] It was a purpose that the early humanists could not have approved more heartily. The two pairs of imperial lives each included a bad and a good prince; they were, Wotton agreed, "the properest Instances to set Virtue and Vice, and the Consequences of them both in a clear and full Light."

Unfortunately, the young boy died before the work was completed. Wotton therefore decided to take the fragments and connect them with the missing narrative: that is, the several reigns and twenty-six years that lay between the two pairs of emperors. This would make the history complete and continuous and much more intelligible. No doubt it was at this time that he also added the elaborate scholarly apparatus that makes the work distinctive, a learned commentary that attempts to summarize the state of classical scholarship on his subject. Although in a sense his theme cried out for rheotrical treatment, for a style that would, according to classical theory, dramatize or entertain, Wotton thought that end undesirable and largely impossible, at least for the way in which he intended to treat his subject. "Affectation of Eloquence becomes History the least of anything, especially such an History as this, which like Mosaic Work must be made up and interwoven with the Thought and Sentences of other Men, and where to add to, or diminish from ones Authors, may be of ill consequence." He strove for simplicity and clarity and above all for accuracy, rather than for literary finish. Under the circumstances, his work read well enough though without distinction. Wotton managed his erudition without interfering with his narrative, largely (though not entirely) by relegating it to an elaborate series of notes, which he placed at the end of the work.[39]

It is these that are the most interesting part of the history. As he had promised in his introduction, he uses them, with some discussion in the text, to describe his sources and to consider problems of interpretation and disagreement among scholars. If he follows rather closely the recent works of Tillemont and Dacier, it is because they employed all the ancient sources. Still, he does not follow them slavishly; indeed, he exhibits firsthand acquaintance not only with the ancient narratives in Greek and Latin but with inscriptions and monumental remains, especially with the ancient coins, "those undisputed Monuments of Antiquity" that he noticed, "explain many things which the Historians do very lamely tell us." Here was a field only recently cultivated, a "modern" achievement, an immensely popular antiquarian pastime but also a science indispensable to writing the history of the ancient world. Like its kindred disciplines epigraphy, chronology, and diplomatics (all familiar to Wotton and employed more or less in his work), numismatics had been first discovered in Renaissance Italy among the humanists who were eager, in their recovery of ancient literature, to employ whatever evidence might illuminate their texts. In two centuries it had made steady progress in that regular and cumulative fashion that Wotton took to be characteristic of all historical scholarship. By 1700 it was widely acknowledged by amateurs and collectors, as well as by scholars, to be a useful aid to classical history. Thus, even on so elementary a point as to whether to call the emperor Elagabalus or Heliogabalus, Severus Alexander or Alexander Severus, Wotton saw that the coins could be decisive. He naturally sided with the modern antiquaries against the ancient writers—the authors, in this case, of the *Historia Augusta*. "When disputes arise of this kind," he claimed, "Medals are the only proper Authoritys by which they can be decided." And though their authority, like the written sources, could also be questioned at times, wherever they agreed, their testimony was decisive; they were "the truest Monuments of Antiquity." No modern scholar would disagree.[40]

There is not space in this essay to track Wotton through his sources or to show his mastery of humanist scholarship and criticism. His work, in its conclusions and techniques, is impossible to imagine without the collective labor that had accumulated since the Renaissance and without his understanding of the methods of classical scholarship as they had been practiced for generations. But were they applicable to English history also? It is not surprising, perhaps, to find classical scholarship on a classical theme, but what about the history of later times? How would the period of Temple's *Introduction* be treated by a philologist or antiquary?

Inevitably, Wotton's interests extended to these matters as well; there was no area of contemporary scholarship that he did not know. If he was quick enough to pick out the flaws in Temple's work, he understood that there was an even more fundamental weakness to his undertaking. Temple, like all the narrative writers before him, had been debarred from understanding his subject by his ignorance of Anglo-Saxon. How could one pretend to understand the customs, institutions, social life, even the laws and politics of early England without access to all those sources written in the native language? No more than Daniel or Milton before him does this seem to have bothered Temple; the tradition of humanist rhetoric did not encourage researches of this kind. But from the moment antiquarian study began in England under the influence of humanist scholarship, the problem was evident. With John Leland and Robert Talbot early in the sixteenth century, the revival of the ancient languages of Great Britain began. It was no coincidence that Celtic and Anglo-Saxon philology took their first tentative steps just when classical philology was introduced into England and began its special English task of recovering Roman Britain. Nor was it surprising that they continued to borrow their techniques in subsequent generations.[41]

By Wotton's day the development of Anglo-Saxon philology had far advanced. In fact, just as he was preparing the 1705 *Reflections,* it reached its climax with the appearance of George Hickes's *Thesaurus of the Northern Tongues.* Wotton was able to celebrate that work (along with Newton's *Optics*) as one of the latest and greatest of modern achievements. Hickes's three large folios, even weightier and more impressive than the *Complete History,* provided the missing key to Anglo-Saxon history and culture. It was only now possible, Wotton wrote, "to draw up an Accurate History of the Alterations of our Language since we were a People, to this Time, to ascertain the true Original of almost every Word." And, as a result, it was only now reasonable to expect "to see the Learning of our Northern Ancestors better known to us, than it ever was to them in any single Age in which any of them lived." The advantages of classical philology, won by the labors of generations of humanists and finally applied fully to a foreign field, were at last capable of recapturing the old Germanic culture of the North—and with the same usefulness to history. Wotton at once set about writing an abridgement of Hickes's work in order both to advertise and to simplify the original.[42]

It was no easy task. Not only was the *Thesaurus* massive; it was frightfully complex. For one thing, it was not really the work of a single author but rather a collaborative achievement that Hickes had masterminded, a whole series of Latin treatises of different kinds and lengths devoted to aspects of the northern languages and culture. It contained three grammars (Anglo-Saxon, Gothic, and Icelandic, the first of their kind), a treatise by Andrew Fountaine on Anglo-Saxon coins, and (occupying an entire volume) a catalog of all the Anglo-Saxon manuscripts that could be traced and described by Hickes's brilliant young assistant, Humfrey Wanley. These were surrounded by lengthy prefaces, engraved plates, six indexes, and a most valuable dissertation on the excellence and usefulness of the northern languages. Dozens of contributors were credited in the preface and throughout the various parts. In its form, or formlessness, it was only too characteristic of seventeenth-century erudition. But if it was a natural target for the satire of literary gentlemen, it was, in the long run, indispensable to the historians of early Britain.

Hickes's preliminary dissertation alone should have made it so. It was both a discussion of the sources and problems in understanding Anglo-Saxon culture and a description of some of the institutions and customs of that period. Among other novel things, Hickes considered place names, wills, coins, and charters; his discussion of the last is perhaps the most valuable. As Wotton saw, "nobody can rightly distinguish these Charters, especially if Originals, whether they be spurious or genuine," unless he was aware of the history of Anglo-Saxon handwriting and "of the Phrases and Manners of Speech proper to every Age." As demonstration, Hickes was able to show that the whole series of charters in the medieval chronicle of Ingulf were forged; his technique was exactly like Bentley's for Phalaris. The charters were false because they were anachronistic in both language and content. But it was only through close and painstaking attention to detail (the "pedantry" of Temple and Swift) that such knowledge was possible. How the signs of the cross were made in official documents, "how frivolous and minute soever they may seem to those who are not curious, and make but light of Charters, are nevertheless of no little moment"; by them the age and authenticity of the texts might well be determined.[43]

Of course, Hickes and Wanley and their cohorts were only doing in England what Mabillon and Montfaucon (whose works they knew) were doing in France, and what all Europe had cooperated in doing for classical Greece and Rome. And Hickes was fully conscious of the long development of Anglo-Saxon studies that had preceded his day and to which he was immediately indebted. In the *Thesaurus,* the application of these philological and historical techniques paid immediate dividends for understanding life in early Britain. Hickes had much to say, for example, about Anglo-Saxon courts and legal institutions, about the religion, taxation, and topography of the early period. Wanley's catalog may still be used to guide the student to and through the sources of Anglo-Saxon history. And there were a host of other uses to which the work might be put, too extensive to discuss here. In Wotton's words, it was "a Treasure that revives the Heroic Deeds of our Ancestors . . . that either contains in itself all the Laws, Customs, and Manners of our Country, or will at least illustrate whatever is elsewhere contained of them in Books that have hitherto been scarce, if at all, understood."

(4)

Nevertheless, the *Thesaurus* was only one work in the collective enterprise of the antiquaries to recover the early history of England. Britain had had a Celtic and a Roman history also, not to say a later medieval and modern history, all equally or at least potentially amenable to the skills of the philologist and antiquary. Looking back across the two centuries that separated Hickes and his friends from John Leland and his successors, one can see a single great antiquarian dream being slowly realized. Leland had never passed beyond announcing it and accumulating notes for it, but he understood virtually every one of the great antiquarian tasks of the next generations. The plans he laid for his interminable projects—all unrealized—remind one exactly of the plans still being proposed by Humfrey Wanley for the new Society of Antiquaries in 1707.[44] Was it surprising that Leland's notes were read with consuming interest by the antiquaries of the later seventeenth century (as they had been read continually from the time he penned them) and that various plans for their publication were soon realized?[45] The great Camden had been accused a hundred years before of plagiarizing them; now Camden's *Britannia* (1695) was revived along with Leland and characteristically enlarged and updated by a team of antiquaries in what constitutes the most impressive single achievement in the long and gradual recovery of ancient Britain. One of the contributors to that enterprise was a Welshman named Edward Lhwyd, who spent years doing for the Celtic language and culture exactly what Hickes had done for the Anglo-Saxon. His *Archaeologica Britannica* (1707) is a philological and historical achievement that properly belongs with Bentley's *Dissertation* and the *Thesaurus* and shows how general and how continuous was the conception of the historian's task—or more accurately the task of the philologist-antiquary—at the end of the period.[46]

Yet oddly enough, all this scholarly accomplishment did not transform itself at once into modern historiography. The works of Hickes and Lhwyd and the new *Britannia* were in a real sense the climactic achievements of Renaissance antiquarianism rather than the harbingers of anything new. Like the *Complete History,* they summarized the achievement of the whole age. It was more than a century before any marked progress occurred. Hickes and Wanley, for example, were more advanced in their Anglo-Saxon competence and learning than anyone would be for generations. In part this was a result of the continued separation of narrative from research; eighteenth-century historians learned very little from the *Thesaurus*. In part it is because the motives that first engendered antiquarian enthusiasm subsided somewhat in the eighteenth century. From its beginnings, Anglo-Saxon research had been undertaken especially by churchmen anxious to find evidence in the early records to support their position. This was true of the circle around Archbishop Parker, which initiated these studies under Queen Elizabeth, and it was still true of the circle around Hickes. Political controversy served the same interests and died away in the same fashion at about the same time. Having lost impetus, the antiquarian movement had to stumble against the powerful opposition of that other humanist current, the hostility of the ancients to all medieval study and their loathing for the pedantry of scholarship. It is not surprising that among the few achievements that followed upon our period, it was the study of Roman (rather than Saxon or Celtic) times that was least inhibited. It is only in the nineteenth century that one can speak again of great and rapid change, a "revolution" in historiography. It is only then that narrative and scholarship lost their independence and were transformed into "modern" history. But that, of course, is another story.

CHAPTER 7

Edward Gibbon and the Quarrel
between the Ancients and the Moderns

It was perhaps inevitable that Edward Gibbon should take sides in the quarrel between the ancients and the moderns. It used to be said that the contest had ended long before his time, won decisively early in the eighteenth century by the moderns both in England and France, and that the idea of progress had triumphed over every backward look. But even the most cursory inspection turns up evidence to the contrary, and it is plain that the quarrel continued unresolved for generations and that the ancients, unabashed, still had a good deal left to say.[1] It was, after all, Swift and Pope who spoke out most effectively in England, while Boileau and Mme Dacier were only slightly less audible—and equally unrepentant—in France. Indeed, it looks rather as though it was *ancienneté* (ancientness) that still continued to dictate the terms of the argument, if not the outcome, and it was a long time before the question appeared so settled that a gentleman or a scholar could feel free of all need to declare himself. Gibbon, who considered himself both a scholar and a gentleman, certainly felt under obligation and early and continuously pronounced on the argument. The quarrel was not the only and probably not the most important influence upon Gibbon's thought, but it was a crucial ingredient in the formation of his mind and an essential part of that elaborate setting in which we can hope to measure his achievement.[2]

Among many examples of the persistence of the quarrel, I shall single out only one or two here that were certainly known to Gibbon. Throughout his life, Gibbon read and admired Voltaire. He considered him the first writer of the age, and though he came to have some doubts about his wisdom and judgment, it is clear that the old man exercised a continuing fascination for him.[3] For Voltaire, who was brought up amid the *querelle* and who visited England just in time to witness the dying embers of the battle of the books, the issues in the contest remained a lifelong preoccupation. Already in England in 1726–29, he entered into controversy with an essay on epic poetry that drew a tart reply from another visitor, the Italian Paolo Rolli. The immediate question was the precedence in epic of ancients or moderns: in brief, whether Homer, as the prince of poets, was altogether unassailable or not, a point that had exercised the best wits in France for two generations.[4] In this matter, Voltaire inclined toward the moderns, though cautiously, compared with La Motte and Terrasson, ready to find some fault with Homer and much merit in Virgil and Tasso, and eager to liberate the poet from the necessity of slavish imitation. Even so, he managed to offend the antique sensibilities of Rolli, who accepted Voltaire's premise (borrowed, incidentally, from the modern Fontenelle) that human nature was the same in all ages, only to insist on the justice of using Homer as a timeless standard for all poetry and to reaffirm the superiority of the *Iliad*.[5] The contest, as usual, was a draw.

Sometime later, Voltaire wrote an essay on the ancients and moderns, which he included in the *Philosophical Dictionary*. He reviewed the whole quarrel there, noticing ruefully that "men had always pretended that the good old times were much better than the present" and that the ancients themselves had in the Silver Age debated the question.[6] As for the uniformity of human nature, Voltaire pointed out that that hardly settled the question on either side. It was not whether nature *could* produce a genius in modern times equal to the ancients but whether in fact she *had*. Was antiquity actually superior in genius to the Italian Renaissance or the age of Louis XIV? (Voltaire, typically, discarded the Middle Ages altogether.) Once again, Voltaire attempted a moderate position: the ancients, he argued against La Motte, should be *esteemed* without being *adored*. Their languages, he agreed, "were richer and more harmonious than our modern tongues which are a mixture of corrupt Latin and the horrible jargon of the Celts." But in many other respects the moderns had to be awarded the palm. Sir William Temple had been wrong to claim the classical temples above any others: "Englishman that he was, he should have allowed that St. Peter's at Rome is incomparably more beautiful than the Capitol." (Gibbon emphatically agreed.)[7] As for the sciences, Temple had been altogether blind. At least Boileau and Racine had known enough to leave them out of their quarrel with Perrault.[8] In an imaginary dialogue set in the boudoir of Mme de Pompadour, Voltaire once again took up the question, largely to advance the cause of the moderns in literature, science, and comfort.[9] (In the course of the conversation, a servant brings the company a tray of coffee, tea, and chocolate, to the astonishment of a visitor freshly arrived form ancient Rome. One is reminded of Gibbon's remark about the Emperor Augustus, "that he had neither glass to his windows nor a shirt to his back.")[10] The point is reinforced in Voltaire's historical works, which, of course, Gibbon studied with special care.[11] Of the four great ages of human achievement, the most recent, the age of Louis XIV, was superior to the rest in reason and science but not in the arts. Newton was the first to discover gravity and dispel the ignorance of the ages, but Greece, Rome, and Florence could still claim precedence in other matters.[12]

In short, it looked to Voltaire and to others that there was not just one simple quarrel in progress but one for every field and at least two main battlegrounds: one for the arts and literature, the other for the sciences.[13] And though it was becoming increasingly difficult to deny the modern achievement in the knowledge and mastery of nature, it was not necessarily so for other things. One of Gibbon's fondest possessions was a run of the *Memoirs* of the Academy of Inscriptions, the first twenty volumes of which he purchased for twenty pounds and read with lasting pleasure.[14] There he found, with much else that was useful, an essay by the abbé Gedoyn of 1736, posing the still topical question "whether the ancients were more learned than the moderns and how far one ought to appreciate the merits of the one or the other."[15] Let us allow the ancients, began the abbé, the glory of having surpassed us in eloquence and poetry and take them for our masters in all things that require taste and sentiment. The point was too obvious to elaborate. At the same time, he continued, "let us recognize that the moderns have been more laborious, more avid of knowledge, more exact in the observation of nature, more attentive and profound in their researches, and in a word, more incomparably universal and learned." Each, therefore, deserved esteem for its own achievement. It was no doubt a judicious conclusion, though of course not everyone agreed, and it shows how plausible it was to be an ancient with respect to some things and a modern with respect to others, a fact that has confounded some recent students of the quarrel.[16]

For the rest of the eighteenth century, it was in literature and the arts, where progress was harder to define and where it was not at all clear that the moderns could claim superiority, that the chief battles remained to be fought. In an essay of 1754 by Joseph Warton in the *Adventurer* No. 127, Gibbon read: "That age will never again return, when a Pericles after walking with Plato in a portico built by Phideas and painted by Apelles, might repair to hear a pleading of Demosthenes or a tragedy of Sophocles."[17] It was too easy for Gibbon to point out that that age would never return because it had never existed, since the chronology was all askew.[18] Warton had plausibly carried the main point, upholding Homer against all the modern poets; the Greek tragedies against Shakespeare, Corneille and Racine; Demosthenes and Cicero against any modern oratory, and declaring the improvements of all modern architecture to be absolutely dependent on classical precedent. Only in painting was he willing to allow a successful challenge. As for history, Warton was confident that here too the ancients would triumph in any match-up: Tacitus over Machiavelli; Sallust and Plutarch over Thuanus; Livy and Herodotus over Davila; Xenophon, Caesar, and Polybius over any modern memoir. The classical historians remained for him models for content and style. Although Gibbon did not make every one of these comparisons, it is pretty clear from the scattered comments in his writings that he was willing to accept almost every one of these judgments. Warton became a friend and remained a favorite writer.

What kept the controversy going, no doubt, was the integrity of classical education.[19] Gibbon's own schooling was irregular and had to be reinforced after he left Oxford for Lausanne, but he always defended the public schools and "all they pretend to teach, the Latin and Greek languages . . . the keys to two valuable chests."[20] Classical education meant classical imitation, and it is not surprising that the quarrel between the ancients and the moderns was fueled by differences over the relative advantages of imitation and originality, differences that could be found in the ancients themselves, in Quintilian and Tacitus, for example, and in the Ciceronian combatants of the Renaissance, all of whom Gibbon knew directly.[21] One of his first and most ambitious literary efforts was a reply to Richard Hurd, who had interpolated an essay on "poetic imitation" into his commentary on Horace. Hurd argued in favor of imitation on the ground that a timeless human nature and a repertoire of similar circumstances were bound to produce a similar poetry, even without deliberate copying.[22] Gibbon replied by noticing first that the disposition to imitate was the result of education and habit and that that was enough to cause one to look out on the world "and see it with the eyes of the ancients." There was nothing either necessary or inevitable about this, and Gibbon thought that it must still be possible to describe nature with some originality and thus avoid the need to imitate pedantically. "He would desire Mr. Hurd . . . for a precise answer, at what period of the history of letters, the scene had been closed, nature exhausted, and succeeding writers reduced to the hopes of imitating successfully?"[23] It was a good modern riposte, yet Gibbon's description of the actual situation, of the education and habits and consequently the "veneration" for antiquity of his contemporaries, makes it easy to see why *ancienneté* would not die.[24]

Gibbon's interest in the quarrel was thus engendered by a vigorous contemporary discussion for which there is much additional evidence. But Gibbon discovered it also by reading directly in the original authors of the French *querelle* and the English battle of the books. His first published effort, the French *Essay on the Study of Literature,* which he wrote between 1759 and 1761, may be seen as a deliberate effort to resolve some of the issues raised by these earlier writers. In particular, its main theme is an attempt to defend the conjuncture between classical taste and classical erudition, between imitation and learning, which the two parties had deliberately split asunder. The moderns (Fontenelle, La Motte, Terrasson), had according to Gibbon, employed reason, style, and jest to try to reduce Homer to the pitiful level of Chapelain. The ancients had opposed to this "only an attachment to minutiae" and "prejudices, railings and quotations." As a result, ridicule had triumphed, and modern philosophers found it astonishing "that men can spend a whole life in collecting facts and words, and in loading the memory instead of enlightening the mind."[25] The ancients were saddled with contempt, and what used to be proudly called *belles lettres* was now despised as *erudition*. For Gibbon, all this was unfortunate. "The ancient authors," he continued to insist, "have left models for those who would dare to follow in their footsteps."[26] This did not mean servile submission, for understanding and imitation depended not only on gaining a "minute acquaintance" with ancient times but on grasping the spirit of ancient literature as well. Gibbon remembers the modern Perrault, who was shocked by the gross manners of Homer's heroes. "In vain did Boileau remonstrate with him, that Homer wished and ought to depict the Greeks and not the French."[27] Gibbon read the *Iliad* through in Greek with the commentaries (which Perrault had not), and he did not forget the quarrel about Homer in the footnotes to the *Decline and Fall*.[28]

Already in the *Essay*, Gibbon hoped to join the virtues of the ancients and the moderns, style and good sense with erudition. It is the program of the *Decline and Fall*. "If philosophers are not always historians, it were, at any rate, to be wished that historians were always philosophers."[29] By philosophy, Gibbon seems to have meant two things: the outlook and values of the enlightened men of his time, the philosophes; and, with respect to history in particular, an understanding of the causes and connections between events. His classical model is Tacitus, even above Livy, because he is more "philosophical," though both knew how to rise above those raw compilers who are satisfied with the facts alone.[30] It is no coincidence that the *Decline and Fall* begins just where Tacitus left off, that Gibbon's views about his subject so often echo the Roman, or that he is continuously praised in its notes; both Gibbon's friends and enemies noticed the resemblance.[31] Arnaldo Momigliano has pointed out the reluctance of the humanists to attempt ancient history directly; Gibbon is no bolder, content to start his own work just at that moment when the long train of classical histories had begun to peter out.[32] In choosing to write his work in the form of a narrative (even including battle descriptions and set speeches), he was self-consciously assuming the posture of his classical models and betraying a genuine *ancienneté;* in infusing it with classical scholarship and the values of his philosophical friends, he was, of course, espousing the cause of modernity. The result was nothing less than a heroic attempt to resolve the age-old quarrel at its very center by joining the views of both ancients and moderns about the nature and purpose of history, and by marrying the two methods of approaching the past that were so generally kept apart.[33]

It was in the battle of the books that this issue had been most clearly and decisively raised.[34] Temple, who had begun the fracas in 1690, had set the ancients unreservedly above the moderns in history as in everything else: Herodotus and Livy above Davila and Strada, Caesar above Sleidanus. The ancients, he insisted, had alone combined the virtues of style and content, eloquence and political experience. When Temple himself attempted a history, it turned out as we have seen to be a graceful narrative, unpretentious in research, essentially a rewrite of Samuel Daniel's earlier work. Gibbon owned a copy of Temple's complete works and enjoyed reading them, but he was contemptuous of his scholarship.[35] So indeed was Temple's original opponent, William Wotton, who did not hesitate to point out some of the "strange" factual mistakes that marred his history. Unlike some of the French moderns, Wotton was looking for a middle way between the extremes of too much deference to the ancients and too much irreverence, and he was eager to divide the field and to assign most of the humanities to the ancients, while claiming most of the sciences for the moderns. In this he pretty much anticipated Voltaire and the abbé Gedoyn, not to say Gibbon himself. On the vexed question of imitation, he agreed that "the Masters of Writing in all their several Ways, to this day, appeal to the Ancients, as their Guides, and still fetch Rules for them, for the Art of Writing." The superiority of the classical languages assured the ancients of the advantage. Wotton only wished to allow the possibility that the moderns might some day catch up and produce another Cicero or Virgil.[36]

As for history, Wotton was willing to concede that the ancients still had the advantage in narrative, though he thought that some of the moderns could hold their own with them in content, particularly Paolo Sarpi, whose *History of the Council of Trent* Gibbon also admired extravagantly.[37] It was elsewhere with the invention of philology and antiquities that the moderns had a clear and definite advantage over anything the ancient world had known. Here, it seemed to Wotton, a new world of historical understanding had opened of almost limitless possibility. When Temple denied the usefulness of this (in the essay printed by the young Jonathan Swift), it was because he thought that the scholars' concern for detail had become excessive and actually had begun to obscure rather than illuminate the meaning of the classical texts.[38] A Dutch variorum, a text surrounded and dwarfed by commentary, was a mockery of the easy lucidity that was Temple's ideal.[39]

When, therefore, Richard Bentley entered the contest and showed that Temple's endorsement of the ancient writers was based on ignorance and that his choice of Phalaris as the oldest and (therefore) the best of the Greeks was mistaken because the epistles were the fabrications of a late and rather incompetent sophist, it began to appear that *ancienneté* was a devotion that depended on some—but not too much—knowledge of antiquity and that classical learning was itself the most insidious enemy of classical imitation. Wotton and Bentley knew vastly more about the ancients than did Temple—who had, to his embarrassment, lost his Greek altogether—and *they* were the moderns in the battle of the books. The Christ Church wits who banded together to answer Bentley, as well as Swift and Pope, who rallied to the ancient cause, remained at the same fundamental disadvantage as Temple. But they were not the less sincere in their *ancienneté* and could argue plausibly that despite or perhaps because of their indifference to detail, they understood better the spirit of the classical works and how to use them—better certainly than their opponents, whose prose was clumsy and whose thought was clouded with pedantic learning.[40] Did they not prove it with their classical rhetoric?

Now it is one of the complications of this situation that the philosophes of the next generation, like Voltaire and d'Alembert,[41] lined up with the ancients in their disparagement of modern learning and the moderns in their belief in science and their hopes for the future.[42] They were thus less modern than they sometimes pretended. It is to Gibbon's credit that he saw something to both sides of the argument. He had won his own way to erudition by a long, self-regulated course in the antiquarian and philological scholarship of two centuries. Even as a child he set himself problems in chronology and textual criticism, and as a young man he crossed swords with the experts in a learned correspondence where he tried his skills at dating and emendation. Some of this scholarship he learned at second hand, reading the *Diplomatica* of Mabillon and the *Paleographia* of Montfaucon, visiting the Academy of Inscriptions in Paris and studying the numismatics of Ezechiel Spanheim—picking up, as he said, the theory without ever attaining the practice but acknowledging the achievement and employing the results.[43] As much as he valued the learning of classical scholarship, he seems never to have stopped worrying about its excesses or thought of it as an end in itself. The footnotes of the *Decline and Fall* provide a running commentary on the flaws as well as on the uses of erudition, on the failures of judgment and common sense of the great men of learning—every one of whom, it seems, Gibbon used in his work. Gibbon's attitude toward the "minute diligence" of the antiquaries was thus a nicely calculated balance between the extremes of ancient and modern sensibility.[44]

It is only toward the end of the *Decline and Fall* that Gibbon pronounced directly on the battle of the books. He is describing the fall of Egypt to the Saracens, and he considers the destruction of the famous Alexandrian Library. Although he is dubious of both the fact and its consequences, he wonders for a moment what its loss would have entailed. If it were only the destruction of the "ponderous" mass of theological controversy, a philosopher, he thinks, might smile and find it to the ultimate benefit of mankind. As for its classical contents, it seems to Gibbon that the survival of the ancient works is more surprising than their destruction. True, the three great historians of Rome have come down to us imperfectly, and some worthy poetry has been lost forever, "yet we should gratefully remember that the mischances of time and accident have spared the classic works to which the suffrage of antiquity had adjudged the first place of genius and glory." A footnote here recalls Quintilian's authoritative list of classics. "Nor can it fairly be presumed that any important truth, any useful discovery in art or nature, has been snatched away from the curiosity of modern ages." Here another footnote reminds us of William Wotton, who had argued "with solid sense against the lively fancies of Sir William Temple."[45]

To be fair, neither Wotton nor the battle of the books is very conspicuous in Gibbon's work, and it looks as though he may have come upon them only after his mind had already been formed, after he had confronted some of the same issues in the French *querelle*. Nevertheless, it is clear from scattered references in the *Decline and Fall* that Gibbon associated himself generally with those moderate defenders of modernity like Wotton and Bentley, whose philology and criticism he specifically admired—rather than with the French radicals like Perrault, La Motte, and Terrasson, whose learning was so obviously superficial—and that it was they who helped him to define and reinforce his position.[46] Like Wotton, he believed confidently in the achievement of modern science and technology, though he knew much less about it; he wanted also to give antiquity its due, to recognize its superiority in certain matters like the Greek language, which was "doubtless the most perfect that has ever been contrived by the art of man,"[47] and to see it as the stock on which modern learning and civilization had built and still could grow. Gibbon had much respect for Arabic learning, but he thought that the Moslems had deprived themselves "of the principal benefits of a familiar discourse with Greece and Rome, the knowledge of antiquity, the purity of taste, and the freedom of thought."[48]

Like Wotton therefore and some of the other eighteenth-century moderns, Gibbon was half an ancient. Civilization was for him inconceivable without Homer, Plutarch, and Livy. "Our education in the Greek and Latin schools," he was willing to concede, "may have fixed in our minds a standard of exclusive taste, and I am not forward to condemn the literature and judgment of nations of whose language I am ignorant." (In this he would not make Temple's mistake.) "Yet I *know* that the classics have much to teach, and I *believe* that the Orientals [and, he might have added, the moderns] have much to learn; the temperate dignity of style, the graceful proportions of art, the forms of visible and intellectual beauty, a just delineation of character and passion, the rhetoric of narrative and argument, the regular fabric of epic and dramatic poetry." The aesthetic and moral standards of ancient Greece and Rome remained for him, like human nature itself, universal and timeless in their character and authority. "Shakespeare had never read the poems of Gregory Nazianzen, he was ignorant of the Greek language; but his mother-tongue, the language of nature, is the same in Cappodicia and in Britain."[49] The great and celebrated Church of Santa Sophia in Constantinople, to choose but one example, disappointed Gibbon by its "irregular prospect of half domes and shelving roofs," as, inevitably, did the whole of Western Gothic architecture.[50] On the other hand, he could not imagine a more perfect example of moral and political virtue than Cicero, the hero of more than one eighteenth-century modern and a model for all time.[51]

Did Gibbon believe, then, in progress? Undoubtedly, though with all those familiar qualifications of the eighteenth-century modern who was at heart still half an ancient. In some matters he did not hesitate, like mathematics, for example, where there was always advance;[52] or the sciences and technology, where retreat was unlikely. But progress was less clear in literature and the arts, where classical models and standards remained supreme, however hopefully Gibbon might look to modern emulation. And in politics and life there was even more ambiguity. Gibbon was pleased to write his history in "a free and civilized country, in an age of science and philosophy." He believed that the modern English government with its constitutional safeguards for liberty was a triumph of human ingenuity unlikely to be improved.[53] Yet the *Decline and Fall* opens by recalling as the "happiest period in history" the imperial age from Domitian to Commodus.[54] Gibbon writes frequently of the many "revolutions" that have transformed the past, but he usually retains something of the etymological sense of the word; i.e., a return to a state of affairs that once had been. There is, therefore, a bit of the classical cyclical view still in Gibbon's notion that all nations pass through a "slow but sure progression . . . from barbarism to industry, arts, luxury, and effeminacy," ancients and moderns alike.[55] Moreover, if there was a touch of *ancienneté* to his view of past progress, there was even more to his doubts about future progress. As with Voltaire and David Hume, Gibbon was compelled to believe that the age of reason ("this enlightened age") was a kind of stopping point for history.[56] Since human nature was always the same (a notion that had come to be shared by both the ancients and the moderns), there was inevitably a certain sameness about human history and a conviction, finally, that there was little real difference, alas, between civilized and savage man.[57] "The silent and irreversible" progress that Gibbon sometimes talked about was a progress toward the reason of the reasonable man—no new invention of the eighteenth century, though epitomized certainly in the philosophes and in Gibbon himself. Perfectibility, at any rate, was no part of Gibbon's expectation.

Gibbon's very choice of subject reflects his ambivalence. He had chosen to write of decline, of the triumph of barbarism and religion and the downfall of civilization, but his work ends with renewal. His view of the Renaissance, of the revival of antiquity, is a characteristic blend of ancient and modern sensibility. He dismisses the Middle Ages as all ignorance and superstition. Only after many dark centuries was the eloquence and reason of ancient Greece and Rome reintroduced into the West. "Such an intercourse," Gibbon reminds us, "must tend to refine the taste, and to elevate the genius of the moderns."[58] Yet it did not happen all at once: "the spirit of imitation is of a servile cast, and the first disciples of the Greeks and Romans were a colony of strangers in the midst of their age and country."[59] For a long time, men were content to become mere wards of Aristotle or repeat the thoughts and words of the Augustans, even to look at nature simply through the eyes of Pliny or Theophrastus. It would be hard, Gibbon thought, to find in that period a single real discovery of science or a work of invention or eloquence worth recalling. "But as soon as it had been deeply saturated with the celestial dew, the soil was quickened into vegetation and life; the modern idioms were refined; the classics of Greece and Rome inspired a pure taste and a generous emulation; and in Italy, as afterwards in France and England, the pleasing reign of poetry and fiction was succeeded by the light of speculative and experimental philosophy." The Enlightenment, Gibbon's age, was thus both the true heir to antiquity and at the same time the beginning of modern superiority. "In the education of a people," Gibbon concludes, "as that of an individual, memory must be exercised, before the powers of reason and fancy can be expanded; nor may the artist hope to equal or surpass, till he has learned to imitate the work of his predecessors."[60] Progress was thus possible in art as well as life, though the terms remained largely set by the timeless values of antiquity. Nor did Gibbon believe that the gains, once made, were any longer reversible. In a long essay that he appended to the first half of his history, "Observations on the Fall of the Empire in the West"—which continues to sound like William Wotton—he argued that the new barbarians could only succeed in overrunning the new Augustans by first taking up the modern achievements of the West: "Before they can conquer they must cease to be barbarians."[61]

To imitate one's predecessors was thus the first and necessary preliminary to improvement. One had first to go backward in order to go forward. This had been Wotton's plea in the battle of the books, and now it was Gibbon's in the *Decline and Fall*. In the same way, Gibbon had followed Wotton in preaching the virtues of erudition as well as eloquence. It is tempting, therefore, to ascribe a direct influence to Wotton, especially when one discovers that he also anticipated Gibbon by actually writing a history that covers much of the same ground as the first volume of the *Decline and Fall*, where it is cited half a dozen times.[62] *The History of Rome from the Death of Antoninus Pius to the Death of Alexander Severus* (1701) is a full narrative with the unusual distinction of adding an elaborate scholarly commentary in the form of a generous set of notes at the end of the work—just where Gibbon had originally intended his.[63] Inscriptions, coins, and monumental remains are all dexterously employed there to elucidate the obscure points in the story that were blurred by the inadequate and problematical literary sources. In its way, it is an exemplary and original performance, but I do not think it did much to shape Gibbon's work. It was too modest in its literary pretensions, too "unphilosophical" in its outlook.[64] Gibbon no doubt learned something from it, but it is more interesting, I believe, as an anticipation of how Gibbon was trying to solve the same kind of problem on a more ambitious scale. Above all, it is further evidence of the framework of thought within which Gibbon worked, of the continuing existence of the problems and opportunities that the quarrel between the ancients and the moderns raised for the theory and practice of history. From that perspective, it looks as though the *Decline and Fall* was the true culmination of the quarrel, the most ambitious attempt ever made to sum up the whole course of the long argument and to resolve its many issues.

Yet Gibbon's great work was also the last of its kind, for while it had many readers, it had no real successors. Erudition was advancing according to the prescriptions of the moderns, and it was becoming impossible, even with a generous private income and absolute dedication, to master the books and to bring them together in one's own library.[65] Furthermore, the new historical erudition was reaching out ever more insistently beyond the books to the documents themselves, and the German reviewer of Gibbon is already critical of his old-fashioned scholarship.[66] Perhaps more profoundly, there was at last a revolutionary new spirit abroad dissolving that final bulwark of both ancients and moderns, the belief in the timelessness and universality of human nature and value—a new relativity or historicism that would have astonished Gibbon. To all these things Gibbon had little to contribute and much to fear. His modernity, I think, like that of the Enlightenment in general, was still too tied up with his *ancienneté,* too much a part of the battle of the books, to be altogether familiar to us. But that, perhaps, is part of his continuing appeal.

CHAPTER 8

Eighteenth-Century Historicism
and the First Gothic Revival

Let us begin with two scenes set in the historical imagination of the later eighteenth century. In the first, which is of course very familiar, Edward Gibbon sits in the ruins of the Capitol and watches with regret as the barefooted friars of St. Francis tread on the ruins of empire. In the second, perhaps less well known, Gibbon's friend Thomas Warton sits in the Gothic ante-chapel of New College Oxford and looks with pleasure at the new stained glass windows of Sir Joshua Reynolds, come to replace the medieval panels that once illuminated the spot. A comparison of these two scenes may help to get at the rather awkward and elusive problem, the extent and limits of historical thinking in the period, of what I shall try to define later as historicism.

Gibbon, it will be remembered, describes his melancholy scene in the last chapter of the *Decline and Fall*, and again in his autobiography: "It was at Rome, on the 18th of October, 1764, as I sat musing amidst the ruins of the Capitol, while the barefooted fryars were singing vespers in the Temple of Jupiter, that the idea of writing the decline and fall of the city first started to my mind." By the time Gibbon wrote these words in 1790, the "melancholy" reaction to classical ruins was an old and familiar story, and Gibbon himself concludes the *Decline and Fall* by recalling the similar sentiments of the Italian humanist Poggio, three centuries before.[1] He may also have been thinking of John Dyer's popular poem on "The Ruins of Rome" (1740), as he was surely remembering Conyers Middleton on the same subject, though he does not say so here. Middleton had written a very successful life of Cicero (1741) in which he describes the great man's villa and continues: "But there cannot be a better proof of the delightfulness of the place, than that it is now possessed by a Convent of Monks, and called the Villa of St. Dominic. Strange revolution! to see Cicero's portico's converted to Monkish cloisters! the seat of the most refined reason, wit and learning, to a nursery of superstition, bigotry and enthusiasm! What a pleasure it must give to these Dominican Inquisitors, to trample on the ruins of a man whose writings, by spreading the light of reason and liberty thro' the world have been one great instrument of obstructing their unwearied pains to enslave it."[2] Middleton, Gibbon believed, was a man "endowed with penetration and learning," and he subscribed to many of the same sentiments, not least to that "religious scepticism and cultural nostalgia" which more than one writer has seen as the key to the many "revolutions" of the *Decline and Fall.* The fact that Gibbon later rewrote his account of how he first conceived his subject—changing his original version which read, "musing in the church of the Zoccolanti" to musing in the Capitol—has provoked suspicion. Did it really happen that way in 1764 when, after a sleepless night, Gibbon remembered climbing to the top of the forum and noting just where Romulus stood and Cicero spoke and Caesar fell? Or was it only the way Gibbon wanted his readers to think it had happened when, some twenty-five years later, he set out to explain and justify his life work?

Perhaps it does not really matter. If art was then supposed to imitate life, then sometimes surely life must have imitated art. In either case, the scene provides a perfect summary depiction of Gibbon's stance toward his subject, and it should have happened that way even if it did not. Many others had noticed the same contrast between Rome risen and fallen, between classical and Christian culture, but no one yet had chosen to describe the whole course of that long descent—the triumph, as Gibbon says, of barbarism and religion. And it was indeed a somewhat perverse thing to do for one whose heart was set in the silver age of the Antonines, or better yet, in the golden age of the Hanoverians. What was it, then, that led Gibbon to think of dwelling for so many years in that "long period of distress and anarchy, in which empire and arts and riches migrated from the banks of the Tiber?" No doubt the clue lies in that same self-satisfied, commonplace eighteenth-century point of view; for if Gibbon's subject was the Middle Ages, his perspective was resolutely contemporary—that is to say, neoclassical—and his long story has a happy beginning and a happy end.

The fact is that Gibbon accepted without hesitation the values of his own time, both moral and aesthetic, and he saw them as universally applicable to past and present. Throughout the six quarto volumes of his immense work, he never fails to extol all those who had measured up, from Cicero to Middleton, or condemn the many others who had so often faltered. Gibbon recognized, even relished, the vast diversity of customs and manners, laws and institutions, that set off most of his subjects from polite and civilized modern Europe. He had always been fascinated with the exotic, and his history encompasses Germanic and Scandinavian tribes, Arabs, Turks and Tartars, Byzantines, and even Chinese, not to mention Gothic Europeans—a vast panoply of foreign cultures. But Gibbon looks down on each with the bemused "philosophical" eye of someone quite outside the follies of history and impervious to its errors. The lessons of history, like Gibbon's famous irony, derived entirely from this Olympian view.

In short, Gibbon lacked one element, at least, of the modern historical consciousness—that which we may call, for want of a better term, historicism. That this was a limitation we may be sure, for whatever other value we may want to assign to his history, it no longer seems of much use as an account of any of those distant cultures. Lack of sympathy, it is usually said, kept Gibbon from any real understanding of the many peoples whose manners and customs he found barbarous. The history of the Middle Ages could only be written properly when its values began to make sense to a later generation. A nostalgia for Cicero did not help Gibbon, or anyone else in the eighteenth century, to understand the barefooted friars who succeeded the ancients.

Now modern historicism seems to develop in two stages. First there is the recognition, which Gibbon certainly understood, that all human activities are historical: that is to say, conditioned by time and place. Then there is a further stage, which Gibbon did not know, when it is alleged that all human values and even human nature itself are also conditioned by the circumstances of history. In the first stage it is apparently possible to view the variety of the past and its dissimilarity from the present and yet continue to maintain the universality and constancy of human nature and values.[3] In the second stage, however, all is flux; the historian himself is seen to be a part of the historical process and a result of history, and a fixed vantage point is no longer thought to be possible or desirable. We have arrived at the notion of cultural relativism. This stage Gibbon never reached, nor does it appear that anyone else did either in the eighteenth century—not even Vico or Herder, the best candidates in that period, and certainly not anyone in England.[4]

We may take as an example of this reluctance, a little essay by Jonathan Richardson the younger, published in 1776, the same year that Gibbon's *Decline and Fall* began to appear. Richardson reflects in it on the vast diversity of human manners and customs and seems about to draw some startling conclusions. Men have agreed so little, he writes, about religion, politics, fashions—even about such fundamental matters as the difference between right and wrong—"that it would almost incline us to doubt whether these have any fixed point in the nature of things, and do not almost depend on accidental convenience, and the various circumstances of time and place." Richardson is *almost* prepared for a full-fledged historical relativism. "For what critiera can we have? and who shall be the judge?"[5] For a moment, reason itself—the universal, reassuring, self-evident reason of the eighteenth century—looked dangerously uncertain, perhaps nothing more than local custom, just the familiar custom, Richardson says, that we are used to. But characteristically, Richardson draws back from the brink, much as Carl Becker assures us, did all his greater contemporaries, and carries us through the rest of his miscellaneous reflections by assuming once again a universal human nature subject to the same pride and prejudice and the same ultimate values that are to be found at all times and places.[6]

Perhaps the best test case of this eighteenth-century ambivalence, however, is Thomas Warton and his circle. Warton and his friends are a better test than Gibbon or Richardson because they represent a historical viewpoint that was distinctly more enthusiastic about the Middle Ages and more open to the possibility of a nonclassical perspective. Warton and his older brother, Joseph, helped to lead the "Gothic revival," and they have usually been placed among the "pre-Romantics" and thought to anticipate the nineteenth century.[7] If we would like to know how far eighteenth-century historicism extended, it is probably to the Wartons and their friends (Gray, Hurd, Lowth, Percy, and the rest) that we should go. It used to be thought that the two brothers were taught to look sympathetically upon the Gothic Middle Ages by their father, who took them on walking tours to visit old castles and churches and who introduced them to the poetry of Spenser and Milton. There is still something to this, although it now looks rather as thought the two adolescent boys caught something in the air in the 1740s and made their own discovery of the appeal of Gothic poetry, even to rewriting and publishing their father's works after his early death.[8] Perhaps it was the very triumph just then of the neoclassical style in Alexander Pope's poetry and the Earl of Burlington's architecture that finally interrupted that long continuity of the Gothic tradition in England and that inadvertently and paradoxically raised a nostalgia for the culture of the later Middle Ages. If so, it would be curiously reminiscent of that other great breach of cultural continuity that occurred when Gothic style itself arose at the end of the medieval period and cut off the classical connection that had held on tenuously for so many centuries and so (perhaps) helped to set the stage for the humanist revival of antiquity.[9]

Whatever it was, the two young brothers wrote and published a number of pieces in these early years that introduced some new "romantic" themes into English poetry and helped to break the spell that Pope and his disciples had cast. Perhaps as early as 1740, Joseph Warton wrote *The Enthusiast, or the Lover of Nature*, in which the palaces and gardens at Stowe and Versailles are contrasted unfavorably with an unadorned nature; the polished manners and pomp of modern life with a pristine simplicity; and in which the "ruin'd tops of Gothic battlements" help pleasantly to set the scene. In his "Ode to Fancy" (1746), we view again with pleasure the "Gothic churches, vaults, and tombs" and the "mould'ring tow'rs" of an ancient abbey; there are echoes of Spenser, Milton, and Shakespeare; and imagination is exalted over reason.[10] The "Ode to Fancy" appeared in a collection of poems by all three Wartons with a preface by Joseph that boldly declares for the literature of fancy over the prevailing didactic and moralizing mode and that pleads for a "return" to a former path.[11] Ten years later, the young poet completed his polemic and made his reputation with the first volume of his *Essay on the Genius and Writings of Pope*.

Yet curiously, even in the *Essay*, Joseph is decidedly ambivalent toward his subject. To some extent this may have been due to constraints put upon him by his publisher, Robert Dodsley,[12] but it was more likely due to a genuine neoclassical sympathy and a lingering affection for Pope. Even among the early poems that Warton admired and printed, there is one—"To a Gentleman upon his Travels thro' Italy"—that laments the destruction of classical culture by the barbarous Goths and superstitious monks and might well have been written by the young Gibbon.[13] In a youthful essay written for the *World* (1753), Warton declared his neoclassical taste in the arts and architecture, decrying the new barbarism that sought to mix "Gothic whimsies" with a pure and simple Greek style. And in a pair of essays written in the next year for the *Adventurer*, he argued for the general superiority of the ancients over the moderns, excepting only some minor species of poetry.[14] He soon stopped writing his own poetry and turned instead to editing and translating Virgil in the company of some of Pope's most ardent followers.[15] In the *Essay on Pope*, Warton continued to rank the poet beneath the best of the moderns as lacking in imagination and unable to attain to either the sublime or the pathetic. Yet he did not fail to mete out some praise for what he thought Pope had achieved and to single out some beauties as well as some blemishes in the poems. Even more to the point, he insisted that generally speaking, the arts and literature had reached their acme at the beginning of the eighteenth century, one of those golden periods like Alexandrian Greece and Augustan Rome that had occasionally distinguished the past. Dryden's poetry and Boileau's criticism remained for him unsurpassed.[16] Perhaps it is not surprising that Samuel Johnson, who prized Pope a good deal more than Warton and Gothic a good deal less, could review the *Essay* and give it grudging approval.[17]

With the passage of time and a post at Winchester College, Joseph Warton became increasingly orthodox in his opinions. Eventually, he returned to Pope, this time to edit his works and to subscribe forthrightly to many of his views. Now he was prepared to dissent even from

Edward Young—a youthful hero whose *Conjectures on Original Composi-*
tion had been another early effort to get out from under the constraints
of Augustan neoclassicism—by approving Pope's famous couplet:

> Learn hence for ancient rules a just esteem,
> To copy nature is to copy them.[18]

Had there ever been a more succinct expression of that special conjunction of the classical and the universal which held the eighteenth century
in thrall? But the closer one looks at Warton, the less "romantic" he
appears to be. When the second volume of the *Essay* finally appeared,
after a long delay, a writer in the *Gentleman's Magazine* thought that Pope
himself would have been satisfied with it.[19] Warton spent his declining
years in happy communion with the members of Johnson's club, among
them Gibbon and Joshua Reynolds, projecting a history *not* of the Middle Ages but of the revival of classical learning.[20]

With Thomas Warton, who was always close to his brother, this ambivalence was more persistent and probably more profound. He had
contributed to the *Odes on Various Subjects* of 1746; the next year, at the
age of nineteen, he published an important poem of his own, "The
Pleasures of Melancholy," a mood piece that anticipates the "graveyard"
poetry soon to become fashionable.[21] Here again, we find Spenser
placed above Pope; imagination above reason and the rules; nature wild
and unadorned; a ruined abbey and Gothic vaults. Thomas went on to
Oxford, where he studied and taught for the rest of his life. In some
ways he became the typical Oxford don of the period, like the ones
remembered in Gibbon's autobiography, not much burdened by teaching and free to celebrate his long vacations with antiquarian tours of the
countryside.[22] He kept up his poetry sufficiently to become the Oxford
Professor as well as poet laureate, but he won his first real fame in 1754
with his *Observations on the Faerie Queene.*

Warton brought to his subject a fresh vision. He saw that the Elizabethan Spenser could only be understood and appreciated by restoring
his original cultural context. "In reading the work of an author who
lived in a remote age, it is necessary that we should look back upon the
customs and manners which prevailed in his age; that we should place
ourselves in his situation, and circumstances; that so we may be the
better enabled to judge and discuss how his turn of thinking, and manner of composing were bias'd, influenc'd, and, as it were, tinctur'd, by
very familiar and reigning appearances, which are utterly different from
those with which we are at present surrounded." "For this purpose," he
wrote later, "I have considered the customs and genius of his age, I have
searched contemporary writers and examined the books in which the

peculiarities of his style, taste, and composition are found."[23] Samuel Johnson at once appreciated Warton's accomplishment: "The reason why the authors which are yet read of the sixteenth century are so little understood is that they are read alone; and no help is borrowed from those who lived with them or before them."[24]

Now it is true that at least one of Warton's predecessors, John Hughes, had seen that the *Faerie Queene* could not be judged by classical standards: "To compare it with the Models of Antiquity, wou'd be like drawing a Parallel between the Roman and the Gothick Architecture." Unfortunately, Hughes did not have the historical equipment to find out much about what Spenser was really doing or enough sympathy with his purpose to get out of his own neoclassical prejudices.[25] A much better model for Warton was Lewis Theobald, who had quarreled with Pope's edition of Shakespeare and supplied a new version of his own, showing exactly how useful a knowledge of contemporary Elizabethan language and literature could be in explicating an old poet. (Theobald was, incidentally, borrowing *his* method from classical philology, where it had been applied for centuries to elucidate the classical poets; his particular model was Richard Bentley.)[26] For this offense Pope put Theobald (along with Bentley) in the *Dunciad*. Warton however defends him vigorously: "If Shakespeare is worth reading, he is worth explaining; and the researches used for so valuable and elegant a purpose, merit the thanks and candour, not the satire of prejudice and ignorance."[27]

Still, if it was easy to see that neither Shakespeare nor Spenser was writing according to classical rules, it was another thing to discover just what they *were* doing; and it was still another thing to come to appreciate, perhaps even to prefer, an alternative to neoclassicism. Warton saw that Spenser had tried to write not like Homer or Virgil but like the modern Ariosto, and that the medieval romances were his chief source and inspiration. "It is absurd," he continued, "to think of judging either Ariosto or Spenser by precepts which they did not attend to. We who live in the days of writing by rule, are apt to try every composition by those laws which we have been taught to think the sole criteria of excellence." We must take Spenser as we find him, "destitute," it is true, "of that arrangement and economy which epic severity requires" but compensating with something else, "something which engages the affections, the feelings of the heart, rather than the cold approbation of the head." "In reading Spenser," Warton concludes, with characteristic ambivalence, "if the critic is not satisfied, yet the reader is transported."[28]

No doubt this was unorthodox enough, a reversal certainly of the usual emphasis on reason. But Warton was not ready to take the next step. He was, no more than his brother, willing to abandon classical standards for another alternative; apparently, he merely wished to rejuvenate what he thought was a flagging neoclassical imagination. The *Observations* opens thus: "When the works of Homer and Aristotle began to be restored and studied in Italy, when the genuine and uncorrupted sources of antient wisdom were opened, and every species of literature at last emerged from the depths of Gothic ignorance and barbarity; it might have been expected, that instead of the romantic manner of poetical composition . . . a new and more legitimate taste of writing would have succeeded." This did not happen at once, for there was a cultural lag that explains for Warton why Ariosto continued to prefer "the ridiculous and incoherent excursions of Boiardo to the propriety and uniformity of the Grecian and Roman models," and why Spenser remained still a "romantic poet."[29] Warton found much to admire in the Elizabethans, but he never suggested that they were superior to the best of the ancients. Indeed, the *Observations* contains so many pages pointing out Spenser's shortcomings that the author felt he must apologize. As Warton put it later about himself, he "so far conformed to the reigning notions of modern criticism as . . . to recommend classical propriety," even while he hoped that the beauties of the "dark ages" might also be made to contribute to reinvigorating the powers of imagination and fancy.[30]

In 1762, Warton brought out a second edition of the *Observations* in which he developed his ideas further. One long interpolation drew immediate attention. In glossing a line of Spenser's, where the poet had referred to "Doric" columns, Warton was led to write a whole disquisition tracing "the beginning and progressive state of architecture in England" from the early Middle Ages to Spenser's time. Though brief, it was a tour de force, for nothing quite like it had ever been attempted before.[31] In a few concise pages Warton set out, with dates and examples, the basic stages through which medieval architectural style had passed in England. He begins with what we should now call Romanesque but which he calls Saxon and proceeds through early English (or "Saracenic," a term that Warton borrowed from Christopher Wren)[32] to "true or absolute" Gothic, ornamental and then florid Gothic, and finally the hybrid Elizabethan variety, a composite of Gothic with the new taste for the classical. Warton saw the difficulty of differentiating these "gradations" of style, which required "ocular demonstration, and a conversation on the spot, to be clearly proved and illustrated."[33] But he was confident that he could not only describe the basic characteristics of each—the changes that had occurred in columns, arches, vaulting, and windows—but that he could date them and relate them to contemporary literature. He believed that he could reconstruct the stages in the making of a particular building by the successive styles that appeared there. Even the Gothicist Horace Walpole was deeply impressed by Warton's skill.

"How can you, Sir, approve such hasty superficial writings as mine," he wrote, upon receiving a copy of the *Observations,* "you who in the same pursuits are so much more correct, and have gone so much deeper? . . . Compare your accounts of Gothic architecture with mine; I have scarce skimmed the subject; you have ascertained all its periods."[34]

Warton's confidence in these matters was the result of a long intimacy with the buildings themselves, combined with a close study of the documents. The notebooks that he kept on his travels show him every year in his summer holidays observing carefully the surviving castles, churches, and abbeys of the later Middle Ages, copying down their characteristic features and occasionally sketching them. He was, apparently, preparing a more ambitious work to be called "Observations Critical and Historical on Churches, Monasteries, Castles and other Monuments of Antiquity in Various Counties of England and Wales."[35] His model was the antiquarian "itinerary," an old genre introduced into England by John Leland and known to Warton through Thomas Hearne's recent edition; but where Warton's predecessors were pretty well indiscriminate in their interest in everything old, Warton confined himself largely to the later Middle Ages.[36] Warton never seems to have gotten much north of Lincoln Cathedral, but he traveled everywhere else in the south and west, often repeating his visits.[37] Between times, he read in the chronicles and ecclesiastical records, trying to discover what he could about the foundations and alterations of all the early buildings. Once, at least, he began to recast his notes for publication and formally promised a larger work, but when he died in 1791, it was only the digression that remained. Yet even that was several times thought worthy of republication and helped to usher in the full-fledged Gothic revival of the nineteenth century.[38]

The notebooks show that Warton's method for studying architecture, like his concern for literature, was borrowed ultimately from the study of the classics. Like Gibbon, and indeed like everyone else with a formal education, Warton had been brought up with the language and literature of ancient Greece and Rome, and there are many marks of their influence throughout his manuscripts. (There are, for example, many translations and imitations, including an elegant version of Cicero's defense of poetry, the *Pro archia.*)[39] Gibbon, too, had started out thinking of a literary career and as a youth had tried his hand at textual criticism and emendation, but Warton became a professional. At Oxford he was elected professor of poetry, a job that his father had held before him, and for ten years (1757–67) he lectured on the Greek poets.[40] During this time he also wrote several textbooks, including two selections of metrical inscriptions, one in Latin (1758), the other in Greek (1766); projected a translation of Apollonius Rhodius; and actually completed a critical edition of his favorite poet, Theocritus. Warton found much help for the latter among the papers of the classical philologist James St. Amand in the Bodleian Library.[41] His friend William Warburton introduced him to the best Greek scholar of his generation, the able if irascible Jonathan Toup (the Richard Bentley of his generation, according to one correspondent),[42] who furnished him with copious animadversions. Theocritus appeared belatedly in 1770 with one of Warton's early lectures prefixed, "De poeti Graecorum bucolica." It was a creditable effort at classical philology and won him sufficient contemporary esteem.[43]

It appears that Warton owed much of his inspiration as a critic and historian to this continuous absorption in classical letters. It was, of course, the Renaissance humanists and their scholarly successors who had first discovered how to retrieve and appreciate the lost languages and literature of an earlier time and so invented modern criticism and historiography; Warton and his friends had no doubt that this was a great and beneficent "revolution." His brother Joseph and his friend Anthony Collins had both set out to tell the story of the "restoration of letters"[44] but it was Thomas who actually succeeded in recounting it, for England anyway—first in his *Life of Sir Thomas Pope* (1772) and then more elaborately in his *History of English Poetry* (1774). The revival of antiquity, he thought, should more properly be called "the restoration of good sense and useful knowledge." It had brought true taste and propriety, rectitude of thinking and judging; it had civilized mankind and reformed religion.[45] As a scholar, therefore, Warton felt himself to be working within a long tradition that reached back beyond Erasmus to the Italian humanists and that had continued without interruption to his own time. Gibbon felt much the same when he wrote his own history of the revival in the last volume of the *Decline and Fall*. Both men looked back upon the oscillations of Western culture from pretty much the same vantage point, though Warton was harder on the Goths, Gibbon on the monks, as the principal agents of decline.

Among the many lessons that Warton learned from his classical studies was, therefore, something about the preliminary skills that were required to revive the past—philology, textual criticism, lexicography, diplomatics, and so on—as well as the formal means of communicating that learning: the commentary, footnote, index, and appendix. But if the classicists had insisted on confining themselves to the ancient Greek and Latin writers, we have seen how there had early been some moderns willing to extend their methods to more recent cultures, notably in England to the Anglo-Saxons, whenever politics and religion whetted interest. Warton knew the work of George Hickes and his circle; he had read the *Thesaurus* of 1705, which was the culmination of the work of a century and a monument to recent Oxford scholarship.[46] In one sense, Warton merely set out to do for the later Middle Ages what had been accomplished already for the earlier period—and what had been done even better for antiquity—that is, recover another complete culture: its customs, institutions, art, and literature. Like Richard Hurd, who admired his work and became a friend, Warton saw a connection between feudalism, chivalry and romance, and the need to reintegrate them into an intelligible whole that could be understood in its own terms.[47] He had begun by explicating Spenser, the ripe fruit of that lost civilization, as a classicist might choose Virgil;[48] and he saw that to understand the poet, no aspect of his culture was irrelevant—not the language, not the customs, not the architecture of the period, all of which had usually been ignored and dismissed as barbarous.[49]

Warton learned another thing from the classicists and equally important: an appreciation of style and a notion of development. Cicero and Quintilian had long before pointed the way in reviewing classical letters, and the Renaissance critics resumed their task, extending it (in the work of Vasari and his followers) to the fine arts and architecture.[50] Here again it was Warton's achievement to transfer to the later Middle Ages a point of view that had been applied to ancient literature and modern art; to apply to Gothic style the same kind of criticism and the same notion of development that had been worked out for the classics, with the Elizabethans taking the role that had been originally played by the Augustans. It was no use, however, pretending that medieval writers and artists had composed according to classical rules. As Hurd put it in his *Letters on Chivalry and Romance,* "When an architect examines a Gothic structure by Grecian rules, he finds nothing but deformity. But the Gothic architecture had its own rules, by which when it comes to be examined, it is seen to have its merits as well as the Grecian."[51] "We must not," Warton added later, "try the modes and notions of other ages, even if they have arrived to the same degree of refinement, by those of our own."[52] Warton knew a lot more about the nature and merits of Gothic culture than Hurd and he shared with his friend the notion that it must be tried by its own nonclassical standards; the two critics were thus taking a bold step toward modern historicism. Yet, as we shall see, it looks as though neither man was quite prepared to escape altogether from the confines of the neoclassical perspective.[53]

Finally, Warton learned another valuable lesson from the classicists; he learned from them the importance of looking at the artifacts of the past as well as its literature and of seeing a relationship between the two. He discovered how to look at the monuments of the Middle Ages in much the same way that the humanists had looked at the ruins of ancient Rome, not only with melancholy and nostalgia but with the same practical purpose of using them to divine and illustrate the meaning of past history and poetry, as well as vice versa.[54] Warton had grown up among antiquaries as well as poets, and he learned from them (just as Gibbon was doing about the same time in Paris) something of that whole archaeological armory that had been accumulating over the centuries: the use of coins, inscriptions, charters, and monumental remains, as a way of recreating the past. A phrase in Spenser about Doric columns could lead therefore to a discussion of the reappearance of classical ornaments under Elizabeth; while a quotation from Chaucer or Piers Ploughman could help to illuminate a style in the development of medieval building practice.[55] In one remarkable passage, Warton shows how the seals of the English kings could be used to describe and date the very same sequence of changes in architecture that he could observe in the cathedrals and that was paralleled in contemporary literature.[56] To repeat: Warton's technique was all borrowed, but his originality lay in his attempt to apply the time-honored methods and insights of classical scholarship—that is to say, classical philology, criticism, and antiquities—to the very period that had always seemed most antithetical to the classical ideal, the Gothic Middle Ages. This attempt to apply a neoclassical technique to a nonclassical subject matter was undoubtedly one main source of Warton's ambivalence.

It is, at any rate, clear from a reading of his work that Warton never really did mean to free himself from the neoclassical perspective of his time. It is true that he saw that understanding the poetry of the past required that the critic place himself in the writer's situation and circumstance,[57] and this was an insight of immense significance in the development of modern historicism. And it is true that Warton, more than Hurd and perhaps any other Englishman of his time, understood how to do this and committed himself to the task.[58] But Warton did not intend thereby to give up his classical allegiance. He continued to find great value in the study of medieval poetry, historical and literary, for learning about the customs and usages of one's ancestors and as a continuing source of inspiration for the modern writer. But Warton's praise was always qualified by reservations. So, for example, he pleads that one should read widely in the literature of the Middle Ages, "however monstrous and unnatural these compositions may appear to this age of reason and refinement"; and one should come to terms with the despised culture of chivalry, even if it appeared only as "a barbarous sport, an extravagant amusement, of the dark ages." In short, chivalry and romance had once had a civilizing effect and could still afford some stimulus to the poetic imagination, but they were not to be confused with the superior models of antiquity.[59] Warton had a genuine appreciation for medieval culture and never failed to distinguish its beauties from its defects, its successes from its failures; but he never thought of Gothic style in the arts or literature as an *alternative* to classical culture, merely as one means of augmenting and reinvigorating it.[60]

Already in the *Observations,* Warton had attempted a brief retrospect of English poetry up to the age of Spenser.[61] By 1762 he was planning a full-fledged history of English poetry, a project that had first been proposed by Pope and Thomas Gray and that had long been on his mind. "You have," Hurd had written to him on receiving a copy of the *Observations,* "taken the only way to penetrate the mysteries of this poet, I mean by investigating the manners and fictions of Chivalry and Romance." Now, he praised Warton's new plan: "It is true, a work of this sort requires the Antiquarian, as well as the Critic. But you are both."[62] For the rest of his life, Warton labored over this vast undertaking, trying to combine the historiographical skills of the philologist and antiquary with the sympathetic insight of the critic in order to tell the whole story of English literature from the Middle Ages to modern times, and to tell it well. In its double ambition it was undoubtedly a formidable project.

Though others had doubts, Warton liked to think of himself as living in a period when "the curiosity of the antiquarian is connected with taste and genius, and his researches tend to display the progress of human manners, and to illustrate the history of society."[63] His project was not unworthy of Gibbon, who shared many of the same sentiments. Both men hoped to find an appropriate form in which to cast their medieval researches, a form that would combine the precision and detail of the scholar (including all the paraphernalia of modern scholarship) with the style and polish of the man of letters. But this was not easy to do at a time when the wits had turned all their mockery against the pedantry of learning and when the two activities remained largely separate.[64] Both Gibbon and Warton appreciated the possibilities of scholarship while lamenting its tendency to dullness and pedantry. Gibbon defended learning in his first published work, the *Essay on Literature* (1761), against frivolous criticism, but in his footnotes to the *Decline and Fall* he was never at a loss to detect its excesses. Warton poked occasional fun at the antiquaries, but he never missed a chance to commend and employ them in his *History of English Literature.*[65] If, in the end, Gibbon was able to marry the two modes of learning and polish more successfully than Warton,[66] it was probably because he had a venerable tradition of historical narrative handy on which to peg his learning, as well as a unique prose style. It was more difficult, and certainly more original, for Warton to attempt to cast his design into a readable form.[67] But when the first volume of his work appeared, it was widely though not universally believed that Warton had succeeded. "This elegant writer," applauded the *Gentleman's Magazine,* "already well known to the learned world as a poet, a critic, and an antiquary, opposite as these characters would seem to be, has here in some measure united them all."[68] "When antiquarians treat their subject thus," commented Warburton, "they become the most usefull as well as interesting Writers."[69] As the work grew in length, however, not everyone was so sure. William Mason wrote to Walpole in 1781, "I will thank you . . . for saving us the trouble of reading Mr. Gibbon and for doing your best to save us from reading T. Warton, but in this latter author's antiquarian mind we are already above knee deep and we must on as fast as we are able." He wished the work, grown now to three quartos, could be abridged, but added, "Nevertheless, let us do him justice, when he writes on a good subject few write better."[70]

The trouble, Walpole agreed, was with the subject; for all the growing fad for Gothic, the culture of the Middle Ages still held little general appeal. "Well, I have read Mr. Warton's book," Walpole wrote to Mason on receiving the first volume, "and shall I tell you what I think of it? I never saw so many interesting particulars crowded together with so little entertainment and vivacity. Mr. Warton has amassed all the parts of learning of four centuries, and all the impression that remains is, that those four ages had no parts or learning at all. There is not a gleam of poetry in their compositions between the skalds and Chaucer." It was too bad, he concluded, that Warton had developed "such affection for his materials, even to preferring the original Chaucer to the adaptations of Dryden and Pope!"[71] This was, of course, the same Walpole who had built Strawberry Hill, written the *Castle of Otranto*, and approved Percy's *Reliques of Ancient English Poetry*. His Gothic taste seems always to have been encapsulated in an invincible neoclassical sensibility. What then should we expect from the rest of Warton's readers?[72]

The *History of English Poetry* appeared in three volumes between 1774 and 1781.[73] It was meant to cover the period from the end of the eleventh century to the beginning of the eighteenth, but Warton never got past the Elizabethans to complete his work. Warton described his first volume in a letter to Thomas Gray in 1770: "I begin with a . . . general dissertation, as you intended, on the Northern Poetry, with its introduction into England by the Danes and Saxons and its duration. I then begin my History at the Conquest which I write chronologically in sections." He had decided a little reluctantly to exclude the drama because of its bulk. "One of my sections, a very large one, is entirely on Chaucer. . . . In the course of my Annals, I consider collaterally the Poetry of the different Nations as influencing our own. . . . Although I proceed chronologically, yet I often stand still to give some general view."[74] Long quotations give the work something of the deliberate character of an anthology, and there is copious bibliography and much digression.

Perhaps there is no need to describe the work any further here, except to say that it carries on in much the same spirit as the *Observations*. The author still wavers between the fixed vantage point of his own time, with its universal neoclassical values, and a bold but distinctly subordinate historicism that proposes the need to know and appreciate the past on its own terms. "We look back on the savage condition of our ancestors with the triumph of superiority, and are pleased to mark the steps by which we have been raised from rudeness to elegance."[75] The history of English poetry is the story of its rise from a rude and obscure beginning "to its perfection in a polished age," under the tutelage of classical Greece and Rome. The Renaissance was a "mighty deliverance, in which the moulding Gothic fabrics of false religion and false philosophy fell together."[76] So far we might be reading Gibbon (who, incidentally, welcomed Warton's book by saying that it illustrated "the taste of a poet and the minute diligence of an antiquarian"), except that here and there Warton allows an unexpected "gleam of light" to the earlier age.[77] To what extent, then, had the "revolution" that led to modern taste been gain? The moderns, he replied (echoing Hurd), had won "much good sense, good taste, and good criticism. But in the meantime, we have lost a set of manners, and a system of machinery, more suitable to the purposes of poetry, than those which have been adopted in their place. We have parted with extravagances that are above propriety, with incredibilities that are more acceptable than truth, and with fictions that are more valuable than reality."[78] "The faultless models of Greece and Rome" had cleared away the rubbish of medieval barbarism but only to produce, "that bane of invention, Imitation."[79] For Warton, it was the Elizabethan period, not the eighteenth century, that was the golden age of English poetry, just because it had balanced classical interest with Gothic inspiration.[80] Perhaps that was one reason that Warton never finished his work and brought it down to his own time.

And so, at last, we come to the scene in the antechapel of New College, Oxford, 1782. Some years earlier, the fellows of the college began to attend to the fourteenth-century glass of the founder, William of Wykeham, which had suffered much during the Reformation. From 1736 they hired several glass painters in succession to replace the old glass with new, in both the chapel and the antechapel. Still they were not satisfied, and so in 1777 they turned to Sir Joshua Reynolds for help, using the good offices of Joseph Warton as intermediary. Warton was very pleased: "I really cannot sufficiently applaud your Zeal and Attention in carrying on a Scheme so much for the Credit and ornament of our Sister College and which will make your Chappell one of the finest Rooms in Europe."[81] He agreed to approach his old friend and even pledged twenty pounds of his own to promote the new plan. Reynolds was equally delighted with the commission and hoped that Thomas War-

The West Window of the Chapel, New College, Oxford, c. 1780, designed by Sir Joshua
Reynolds and engraved by Richard Earlom. Yale Center for British Art, Paul Mellon
Collection.

Central panel of the Reynolds window. Sir Joshua's paintings were translated to glass by John Jervais.

ton would show him around the college when he arrived and inform him "what is to be done and everything about it."[82] (In the event, Warton seems to have gone off on one of his rambles when Reynolds arrived later that summer.) It was eventually agreed that the artist should supply one figure each for eight compartments, which would then be transferred to the windows by the glass painter John Jervais.

Once Reynolds visited the site, however, the scheme was transformed. It was now agreed that all the figures could be brought together in a single large design for the great west window. Jervais thought the stonework could be altered somewhat to create a space in the center for a focal picture that would produce a great effect. Reynolds was soon able to report that everyone approved the new design, including the architect, Sir William Chambers, and Thomas Warton. "My idea," Reynolds wrote to the warden, "is to paint in the great space in the centre, *Christ in the Manger,* on the principle that Correggio had done it, in the famous picture called the *Notte,* making all the light to proceed from Christ. . . . I shall fill . . . the seven divisions below with the figures of Faith, Hope and Charity, and the four Cardinal Virtues, which will make a proper rustic base, or foundation, for the support of the Christian religion." "Mr. Thomas Warton amongst the rest thinks the beauty of the window will be much improved, supposing the Pictures which are occupying the space out of the question." The change, Reynolds hastened to add, would by no means weaken the structure of the window. He hoped his picture would be "the first work of this species of Art that the world has yet exhibited."[83]

Reynolds had meant to supply only cartoons for Jervais to work from but decided instead to furnish paintings because, as he explained, he found it easier to paint than to draw, and Jervais would have a better original to copy. Between 1778 and 1781, he exhibited these panels at the Royal Academy with great success; the nativity scene alone fetched the highest price that had ever been paid for an English painting. Unfortunately, when they were translated to glass, it was generally agreed with Horace Walpole that their effect had been lost because of their opaque colors. Even Reynolds himself seems to have been disappointed.[84]

Not Warton. He described his own satisfaction in an eight page poem about the glass which begins with a descripton of himself.

> For long, enamour'd of a barbarous age,
> A faithless truant to the classic page;
> Long have I lov'd to catch the single chime
> Of minstrel-harps, and spell the fabling rime;
> To view the festive rites, the knightly play,
> That deck'd heroic Albion's elder day,

> To mark the mouldering halls of barons bold,
> And the rough castle, cast in giant mould;
> With Gothic manners, Gothic arts explore,
> And muse on the magnificence of yore.

Chiefly, he continues, he loved to roam the Gothic churches,

> Where Superstition with capricious hand
> In many a maze the wreathed windows plann'd.

Now, abruptly, he looks at Reynolds' windows, and when he sees their chaste design and just proportions, he grasps the true dimensions of Attic art:

> Sudden, the sombrous imagery is fled,
> Which late my visionary rapture fed.
> Thy powerful hand has broke the Gothic chain,
> And brought my bosom back to Truth again.
> To truth, by no peculiar taste confin'd,
> Whose universal pattern strikes mankind.

And so on, to the conclusion:

> No more the Sacred Window's round disgrace,
> But yield to Grecian groupes the shining space.

Reynolds had added new luster to religious light and managed to reconcile "the willing graces to the Gothic pile."[85]

In a word, it appeared that Warton was renouncing his Gothic allegiance for Reynolds' neoclassical point of view, for the view that Reynolds was just then offering publicly in his famous lectures, that timeless generalizing perspective that is the very reverse of historicism.[86] Did Warton really mean it? Had he in fact been moved in the New College antechapel in the way he describes? Reynolds himself doubted it, though he enjoyed the compliment: "I owe you great obligations for the sacrifice you have made, or pretended to have made, to modern art. I say pretended, for though you . . . have opposed the two different styles with the skill of a Connoisseur, yet I may be allowed to entertain some doubts of the sincerity of your conversion. I have no great confidence in the recantation of such an old offender."[87] Indeed, it was hard to see how a man who had committed his whole career to the resurrection of the forgotten poets of the Middle Ages, who had spent all his leisure seeking out the monuments of Gothic art and architecture, and who had so often proclaimed the value of the medieval imagination to the reinvigorating of modern culture could so cheerfully and easily seem to disavow it all.

Yet Warton was, I think, more consistent than first appears, even allowing for his obvious flattery of Reynolds.[88] We have seen how, throughout his work, he had always managed to contain his Gothic enthusiasm within a broadly neoclassical framework. If he never quite sneered at the Middle Ages, like Gibbon and Walpole, he nevertheless insisted always on the inadequacies of even its finest achievements. Chaucer and Salisbury Cathedral were each admirable in their own Gothic ways, but each suffered from irremediable faults from Warton's eighteenth-century perspective. Once, the two Wartons were discussing Shakespeare, that last flower of preclassical English culture. "I do not wonder," Joseph wrote, "at your fondness for the writings of Shakespeare. Among his various excellencies you seem to be particularly struck by the little *strokes of nature* which you say, scarce any writer but he and Homer have had either Feeling of Judgment enough." Apparently, Thomas had wondered whether the Greek tragedies could in that respect hold their own. He had allowed that "in the Disposition of their Dramas, in supporting their characters, in the Purity of their Diction and Sublimity and Propriety of their Sentiments," they were unsurpassed. "But—cryed you—tell me if Sophocles and Euripides have so many delicate Strokes of Nature as our English poet?"[89] It was not an easy balance to strike, and it is always possible to read Warton in two ways. But it seems clear enough that if the classics had their occasional deficiencies, they remained for him—in most things anyway—the supreme examples of their kind, needing only a bit of Gothic fancy to brighten them up for present use.

Is it possible to find a Gothicist in the period who was prepared to go further? I doubt it. If there was an exception it would likely have been among the antiquaries, who were always first in their nostalgia for the past and less sensible of the constraints of good taste. William Stukeley is an obvious candidate, an antiquary who kept the cause alive just when it appeared to be seriously slipping but whose extravagant theories about the ancient Druids caused much amusement then and now.[90] Stukeley was a founding member of the Society of Antiquaries, and he shared his colleagues' somewhat indiscriminate enthusiasm for everything old, whether Celtic or Roman, Saxon or Gothic—though to be sure, it was the Roman remains that always took precedence. Nevertheless, when Stukeley reached York on a June day in 1740, he was so ravished by the great church there that he preferred it, so he wrote in his diary, either to St. Peter's in modern Rome or to the Pantheon in antiquity. He particularly admired the stained glass windows, whose destruction elsewhere he frequently lamented, and he managed—like Walpole a little later—to collect some fragments from the local churches in Stamford and install them in his own house.[91] He was obviously moved by the grandeur and beauty of York Minster (and nearby Beverly), but his appreciation was certainly less informed than Warton's and probably more influenced by purely historical and associative considerations.[92]

Indeed, one may be permitted to wonder how profound Stukeley's Gothic taste was and whether he ever thought of it as an alternative to classicism. Even while at York, he particularly admired the new Assembly Rooms designed by the Earl of Burlington in the Palladian style, the very quintessence of neoclassicism, and in a previously published work he specifically welcomed many of the modern "improvements" that had come to Gothic Oxford.[93] He remained enormously impressed by the Roman roads and ruins, which he traced in his travels: "For arts military and civil that became a most wise government," he was convinced, "the Romans beyond compare exceeded all nations." "As well use, they studied eternity in all their works." When he reached Canterbury, he was a little disappointed; it was "much too high for its breadth, as all Gothic buildings were."[94] Stukeley genuinely liked Gothic, perhaps more so with the passage of time; he sketched it often in his notebooks and even designed a Gothic structure or two of his own. But he continued to admire the classical at least as well, and he never found anything to surpass the ancient sculpture that he had seen as a young man in the collections of the Earls of Pomfret and Pembroke. Fortunately, perhaps, as more an antiquary than a critic, he did not feel compelled to choose.

For Warton, as for Walpole, the choice was more insistent. When Walpole made his comparison between Gothic and classical, he hastened to add that he had not meant to deny the classical superiority but merely to affirm that there was more knowledge and taste in the Gothic buildings than was generally allowed. "Our buildings," he added, "must be as Vitruvian as writings in the days of Erasmus were obliged to be Ciceronian."[95] And when Warton, in the course of writing the *History of English Poetry,* came to consider the reappearance in Britain of the classical style in the arts and literature, he was ready to welcome it unreservedly. Like Stukeley, he applauded the belated appearance of the Renaissance in Gothic Oxford. In writing the life of the benefactor of his college, Ralph Bathurst, Warton described him as "the first who introduced the just and genuine proportions of Grecian architecture into the university, which have ever since been so successfully followed. The venerable beauties of Gothic architecture alone prevailed, till his new court at Trinity College appeared." Until the new chapel was built there, Warton points out, the splendid decorations and exquisite furnishings of "modern art" had been absolutely unknown in Oxford.[96] A Thomas Hearne might, with antiquarian pedantry, regret the improving spirit of English classicism; Warton did not. "Our liberal ancestors spared no costs in erecting strong and durable Edifices, but they seem to have had very little notion of Elegance, Convenience and Propriety."[97] Thomas Warton's admiration for the art of Reynolds (who, by the way, painted both the brothers' portraits) was thus perfectly sincere. And like his brother Joseph, he seems to have endorsed the new windows from the start.

Yet even so, it is hard to see how Warton, with his remarkable feeling for cultural anachronism, could have approved a neoclassical window in a Gothic setting. Even Christopher Wren had chosen to repair a Gothic fabric in a Gothic style.[98] Warton was wonderfully attuned to the many anomalies of style that he observed around him. We smile, he says with a touch of Gibbonian superiority, when we discover the anachronistic errors of Chaucer, Gower, or Shakespeare—when, for example, Hector quotes Aristotle, or Ulysses learns rhetoric from Cicero.[99] And when Pope tried to correct Chaucer's (admitted) extravagances in the *House of Fame* by intruding his own elegant diction and harmony of versification, Warton believed he was making a mistake: "An attempt to unite order and exactness of imagery with a subject formed on principles so professedly romantic and anomalous, is like giving Corinthian pillars to a Gothic palace. When I read Pope's elegant imitation of this piece, I think I am walking among the modern monuments unsuitably placed in Westminster Abbey."[100]

But Warton did not want to accept a Gothic imitation either, and in this, I think, we can see both the extent and the limits of his historicism. Warton believed that Gothic style belonged entirely to its own age, that it was embedded in a whole "system" of cultural relations in which feudalism, chivalry, romance, Christian superstition, Gothic architecture, and stained glass windows were some of the component parts. (Warton, incidentally, seems to have entertained writing a history of stained glass as part of his projected history of Gothic architecture in England.)[101] It was the controversy over the Rowley poems, the alleged fifteenth-century poetry foisted onto an enthusiastic public by Thomas Chatterton in 1777, that forced Warton to reconsider the subject most fully. That the poems were actually eighteenth-century compositions he had not the slightest doubt, for if it were true that they had been written in the reign of Edward IV, his whole "system" must fail. Warton's view that the culture of the later Middle Ages was *sui generis* was predicated on his notion of development. The first English poetry was necessarily rude and imperfect and had to be polished over time.[102] If the Rowley poems were genuine, "the entire system that has hitherto been framed concerning the progression of poetical composition, and every theory that has been established on the gradual improvement of taste, style, and language, will be shaken and discouraged." The Rowley poems, in fact, reflected "the accumulated practice, experience, and invention, of previous writers." Poetry, like all other human effort, required a long collaborative labor of improvement.[103] The proof was that it was impossible to go backward and pretend now to write—or to build—with the innocence and simplicity of the Middle Ages. "A builder of ruins is seldom exact throughout, in his imitation of old-fashioned architecture. Some modern moulding or ornament will here and there unfortunately be detected, in the bend of an arch, the tracing of a niche, or the ramifications of a window." Warton found no trouble showing the anachronisms of style, language, meter, and historical allusion in the fraudulent Rowley poems.[104]

Where Warton *was* inconsistent, however, was in his view of classical style. While he was staunchly opposed to a literal imitation of classical models, he seems nevertheless to have continued to take for granted the essentially timeless character of the classical achievement. Most poetry and architecture was relative to time and place, he thought; but there was something about perfection, once it was achieved, that was changeless and could only be reiterated. As a result, the values that informed both life and art were not for Warton endlessly variable in themselves but still lay outside and apart from history. (Thus for Reynolds, Gothic style *appeared* to be older than classical.)[105] It was thus neither possible nor desirable to replace a Gothic stained glass window with a Gothic imitation, which must immediately betray itself and would not in any case suit a modern sensibility, but a neoclassical painting was perhaps another matter.[106] Reynolds did not share Warton's taste for Gothic, but Warton, it appears (with all the other Gothicists), did share Reynolds' taste for the antique. "If a portrait by Hans Holbein was to be retouched, or rather repainted by Reynolds," Warton wrote in 1782, "it would undoubtedly be made a much finer picture. But it would not be a picture by Hans Holbein."[107] Apparently, one might reasonably find pleasure in either one or the other, but Warton believed that one should never mistake the one for the other.

What I have been suggesting, then, is that while Warton went far beyond Gibbon and most of his contemporaries in his understanding and appreciation of the nonclassical medieval achievement, he was yet constrained by some of the same assumptions about the permanence and universality of human nature that he continued to associate with the best of the ancients and so was unwilling still to take that last radical step into historicism that awaited the nineteenth century. In this he was typical of that whole band of Gothic enthusiasts, most of them friends and associates, who did so much to conjure up and make plausible an alternative to classical culture without ever actually accepting it for themselves.[108] It is plain that until the ancients were once and for all de-throned and the values of classical life and literature reduced to time and place, historicism in its full meaning could remain only partial and halfhearted. To the extent that the Gothicists contributed to that eventual upheaval, they did so unwittingly; nor does it seem likely that they would have altogether approved the consequences. Still, we must give them full credit for taking a giant step toward the forging of the modern historical consciousness, even while they remained thoroughly at home in their own age.

Notes

Preface

1. I find my theme anticipated by at least one distinguished historian. In 1968, Herbert Butterfield wrote, "If we speak of an 'evolution of British historiography' we have to remember that it is one which draws heavily on foreign influences, heaviest of all on classical antiquity. The modern history of historiography must not only take note of this—it must deal with those people who, from the time of the Renaissance were advancing the study of Greece and Rome. For this reason, it cannot be sharply separated from the history of classical scholarship" ("Narrative History and the Spade-Work behind It," *History*, 53 [1968], 173). I do not know of any general work that takes this into account or that in any way attempts to treat the whole period from the vantage point of historiography. Of previous studies that consider a part of the subject, the best remain those that deal with the sixteenth century: F. J. Levy, *Tudor Historical Thought* (San Marino, Calif., 1967), and Arthur Ferguson, *Clio Unbound* (Durham, N.C., 1979), each of which gives some attention to humanism. Other special studies are acknowledged in the footnotes to the essays.

2. Paul Oskar Kristeller, *Renaissance Thought: The Classic, Scholastic and Humanistic Strains* (New York, 1961), p. 10. For the invention of the term, see also Augusto Campagna, "The Origin of the Word Humanist," *Journal of the Warburg and Courtauld Institutes*, 9 (1946), 60–73; and for a good short survey with copious bibliography, Charles Trinkaus, "Humanism," *Encyclopedia of World Art*, VII (New York, 1963).

3. C. S. Lewis, *English Literature in the Sixteenth Century* (Oxford, 1954), pp. 18–19.

4. The humanists, Kristeller says (p. 98), were the proper ancestors of modern philology and history. Unfortunately, the history of scholarship has had relatively little attention (for England especially). For a detailed survey, one must go back to J. E. Sandys, *A History of Classical Scholarship*, 3 vols. (Cambridge, 1903–8); and for the best summary treatment, to Ulrich von Wilamowitz-Moellendorf, *A History of Classical Scholarship* (1921), trans. Alan Harris (London, 1982). The second volume of Rudolf Pfeiffer's *History of Classical Scholarship from 1300 to*

1850 (Oxford, 1976) is useful but disappointing after the magisterial first volume that preceded it.

5. An interesting parallel to this contrast could be made in the next generation when the humanist Polydore Vergil and the scholastic John Major set about solving a similar problem with similar results, this time questioning the reliability of the early British history. Again each reached a "correct" result, though by very different methods. Compare the account in the *Anglica historia* (cited in the Caxton essay below) with Major's *A History of Greater Britain* (1521), trans. Archibald Constable, Scottish History Society, 10 (Edinburgh, 1892). Once again, it was the humanist who made the contribution to subsequent historiography.

6. I have not bothered to update the bibliography either in chap. 2 (first published in 1973) or elsewhere. The notes throughout were offered primarily to support and illustrate the arguments as originally formulated, and it would be a little misleading to alter them now without rewriting the whole. I have, however, made a change or two where subsequent scholarship has seriously modified my original view.

7. The closest thing would seem to be the essays collected in *English Historical Scholarship in the Sixteenth and Seventeenth Centuries*, ed. Levi Fox (London, 1956), especially Stuart Piggott, "Antiquarian Thought in the Sixteenth and Seventeenth Centuries," pp. 93–114; and Piggott's *Ruins in a Landscape* (Edinburgh, 1976).

8. This is not the place for polemics, so I will only refer the reader to the fine piece by Adrian Kuzminski, "Defending Historical Realism," *History and Theory*, 18 (1979), 316–49; and to the suggestive essay by Louis Mink, "Narrative Form as Cognitive Instrument," in *The Writing of History*, ed. Robert H. Canary and Henry Kozicki (Madison, Wis., 1978), 129–49. My own allegiance is to R. G. Collingwood, to whom I have paid respects in "The Autonomy of History: R. G. Collingwood and Agatha Christie," *Clio*, 7 (1978), 253–64; and "Collingwood, Vico, and the Autobiography," *Clio*, 9 (1980), 379–92. I have enlarged my own views further in an article in the *Annals of Scholarship*, 3 (1986), 37–60, entitled "Method in the History of Ideas: More, Machiavelli, and Quentin Skinner."

9. See my article "Natural History and the History of the Scientific Revolution," *Clio*, 13 (1983), 57–75. I have indicated connections throughout my book *Dr. Woodward's Shield: History, Science, and Satire in Augustan England* (Berkeley, Calif., 1977).

10. For a précis and critique of the literature, see my essay, "Ancients and Moderns Reconsidered," *Eighteenth Century Studies*, 15 (1981), 72–89; and more recently, "The Battle of the Books and the Shield of Achilles," *Eighteenth Century Life*, 9 (1984), 33–61.

1. Caxton's Histories

A preliminary version of this paper was given at the English Society for Renaissance Studies, Hertford College, Oxford, June 1985.

1. See, e.g., Charles L. Kingsford, *English Historical Literature in the Fifteenth Century* (Oxford, 1913); Antonia Gransden, *Historical Writing in England* II (Ithaca, 1982).

2. Caxton's relationship to contemporary taste is considered by the following: H. B. Lathrop, "The First English Printers and Their Patrons," *The Library*, 4th ser., 3 (1922–23), 69–96; A. T. P. Byles, "William Caxton as a Man of Letters," ibid., 15 (1934), 1–25; H. S. Bennett, "Caxton and His Public," *Review of English Studies*, 19 (1943), 113–19; Bennett, *Chaucer and the Fifteenth Century* (Oxford, 1947), pp. 206–8; Curt Buhler, *William Caxton and His Critics* (Syracuse, N.Y., 1960), p. 13. For Caxton in general, I have found these sources especially useful: Nellie Slayton Aurner, *Caxton: Mirror of Fifteenth-Century Letters* (London, 1926); W. J. B. Crotch, introduction, *The Prologues and Epilogues of William Caxton*, Early English Text Society, orig. ser., 176 (London, 1928); N. F. Blake, "William Caxton: His Choice of Texts," *Anglia*, 83 (1965), 289–307; Blake, *Caxton and His World* (London, 1969); George D. Painter, *William Caxton: A Biography* (New York, 1977); "Papers Presented to the International Congress 1976," *Journal of the Printing Historical Society*, 11 (1976–77); Lotte Hellinga, *Caxton in Focus: The Beginning of Printing in England* (London, 1982).

3. C. S. Lewis doubted that any Middle English author, including Chaucer, clearly believed he was writing a fiction: "They all proceed as if they were more or less historians" ("The English Prose *Morte*," in *Essays on Malory*, ed. J. A. W. Bennett [Oxford, 1963], p. 22; cf. Larry D. Benson: "Every romancer must claim a source even when he is being most original," *Malory's Morte Darthur* [Cambridge, Mass., 1976], p. 67. For examples in other genres, see C. W. C. Oman, "Some Medieval Conceptions of Ancient History," *Trans. Royal Hist. Soc.*, 4th ser., 4 (1921), 1–22; Christopher Brooke, *Medieval Church and Society* (London, 1971), p. 119; H. L. Levy, "As myn aucthour seyeth," *Medium Aevum*, 12 (1943), 25–39; Brian S. Lee, "This Is No Fable: Historical Residues in Two Medieval Exempla," *Speculum*, 56 (1981), 729. For theory, see A. C. Spearing, *Criticism and Medieval Poetry*, 2d ed. (New York, 1972), pp. 74–75.

4. The one general work on the subject seems to be William Nelson's suggestive little book, *Fact and Fiction: The Dilemma of the Renaissance Story-Teller* (Cambridge, Mass., 1973).

5. *The Recuyell of the Historyes of Troye* (1474), ed. H. Oskar Sommer (London, 1894), 1, 10. The work was begun at Bruges in 1464 and published, according to Hellinga, late in 1473 or early 1474 (*Caxton in Focus*, p. 83). The term "euhemerism" derives from the Greek romance by Euhemerus (c. 300 B.C.), translated into Latin by Ennius. Though both versions were lost in antiquity, their doctrine survived in other classical works and was transmitted to the Middle Ages by the early church fathers and Virgilian commentators: see Jean Seznec, *The Survival of the Pagan Gods*, trans. Barbara F. Sessions, Bollingen Series, 38 (Princeton, N. J., 1940); John Daniel Cooke, "Euhemerism: A Medieval Interpretation of Classical Paganism," *Speculum*, 2 (1927), 296–410.

6. See, lately, Margaret Kekewich, "Edward IV, William Caxton, and Literary Taste in Yorkist England," *Modern Language Review*, 66 (1971), 481–87; Gordon Kipling, *The Triumph of Honour: Burgundian Origins of the Elizabethan Renaissance* (London, 1977); "Henry VII and the Origins of Tudor Patronage," in *Patronage in the Renaissance*, ed. Guy Lytle and Stephen Orgel (Princeton, N.J., 1981), pp. 117–64; Blake, *Caxton and His World*, pp. 68–70. The classic treatment of Burgundian culture in this period remains J. Huizinga, *The Waning of the Middle Ages*

(London, 1924); still useful is George Doutreport, *La littérature française à la cours des ducs de Bourgogne* (Paris, 1909); Otto Cartellieri, *The Court of Burgundy*, trans. Malcolm Letts (London, 1929). Very little is known about Lefevre.

7. Epilogue to bk. 2, in Crotch, *Prologues and Epilogues*, pp. 6–7. I have modernized quotations throughout.

8. Epilogue to bk. 3, ibid., pp. 7–8.

9. Boccaccio's *Genealogia* was begun between 1347 and 1350 and revised afterward; it was published eventually in 1473. It received an early translation into French by Laurent Premierfait, which was not printed until 1499. See Henri Hauvette, *Boccace* (Paris, 1914), pp. 413–30; Cornelia C. Coulter, "The *Genealogy of the Gods*," in *Vassar Medieval Studies*, ed. Christobel F. Fiske (New Haven, Conn., 1923), pp. 317–41; Charles C. Osgood, introduction to Boccaccio, *On Poetry* (Princeton, N.J., 1930).

10. Guido de Columnis, *Historia destructionis Troiae*, ed. Nathaniel E. Griffin (Cambridge, Mass., 1936). The colophon (p. 276) says it was composed in 1287. There is a translation of the *Historia* with a useful introduction on Guido's sources and his views about history and fiction by Mary Elizabeth Meek (Bloomington, Ind., 1974). For the *Roman de Troie*, see the edition by A. Joly (Paris, 1870), who dates it between 1175 and 1180 (p. 109). Raffaele Chianterá, *Guido delle Colonne* (Naples, 1955), pp. 158–243, argues that Guido used other sources besides Benoit. Among other early versions of the Troy story using Benoit, see *The Seege or Batayle of Troye*, ed. Mary E. Barnacle, Early English Text Society, orig. ser., 172 (London, 1927), p. lvii; and Kathleen Chesney, "A Neglected Prose Version of the *Roman de Troie*," *Medium Aevum*, 11 (1942), 46–67. For anachronistic illuminations in the Troy stories of Guido, Benoit, et al., see Hugo Buchthal, *Historia Troiana: Studies in the History of Medieval Secular Illustration*, Studies of the Warburg Institute, 32 (London, 1971).

11. See Nathaniel Griffin, *Dares and Dictys* (Baltimore, Md., 1907); Griffin, "Un-Homeric Elements in the Medieval Story of Troy," *JEGP*, 7 (1907–8), 35–52. There is a translation by R. M. Frazer, Jr., *The Trojan War: The Chronicles of Dictys and Dares* (Bloomington, Ind., 1966). For a recent effort at an appreciation, see Robert M. Lumiansky, "Dares's *Historia* and Dictys's *Ephemeris*: A Critical Comment," in *Studies in Language, Literature and Culture of the Middle Ages and Later*, ed. E. B. Atwood and A. H. Hill (Austin, Tex., 1969), pp. 200–210.

12. So Chaucer in the *House of Fame*: "One said that Homer made lies, feigning in his poetry, and was to Greeks favorable, therefore held it be but fable" (ll. 1477–80). For the Trojans as founders of the Western nations, see, for example, Robert Fabyan, *The New Chronicles of England and France* (1516), ed. Henry Ellis (London, 1811), p. 55.

13. Doubters included Salutati, Vives, Xylander, and Joseph Scaliger, but it was only Perizonius who took the trouble to examine the subject systematically in the dissertation that he prefixed to the Delphin edition of Dares and Dictys by Anne Dacier (Amsterdam, 1702). Dares was still being published in French translation in 1572 as *L'histoire véritable de la guerre des Grecs et des Troyens*. In England, about the same time, Philip Sidney was still taking it at face value, preferring it to the *Aeneid*: see the *Defence of Poesie* (1595), in *The Prose Works*, ed. Albert Feuillerat (Cambridge, 1963), III, 16.

14. "I know of no exception to the rule that the classical themes transmitted to medieval artists by texts were anachronistically modernized." This is Panofsky's famous "principle of disjunction," that themes borrowed from antiquity were always reproduced in nonclassical guise: see Erwin Panofsky, *Renaissance and Renascences in Western Art* (New York, 1968), pp. 84–87, et passim. It would be pointless to try to multiply literary examples, but see Beryl Smalley, *English Friars and Antiquity in the Early Fourteenth Century* (Oxford, 1960), pp. 10–11; and for chronicles (besides Oman, "Medieval Conceptions"), see T. F. Tout, *The Study of Medieval Chronicles* (Manchester, 1922), pp. 11–12. Morton W. Bloomfield has argued that Chaucer at least had a "sense of history" but has to admit that he too was full of anachronisms ("Chaucer's Sense of History," in *Essays and Explorations* [Cambridge, Mass., 1970], pp. 13–26). More recently, C. David Benson has tried to do the same thing for Lydgate ("The Ancient World in John Lydgate's *Troy Book*," *American Benedictine Review*, 24 [1973], 299–312). Needless to say, the attempt to present fiction in the guise of history is characteristic of the period and neither Chaucer nor Lydgate makes much of an effort to get at the real past. See, further, G. L. Kittredge, "Chaucer's Lollius," *Harvard Studies in Classical Philology*, 28 (1917), 47–133; C. S. Lewis, "What Chaucer Really Did to *Il Filostrato*," in *Chaucer Criticism*, ed. R. J. Schoeck and Jerome Taylor (Notre Dame, Ind., 1961); A. J. Minnis, *Chaucer and Pagan Antiquity* (Cambridge, 1982), pp. 6ff.

15. John Lydgate, *Troy Book*, ed. Henry Bergen, Early English Text Society, extra ser., 97 (London, 1906). See Walter F. Schirmer, *John Lydgate*, trans. Ann E. Keep (London, 1952), pp. 42–58; Derek Pearsall, *John Lydgate* (London, 1970), pp. 122–59. Two other renderings of Guido's story into English are the *Gest Hystoriale of the Destruction of Troy*, ed. George A. Pantin and David Donaldson, Early English Text Society, orig. ser., 43 (London, 1874) and the *Laud Troy Book*, ed. J. E. Wulfing, Early English Text Society, orig. ser., 89 (London, 1902). In general, see Margaret R. Scherer, *The Legends of Troy in Art and Literature* (New York, 1963); C. David Benson, *The History of Troy in Middle English Literature* (Woodbridge, Suffolk, England, 1980).

16. Lydgate, *Troy Book*, prologue, ll. 217–20, 362–65. See Lois Ebin, "Lydgate's Views on Poetry," *Annuale Mediaevale*, 18 (1977), 76–105; Robert W. Ayers, "Medieval History, Moral Purpose, and the Structure of Lydgate's *Siege of Thebes*," *PMLA*, 73 (1958), 463–74.

17. Benson, *History of Troy*, pp. 101–2.

18. Robert Braham, "To the Reader," printed in the *Troy Book*, pp. 62–65. When Caxton discovered that the manuscript from which he had printed the *Canterbury Tales* was a bad one, he reedited the work from a better but thought neither to collate nor to make a new transcript: see Beverly Boyd in *Editing Chaucer*, ed. Paul G. Ruggiers (Norman, Okla., 1984), pp. 13–34. Despite Braham's pretensions and his view that scholarship had greatly improved since Caxton's time, "when all good letters were almost asleep," his edition makes no actual improvement. Progress in these matters was (as we shall see) painfully slow, though the idea at least was afoot.

19. The definition of "romance" is notoriously difficult to establish. For some recent discussion, see A. C. Baugh, "The Middle English Romance: Some Questions of Creation, Presentation and Preservation," *Speculum*, 42 (1967), 1–32;

Paul Strohm, "Storie, Spelle, Geste, Romance, Tragedie: Generic Distinctions in the Middle English Troy Narratives," *Speculum*, 46 (1971), 348–59; Dieter Mehl, *The Middle English Romances of the Thirteenth and Fourteenth Centuries* (London, 1967); Derek Pearsall, "The English Romance of the Fifteenth Century," *Essays and Studies*, 29 (1976), 56–83.

20. *The History of Jason*, ed. John Munro, Early English Text Society, extra ser., 111 (London, 1913); Crotch, *Prologues and Epilogues*, pp. 32–34. See Ruth Morse, "Problems of Early Fiction: Raoul Le Fevre's *Histoire de Jason*," *Modern Language Review*, 78 (1983), 34–45. Morse has written two other important articles that deal with the relationship between history and fiction in Burgundian culture: "Historical Fiction in Fifteenth Century Burgundy," *Modern Language Review*, 75 (1980), 48–64; and "This Vague Relation: Historical Fiction and Historical Veracity in the Later Middle Ages," *Leeds Studies in English*, 13 (1982).

21. *History of Jason*, p. 9. Lydgate also wrote a *Siege of Thebes*, ed. Axel Erdmann and E. Ekwall, Early English Text Society, extra ser., 108, 120 (London, 1911, 1930).

22. *Godefroy of Bologne*, ed. Mary Noyes Colvin, Early English Text Society, extra ser., 64 (London, 1893), prologue, p. 4. William of Tyre's history has been translated as *A History of Deeds Done beyond the Sea* by Emily A. Babcock and A. C. Krey with a good introduction (New York, 1943). Heinrich von Sybel was the first to subject the work to systematic criticism: see *The History and Literature of the Crusades*, trans. Lady Duff Cooper (London, n.d.), p. 197. Caxton's prologue appears in Crotch, *Prologues and Epilogues*, pp. 48–49.

23. See James R. Rorimer, *Bulletin of the Metropolitan Museum of Art*, 34 (1939), 224–27; Scherer, *Legends of Troy*, pp. 239–41; Horst Schroeder, *Der Topos der Nine Worthies in Literatur und bilden der Kunst* (Gottingen, 1971); I. Gollancz, introduction to *The Parlement of the Thre Ages*, Roxburghe Club (London, 1897); Roger S. Loomis, "Verses on the Nine Worthies," *Modern Philology*, 15 (1917–18), 211–12. Eventually there were nine antiheroes as well: see Bruce Dickins, "The Nine Unworthies," in *Medieval Literature and Civilization: Studies in Memory of G. N. Garmonsway*, ed. A. D. Pearsall and R. A. Waldron (London, 1969), pp. 328–32.

24. *Charles the Grete*, ed. Sidney J. H. Herrtage, Early English Text Society, extra ser., 37 (London, 1881), prologue, pp. 1–3; Crotch, *Prologues and Epilogues*, pp. 97–98.

25. *Blanchardyn and Eglantine*, ed. Leon Kellner, Early English Text Society, extra ser., 58 (London, 1890); Crotch, *Prologues and Epilogues*, pp. 104–5; *Paris and Vienne*, ed. MacEdward Leach, Early English Text Society, orig. ser., 234 (London, 1957). The education of Blanchardyn is instructive. He is "endoctrined in literature and good manners" by a clerk. One day he enters a chamber of the palace and sees tapestries depicting the destruction of Troy. He insists on learning the history, and his master recounts the whole story. He is so moved and stirred by it that he gains "the will for to be like unto those noble and worthy knights, whereof he saw the remembrances" (pp. 14–15).

26. I use the text of *The Golden Legend* as edited by Henry Ellis, 7 vols. (London, 1900); see Crotch, *Prologues and Epilogues*, pp. 70–76. See also Pierce Butler, *Legenda aurea–Légende dorée–Golden Legend* (Baltimore, Md., 1899). For

the author, see Ernest C. Richardson, *Materials for a Life of Jacopo da Varagine* (New York, 1935); Giovanni Monleone, *Jacopo da Varagine e la sua cronica di Genova* (Rome, 1941).

27. For the relationship of the different versions, see articles by Sister Mary Jeremy in *Modern Language Notes*, 59 (1944), 181–83; *Speculum*, 21 (1946), 212–21; *Medieval Studies*, 8 (1946), 97–106; and *Traditio*, 4 (1946), 423–28. See also Auvo Kurniven, *Neuphilologische Mitteilungen*, 60 (1959), 353–75; Werner W. Krapp, *Hagiography and Medieval Literature* (Odense, 1981), p. 67; Robert Seybolt, "Fifteenth-Century Editions of the *Legenda Aurea*," *Speculum*, 21 (1946), 327–42, 500–504. Caxton turned hagiographer also in printing the *Liber Festivalis* (i.e., Mirk's *Festial*), ed. Theodore Erbe, Early English Text Society, extra ser., 96 (London, 1905); and at the very end of his life when he prepared a collection of the desert fathers, a *Vitas Patrum*, which his assistant, Wynkyn de Worde, printed in 1495 from a manuscript completed on the last day of Caxton's life late in 1491; see Painter, *William Caxton*, p. 187.

28. Sister Mary Jeremy, "Caxton's *Golden Legend* and Varagine's *Legenda Aurea*," *Speculum*, 21 (1946), 215–17.

29. Hippolyte Delehaye, *The Legends of the Saints*, trans. Donald Attwater (London, 1962), pp. 53–60, 91, et passim; and Delehaye, *The Work of the Bollandists* (Princeton, N.J., 1922). See also René Aigron, *L'hagiographie: Ses sources, ses méthodes, son histoire* (Poitiers, 1953), pp. 128ff., 167ff., 195ff.

30. Caxton followed the version in the *Gilte Legende* for his story in the *Golden Legend*: see W. McLeod, "Alban and Amphibal: Some Extant Lives and a Lost Life," *Medieval Studies*, 42 (1980), 407–30. Lydgate devoted a separate work to the subject, *St. Alban and St. Amphibalus*, ed. George F. Reinecke (New York, 1985). See also J. S. P. Tatlock, "St. Amphibalus," *Essays in Criticism*, 2d ser., *Univ. Cal. Pubs. in Eng.*, 4 (1934), 249–57, 268–70; Florence McCulloch, "Saints Alban and Amphibalus in the Works of Matthew Paris," *Speculum*, 56 (1981), 761–85.

31. Ellis, *Golden Legend*, III, 126–34; cf. *The Golden Legend*, trans. Granger Ryan and Helmut Rippinger (New York, 1941), pp. 232–38 (based on the only modern Latin edition, by Johann Graesse [Leipzig, 1850]). For St. George, see Hippolyte Delehaye, *Les passions des martyrs*, 2d ed. (Brussels, 1966), pp. 283–85; Delehaye, *Legends*, p. 88; John E. Matzke, "Contributions to the History of the Legend of St. George," *PMLA*, 17 (1902), 464–535, and 18 (1903), 99–171. According to Delehaye, St. Gelasius had already cast doubt on St. George in 494 A.D. (*Les légendes grecques des saints militaires* [Paris, 1909], pp. 45–76). Even so, Alexander Barclay was still defending the saint against all doubts in his translation of Mantuan's Latin life (1515); see *The Life of St. George*, ed. William Wilson, Early English Text Society, orig. ser., 230 (London, 1955), pp. 7–8.

32. Kenneth Sisam, ed., *Fourteenth-Century Verse and Prose* (Oxford, 1921), p. xiii. See also Mehl, *Romances*, pp. 17–20; Bloomfield, *Essays*, pp. 119–21.

33. *Nova legenda Anglie*, printed by Wynkyn de Worde (1516) from a work that goes back to the mid-fourteenth century. "He exercises no criticism, no judgment, his credulity is unbounded. He takes in everything, believes in everything": see the edition and introduction by Carl Horstman (Oxford, 1901), p. lxvi.

34. See the articles in *Medieval Hagiography and Romance*, ed. Maurice Clogan,

in *Medievalia et Humanistica*, new ser., 6 (1975), 41–49, 91–101, 121–37; O. T. Wolpers, *Die englischen Heiligenlegende des Mittelalters* (Tübingen, 1964), pp. 188ff., 253ff. Already in the thirteenth century, Thomas Cobham praises the *joculatores*, "who sing about the deeds of princes and the lives of the saints and bring consolation to men in sickness or hardship" (*Penitential*, 1, 59, in E. K. Chambers, *The Medieval Stage* [Oxford, 1903], 1, app. G., pp. 262–63).

35. *The High Book of the Grail*, trans. Nigel Bryant (Cambridge, 1978), p. 11. See William Nitze, *Perceval and the Holy Grail*, University of California Publications in Modern Philology, 28, no. 5 (Berkeley, Calif., 1949); Fanni Bogdanow, *The Romance of the Grail* (Manchester, 1966).

36. Bogdanow, *Grail*, p. 10. See also E. K. Chambers, *Malory*, English Association Pamphlet, 51 (London, 1922), p. 9; P. E. Tucker, "The Place of the *Quest of the Holy Grail* in the *Morte Darthur*," *Modern Language Review*, 48 (1953), 391–97; Charles Moorman, "Malory's Treatment of the Sankgreall," *PMLA*, 71 (1956), 497–504, and various essays in *Aspects of Malory and Arthurian Literature*, ed. T. Takamiya and Derek Brewer (Cambridge, 1981).

37. *Brut*, ed. W. D. Brie, Early English Text Society, orig. ser. 131 (London, 1906–8). See Brie, *Geschichte und Quellen der mittelenglischen Prosachronik* (Marburg, 1905); Kingsford, *English Historical Literature*, pp. 113–39; Gransden, *Historical Writing*, pp. 220–48.

38. Caxton, *The Cronycles of Englond* (London, 1482), ch. 1, "How the land of England was first named Albion," sig. a2–a3; *Des Grantz Geantz*, ed. G. E. Brereton, Medium Aevum Monographs, 2 (Oxford, 1937); Smalley, *English Friars*, pp. 17–18.

39. For the Ursula story, see J. S. P. Tatlock, *The Legendary History of Britain* (Berkeley, Calif., 1950), pp. 237–41, based on Wilhelm Levison, *Das Werden der Ursula-Legende* (Cologne, 1928), pp. 1–164. Jacopo da Varagine had a particular interest in this legend, having gone to some trouble to procure a head of one of the virgins for his monastery (Richardson, *Materials*, pp. 119–20).

40. Ralph Higden, *Polychronicon*, ed. Churchill Babington, 9 vols., Rolls Series, (London, 1865–86). This edition contains the Latin original with two English translations, Trevisa's and a second anonymous one. See John Taylor, *The Universal Chronicle of Ranulf Higden* (Oxford, 1966); "The Development of the *Polychronicon* Continuation," *English Historical Review*, 76 (1961), 20–36; A. C. Crawley, "Relationships of the Trevisa Manuscripts and Caxton's *Polychronicon*," *London Medieval Studies*, 1, pt. 3 (1948), 463–82.

41. *Polychronicon*, 1, 9, 17.

42. V. H. Galbraith, "The Autograph Manuscript of Ranulph Higden's *Polychronicon*," *Huntington Library Quarterly*, 23 (1959), 1–18. There is an enlarged version incorporating much hagiographical material; see Galbraith, "The *Historia Aurea* of John, Vicar of Tynmouth and the Sources of the Saint Albans Chronicle," in *Essays in History Presented to Reginald Lane Poole* (Oxford, 1927), pp. 379–95.

43. *Polychronicon*, 1, 19.

44. At least two entirely legendary heroes became familiar figures in the chronicles, Havelock the Dane and Guy of Warwick: see Laura A. Hibbard, *Medieval Romance in England* (Oxford, 1924), pp. 103, 109, 127–39. By the

fourteenth century, knights are writing chivalric history, e.g., Sir Thomas Gray's *Scalacronica* and the Chandos Herald's *Life of the Black Prince*; see Gransden, *Historical Writing*, pp. 92–100. For the difficulty of distinguishing romance and chronicle as genres, see Mehl, *Romances*, pp. 20–22.

45. Higden's sources remain obscure; he probably took the Alexander story from Vincent of Beauvais, though he used other sources also; see G. H. V. Bunt, "Alexander and the Universal Chronicle," in *The Medieval Alexander Legend and Romance Epic: Essays in Honor of David Ross*, ed. Peter Noble, et al. (New York, 1982), pp. 3–8. For the legendary sources of Alexander, see *The Pseudo-Turpin* (c. 1140–50), ed. H. M. Smyser (Cambridge, Mass., 1937); *The Romance of Alexander the Great by Pseudo-Callisthenes* (probably before the fourth century A.D.), ed. Albert M. Wolohojian (New York, 1969); *The Gests of Alexander of Macedon*, ed. Francis P. Magoun (Cambridge, 1929); George Cary, *The Medieval Alexander*, ed. D. J. A. Ross (Cambridge, 1956).

46. Bartholemew's *De proprietatibus rerum* was written about 1230 and fills nineteen books with natural lore borrowed from a wide reading of miscellaneous works. It was very popular and was translated by Trevisa in 1398 and published by Wynkyn de Worde in 1494, apparently from a copy prepared by Caxton. It was reworked for the Elizabethans by Stephen Bateman (1582); see the excerpts in *Medieval Lore from Bartholemew Anglicus*, ed. Robert Steele (London, 1893), who lists many editions in Latin, French, Dutch, Spanish, and English. A critical edition of Trevisa's version has been newly edited by M. C. Seymour and Gabriel Liegey, *On the Properties of Things*, 2 vols. (Oxford, 1974). See also Lynn Thorndike, *A History of Magic and Experimental Science* (New York, 1923), II, 401–35.

47. Smalley, *English Friars*, p. 21.

48. *Polychronicon*, I, 17; II, 281–83; II, 420–23; II, 430–31; I, 94; II, 423.

49. Ibid., II, 83.

50. Ibid., II, 360.

51. Ibid., II, 370; Isidore of Seville, *Etymologiarum sive Originum*, ed. W. M. Lindsay, 2 vols. (Oxford, 1911), I, xl, *De fabula*. For Isidore, see Ernest Brehaut, *An Encyclopedist of the Dark Ages: Isidore of Seville* (New York, 1912); for Isidore's poetics, Ernst Robert Curtius, *European Literature and the Latin Middle Ages*, trans. Willard Trask (1953; reprinted, New York, 1963), pp. 450–57.

52. *Polychronicon*, II, 372. See Augustine, *Contra Mendacio*, in *Seventeen Short Treatises* (Oxford, 1847), pp. 426–69, esp. pp. 448–50. Various other passages from Augustine are collected in Concetta C. Greenfield, *Humanist and Scholastic Poetics, 1250–1500* (Lewisburg, Penna., 1981), pp. 29–31.

53. *Polychronicon*, II, 372–74. Neckham's commentary remains in manuscript, but an edition is promised; see R. W. Hunt, *The Schools and the Cloister: The Life and Writings of Alexander Nequam (1157–1217)* (Oxford, 1984), pp. 128–29. Macrobius' commentary on Cicero's *Dream of Scipio* has been translated by William Harris Stahl (New York, 1952); see esp. pp. 82–84. For its uses in the later Middle Ages, see Peter Dronke, *Fabula: Explorations in the Uses of Myth in Medieval Platonism* (Leiden, 1974), pp. 14–78; Paula Demats, *Fabula: Trois études de mythographie* (Geneva, 1973).

54. *Polychronicon*, II, 375. There is an *ars praedicandi* that has been attributed to

Higden: see G. R. Owst, *Preaching in Medieval England* (Cambridge, 1926), p. 247.

55. See n. 9 above. Charles G. Osgood has translated the last two books of the *Genealogy*, edited recently by Jeremiah Reedy (Toronto, 1978). See also Edmund Reiss, "Boccaccio in English Culture of the Fourteenth and Fifteenth Centuries," in *Il Boccaccio nella cultura Inglese e Anglo-Americana*, ed. Giuseppe Galigani (Florence, 1974), pp. 15–26.

56. The basic texts are Dante, *Convivio*, ii.i, and *Letter to Can Grande* (now generally accepted as genuine); Petrarch, *Rerum familiarum*, x.4, and *Coronation Oration*, trans. Ernest H. Wilkins, *PMLA*, 68 (1953), 1246. The enormous controversy over Dante's distinction between the allegory of the theologians and the allegory of the poets is perhaps beside the point for us, though the literature is richly suggestive as to medieval notions of fiction: see Robert Hollander, *Allegory in Dante's Commedia* (Princeton, N.J., 1969); "Dante Theologus-poeta," *Dante Studies*, 94 (1976), 91–136; Alarano Lanapoppi, "La *Divina Commedia*: Allegoria del poeti o allegoria di theologi?" *Dante Studies*, 86 (1968), 17–40, with references to articles by Charles Singleton, Richard Green, Joseph Mazzeo, and Bruno Nardi.

57. See M. Souverain, *Platonism Unveil'd* (London, 1700), p. 91; for recent commentary, Etienne Gilson, "Poésie et verité dans la *Genealogia* de Boccace," *Studi sul Boccaccio*, 2 (1964), 253–82; Leo Spitzer, "The Prologue to the *Lais* of Marie de France and Medieval Poetics," *Modern Philology*, 41 (1943–44), 96–102. In general, see Curtius, *European Literature*, pp. 204–5; Jean Pepin, *Myth et allégorie* (Paris, 1958); and above all, Henri de Lubac, *Exégèse mediévale*, 4 vols. (Paris, 1959–64), esp. iv, 182–208.

58. Christine de Pizan, *Epistle of Othéa*; see the introduction to the Scrope version by Curt Buhler, Early English Text Society, orig. ser., 264 (London, 1970), and the versions published by George Warner (London, 1904) and James D. Gordon (Philadelphia, 1942). For Christine, see S. Solente, "Cristine de Pisan," *Histoire littéraire de la France*, 40 (1974), 335–422; Charity C. Willard, *Christine de Pisan: Her Life and Works* (New York, 1984); J. C. Laidlaw, "Christine de Pizan: An Author's Progress," *Modern Language Review*, 78 (1983), 532–50. For Scrope, see Buhler's introduction to *The Dicts and Sayings of the Philosophers*, Early English Text Society, orig. ser., 211 (London, 1941). *Othéa* was very popular in France and exists in many manuscripts and two printed versions (1499, 1522), but it has not yet received a modern edition; see Gianni Mombello, *La traduzione manuscritta dell'Epistre Othéa di Christine de Pizan* (Turin, 1967).

59. For Christine's sources, see P. G. C. Campbell, *L'Epitre d'Othéa* (Paris, 1924); for the *Histoire*, Paul Meyer, "Les premiers compilators françaises d'*Histoire ancienne*," *Romania*, 14 (1885), 36–76; for the *Ovide moralisé*, the nice summary in Panofsky, *Renaissance and Renascences*, pp. 78–80. For the illustrations, see Millard Meiss, *French Painting in the Time of Jean de Berry: The Limbourgs and Their Contemporaries*, 2 vols. (New York, 1974), I, 23ff.

60. The phrase is from the English translation of Harl. MS., 838 by Gordon, *The Epistle of Othea* (Philadelphia, 1942), p. xxxviii; Rosamund Tuve, *Allegorical Imagery* (Princeton, N.J., 1966), p. 289. The printed version by Robert Wyer

(1540) includes a colophon referring to the work as *The C Hystories of Troye.* More than half the text, however, deals with other things.

61. Scrope version, p. 33.

62. Ibid., p. 55.

63. Sister Mary Ignatius, "Christine de Pizan's *Epistre d'Othéa:* An Experiment in Literary Form," *Medievalia et Humanistica,* n.s., 9 (1979), 130.

64. E. K. Rand, *Ovid and His Influence* (Boston, 1925), p. 58.

65. See Smalley, *English Friars;* Judson Boyce Allen, *The Friar as Critic: Literary Attitudes in the Later Middle Ages* (Nashville, Tenn., 1971). For Ovid's medieval fame, see (besides Rand) Lester K. Born, "Ovid and Allegory," *Speculum,* 9 (1934), 362–79; Fausto Ghisalberti, "Medieval Biographies of Ovid," *Journal of the Warburg and Courtauld Institutes,* 51 (1946), 10–59; L. P. Wilkinson, *Ovid Recalled* (Cambridge, 1955), chaps. 11–12. For an English paraphrase and explication of the *Metamorphosis,* see Thomas Walsingham, *De archana deorum,* ed. Robert A. van Kluyve (Durham, N.C., 1968). Walsingham was also a chronicler and the author of an elaboration of Dictys, as well as of a *Historia Alexandri,* among other historical and pseudohistorical works.

66. Only the second half of Caxton's manuscript of Ovid was known for a long time; it was edited by S. Gaselee and H. F. B. Brett-Smith (Oxford, 1924). The first half reappeared in 1964 and has been reunited with the original at Magdalen College. I have used the facsimile edition printed by George Braziller (New York, 1968). Mansion's work is noticed by Painter, *William Caxton,* p. 102; it became the basis for a version known as the *Bible des poètes* and remained very popular in France for many years; see Ann Moss, *Poetry and Fable: Studies in Mythological Narrative in Sixteenth-Century France* (Cambridge, 1984), pp. 7ff.

67. Basil's work can be read in a translation by F. M. Padelford, *Essays on the Study and Use of Poetry* (New York, 1902); Caxton's preface is considered in Robert L. Montgomery, "William Caxton and the Beginnings of Tudor Critical Thought," *Huntington Library Quarterly,* 36 (1973), 91–103.

68. Wilkinson argues that Ovid did not hesitate to invent, but since most of his sources have perished, it is not obvious one way or the other (*Ovid Recalled,* p. 146).

69. The last quotation is from the prologue to bk. 1; the rest from the general prologue to the whole. Caxton's sources were probably, like Mansion's, a fifteenth-century prose redaction of the *Ovide moralisé* and the Latin *Ovidius moralizatus* of Pierre Bersuire; see Moss, *Poetry and Fable,* p. 7. Cf. the twelfth-century poet, "Servants of God, listen to my story; it is very simple and seems unadorned, but it is full of meaning (*sens*) and matter. The story is chaff, the meaning wheat, the meaning is the fruit, the story the branch" (quoted in William Nitze, "*Sens et Matière,*" *Romania,* 44 [1915], 14–16).

70. When Caxton comes to the battle of Troy (bk. 12), he once again notices the different accounts of Dares and Dictys, Guido and Homer, but leaves it to the reader to sort things out.

71. Boccaccio, *On Poetry,* 14.ix (p. 48); xiii (p. 67). Cf. Petrarch, "To make up all that one writes is to be a fool and a liar rather than a poet," *Coronation Oration,* p. 1246; Edward Moore, *Studies in Dante,* 2d ser. (Oxford, 1899), pp. 132–33.

Petrarch thought he was the first to have made the discovery about the discrepancy in the Dido-Aeneas story, but he was preceded by the English friar John Ridewall (Smalley, *English Friars*, p. 130).

72. Allen, *Friar as Critic*, pp. 4, 74, et passim; Eugene Vinaver, *The Rise of Romance* (Oxford, 1971), p. 18; A. J. Minnis, "The Influence of Academic Prologues on the Prologues and Literary Attitudes of Late Medieval English Writers," *Medieval Studies*, 43 (1984), 342–83. The three- or fourfold sense of scripture could sometimes be extended to seven or more: see Harry Caplan, "The Four Senses of Scriptural Interpretation and the Medieval Theory of Preaching," *Speculum*, 4 (1929), 282–90.

73. A useful survey remains E. Harris Harbison, *The Christian Scholar in the Age of the Reformation* (New York, 1956). For the humanist-Protestant criticism of the fourfold sense, see Frederic W. Farrar, *History of Interpretation* (London, 1886).

74. *Caxton's Aesop*, ed. R. T. Lenaghan (Cambridge, Mass., 1967), p. 89.

75. Crotch, *Prologues and Epilogues*, p. 62; *The History of Reynard the Fox*, ed. N. F. Blake, Early English Text Society, orig. ser., 263 (London, 1970). This time Caxton used a Dutch original.

76. See app. 25, G. G. Coulton, *Five Centuries of Religion* (Cambridge, 1923), I, 543–44.

77. Only fragments survive from the 1509 edition of Stephen Hawes, *The Pastime of Pleasure*; the 1517 edition has been edited by William Edward Mead, Early English Text Society, orig., ser., 173 (London, 1928); see ll. 708ff., 932–52, 981–85, 1072ff.

78. Crotch, *Prologues and Epilogues*, p. 62.

79. "The principle that oral witness deserves more credence than written evidence was a legal commonplace" (M. T. Clanchy, *From Memory to Written Record: England 1066–1307* [London, 1979], p. 210).

80. "It is much more important—and infinitely more arduous—to interpret witnesses than to glean one's information from books" (Polybius, XII.27.1–6). For this "typical animus against written records," see C. R. Ligota, "The Story Is Not True: Fact and Fiction in Antiquity," *Journal of the Warburg and Courtauld Institutes*, 45 (1982), 1–13.

81. Giraldus Cambrensis, *Opera*, ed. J. S. Brewer, Rolls ser., 21 (London, 1861–91), I, xlv. Cf. John of Salisbury, preface to *Historia pontificalis*, ed. Marjorie Chibnall (London, 1956), p. 4.

82. Trial by ordeal was thought to be more efficacious than reconstruction of the crime, even perhaps after the more primitive kinds of the former began to disappear; see R. van Caenegen, "The Law of Evidence in the Twelfth Century," *Proceedings of the Second International Congress of Medieval Canon Law* (1965), 297–310; John W. Baldwin, "The Intellectual Preparation for the Canon of 1215 against Ordeals," *Speculum*, 36 (1961), 613–36.

83. John Bromyard, quoted in G. R. Owst, *Literature and Pulpit in Medieval England* (Cambridge, 1933), p. 155; Allen, *Friar as Critic*, p. 68n.

84. Samuel K. Workman, "Versions of Skelton, Caxton and Berners of a Prologue by Diodorus Siculus," *Modern Language Notes*, 56 (1941), 252–58; N. F. Blake, "Caxton's Language," *Neuphilologische Mitteilungen*, 67 (1966), 122–32.

Caxton's friend, John Skelton, was translating Diodorus just about this time; see the edition by F. M. Salter and H. L. R. Edwards, Early English Text Society, orig. ser., 233, 239 (London, 1956–57), pp. 5–12 (*proheme*).

85. Crotch, *Prologues and Epilogues*, pp. 64–67. Caxton furnished an index to the *Polychronicon*, the first for an English printed book. "History," says Blake, "has become a series of examples which a reader can select at will" (*Caxton and His World*, p. 115).

86. Caxton, preface to *Canterbury Tales* (2d ed., 1483), in Crotch, *Prologues and Epilogues*, pp. 90–91; Painter, *William Caxton*, pp. 132–34. *The Stanzaic Life of Christ* also employs the *Polychronicon* and the *Legenda aurea* and proclaims their equal truth; ed. Francis A. Foster, Early English Text Society, orig. ser., 166 (London, 1926), p. xix.

87. Froissart, *The Chronicle*, trans. Lord Berners, ed. William Paton Ker, 6 vols. (London, 1901), prologue, 1, 3–7. For Berners, see *The Boke of Huon of Bordeux*, ed. S. L. Lee, Early English Text Society, extra ser., 40–41 (London, 1882–83), p.xl; N. F. Blake, "Lord Berners: A Survey," *Medievalia et Humanistica*, new ser., 2 (1971), 119–32.

88. The first part of the work is based largely on the chronicle of Jean le Bel. For Froissart, see William Paton Ker, "Froissart," in *Essays in Medieval Literature* (London, 1905), pp. 135–238; F. S. Shears, *Froissart: Chronicler and Poet* (London, 1930); and the essays in *Froissart–Historian*, ed. J. J. N. Palmer (Woodbridge, Suffolk, 1981).

89. Huizinga, *Waning*, p. 67; J. W. Sherborne in Palmer, *Froissart–Historian*, p. 50.

90. Epilogue, *Book of the Order of Chivalry*, in Crotch, *Prologues and Epilogues*, p. 83.

91. *The History of the Valiant Knight Arthur of Little Britain*, ed. E. V. Utterson (London, 1814), prologue, pp. liv–lv. See Kenneth Oberembt, "Lord Berners' Translation of *Artus de la Petite Bretagne*," *Medievalia et Humanistica*, 5 (1974), 191–99.

92. Edward D. Kennedy, "Malory's Use of Hardyng's *Chronicle*," *Notes and Queries*, 214 (1969), 167–70; Kennedy, "Malory and his English Sources," in Takamiya and Brewer, *Aspects of Malory*, pp. 42–48; Robert H. Wilson, "More Borrowings from Hardyng's *Chronicle*," *Notes and Queries*, 215 (1970), 208–10. The preface to Hardyng by Richard Grafton (1543) typically denies responsibility for the truthfulness of the history, claiming only to reproduce the sources faithfully; see *The Chronicle of Iohn Hardyng*, ed. Henry Ellis (London, 1812), p. 10.

93. The modern literature on Malory begins with G. L. Kittridge, "Who Was Sir Thomas Malory?" *Harvard Studies and Notes in Philology and Literature*, 5 (1897), 85–106, and continues through full-length studies by Edward Hicks, *Sir Thomas Malory* (Cambridge, Mass., 1928), and William Matthews, *The Ill-Famed Knight* (Berkeley, 1966), and a host of articles among which those by P. J. C. Field may be the most interesting: see the *Bulletin of the Institute of Historical Research*, 47 (1974), 24–35; *Medium Aevum*, 48 (1979), 213–39; *Bulletin of the John Rylands Library*, 64 (1982), 433–56.

94. Thomas Malory, *Works*, ed. Eugene Vinaver, 2d ed., 3 vols. (Oxford,

1967), II, 1036. Lancelot fears that "men shall chronicle after me" (II, 1202–3). Caxton's text of the *Morte Darthur* has been freshly edited by James W. Spisak and William Matthews, 2 vols. (Berkeley, Calif., 1983).

95. Lydgate, *Fall of Princes*, VIII, 2780–83, ed. Henry Bergen, 4 vols., Early English Text Society, extra ser., 121–24 (London, 1924–27), 901. The prologue to the *lai de Tyolet* also has Arthur's knights return from their adventures, tell their tales, and have clerks at once write them down: see "*Lai de Tyolet*," trans. Margo Vinney, *Allegorica*, 3 (1978), 6–41, ll. 25–35.

96. Malory, *Works*, III, 1242.

97. See, e.g., Eugene Vinaver, *Malory* (Oxford, 1970), pp. 64, 90; Malory, *Works*, III, 1617n.; Vida Scudder, *Le Morte Darthur: A Study of the Book and Its Sources* (London, 1920), p. 185; D. S. Brewer, "The Hoole Book," in *Essays on Malory*, ed. J. A. W. Bennett (Oxford, 1963), pp. 49–50; Mark Lambert, *Malory: Style and Vision in Le Morte Darthur* (New Haven, Conn., 1975), pp. 126, 134–35; Larry D. Benson, *Malory's Morte Darthur* (Cambridge, Mass., 1976), pp. 8–9, 73, 137, et passim.

98. There is a long tradition of interpretation that sees the *Morte Darthur* as reflecting fifteenth-century events even while it purports to describe the world of Arthur. See Nellie S. Aurner, "Sir Thomas Malory—Historian?" *PMLA*, 48 (1933), 362–91; Vinaver, in Malory, *Works*, I, xxxi–xxxii; R. R. Griffith, "The Political Bias of Malory's *Morte Darthur*," *Viator*, 5 (1974), 355–86; and the Field articles cited in n. 93 above.

99. N. F. Blake, "Caxton Prepares His Edition of the *Morte Darthur*," *Journal of Librarianship*, 8 (1976), 272–85. Caxton's prologue may be found in Crotch, *Prologues and Epilogues*, pp. 92–95.

100. Most modern opinion is against the book, which in any event could not have been very old. For a recent effort to resuscitate Geoffrey's source, see Geoffrey Ashe, "A Certain Very Ancient Book: Traces of an Arthurian Source in Geoffrey of Monmouth's *History*," *Speculum*, 56 (1981), 301–23. In a vast literature, see E. K. Chambers, *Arthur of Britain* (London, 1927); J. S. P. Tatlock, *The Legendary History of Britain* (Berkeley, Calif., 1950); John Edward Lloyd, "Geoffrey of Monmouth," *English Historical Review*, 58 (1942), 460–68; John J. Parry and R. T. Caldwell, "Geoffrey of Monmouth," in *Arthurian Literature in the Middle Ages: A Collaborative History*, ed. Roger S. Loomis (Oxford, 1959), pp. 72–93; Stuart Piggott, "The Sources of Geoffrey of Monmouth," *Antiquity*, 15 (1941), 269–84; Valerie Flint, "The *Historia Regum Britanniae* of Geoffrey of Monmouth: Parody and Its Purpose, A Suggestion," *Speculum*, 54 (1979), 447–68; Neil Wright, "Geoffrey of Monmouth and Gildas," *Arthurian Literature*, 2 (1982), 1–40.

101. William of Newburgh, *Historia Rerum Anglicarum*, ed. Richard Howlett, Rolls ser., 83 (London, 1884); trans. Joseph Stevenson, in *Church Historians of England*, IV (London, 1856), p. 398. See Nancy Partner, *Serious Entertainments: The Writing of History in Twelfth-Century England* (Chicago, 1977), pp. 51–140. Giraldus Cambrensis expressed doubts even earlier but nevertheless used much of the fabulous material in his work. For the use and development of the legendary history, see Robert H. Fletcher, *The Arthurian Material in the Chronicles* (1906; reprinted, New York, n.d.); Laura Keeler, *Geoffrey of Monmouth and the Later*

Latin Chroniclers (Berkeley, Calif., 1946); J. D. Bruce, *The Evolution of Arthurian Romance*, 2 vols. (Baltimore, Md., 1923); Loomis, *Arthurian Literature in the Middle Ages*. Political uses may have helped its acceptance; see articles by Gordon G. Gerould, Mary E. Griffin, and R. S. Loomis in *Speculum*, 2 (1927), 33–51; 16 (1941), 109–20; 28 (1953), 114–27.

102. *Polychronicon*, v, 328–37.

103. See Gransden, *Historical Writing*, p. 49.

104. *Polychronicon*, v, 337. For a preliminary comparison, see John E. Housman, "Higden, Trevisa, Caxton and the Beginnings of Arthurian Criticism," *Review of English Studies*, 23 (1947), 209–17. For Trevisa, see Aaron J. Perry, introduction to Trevisa, *Dialogus inter Militem et Clericum*, Early English Text Society, orig. ser., 167 (London, 1925), pp. lv–lxxvii; David C. Flower, "John Trevisa and the English Bible," *Modern Philology*, 58 (1960–61), 81–98; Flower, "More about John Trevisa," *Modern Language Quarterly*, 32 (1971), 243–51.

105. John Rous's work was edited by Thomas Hearne, *Joannis Rossi Antiquarii Warwicensis Historia Rerum Angliae* (Oxford, 1716); for Hardyng, see n. 92 above; for both, Gransden, *Historical Writing*, II, 274–87, 309–27.

106. Caxton's editing has been the subject of much discussion and controversy. The Winchester manuscript, newly come to light, does not seem to have been Malory's principal source, though it may have been known to him; see Lotte Hellinga and Hilton Kelliher, "The Malory Manuscript," *British Library Journal*, 3 (1977), 91–113. On the whole, it looks as though Caxton was typically faithful to his text, though he added book divisions and chapters; see Sally Shaw, "Caxton and Malory," in Bennett, *Essays on Malory*, pp. 114–45. Nevertheless, on at least one occasion, when Malory was following the English alliterative *Morte Arthure* (for bk. 2), Caxton radically altered and abbreviated it so as to make it his own. In this respect Caxton treats Malory in the same way that Malory had treated his source; see Terence McCarthy, "Caxton and the Text of Malory's Book 2," *Modern Philology*, 71 (1973), 144–52; Tania Vorontzoff, "Malory's Story of Arthur's Roman Campaign," *Medium Aevum*, 6 (1937), 199–221; Michael Stroud, "Malory and the Chivalric Ethos: The Hero of *Arthur and the Emperor Lucius*," *Medieval Studies*, 36 (1974), 331–53.

107. So Painter, *William Caxton*, p. 147; Hellinga and Kelliher, "Malory Manuscript," pp. 154–55; Hellinga, *Caxton in Focus*, p. 89.

108. Prologue to *Polychronicon*, in Crotch, *Prologues and Epilogues*, pp. 65–66; see W. A. Nitze, "The Exhumation of King Arthur at Glastonbury," *Speculum*, 9 (1934), 355–61; Geoffrey Ashe, ed., *The Quest for Arthur's Britain* (New York, 1968), pp. 126–27.

109. Crotch, *Prologues and Epilogues*, p. 97.

110. See Roberto Weiss, *Humanism in England during the Fifteenth Century*, 2d ed. (Oxford, 1957), pp. 13–21.

111. Prologue to *Caton* (1483) in Crotch, *Prologues and Epilogues*, pp. 77–78. Caxton's *Aesop* includes a selection from Poggio's *Facetiae*: see R. H. Wilson, "The Poggiana in Caxton's *Aesop*," *Philological Quarterly*, 30 (1951), 350. Caxton's friend Skelton translated Diodorus from Poggio's Latin version.

112. One of the Italian works was Lorenzo Traversagni's *Nova rhetorica*, which

Caxton published in 1479 (with an *Epitome* the following year), ed. R. H. Martin and J. E. Mortimer, *Proc. Leeds Phil. and Lit. Soc.*, 14 (1971). James Murphy casts some doubt on its Renaissance character but does find a more "modern" view of rhetoric in it than in the thoroughly medieval *Court of Sapience* (1481?), which Caxton also printed and which was probably closer to his own ideas; see "Caxton's Two Choices: 'Modern' and 'Medieval' Rhetoric in Traversagni's *Nova rhetorica* and the anonymous *Court of Sapience*," *Medievalia et Humanistica*, new ser., 3 (1972), 241–55. For Traversagni, see Weiss, *Humanism*, pp. 162–63; Wilbur S. Howell, *Logic and Rhetoric in England 1500–1700* (Princeton, N.J., 1967), pp. 78–81. The *Court* has been edited by Robert Spindler and is discussed by Curt Buhler in two issues of the *Beiträge zur Englischen Philologie* (1927, 1932). Two other brief Latin works of a vaguely humanist character, both probably commissioned by the authors, are the speech of John Russell, *Propositio Johannis Russell* (c. 1477–78) and the *Sex epistolae* of Petrus Carmelianus (1483); see Painter, *William Caxton*, pp. 94–95, 135–36. The Ciceronian works are *De senectute* (*Tully of Old Age*, 1481) translated from the French of Laurent Premierfait, possibly by Stephen Scrope, as revised by William Worcester; and the *De Amicitia* (*Of Friendship* with *A Declamation of Nobility*, 1481), probably directly from Latin by John Tiptoft; see Painter, *William Caxton*, pp. 111–13, relying on Curt Buhler's introduction to the *Dicts and Sayings of the Philosophers*, p. xii.

113. Edward Gibbon, *Miscellaneous Works* (London, 1814), III, 563–64. See also John Lewis, *The Life of Mayster Wyllyam Caxton* (London, 1737), pp. 63, 119; Thomas Warton, *History of English Poetry* (London, 1778), II, 123. The view is still endorsed in John M. Berdan, *Tudor Poetry* (New York, 1920), p. 26.

114. Caxton specifies Virgil, Ovid, Cicero, "and all the other noble poets and orators to me unknown," *Eneydos* (1490), ed. M. T. Culley and F. J. Furnivall, Early English Text Society, extra ser., 57 (London, 1890), prologue, pp. 1–4; Crotch, *Prologues and Epilogues*, pp. 107–10. For Skelton's "humanism," see William Nelson, *John Skelton Laureate* (New York, 1939), pp. 38–39, 40–58; R. L. Dunbabin, "Skelton's Relation to Humanism," *Modern Language Review*, 12 (1917), 129–37; J. Lloyd, "John Skelton and the New Learning," *Modern Language Review*, 24 (1929), 445–46.

115. Caxton, *Mirror of the World*, ed. O. H. Prior, Early English Text Society, orig. ser., 110 (London, 1913), chap. 13, pp. 157ff. For Virgil legends, see Domenico Comparetti, *Virgil in the Middle Ages*, trans. E. F. M. Benecke (London, 1895); J. W. Spargo, *Virgil the Necromancer*, Harvard Studies in Comparative Literature, 10 (Cambridge, Mass., 1934); "Virgilio nel Medio Evo" (articles by V. Ussano, E. K. Rand, and others), *Studi Medievali*, 5 (1932); John Savage, "Some Possible Sources of Medieval Conceptions of Virgil," *Speculum*, 19 (1944), 336–43.

116. *Eneydos*, p. 120. The *Livre des Enéides* was a fourteenth-century romance adapted from Virgil and from Boccaccio's *Fall of Princes*. It was printed in 1483, but Caxton used a manuscript; see Louise B. Hall, "Caxton's *Eneydos* and the Redactions of Virgil," *Medieval Studies*, 22 (1960), 136–47; Painter, *William Caxton*, p. 174.

117. *Eneydos*, p. 23. Lydgate's version of Boccaccio (n. 95 above) (c. 1438–39)

was based on a French amplification by Laurent Premierfait (1400), first printed in 1483. The additions include much material drawn from the *Metamorphoses* and the *Genealogia Deorum* and constitute a kind of history of the world.

118. *Virgil's Aeneid*, trans. Gavin Douglas, ed. David Coldwell, Scottish Text Society, ser. 3, 25, 27, 28, 30 (Edinburgh, 1957–64), I, prologue, ll. 143, 262. The translation was made 1512–13; it was first printed, somewhat anglicized, by William Copeland in 1553.

119. Ibid., p. 39: "But ye shall know that the principal interest of Virgil was to extol the Romans, and in special the clan or family of Julian . . . because the emperor August Octavian, to whom he dedicated his work, was of that house and blood, and sister to Caesar Julius." To make his point, Douglas uses Caesar, Lucan, and Suetonius. That he had a parallel political purpose of his own is suggested by his editor (pp. 33–37) and by Bruce Dearing, "Gavin Douglas's *Aeneid*: A Reinterpretation," *PMLA*, 67 (1952), 845–62. Douglas seems to have used the Latin edition of Jodicus Badius Ascensius (1507); see Priscilla Bawcutt, "The Source of Gavin Douglas's *Eneados* IV Prologue 92–9," *Notes and Queries*, 214 (October 1969), pp. 366–67. For the resuscitation of the historical Virgil, see Duane Reed Stuart, "Biographical Criticism of Virgil since the Renaissance," *Studies in Philology*, 19 (1922), 1–30.

120. By Ezra Pound, C. S. Lewis, and others. Lewis, it should be said, finds the work still "medieval" (*English Literature in the Sixteenth Century* [Oxford, 1954], pp. 81–90), though his comparison is with Dryden rather than with Caxton or Chaucer, as Douglas intended. Douglas came to know Polydore Vergil, among other humanists; according to John Major, he shared their antipathy to scholasticism. See the introduction to Gavin Douglas, *Poetical Works*, ed. John Small, 4 vols. (Edinburgh, 1874), I, clviii–clxii. Douglas's commentary was left incomplete in manuscript; it can be read in Small's edition (II, 283ff.) or as footnotes in Coldwell's edition. See also Louise B. Hall, "An Aspect of the Renaissance in Gavin Douglas's *Aeneid*," *Studies in the Renaissance*, 7 (1960), 184–92; Robert Fulton, "Douglas and Virgil," *Studies in Scottish Literature*, 18 (1983), 121–28.

121. Some general surveys are: Huizinga, *Waning*, pp. 67–74, 94, 101; J. H. Huizinga, "Chivalric Ideas in the Late Middle Ages," in *Men and Ideas*, trans. J. S. Holmes and Hans van Marle (London, 1960), 196–206; Raymond L. Kilgour, *The Decline of Chivalry* (Cambridge, Mass., 1937); Arthur B. Ferguson, *The Indian Summer of English Chivalry* (Durham, N.C., 1960); Sidney Painter, *French Chivalry* (Baltimore, Md., 1940); Helen M. Cam, "The Decline and Fall of English Feudalism," *History*, new ser., 25 (1940–41), 216–33; Richard Barber, *The Knight of Chivalry* (London, 1970); Richard Barber, *Chivalric Literature: Essays in the Relationship between Literature and Life in the Later Middle Ages* (Kalamazoo, Mich., 1980); K. B. McFarlane, "Bastard Feudalism," *Bulletin of the Institute of Historical Research*, 20 (1945), 161–80; G. L. Harris, ed., *England in the Fifteenth Century* (London, 1981). See also M. G. A. Vale, "New Techniques and Old Ideals: The Impact of Artillery on War and Chivalry at the End of the Hundred Years War," in *War, Literature and Chivalry in the Late Middle Ages*, ed. C. T. Allmand (Liverpool, 1976), pp. 57–72; M. G. A. Vale, *War and Chivalry* (Athens, Ga., 1981), pp. 147–74.

122. *Pageant of the Life and Death of Richard Beauchamp, Earl of Warwick* (at-

tributed to John Rous), ed. Viscount Dillon and W. H. St. John Hope (London, 1914); Samuel Bentley, ed., *Excerpta Historica* (London, 1831), pp. 171–222, 223–39. See too the letter of John to Margaret Paston, July 8, 1468, describing the jousts and pageantry at Bruges (*Paston Letters*, ed. Norman Davis, 2 vols. [Oxford, 1971–76], I, 538–40).

123. Epilogue to the *Fayttes of Armes* (1489) in Crotch, *Prologues and Epilogues*, pp. 183–84. For an account of the tournament held at Westminster in 1494 at the creation of the Duke of York, see *Letters and Papers of Richard III and Henry VII*, ed. James Gairdner, 3 vols., Rolls ser. (London, 1861), I, 388–404. In general, see Francis H. Cripps-Day, *The History of the Tournament in England and in France* (London, 1918), pp. 83–108; R. Cotman Clephan, *The Tournament, Its Periods and Phases* (London, 1919), pp. 38ff.; Sidney Anglo, *The Great Tournament Roll of Westminster* (Oxford, 1968); Sidney Anglo, *Spectacle, Pageantry and Early Tudor Policy* (Oxford, 1969).

124. For Malory's view, see *Works*, III, 1229; for Caxton, *The Book of the Ordre of Chyvalry*, ed. Alfred T. P. Byles, Early English Text Society, orig. ser., 168 (London, 1926), epilogue, pp. 121–25; Crotch, *Prologues and Epilogues*, pp. 82–84. Caxton's translation was from a French version of Raymon Lull's thirteenth-century *Libre del Orde de Cavayleria*.

125. Juan Luis Vives, *A Very Fruitful and Pleasant Booke Called the Instruction of a Christen Woman* (London, 1557), translated from the Latin original (1523), sig. Diii; Vives, *De Tradendis Disciplinis* (1531), trans. Foster Watson as *Vives on Education* (Cambridge, 1913), pp. 239, 246, 248–49; Vives, *The Office and Duetie of an Husband*, trans. Thomas Paynell (London, 1550?), sig. vii. Vives considers the whole question of historical truth and fiction in a dialogue, *Truth Dreamed Up, or Of Poetic License: To What Extent Poets May Be Permitted to Vary from the Truth* (1522): see *Opera Omnia* (Valencia, 1782), II, 517–31; summarized in Nelson, *Fact and Fiction*, pp. 45–48.

126. Roger Ascham, *Toxophilus* (1545), in *English Works*, ed. William A. Wright (Cambridge, 1904), pp. xiv–xv; Ascham, *The Scholemaster* (1570), ibid., pp. 230–31. For Erasmus against the Arthurian romances, see *The Education of a Christian Prince*, trans. Lester K. Born (1936: reprinted, New York, 1968), p. 200; *Peregrinatio religionis ergo* (1526), anonymous translation, c. 1536–37 (see *The Earliest Translations of Erasmus's Colloquia 1536–66*, ed. Henry de Vocht [Louvain, 1928], pp. 101–95). For the Erasmians, see Robert P. Adams, "Bold Bawdy and Open Manslaughter: The English New Humanist Attack on Medieval Romance," *Huntington Library Quarterly*, 23 (1959), 33–44; *The Better Part of Valor: More, Erasmus, Colet and Vives on Humanism, War and Peace, 1496–1535* (Seattle, Wash., 1962). The military methods in More's *Utopia*, according to C. S. Lewis, are "mischievously designed to flout the chivalric code at every turn" (*English Literature*, pp. 28–30). Thomas Elyot compares the New Testament with *Troilus and Criseyde* to the same effect in *Pasquill the Playne* (1533); see Alice S. Miskimin, *The Renaissance Chaucer* (New Haven, Conn., 1975), p. 156. And finally, see Cornelius Agrippa, *Of the Vanitie and Uncertaintie of Arts and Sciences* (1530), trans. James Sandford (London, 1575), chap. 4, "Of Poetrie," pp. 13–14. For the post-Erasmians, see Nelson, *Fact and Fiction*, pp. 98–105.

127. Polydore Vergil, *English History*, ed. Sir Henry Ellis, Camden Society 36

(London, 1846), p. 107. The *Anglica historia* was begun in 1506, completed in first draft in 1513, printed in a revised version at Basle in 1534, and translated in manuscript during the Tudor period. See also the Ellis edition, pp. 26, 30–32, 48, 60–61, 122, 126; and Denys Hay, *Polydore Vergil* (Oxford, 1952), pp. 79–168.

128. The best account remains T. D. Kendrick, *British Antiquity* (London, 1950). See also Arthur Ferguson, "John Twyne: A Tudor Humanist and the Problem of Legend," *Journal of British Studies*, 9 (1969), 24–44. William Camden's *Britannia* appeared first in 1586 and was enlarged in subsequent editions. According to Camden, Geoffrey's history was by his time "yet of little authority amongst men of learning" (preface to 1607 ed., trans. Edmund Gibson [London, 1695]). Camden reviewed all the previous accounts from Wethamstede on and concluded that "the whole story is a thing patched of meer incongruities and absurdities" (ibid., p. ix). There is a brilliant short summary by him in the *Curious Discourses*, delivered before the Society of Antiquaries, ed. Thomas Hearne (London, 1771), I, 90–93; and see chap. 3 in this book. Wethamstede, it should be said, still accepted much of Geoffrey's story, and the British history continued to have adherents, despite Camden; see Ernest Jones, *Geoffrey of Monmouth 1640–1800*, University of California Publications in English, 5, no. 3 (Berkeley, 1944), pp. 357–442.

129. Gildas, *De calamitate, excidio et conquestu Britanniae* (Antwerp, 1525); Hay, *Polydore Vergil*, pp. 29–31; Dennis E. Rhodes, "The First Edition of Gildas," *Library*, 6th ser., 1 (1979), 355–60.

130. John Leland's *Assertio inclytissimi Arturii regis Britanniae* (1554) was translated by Richard Robinson (1582) and is reprinted with a useful introduction in *The Famous History of Chinon of England*, ed. W. E. Mead, Early English Text Society, orig. ser., 165 (London, 1925), esp. p. 39. See also Kendrick, *British Antiquity*, pp. 41–43, 78–96; and now James Carley, "Polydore Vergil and John Leland on King Arthur: The Battle of the Books," *Interpretations*, 15 (1984), 86–100.

131. See P. J. C. Field, "The Winchester Round Table," *Notes and Queries*, 223 (1978), 204; Schnolke-Hasselmann, "The Round Table: Idea, Fiction, Reality," *Arthurian Literature*, 2 (1982), 41–75; Leslie Alcock, *Arthur's Britain* (London, 1971), pp. 73–80; Geoffrey Ashe, ed. *Arthur's Britain* (New York, 1968), pp. 126–27, 137, et passim; Antonia Gransden, "The Growth of Glastonbury Traditions and Legends," *Journal of Ecclesiastical History*, 27 (1976), 352.

132. Samuel Daniel, *Collection of the History of England* (1612–18), printed from the 1626 edition in *The Complete Works*, ed. Alexander Grosart (1896; reprinted, New York, 1963), IV, 85–90; John Speed, *Historie of Great Britaine* (London, 1611), pp. 158–70, 316–18.

133. The standard works are Joel E. Spingarn, *A History of Literary Criticism in the Renaissance*, 2d ed. (New York, 1908); Bernard Weinberg, *A History of Literary Criticism in the Italian Renaissance*, 2 vols. (Chicago, 1961); Baxter Hathaway, *The Age of Criticism: The Late Renaissance in Italy* (Ithaca, 1962). A recent translation of the *Poetics* by L. J. Potts entitles it suggestively, *Aristotle on the Art of Fiction* (Cambridge, 1953). For the *Poetics* in the Middle Ages, see W. F. Boggess, "Aristotle's *Poetics* in the Fourteenth Century," *Studies in Philology*, 67 (1970), 278–94; and for the *Poetics* in Tudor England, Myron T. Herrick, "The Early History of Aristotle's *Rhetoric* in England," *Philological Quarterly*, 5 (1926), 242–57.

134. Giraldo Cinthio, *On Romances*, trans. Henry L. Snuggs (Lexington, Ky., 1968), pp. 51, 167. Cinthio answers the claims of Diodorus Siculus (and thus Caxton) for the precedence of history (pp. 51–52). The work was finished in 1549; Cinthio interpolated further remarks for the 1554 edition.

135. Hathaway, *Age of Criticism*, p. 163, who finds Castelvetro's ideas "starkly novel" (p. 177). Ludovico Castelvetro, *On the Art of Poetry*, trans. Andrew Bongiorno (Binghamton, N.Y., 1984), pp. 3ff, 92ff. See H. B. Charleton, *Castelvetro's Theory of Poetry* (Manchester, 1913); Bernard Weinberg, "Castelvetro's Theory of Poetics," in *Critics and Criticism*, ed. R. S. Crane et al. (Chicago, 1952), pp. 249–71. One of the replies to Castelvetro by Jacopo Mazzoni (1587) is excerpted in *Literary Criticism: Plato to Dryden*, ed. Allan H. Gilbert (1940; reprinted, Detroit, 1962), pp. 388–91.

136. Eighteen *artes historiae* are included in the second edition of Johann Wolfius, *Artes historicae penus* (Basle, 1579). Some typical examples influential in England are Simon Grynaeus, *De utilitate legendae historiae* (1530), translated and prefixed to English translations of Sallust (1564), Josephus (1603), and Justin (1606); Thomas Blundeville, *True Order and Methode of Wryting and Reading Hystories* (1574), adapted from works by Patrizzi and Acontius, ed. Hugh G. Dick, *Huntington Library Quarterly*, 3 (1940), 149–70; Jean Bodin, *Methodus ad facilem historicum cognitionem* (1566), chap. 4, translated as "Of the Choice of History" by Thomas Heywood for his translation of Sallust; see the edition by Charles Whibley (London, 1924), pp. 5–48. Bodin had criticized the Brutus legend, but he was very popular in England; see Leonard F. Dean, "Bodin's *Methodus* in England before 1625," *Studies in Philology*, 39 (1942), 160–66.

137. Puttenham, *Arte of English Poesie* (1589), ed. G. D. Willcock and Alice Walker (Cambridge, 1936), p. 40. The tract appeared anonymously and has caused some difficulties as to authorship, though it is usually ascribed to George or (less likely) Richard Puttenham. Philip Sidney's *Defence of Poesie*, though written earlier, appeared in two versions in 1595; see *The Prose Works*, ed. Albert Feuillerat (Cambridge, Mass., 1935), pp. 46–83. For general commentary (besides Spingarn's *Literary Criticism*), see J. M. W. Atkins, *English Literary Criticism: The Renascence* (London, 1947); and for other texts, *Elizabethan Critical Essays*, ed. G. Gregory Smith, 2 vols. (Oxford, 1904).

138. *Advancement of Learning*, in *The Works of Francis Bacon*, ed. James Spedding, Robert Ellis, and D. D. Heath (Cambridge, 1863), VI, 182–83, 189–91, 202–3. See Murray W. Bundy, "Bacon's True Opinion of Poetry," *Studies in Philology*, 27 (1930), 244–64; Leonard F. Dean, "Sir Francis Bacon's Theory of Civil History Writing," *ELH*, 8 (1941), 161–83.

139. *Midsummer Night's Dream*, V.1.12–17.

140. *Wonder of Women or the Tragedy of Sophonisba*, in *The Plays of John Marston*, ed. H. H. Wood (Edinburgh, 1938), II, 5.

141. *The Whore of Babylon*, in *The Dramatic Works of Thomas Dekker*, ed. Fredson Bowers (Cambridge, 1955), II, 497. See also Ben Jonson, prologue to *Epicoene* (1616) in *Works*, ed. C. H. Herford and Percy Simpson, 11 vols. (Oxford, 1925–52), V, 164; *Timber*, ibid., VIII, 609–10, 635; George Chapman, *The Revenge of Bussy D'Amboise* (1613), ed. F. S. Boas (Boston, 1905), p. 168. See also Nelson, *Fact and Fiction*, pp. 34–35, 98–105.

142. Wilkinson, *Ovid Recalled*, p. 416; Douglas Bush, *Mythology and the Renais-*

sance Tradition in English Poetry (London, 1932), pp. 81–85. D. L. Clark speaks of the "displacement of allegory by example" (*Rhetoric and Poetry in the Renaissance* [New York, 1922], pp. 154–61). See also Myrick, *Sidney*, pp. 194–228. For the continued importance of allegory, see the classical statements of Sir John Harington in "A Brief Apologie of Poetrie," the preface to his translation of *Orlando Furioso* (1591), ed. Robert McNulty (Oxford, 1972); and the elaborate commentary by George Sandys for the second edition of his translation of the *Metamorphoses* (1632), ed. Karl Halley and S. T. Vandersall (London, 1970). Even so, there was a distinct movement away from the medieval notion of fable: see Lee T. Pearcy, *The Meditated Muse: English Translations of Ovid 1560–1700* (Hampden, 1984).

143. Francis Bacon, *Advancement of Learning*, bk. 2; *De Augmentis*, bk. 2, ch. 8; *De sapientia veterum*, pref. See C. W. Lemmi, *The Classic Deities in Bacon* (Baltimore, 1933).

144. See R. S. Crane, *The Vogue of Medieval Chivalric Romance during the English Renaissance* (Menasha, Wis., 1919); "The Vogue of *Guy of Warwick* from the Close of the Middle Ages to the Romantic Revival," *PMLA*, new ser., 30 (1915), 125–94; Mead, *Chinon of England*, p. xxi. To be fair, romance did not die easily; see Capt. Cox's list of books (1575) in *Robert Laneham's Letter, New Shakespeare Soc.*, 6 (1890), pp. xii–xiii; Ethel Seaton, "Marlowe's Light Reading," in *Elizabethan and Jacobean Studies Presented to Frank P. Wilson* (Oxford, 1959), pp. 17–35. The *Morte Darthur* was reprinted in 1529, 1537, 1585, and for the last time in 1634. The anonymous editor tries to defend the historicity of the story but allows that "in many places fables and fictions are inserted, which may be a blemish to the reputation of what is true in this history. . . . Therefore, reader, I advertise thee to deal with this book as thou wouldst do with thy house or thy garment; if the one do want but a little repair, thou wilt not pull down (madly) the whole frame."

145. See, for example, "Thomas Newton in Commendation of This Book," in *The Gallant Delectable and Pleasant Hystorie of Garileon of Englande* (London, 1578); and John Webster, verses to Anthony Munday, in *The Third and Last Part of Palmerin of England* (London, 1602). See also Henry Thomas, *Spanish and Portuguese Romances of Chivalry* (Cambridge, 1920); Mary Patchell, *The Palmerin Romances in Elizabethan Prose Fiction* (New York, 1947); Ortega y Gasset as quoted in E. C. Riley, *Cervantes's Theory of the Novel* (Oxford, 1962), p. 22.

146. *Eastward Hoe* (1605), in Jonson, *Works*, IV, 487–619 (the play is now believed to have been written in collaboration with Chapman and Marston). Francis Beaumont's *Knight of the Burning Pestle* (1613) has been edited with a useful introduction by John Doebler (London, 1967).

147. Michael Drayton, *Works*, ed. J. William Hebel, 5 vols. (Oxford, 1961), IV, vii*.

148. Ibid., v, 297ff. See William H. Moore, "Sources of Drayton's Conception of the *Polyolbion*," *Studies in Philology*, 65 (1968), 783–803.

149. See Bernard H. Newdigate, *Michael Drayton and His Circle* (Oxford, 1941), pp. 92ff.; I. Gourvitch, "A Note on Drayton and Philemon Holland," *Modern Language Review*, 25 (1930), 332–36. He was also a friend of Francis Beaumont and his brother (*Works*, III, 230).

150. John Selden's *The Reverse or Backface of the English Janus*, trans. Redmon

Westcot (London, 1682), pp. 8–12, from the *Jani Anglorum facies altera*, which is included in Selden's *Opera Omnia*, ed. David Wilkins (London, 1726).

151. Drayton, *Works*, IV, vi. Selden has still not received a modern biography, but see chap. 3 in this book.

152. Cf. *The History of Tithes* (1617): "The testimonies were chosen by weight, not by number, taken only thence whether the margin directs, never at second hand. . . . The fountains only, and what best cleared them, satisfied me" (Selden, *Opera*, III, 1072).

153. Drayton, *Works*, IV, viii*–xii*, and the notes to pp. 15, 46, 89, 125, 155. See I. Gourvitch, "Drayton's Debt to Geoffrey of Monmouth," *Review of English Studies*, 4 (1928), 394–403. Drayton also knew the saints' lives of the *Golden Legend* and did not forget St. Amphibalus: *Works*, V, 242. See Alice Haussy, *Poly-Olbion, ou L'Angleterre vue par un Elisabéthain* (Paris, 1972), pp. 52–57.

154. Drayton, *Works*, IV, ix*.

155. See Drayton's correspondence with Drummond of Hawthornden, complaining of the publishers' indifference, in Oliver Elton, *Drayton* (1905; reprinted, New York, 1966), pp. 120–28.

2. Reginald Pecock and Lorenzo Valla

1. Nicholas of Cusa in his *De Concordantia Catholica* (1432–35), III.2; cf. *Opera* (Basle, 1565), reprinted in Christopher Coleman, *Constantine the Great and Christianity*, Columbia University Studies in History, Economics and Public Law, 60, no. I (New York, 1914), pp. 228–37. For the use and criticism of the *Donation* in the Middle Ages, J. J. von Döllinger, *Fables Respecting the Popes*, trans. Alfred Plummer (London, 1871), pp. 89–103; F. Zinkeisen, "The *Donation of Constantine* as applied by the Roman Church," *English Historical Review*, 9 (1894), 625–32; Gerhard Laehr, *Die Konstantinische Schenkung in der abendländischer Literatur des Mittelalters* (Berlin, 1926; reprinted, Vaduz, 1965); V. H. H. Green, "The Donation of Constantine," *Church Quarterly Review*, 135 (1943), 39–63; Walter Ullmann, *Medieval Papalism* (London, 1949); Walter Ullmann, *The Growth of Papal Government in the Middle Ages*, 2d ed. (London, 1965); Domenico Maffei, *La Donazione di Costantino nei Giuristi Medievali* (Milan, 1964); Giovanni Antonazzi, "Lorenzo Valla e la Donazione di Costantino nel secolo XV," *Rivista di Storia della Chiesa in Italia*, 4 (1950), 186–223.

2. The *Donation* was defended, for example, by Augustinus Steuchus, *Contra Laurentium Vallum in Falsa Donatione Constantini* (Lyons, 1547), and answered by John Calvin in the *Institutes*, IV.xi.12. For evidence of continuing debate into the seventeenth century, see Richard Crakanthorpe, *The Defense of Constantine* (London, 1621). There are useful citations in Maffei, *La Donazione*, pp. 321ff.; L. D. Ettlinger, *The Sistine Chapel before Michelangelo* (Oxford, 1965), p. 111n.

3. There is, for example, no reason to suppose that Pecock had read Valla, as H. Maynard Smith alleges in his *Pre-Reformation England* (London, 1938), p. 422.

4. For the alleged modernity of Pecock, see most recently Arthur B. Ferguson, "Reginald Pecock and the Renaissance Sense of History," *Studies in the Renais-*

sance, 13 (1966), 147–65. Ferguson speaks of the essentially "medieval" character of Pecock's thought but nevertheless insists upon his anticipation of Renaissance humanism. He does not say much about the *Donation*, however. For the older view in its extreme form, that Pecock was "too modern even for some people who live in the twentieth century," see E. M. Blackie, "Reginald Pecock," *English Historical Review*, 26 (1911), 448–68; and Reginald Pecock, *The Book of Faith*, ed. J. L. Morison (Glasgow, 1909), pp. 76–79. For echoes in the more recent literature, see E. F. Jacob, "Reginald Pecock," *Proceedings of the British Academy*, 37 (1951), 144; V. H. H. Green, "Bishop Pecock and the English Bible," *Church Quarterly Review*, 129 (1940), 281n.

5. For the details of Pecock's life, see John Lewis, *The Life of Reginald Pecock* (London, 1744); Reginald Pecock, *The Repressor of Over Much Blaming of the Clergy*, ed. Churchill Babington, Rolls Series, 19 (London, 1860), I, introd.; V. H. H. Green, *Bishop Reginald Pecock* (Cambridge, 1945); Jacob, "Pecock"; A. B. Emden, *A Biographical Register of the University of Oxford* (Oxford, 1959), III, "Pecock."

6. Charles Mallet, *A History of the University of Oxford* (London, 1924), I, 186.

7. Always excepting Aristotle, whose works were largely known in translation. Even so, it was the logical, scientific, and metaphysical writings that were studied to the neglect of the *Rhetoric* and *Poetics*.

8. *Repressor*, I, ivn. The paradox was continued in the next century when the English Protestants adopted Pecock as a forerunner and placed him thereby back among the Lollards. See, for example, John Foxe, *The Acts and Monuments*, 4th ed., ed. Joseph Pratt (London, 1870), III, 731–34. *The Index Expurgatorius* of Madrid even described him as a Lutheran professor of Oxford (Smith, *Pre-Reformation England*, p. 287).

9. *Repressor*, I, 73, 6.

10. Thomas Gascoigne, *Loci e libro veritatum*, ed. James E. Thorold Rogers (Oxford, 1881), p. xlii. See also *An English Chronicle*, ed. J. S. Davies, (Camden Society (London, 1856), p. 77; *Brief Latin Chronicle* in *Three Fifteenth Century Chronicles*, ed. J. Gairdner, Camden Society (London, 1880), p. 167.

11. William C. Greet, ed., in his preface to Reginald Pecock, *The Reule of Crysten Religioun*, Early English Text Society, orig. ser., 171 (London, 1927), p. xiii; Elsie V. Hitchcock, ed., in her preface to Reginald Pecock, *The Donet*, Early English Text Society, orig. ser., 156 (London, 1921), p. xvii.

12. *Repressor*, I, 49–50.

13. Green, "Bishop Pecock," pp. 84–87; Jacob, "Pecock," pp. 149–50; Greet, *Reule*, pp. xiv–xv.

14. *Repressor*, I, 8; *Book*, pp. 125–26. The arguments of syllogisms give us "well nigh all things which a man know other wise than a beast knows" (E. V. Hitchcock, ed., *The Follower to the Donet*, Early English Text Society, orig. ser., 164 [London, 1924], p. 9).

15. *Reule*, pp. 428–29; *Repressor*, I, 76.

16. *Repressor*, I, 76.

17. *Reule*, pp. 425–26; *Repressor*, I, 42, 97.

18. *Repressor*, I, 99; *Book*, p. 139.

19. *Repressor*, I, 131.

20. "The doom of reason ought not for to be expounded, glossed, interpreted, and brought for to accord with the said outward writing in Holy Scripture"; it is the Bible, not reason, which is malleable (*Repressor*, I, 25–26; *Follower*, p. 10; *Book*, p. 126; *Reule*, p. 464). There are, however, truths known to faith and not to reason (*Reule*, pp. 202ff.). Cf. Everett H. Everson, "Reginald Pecock, Christian Rationalist," *Speculum*, 31 (1956), 235–42.

21. *Reule*, p. 461. He advises the expositor to keep to the literal interpretation, however, and to use interpretations especially of those "wise holy lettered clerks which lived in the time of the apostles and were hearers and scholars of the apostles."

22. *Reule*, p. 133.

23. *Book*, pp. 261ff.

24. Cf. *Reule*, pp. 431ff. For Pecock's source, see S. R. Daly, "Peter Comestor: Master of Histories," *Speculum*, 32 (1957), 62–73.

25. "For else there might none opinion be overcome by strength of argument, how false ever the opinion were, so that he included no repugnance, such as God might not do by miracle" (*Book*, p. 270). For Pecock's general aversion to miracles, see also *Book*, p. 294; *Repressor*, II, 353–54.

26. Morison, introduction to *Book*, p. 76.

27. *Book*, pp. 250–51; cf. *Reule*, p. 433.

28. *Book*, p. 252 (re the Hundred Years War).

29. *Repressor*, I, 81.

30. *Repressor*, II, 322–23, 350ff. For other contemporary references, see Babington, *Repressor*, II, 323n; for the attack on all clerical endowments, John Wyclif, *Dialogus*, ed. A. W. Pollard, Wyclif Society (London, 1856).

31. *Repressor*, II, 351–52, 357–58.

32. For the text of the *Donation*, see Coleman, *Constantine*, pp. 228–37, from Karl Zeumer, *Festgabe für Rudolf von Gneist* (Berlin, 1888), pp. 39ff; for the *Vita Sylvestri*, Coleman, pp. 217–27, from B. Mombritius, *Sanctuarium seu Vitae Sanctorum*, ed. H. Quentin and A. Brunet (Paris, 1910), II, 508–31. The *Life* preceded the *Donation*, apparently dating from the end of the fifth century; see W. Levison, "Konstantinische Schenkung and Silvesterlegende," *Miscellanea Francesco Ehrle* (Rome, 1924), II, 181ff., 239ff.

33. *Reule*, p. 426. See also the manuscript fragment quoted by Lewis, *Life of Pecock*, p. 68.

34. *Repressor*, II, 352–53. The *Tripartite History* was a condensed Latin version by the translator Epiphanius, guided by Cassiodorus, of the *Ecclesiastical Histories* of Socrates, Sozomen, and Theodoret. It seems to have first been criticized by the humanist Beatus Rhenanus in 1523. See M. L. W. Laistner, "The Value and Influence of Cassiodorus' Ecclesiastical History," *Harvard Theological Review*, 41 (1948), 51–67, reprinted in Chester G. Starr, ed., *The Intellectual Heritage of the Early Middle Ages* (Ithaca, 1957), pp. 22–39.

35. *Repressor*, II, 353–54; *Book*, pp. 270, 294. Pecock finds a discrepancy between the Pseudo-Damasus and Jerome that undermines the authority of the *Liber* (*Book*, pp. 354, 359–60).

36. *Repressor*, II, 357–59. Most of this evidence is as suspect as the *Donation*.

37. *Repressor*, II, 374. This is the thirteenth-century chronicler Martinus Pol-

onus, who seems to have supplied most of this information to Pecock. His work is a brief world chronicle, from Creation to 1277. See the recent article by William Matthews in *Medieval Literature and Civilization: Studies in Memory of G. N. Garmonsway* (London, 1969), pp. 275–88.

38. There is a convenient and extensive list of authorities in Ernest C. Richardson, trans., *Eusebius: Constantine* (Oxford, 1890), pp. 336–44, 445ff., and in Coleman, *Constantine*, pp. 25ff. A brilliant account of the sources is included in Norman H. Baynes, "Constantine the Great and the Christian Church," *Proceedings of the British Academy*, 15 (1929), 341–442. Conspicuous by their absence among Pecock's authorities were some important literary works, especially the pamphlet by Lactantius, *On the Deaths of the Persecutors*, usually considered the most trustworthy literary account (see the edition by J. Moreau [Paris, 1954]), but also the evidence of laws, coins, inscriptions, etc.

39. For the problems of the *Liber*, see the useful brief discussion in E. H. Davenport, *The False Decretals* (Oxford, 1916), pp. 64ff.; L. Duchesne, *Le Liber Pontificalis: Texte, introduction et commentaire* (Paris, 1886), I, cix–cxx (text, 170–201). There is an English translation by Louise R. Loomis, *The Book of the Popes* (New York, 1916).

40. Cf. Coleman, *Constantine*, pp. 139, 154ff.; Edward Gibbon, *The History of The Decline and Fall of the Roman Empire*, ed. J. B. Bury (London, 1897–1900), II, 305n.; Baynes, "Constantine," pp. 396–98, 430–31. For the complex problems involved in the interpretation of this work, see esp. H. Grégoire in *Revue de l'Université de Bruxelles*, 36 (1930), 231–72, and *Byzantion*, 13 (1938), 561–83, and *Bulletin de la Classe des lettres et des sciences morales et politiques*, 39 (1953), 462–78. See also G. Downey in *Dumbarton Oaks Papers*, 6 (1951), 57–66. For recent accounts favoring Eusebius, see Andrew Alföldi, *The Conversion of Constantine the Great*, trans. H. Mattingly (Oxford, 1948); A. H. M. Jones, *Constantine and the Conversion of Europe* (New York, 1962), pp. 73–90.

41. See British Museum MS *Cotton Nero* C.vi.fs.51–58v, described by E. F. Jacob, "Florida Verborum Venustas," *Bulletin of the John Rylands Library*, 17 (1933), 274–78. Another reply to Pecock by John Bury is given in extract in Babington's edition of the *Repressor*, II, 567ff.

42. G. Mancini, *Vita di Lorenzo Valla* (Florence, 1891); L. Barozzi and R. Sabbadini, *Studi sul Panormita e sul Valla* (Florence, 1891); Franco Gaeta, *Lorenzo Valla* (Naples, 1955).

43. On the neglect of grammar in fifteenth-century schools, see, e.g., the testimony of William Bingham, *Cal. Pat. Rolls Henry VI*, III, 295. For its subordination to logic, see H. Rashdall, *The Universities of Europe in the Middle Ages*, ed. F. M. Powicke and A. B. Emden (Oxford, 1936), III, 346; J. B. Mullinger, *The University of Cambridge from the Earliest Times to ... 1535* (Cambridge, 1873), I, 361; Gordon Leff, *Paris and Oxford in the Thirteenth and Fourteenth Centuries* (New York, 1968), pp. 120–22; Brother Bonaventura, "The Teaching of Latin in Later Medieval England," *Medieval Studies*, 23 (1961), 1–20.

44. Hanna Gray, "Valla's *Encomium of St. Thomas Aquinas* and the Humanist Conception of Christian Antiquity," in *Essays in History and Literature Presented to Stanley Pargellis* (Chicago, 1965), pp. 37–51. Valla's works have been reprinted by Eugenio Garin in the *Monumenta politica et philosophica rariora*, ser. I, nos. 5–6

(Turin, 1962). Especially relevant besides the *Encomium* are the *Dialectical Disputations* and the *Elegantiae*, and scattered remarks; cf. Francesco Adorno, "Di alcune orazioni e prefazioni di Lorenzo Valla," *Rinascimento*, 5 (1954), 191–225.

45. Eugenio Garin, *Philosophy and Civic Life in the Renaissance*, trans. Peter Munz (Oxford, 1965), p. 54; cf. Gaeta, *Valla*, chap. 3, "La nuova filologia e il suo significato," pp. 77–126. A most useful recent discussion of Valla's philology and its relation to his notion of history is the second chapter of Donald R. Kelley's *Foundations of Modern Historical Scholarship* (New York, 1970), pp. 19–50.

46. Relevant extracts may be consulted in Eugenio Garin, ed., *Prosatori latini del quattrocento* (Milan, 1952), pp. 594–631; commentary in V. Rossi, *Il Quattrocento* (Milan, 1938), pp. 88ff. Even outside Italy, Valla was admired as *linguae latinae restaurator;* cf. Franco Simone, *The French Renaissance*, trans. H. G. Hall (London, 1969), p. 97.

47. *Repressor*, I, 32–33.

48. E. Harris Harbison, *The Christian Scholar in the Age of the Reformation* (New York, 1956), p. 46; Gianni Zippel, "Lorenzo Valla e le origine della storiografia umanistica a Venezia," *Rinascimento*, 7 (1956), 103n.; A. Morisi, "La filologia neotestimentaria di Lorenzo Valla," *Nuova rivista storica*, 48 (1964), 35–49. The text has been newly edited by Alessandro Perosa, *Istituto nazionale di studi sul Rinascimento, Studi e testi*, 1 (1970). For Valla's critical work on the ancient historians, see esp. R. Westgate, "The Text of Valla's Translation of Thucydides," *American Philosophical Society Transactions and Proceedings*, 67 (1936), 240–51; and G. Billanovich, "Petrarch and the Textual Tradition of Livy," *Journal of the Warburg and Courtauld Institutes*, 14 (1951), 137–208.

49. *Book*, pp. 304–5, and in a lost work entitled *The Provoker*; cf. Gascoigne, *Loci*, pp. 104, 209.

50. Hanna Gray, "Renaissance Humanism: The Pursuit of Eloquence," *Journal of the History of Ideas*, 24 (1963), 497–515.

51. "From eldest days continually hitherto, men were wont for to speak and write their words not only in truth but also therewith together for to speak and to write in some gains and beauty and in some deliciosity; and unto this end and purpose they used certain colors of rhetoric that with them their speeches should be more lusty." This was, however, merely spice and sauce for the meat, Pecock argues, and inappropriate for philosophy (*Repressor*, I, 255).

52. Valla, *De rebus a Ferdinando Hispaniarum rege et majoribus ejus gestis*, in Valla, *Opera omnia* (Basel, 1540), II, 6; cf. Garin, *Philosophy*, p. 55; Adorno, *Orazioni*, p. 194. Pecock on the contrary argued specifically against the use of historical examples as a means of furnishing moral wisdom—a commonplace for the humanist rhetoricians. Reason, not examples, was the sole instrument of philosophy (*Reule*, pp. 449–50).

53. Valla's tract, *De falso credita et ementita Constantini Donatione declamatio*, ed. W. Schwahn (Leipzig, 1928), appeared first in 1440. It was published by Ulrich von Hutten in 1519, and this edition was employed for an English translation in 1534 under the imprint of Thomas Godfray, *A treatyse of the Donation Gyven unto Sylvester* (*Short-Title Catalogue 1475–1640*, ed. A. W. Pollard and G. R. Redgrave [London, 1926], no. 5641). The translation appears to be by William Marshall, who also translated the *Defensor Pacis* at about the same time. See James K.

McConica, *English Humanists and Reformation Politics* (Oxford, 1965), pp. 136–37. I have used this translation, which is quite literal except for some minor additions, in preference to the more recent English version by Christopher Coleman (New Haven, Conn., 1922). I have modernized the spelling as I have all the passages from Pecock so that a comparison between the two authors might be more fairly made. For Hutten's edition, see Hajo Holborn, *Ulrich von Hutten and the German Reformation* (New Haven, Conn., 1937), p. 81. For the use of Godfray's work by Thomas Cromwell in the English Reformation, see the *Letters and Papers Foreign and Domestic of the Reign of Henry VIII*, ed. James Gairdner, VII (London, 1883), nos. 422–23.

54. Marshall trans., sig. f ii.

55. Here Valla succumbs to a forgery every bit as obvious as the *Donation;* see Coleman, trans., p. 73n.

56. Sig. g. ii.

57. Sigs. g iv et seq. There are other examples of anachronism here as where Valla exposes the premature reference to Constantinople as a patriarchate. He also criticizes the faulty geography of the forger.

58. Sig. j ii.

59. See, as another example, Valla's ridicule of ·the justification for papal headship, advanced by Pecock and many others, that Cephas was the name given to Peter (Babington, *Repressor*, I, xxiv). For the origin of this error, see Walter Ullmann, *The Individual and Society in the Middle Ages* (Baltimore, Md., 1966), p. 9n.

60. For an example of the modern effort at a constructive argument, see Paul Scheffer-Boichorst, "Neue Forschungen über die Konstantinische Schenkung," in *Mitteilungen des Instituts für österr. Geschichtsforschung*, 10 (1889), 302ff.; 11 (1890), 128ff. Through close examination of the style, vocabulary, and ideas, he places the forgery in the papal chancery of either Stephen II or Paul I, A.D. 752–67, a conclusion generally held today. For other views, however, see Maffei, *La Donazione*, pp. 7–9; Ullmann, *Growth*, p. 74n.

61. Döllinger, as a result, described Valla's work as "an artistic production, an eloquent declamation, [rather] than a calm historical investigation." For this reason he even preferred Pecock (*Fables*, p. 175).

62. Kelley remarks, for example, that while Valla could discriminate with skill among several classical styles and periods (and thus reveal an authentic historical relativism), with the Middle Ages his "sense of discrimination diminished as his disgust grew." With the fall of Rome, for Valla, there was only decline and disintegration. He was thus disinclined to attempt either to date or to discuss the *Donation* in any way except simply to show its nonclassical character (Kelley, *Foundations*, p. 37).

3. The Antiquarian Enterprise

1. Edward Gibbon, *The History of the Decline and Fall of the Roman Empire*, 7 vols., ed. J. B. Bury (London, 1900), VII, lxxi, 302; Poggio Bracciolini, *Ruinarum urbis Romae descriptio*, composed about 1431 and printed in *De varietate fortunae* (1723; reprinted, Bologna, 1969), pp. 5–39. See Angelo Mazzocco, "Petrarcha, Poggio

and Biondo: Humanism's Foremost Intepreters of Roman Ruins," in *Francis Petrarch, Six Centuries Later*, ed. Aldo Scaglione (Durham, N.C., 1975), pp. 353–63.

2. Edward Gibbon, *Memoirs of My Life*, ed. Georges A. Bonnard (London, 1966), pp. 133–34. Gibbon's immediate literary inspiration may well have been Conyers Middleton's *Life of Cicero* (London, 1741); see Melvyn New, "Gibbon, Middleton and the 'Barefooted Fryars,'" *Notes and Queries*, 223 (1978), 51–52.

3. Jacob Burckhardt's chapters in pt. III of *The Civilization of the Renaissance in Italy* (1860), trans. S. G. C. Middlemore (New York, 1929) are still worth consulting, but see now Roberto Weiss, *The Renaissance Discovery of Classical Antiquity* (Oxford, 1969); Arnaldo Momigliano, "Ancient History and the Antiquarian," in *Studies in Historiography* (New York, 1966), pp. 1–39.

4. See Joseph M. Levine, "Ancients and Moderns Reconsidered," *Eighteenth Century Studies*, 15 (1981), 72–89.

5. In Roger Ascham's English works, edited by James Bennet (1771). William Elstob had printed Ascham's Latin letters in 1703; James Upton, the *Scholemaster* in 1743. Lyly's grammar was revised by John Ward in 1732 and further revised for Eton College in 1758.

6. Roberto Weiss, "Petrarch the Antiquarian," in *Classical, Medieval and Renaissance Studies in Honor of B. L. Ullman*, ed. Charles Henderson (Rome, 1964), II, 199–209; Weiss, *Renaissance Discovery*, pp. 30–47; Pierre de Nolhac, *Petrarque et l'humanisme* (Paris, 1882), pp. 263–66; Angelo Mazzocco, "The Antiquarianism of Francesco Petrarch," *Journal of Medieval and Renaissance Studies*, 7 (1977), 203–24.

7. Petrarch, *Rerum familiarum*, VI. 2, trans. Aldo Bernardo (Albany, N.Y., 1975), pp. 290–95.

8. "Modern epigraphy starts in the political sphere." So Fritz Saxl, "The Classical Inscription in Renaissance Art and Politics," *Journal of the Warburg and Courtauld Institutes*, 4 (1941), 19–46.

9. Gibbon, *Memoirs*, p. 134.

10. Poggio to Niccoli, Sept. 27, 1430, *Two Renaissance Book Hunters: The Letters of Poggius Bracciolini to Nicolaus Niccoli*, trans. Phyllis Gordon (New York, 1974), pp. 167–70.

11. H. W. Janson, "Donatello and the Antique," in *Donatello e il suo tempo* (Florence, 1968), pp. 77–96; Isabelle Hyman, ed., *Brunelleschi in Perspective* (Englewood Cliffs, N.J., 1974), pp. 15–19; Richard Krautheimer, *Lorenzo Ghiberti* (Princeton, N.J., 1982), pp. 277–305; Millard Meiss, *Andrea Mantegna as Illuminator* (New York, 1957), pp. 55–56.

12. Edward Gibbon, *Le journal de Gibbon à Lausanne 1763–64*, ed. Georges Bonnard (Lausanne, 1945), pp. 42ff., 89ff. and *Memoirs*, p. 132. For Biondo, see Bartolemeo Nogara, ed. *Scritti inediti e rara di Biondo Flavio* (Rome, 1927); Denys Hay, "Flavio Biondo and the Middle Ages," *Proceedings of the British Academy*, 45 (1959), 99–128; Dorothy M. Robathan, "Flavio Biondo's *Roma Instaurata*," *Medievalia et Humanistica*, n.s. 1 (1970), 203–16.

13. See Petrarch's *De remediis utriusque fortunae*, known in England as the *Physicke against Fortune*, trans. Thomas Twyne (London, 1579), p. 148ᵛ.

14. Flavio Biondo, *Italia illustrata*, bk. viii (1474), trans. Gerald Strauss, in *Sixteenth-Century Germany, Its Topography and Topographers* (Madison, Wis., 1959),

p. 18. See too the vivid letter of Fra Gioconda to Lorenzo de' Medici, quoted by T. M. Greene, *The Light of Troy* (New Haven, Conn., 1982), p. 9.

15. The *Antiquitates divinae et humanae* seems to have given the name to the science; the word is used already in the fifteenth century but, according to Momigliano, received its original Varronian meaning only with Rosinus, *Antiquitatum romanarum corpus absolutissimum* (1583) ("Ancient History," pp. 5–6).

16. Poggio, *Two Renaissance Book Hunters*, pp. 114–15, 127–33; Gibbon, *Memoirs*, pp. 131–32.

17. See Bernard Ashmole, "Cyriac of Ancona," *Proceedings of the British Academy*, 45 (1959), 25–41; Paul MacKendrick, "A Renaissance Odyssey: The Life of Cyriac of Ancona," *Classica et Medievalia*, 13 (1952), 131–45; Edward W. Bodnar, *Cyriacus of Ancona and Athens*, Collections Latomus, 43 (Brussels, 1960). Poggio also collected inscriptions: see Mazzocco, "Petrarcha, Poggio and Biondo," p. 358.

18. See Julian Raby, "Cyriacus of Ancona and the Ottoman Sultan Mehmed II," *Journal of Warburg and Courtauld Institutes*, 43 (1980), 242–46. For the subsequent history of Renaissance epigraphy, see Weiss, *Renaissance Discovery*, pp. 145ff.; Charles Mitchell, "Archaeology and Romance in Renaissance Italy," *Italian Renaissance Studies*, ed. E. F. Jacob (London, 1960), pp. 455–83; Charles Mitchell, "Felice Feliciano Antiquarius," *Proceedings of the British Academy*, 47 (1961), 197–221; Erna Mandowsky and Charles Mitchell, *Pirro Ligorio's Roman Antiquities* (London, 1963), pp. 1–49; F. de Zulueta, *Don Antonio Agustín* (Glasgow, 1939). For a follower of Biondo, see Roberto Weiss, "Andrea Fulvio antiquario romano (c. 1470–1527)," *Annali della Scuola Normale Superiore di Pisa*, ser. 2, 28 (1959), 1–44.

19. Poggio, *On Nobility*, trans. Renée N. Watkins, in *Humanism and Liberty* (Columbia, Mo., 1978), pp. 122–23, 146–47, 166–67. Cf. Thomas Hearne: "The antient Greeks and Romans were very fond of Antiquities, and us'd to look upon them as sacred, and a very great Ornament of their Houses and Palaces. They therefore adorn'd the Vestibules and Porches of their Temples, Halls, etc. with Armour, Weapons, Trophies, Statues, Urns, Tables and Inscriptions, etc. They would not alienate, or part with them upon any price; and . . . the Citizens of Rome have imitated their ancestors in that Caution" (May 15, 1712, *Remarks and Collections*, III, ed. C. E. Doble, Oxford Historical Society, 13 [Oxford, 1889], 419).

20. For examples, see J. A. W. Bennett, *Essays on Gibbon* (Cambridge, 1980), p. 27n.; for Cotton, see Kevin Sharpe, *Sir Robert Cotton 1586–1631* (Oxford, 1979), p. 72; for Poggio, see Weiss, *Renaissance Discovery*, pp. 183–84; Poggio, *Two Renaissance Book Hunters*, pp. 117–18.

21. Roberto Weiss, *Humanism in England during the Fifteenth Century* (Oxford, 1957), pp. 13–21.

22. John Capgrave, *Ye Solace of Pilgrimes*, ed. C. A. Mills (London, 1911); cf. the twelfth-century *Mirabilia Urbis Romae*, trans. Francis M. Nichols (London, 1889) and the similar work of Master Gregorius printed by M. R. James in the *English Historical Review*, 32 (1917), 531–54.

23. For the prior claims of William of Worcestre (1415–82) and John Rous (1411–91), see T. D. Kendrick, *British Antiquity* (London, 1950), pp. 18–33; K. B.

McFarlane, "William Worcestre, A Preliminary Survey," in *Studies to Hilary Jenkinson*, ed. J. C. Davies (Oxford, 1957), pp. 196–221; John H. Harvey, ed. *William of Worcestre: Itineraries* (Oxford, 1969), pp. ix–xii; Antonia Gransden, *Historical Writing in England* II (Ithaca, 1982), pp. 308–41.

24. Kendrick, *British Antiquity*, pp. 45–64; [William Huddesford], *The Lives of Those Eminent Antiquaries John Leland, Thomas Hearne, and Anthony a Wood*, I (Oxford, 1772). For Leland's title "antiquarius," see Momigliano, "Ancient History," pp. 27–28.

25. Many of Leland's *encomia* were published first in 1589 and are reprinted in Hearne, *Remarks*, v, 81–167; see especially the "Instauratio bonarum literarium," p. 137 and Hoyt H. Hudson, "John Leland's List of Early English Humanists," *Huntington Library Quarterly*, 2 (1939), 301.

26. James P. Carley, "Leland in Paris," *Studies in Philology*, 83 (1986), 1–50; for Budé's numismatics, see L. Delaruelle, *Guillaume Budé* (Paris, 1907), pp. 139ff.

27. Leicester Bradner, *Musae Anglicanae* (London, 1940), p. 30; "Some Unpublished Poems of John Leland," *PMLA*, 71 (1956), 827–36; James P. Carley, "John Leland's *Cygnea Cantio*: A Neglected Tudor River Poem," *Humanistica Lovaniensia*, 32 (1983), 225–41. Leland published seven Latin poems between 1542 and 1546.

28. J. R. Liddell, "Leland's Lists of Manuscripts in Lincolnshire Monasteries," *English Historical Review*, 54 (1939), 88–95; James P. Carley has promised an annotated edition.

29. See Margaret Aston, "English Ruins and English History: The Dissolution and the Sense of the Past," *Journal of the Warburg and Courtauld Institutes*, 36 (1973), 231–55.

30. See, for example, Theodor E. Mommsen, "Petrarch's Conception of the 'Dark Ages,'" in *Medieval and Renaissance Studies*, ed. Eugene Rice (Ithaca, 1959), pp. 106–29; Erwin Panofsky, *Renaissance and Renascences in Western Art* (Stockholm, 1960).

31. Burckhardt pointed this out long ago in his *Civilization of the Renaissance in Italy*, pt. III, chap. 8.

32. Leland, *Instauratio Britannicae antiquitatis*, in Hearne, *Remarks*, v, 120.

33. For Celtis, who intended a *Germania illustrata*, and his disciple Aventinus, who closely resembles Leland, see the following works of Gerald Strauss: "Topographical-Historical Method in Sixteenth-Century German Scholarship," *Studies in the Renaissance*, 5 (1958), 87–101; *Historian in an Age of Crisis: Johannes Aventinus 1477–1534* (Cambridge, Mass., 1963); *Sixteenth-Century Germany: Its Topography and Topographers* (Madison, Wis., 1959).

34. Thomas Hearne, *Remarks*, vi, 88.

35. *The Laboryouse Journey & serche of John Leylande for Englandes Antiquitees . . . with declaracyons enlarged by Johan Bale* (London, 1549).

36. Ibid., sig. [C3ᵛ].

37. Leland, *De rebus collectanea*, ed. Thomas Hearne, 2d ed. (London, 1774), IV, 122–25, 134–36, 136–48; Ronald E. Buckalew, "Leland's Transcript of Aelfric's *Glossary*," *Anglo-Saxon England*, 7 (1978), 149–64. It too was published in the eighteenth century as Leland, *Commentarii de scriptoribus Britannicis*, ed. Anthony Hall (Oxford, 1709).

38. *Laboryouse Journey* [sig. F3ᵛ].

39. Ibid., sig. H.

40. Ibid., sig. I.

41. Edmund Gibson, "Life of Camden," prefixed to his edition of Camden's *Britannia* (London, 1695). See also Huddesford, *Lives*, I, 32, 48.

42. Leland, *Collectanea*, IV, 121; Leland, *Itineraries*, ed. Thomas Hearne, 2d ed. (London, 1745), III, 123–72. See N. R. Ker, "Medieval Manuscripts from Norwich Cathedral Priory," *Transactions of the Cambridge Bibliographical Society*, 1 (1953), 3; May McKisack, *Medieval History in the Tudor Age* (Oxford, 1971), pp. 8, 24.

43. Leland, *Itineraries*, IV, 151–52; Huddesford, *Lives*, I, 20–21.

44. Thomas Godwin, *Romanae historiae anthologia . . . An Exposition of the Roman Antiquities for the Use of Abingdon School* (London, 1622). I quote from the 1655 edition, p. 20.

45. Thomas Godwin, *Moses and Aaron: Civil and Ecclesiastical Rites Used by the Ancient Hebrewes* (London, 1624); Francis Rous, *Anthologiae Atticae libri septem* (London, 1637). I quote from the preface to the fourth edition of the latter (London, 1654).

46. *The Travels and Life of Sir Thomas Hoby Kt*, ed. Edgar Powell, Camden Miscellany, 10 (London, 1902), p. 25.

47. William Barkar, *Epitaphia et inscriptiones lugubres* (London, 1566). An earlier edition (1554) seems to have perished; see George B. Parks, "William Barkar, Tudor Translator," *Papers of the Bibliographical Society of America*, 51 (1957), 126–40.

48. William Thomas, *The Historie of Italie* (London, 1549), p. 22. There is a modern abridged version edited by George B. Parks (Ithaca, 1963).

49. For what follows, see Mary F. S. Hervey, *The Life, Correspondence and Collections of Thomas Howard, Earl of Arundel* (Cambridge, 1921); D. E. L. Haynes, *The Arundel Marbles* (Oxford, 1975); Francis C. Springell, *Connoisseur and Diplomat: The Earl of Arundel's Embassy to Germany in 1636* (London, 1963). Both Henry Wotton and Fynes Morrison had to adopt disguises on their visits to Rome; see Logan P. Smith, *Life and Letters of Sir Henry Wotton* (Oxford, 1907), 1, 17–18.

50. Edward Sherburn to Dudley Carleton, July 13, 1616, in W. Noel Sainsbury, *Original Papers . . . of Sir Peter Paul Rubens* (London, 1859), pp. 272–73.

51. Adolf Michaelis, *Ancient Marbles in Great Britain*, trans. C. A. M. Fennell (Cambridge, 1882), pp. 6–41, based largely on *The Negotiations of Sir Thomas Roe to the Ottoman Porte* (London, 1740). For Roe, see Michael J. Brown, *Itinerant Ambassador* (Lexington, Ky., 1970).

52. See Humphrey Prideaux, *Marmora Oxoniensia* (Oxford, 1676); Michael Maittaire, *Marmora Arundellianorum* (London, 1732–33); Richard Chandler, *Marmora Oxoniensia* (Oxford, 1763).

53. Haynes, *Arundel Marbles*, p. 7.

54. *The Diary of John Evelyn*, ed. E. S. de Beer (Oxford, 1955), III, 495–96.

55. Inigo Jones's notes to Book I of Andrea Palladio's *Quattro libri* are reproduced in a facsimile edition by Bruce Allsopp (Oxford, 1970); see also John Summerson, *Architecture in Britain, 1530–1830* (Baltimore, Md., 1963), p. 67.

56. John Webb, "Memoirs of Inigo Jones," in *The Most Notable Antiquity of Great Britain* (London, 1655); see Richard J. Atkinson, "Stonehenge and the History of Antiquarian Thought," in his *Stonehenge* (London, 1956), pp. 181–204.

57. See Leland's poem to Elyot in *Collectanea*, v, 144. Thomas Elyot's *Boke of the Governour* appeared first in 1531. The genre is surveyed by Ruth Kelso, *The Doctrine of the English Gentleman in the Sixteenth Century*, Illinois Studies in Language and Literature, 14 (Urbana, 1929).

58. Henry Peacham, *The Complete Gentleman*, ed. Virgil B. Heltzel (Ithaca, 1962), p. 117; Alan R. Young, *Henry Peacham* (Boston, 1979).

59. Joseph Addison, *Dialogues upon the Usefulness of Ancient Medals* (1703–5), in *Works* (London, 1721), I; John Evelyn, *Numismata* (London, 1697); Joseph Spence, *Polymetis* (London, 1747); Dr. John Arbuthnot, *Tables of Ancient Coins, Weights and Measures* (London, 1705, 1727).

60. See E. S. de Beer, "François Schott's *Itinerario d'Italia*," *Library*, 4th ser., 23 (1942), 57–84.

61. Francesco Ficoroni wrote a popular guidebook, *Le vestigia e rarità di Roma antica* (Rome, 1744). For Byers, see Brinsley Ford, "James Byers, Principal Antiquarian for the English Visitors to Rome," *Apollo*, new ser., 99 (1974), 446–61. Addison's *Remarks on Several Parts of Italy* appeared in London, 1705.

62. Pierre Gassendi, *The Mirrour of True Nobility and Gentility*, trans. W. Rand (London, 1657); Linda van Norden, "Peiresc and the English Scholars," *Huntington Library Quarterly*, 12 (1949), 369–89; Georges Cahen-Salvador, *Un grand humaniste Peiresc, 1580–1637* (Paris, 1951).

63. John Nichols, *Literary Anecdotes of the Eighteenth Century* (London, 1812–15), III, 721–46.

64. *Gentleman's Magazine*, 58 (1788), pt. 2, supp., p. 1149.

65. Cuthbert Tunstall, *De arte supputandi* (London, 1522); Charles Sturge, *Cuthbert Tunstall* (London, 1938). See too Thomas Smith's "Tables of Money," in John Strype, *Life of Sir Thomas Smith* (Oxford, 1820), pp. 263–73.

66. Mention should be made of Thomas Lydiat (1572–1646), who dared to challenge Scaliger in chronology, and John Greaves (1602–52), who had measured monuments in Rome and actually been to Egypt to see and measure the pyramids for himself; his *Pyramidographia* (1646) and *Discourse on the Roman Foot* (1647) are among his *Miscellaneous Works* printed by Thomas Birch in two volumes (London, 1737), with a life. Weights and measures are treated in Latin volumes by Edward Brerewood (1614) and Edward Bernard (1688).

67. Leland, *Itineraries*, I, 140–41.

68. See T. C. Skeat, "Two 'Lost' Works by John Leland," *English Historical Review*, 65 (1950), 506–7.

69. *Laboryouse Journey*, sig. [H3ᵛ].

70. Leland, *Itineraries*, III, 162; Kendrick, *British Antiquity*, pp. 135–36. Subsequent efforts, employing Talbot and Leland, are William Burton, *A Commentary on Antoninus His Itinerary* (London, 1658); and at the end of our period, Thomas Reynolds, *Iter Britanniarum with a New Commentary* (Cambridge, 1799). See F. Haverfield, *The Roman Occupation of Britain*, revised by George Macdonald (Oxford, 1924), pp. 67–75.

71. There was a London edition of Ortelius's *Theatrum orbis terrarum* (1606)

with a life by Francis Sweerts. For Ortelius' correspondence with the English, see *Ecclesiae Londino-Batavae Archivum*, ed. J. H. Hessels (Cambridge, 1887).

72. For Lhuyd, see Theodore M. Chotzen, "Some Sidelights on Cambro-Dutch Relations," in *Transactions of the Honourable Society of Cymmrodorion* (London, 1937), pp. 129–44; Kendrick, *British Antiquity*, pp. 136–38. Lhuyd's epistle to Ortelius (1568) was appended to the *Theatrum*.

73. F. J. Levy, "Daniel Rogers as Antiquary," *Bibliothèque d'Humanisme et Renaissance*, 27 (1965), 444–62.

74. Stephen Bateman, *The Doome of Warning* (London, 1581), pp. 399–400; C. E. Wright, "The Dispersal of the Monastic Libraries and the Beginnings of Anglo-Saxon Studies: Matthew Parker and His Circle," *Transactions of the Cambridge Bibliographical Society*, 1 (1947–53), 208–37; John Strype, *The Life and Acts of Matthew Parker* (London, 1691), esp. pp. 528–40. John Bale should not be forgotten as a link between Leland and the Parker circle: see Honor McCusker, "Books and Manuscripts Formerly in the Possession of John Bale," *The Library*, 4th ser., 16 (1935), 144–65; Honor McCusker, *John Bale: Dramatist and Antiquary* (Bryn Mawr, Pennsylvania, 1942); H. R. Luard, "A Letter from Bishop Bale to Archbishop Parker," *Cambridge Antiquarian Society Communications*, 17 (1878), 157–73.

75. Matthew Parker, *Correspondence*, ed. J. Bruce and T. T. Perowne (Cambridge, 1853), esp. pp. 253–54, 407, 424–26; W. W. Greg, "Books and Bookmen in the Correspondence of Archbishop Parker," *The Library*, 4th ser., 16 (1935), 243–79.

76. *The Testimonie of Antiquitie* (1566); Parker to Cecil, May 9, 1573, in Parker, *Correspondence*, pp. 424–26. See John Bromwich, "The First Printed Book in Anglo-Saxon Type," *Transactions of the Cambridge Bibliographical Society*, 3 (1962), 265–91; Theodore H. Lunbaugh, "Aelfric's *Sermo de Sacrificio* . . . in The Sixteenth and Seventeenth Centuries," in *Anglo-Saxon Scholarship: The First Three Centuries*, ed. Carl T. Berkhout and Milton Gatch (Boston, 1982), pp. 51–68.

77. The first such printed source was Polydore Vergil's edition of Gildas (1525): see Dennis E. Rhodes, "The First Edition of Gildas," *The Library*, 6th ser., 1 (1979), 355–60. A useful enumeration of printed medieval chronicles remains the introduction to the *Monumenta Historica Britannica* by Henry Petrie and John Sharpe (London, 1848). For criticism of the editorial methods of Parker and his contemporaries, see the introductions to the appropriate Rolls Series volumes, e.g. H. R. Luard to Matthew Paris, *Chronica majora*, 2 (1874), pp. xxiii–xxviii; 4 (1876), pp. xvii–xviii; *Flores historiarum*, 1 (1870), pp. xliii–xlv; Frederic Madden, *Historia Anglorum*, 1 (1866), pp. xxxiii–xxxv; William Stubbs (for Henry Savile) to William of Malmesbury, *De gestis regum Anglorum*, 1 (1887), pp. xciii–xcvii.

78. Robin Flower, "Lawrence Nowell and the Discovery of England in Tudor Times," *Proceedings of the British Academy*, 21 (1935), 47–73; Albert H. Marckwardt, "The Sources of Lawrence Nowell's *Vocabularium Saxonicum*," *Studies in Philology*, 45 (1948), 21–36; Albert H. Marckwardt, *Lawrence Nowell's Vocabularium Saxonicum* (Ann Arbor, Mich., 1952); Ronald E. Buckalew, "Nowell, Lambarde and Leland," in Berkhout and Gatch, *Anglo-Saxon Scholarship*, pp. 19–50.

79. William Lambarde, *Dictionarium Angliae Topographicum et Historicum: An*

Alphabetical Description of the Chief Places in England and Wales (London, 1730). Whether Lawrence Nowell was the famous dean or another is considered in Retha M. Warnicke, "Note on a Court of Requests Case of 1571," *English Language Notes*, 11 (1974), 250–56; but see Paula Black, "Lawrence Nowell's Disappearance in Germany," *English Historical Review*, 92 (1977), 345–53.

80. John Petheram, *An Historical Sketch of the Progress and Present State of Anglo-Saxon Literature in England* (London, 1840); Eleanor N. Adams, *Old English Scholarship in England from 1566–1800* (New Haven, Conn., 1917); Rosamund Tuve, "Ancients, Moderns and Saxons," *ELH*, 6 (1939), 165–90; J. A. W. Bennett, "The History of Old English and Old Norse Studies in England from the Time of Francis Junius till the End of the Eighteenth Century" (Ph.D. diss., Oxford University, 1938); "The Beginnings of Runic Studies in England," *Viking Society for Northern Research: Saga Book*, 13 (1950–51), 263–83; Berkhout and Gatch, *Anglo-Saxon Scholarship*.

81. See David C. Douglas, *English Scholars, 1660–1730*, 2d ed. (London, 1951), p. 19.

82. Henry Spelman to Abraham Wheloc, September 28, 1638, in *Original Letters of Eminent Literary Men*, ed. Sir Henry Ellis, Camden Society (London, 1843), pp. 154–55.

83. For the importance of philology to Spelman, see F. M. Powicke, "Sir Henry Spelman and the *Concilia*," *Proceedings of the British Academy*, 16 (1930), 353, 363–66. The difficulty of learning Anglo-Saxon without aids is vividly described by Willaim L'Isle in the preface to his *Saxon Treatise concerning the Old and New Testament* (London, 1623), sig. d.

84. J. G. A. Pocock, *The Ancient Constitution and the Feudal Law* (1957; reprinted, New York, 1967), pp. 91–123, 182–228.

85. H. A. Cronne, "The Study and Use of Charters by English Scholars in the Seventeenth Century: Sir Henry Spelman and Sir William Dugdale," in *English Historical Scholarship in the Sixteenth and Seventeenth Centuries*, ed. Levi Fox, Dugdale Society (Oxford, 1956), pp. 73–91. For Dugdale, see the *Life, Diary and Correspondence*, ed. William Hamper (London, 1827).

86. White Kennett's biography of William Somner is prefixed to Somner's *Treatise on the Roman Ports and Forts in Kent* (Oxford, 1693).

87. Ibid., pp. 5, 10.

88. Ibid., p. 11.

89. Ibid., pp. 23–24; William Somner, *Dictionarium Saxonico-Latino-Anglicum* (Oxford, 1659).

90. Edmund Gibson conflated several versions; he describes his method in a letter to Thomas Tanner, Bodl. MS. Tanner 25, f.12. His magnum opus was the *Codex juris ecclesiae anglicanae* (1713), where in typical antiquarian fashion he declaimed against "superficial secondhand knowledge" and in favor of printing the sources. See Norman Sykes, *Edmund Gibson* (London, 1926), pp. 10, 13. For criticism, see Charles Plummer, introduction to *Two of the Saxon Chronicles Parallel* (Oxford, 1899), pp. cxxiv, cxxix–cxxxi; for an appreciation, Douglas, *English Scholars*, pp. 69–71, 211–13.

91. George Hickes's grammars were published first as *Institutiones grammaticae*

Anglo-Saxonicae (Oxford, 1689). See J. A. W. Bennett, "Hickes's *Thesaurus*: A Study in Oxford Book Production," in *English Studies*, ed. F. P. Wilson (London, 1948), pp. 28–45; Douglas, *English Scholars*, pp. 77–97.

92. See chap. 2 in this book.

93. Edward Lhwyd, *Archaeologia Britannica* (1707; reprinted, Menston, Yorkshire, 1969). This first volume was a "glossography" only but was meant to introduce another on antiquities, on the model of Hickes; see the proposals in *The Life and Letters of Edward Lhwyd*, ed. R. T. Gunther, Early Science in Oxford, 14 (Oxford, 1945), pp. 41–42.

94. "I am very sensible an Account of such Antiquated Languages is in the vulgar Opinion but very jejune stuff" (Lhwyd to Hans Sloane, July 26, 1707, British Museum MS. Sloane 4041, f. 3). A vigorous effort to defend the Saxons was Richard Verstegen, *A Restitution of Decayed Intelligence: In Antiquities* (Antwerp, 1605), chap. 2. The work had five editions by 1673; see Samuel Kliger, *The Goths in England* (Cambridge, Mass., 1952), pp. 115ff.

95. Thomas Tanner, *Notitia Monastica* (London, 1695), preface; see Douglas, *English Scholars*, pp. 161–64. The *Monasticon Anglicarum* was assembled in three massive volumes by Roger Dodsworth and William Dugdale (1655–73); Douglas, pp. 30–61.

96. William Borlase, *Antiquities Historical and Monumental of Cornwall*, 2d ed. (London, 1769), p. v. See Elizabeth Elstob, *An Apology for the Study of Northern Antiquities* (1715), ed. Charles Peake, Augustan Reprint Society, 61 (Los Angeles, 1956), pp. iii, x; see also the dedication to Mrs. Elstob's *English Saxon Homily* (London, 1709). Jonathan Swift's *Proposals for Correcting the English Tongue* had appeared in 1712; see Irvin Ehrenpreis, *Swift* (Cambridge, Mass., 1967), II, 542–49. For Elstob, see Margaret Ashdown, "Elizabeth Elstob, the Learned Saxonist," *Modern Language Review*, 20 (1925), 125–46; Sarah Collins, "The Elstobs and the End of the Saxon Revival," and S. F. D. Hughes, "The Anglo-Saxon Grammars of George Hickes and Elizabeth Elstob," both in Berkhout and Gatch, *Anglo-Saxon Scholarship*, pp. 107–18, 119–47; S. F. D. Hughes, "Mrs. Elstob's Defense of Antiquarian Learning in her *Rudiments of Grammar for the English Tongue* (1715)," *Harvard Library Bulletin*, 27 (1979), 172–91.

97. There are lives of Camden in Thomas Smith, *Camdeni epistolae* (London, 1691); William Camden, *Britannia*, ed. Edmund Gibson (London, 1695); William Camden, *Britannia*, ed. Richard Gough (London, 1789). See Sir Maurice Powicke, "William Camden," *Essays and Studies*, n.s., 1 (1948), 67–84.

98. John Dee to Lord Burghley, Oct. 3, 1574, *Original Letters* (note 82 above), pp. 32–40. Dee's "Supplication to Queen Mary for the Recovery and Preservation of Ancient Writers and Monuments" was printed by Thomas Hearne in his edition of the *Cronica* of John of Glastonbury (Oxford, 1726), p. 490.

99. Camden, "The Author to the Reader," in *Britannia*. For the Camden-Ortelius correspondence, see Hessels, *Ecclesiae*, nos. 71–72, 78, 145; Smith, *Camdeni epistolae*, nos. 9, 21, 25–26, 29, 36, and app., pp. 97–108. Richard DeMolen promises a critical edition of Camden's correspondence for the Royal Historical Society: see "The Library of William Camden," *Proceedings of the American Philosophical Society*, 128 (1984), 327–409.

100. In Camden's *Remaines Concerning Britaine* (London, 1627), p. 23, he pleads for the publication of the works of Nowell, Lambarde, Joscelyn, and Francis Tate. According to John Aubrey, Camden kept a Welsh servant to help him learn the language (*Brief Lives*, ed. O. L. Dick [London, 1950], p. 51).

101. Preface, *Britannia* (Gough edition), 1, xxxv. "Thus the same hand remov'd the Rubbish, laid the Foundation, and rais'd the Fabrick. The old Itinerary was settled, the British and Saxon Tongues conquer'd, our ancient Historians perus'd, several parts of England survey'd, and now he durst think of reducing his Collections to some method and order" (Edward Gibson, *Britannia*, sig. [b2]). Camden's chronicles are in *Anglica, Normannica, Hibernica a veteribus scriptis* (Frankfurt, 1603).

102. For what follows, see F. J. Levy, "The Making of Camden's *Britannia*," *Bibliothèque d'Humanisme et Renaissance*, 26 (1964), 70–97; Stuart Piggott, "William Camden and the *Britannia*," *Proceedings of the British Academy*, 38 (1951), 199–217; Rudolf B. Gottfried, "The Early Development of the Section on Ireland in Camden's *Britannia*," *ELH*, 10 (1943), 117–30.

103. Camden, *Remaines* (London, 1674), p. 407. For other early uses of the term "middle ages" in England, see George Gordon, *Medium Aevum and the Middle Ages* (Oxford, 1925). Camden's poetry is in Smith, *Camdeni epistolae*, app., pp. 97–108; see especially the verses in praise of Roger Ascham (1590) describing the course of early English humanism (pp. 97–98).

104. Levy, "Camden's Britannia," p. 76n.

105. Thomas Fuller, *The Holy State and the Profane State*, ed. James Nichols (London, 1841), p. 135.

106. For two examples from the north of England, see F. Haverfield, "Cotton Julius F vi: Notes on Reginald Bainbrigg of Appleby, on William Camden, and on some Roman Inscriptions," *Transactions of the Cumberland and Westmorland Societies*, n.s., 11 (1911), 343–78; *Selections from the Household Books of the Lord William Howard*, Surtees Society (Durham, 1878), app., pp. 412, 506–7. Many others are cited in the *Britannia*.

107. Kendrick, *British Antiquity*, p. 151n.

108. The importance of seeing for oneself as an antidote to falsehood and credulity is a fundamental antiquarian insight and is repeated again and again, as in the portrait of John Stow drawn by John Strype and prefixed to his new edition of Stow's *Survey of London* (London, 1720), 1, xx.

109. The accusation came from a jealous fellow herald, Ralph Brooke, *A Discoverie of Certaine Errours* (London, 1596); for the resulting controversy, see Nicholas Harris Nicolas, *Memoir of Augustine Vincent* (London, 1827), pp. 20ff. The squabble helped to impose new standards of accuracy on the heralds and antiquaries.

110. William Lambarde to Camden, July 29, 1585, in Smith, *Camdeni epistolae*, pp. 28–29. Lambarde's *Perambulation of Kent* appeared first in 1576; at the end of the second edition (1596), he explains his relation to Camden. There is a good enumeration and description of the flood of local histories that followed in William Nicolson, *The English, Scotch and Irish Historical Libraries* (London, 1736), pp. 10–27; W. G. Hoskins, *Local History in England* (Edinburgh, 1959), pp. 15–

24. For some later works, see *English County Historians*, ed. Jack Simmons (London, 1978). There are biographies by Wilbur Dunkel, *William Lambarde* (New Brunswick, N.J., 1965) and Retha M. Warnicke, *William Lambarde: Elizabethan Antiquary* (London, 1973).

111. For the Society of Antiquaries, see the following works of Linda van Norden: "The Elizabethan College of Antiquaries" (Ph.D. diss., University of California, 1946), some of which has appeared as "Sir Henry Spelman and the Chronology of the Elizabethan College of Antiquaries," *Huntington Library Quarterly*, 13 (1950), 131–60; and "Celtic Antiquarianism in the *Curious Discourses*," in *Essays to Lily B. Campbell* (Berkeley, Calif., 1950), pp. 63–70. See also C. E. Wright, "The Elizabethan Society of Antiquaries and the Foundation of the Cottonian Library," in *The English Library before 1700*, ed. Francis Wormald and C. E. Wright (London, 1958), pp. 176–212; Joan Evans, *History of the Society of Antiquaries* (London, 1956), pp. 1–14. Some of the papers of the society were assembled by Thomas Hearne as *A Collection of Curious Discourses*, new ed. (London, 1775).

112. Weever, "The Author to the Reader," in *Ancient Funerall Monuments* (London, 1631).

113. Hickes to the Bishop of Bristol, May 22, 1714, in Douglas, *English Scholars*, p. 19.

114. Sharpe, *Cotton*, pp. 28–29, 80; Wright, "Society of Antiquaries," p. 207.

115. Selden to Cotton, April 4, 1618, dedication to *The History of Tythes*, in Selden, *Opera Omnia*, ed. David Wilkins (London, 1726), III, 1067.

116. So Archbishop Parker had to apologize for Walsingham's style, "crasso et levidensi" (McKisack, *Medieval History*, pp. 43–44).

117. See Evan Evans, preface to *Some Specimens of the Ancient Welsh Bards* (London, 1764). Evans' whole career is instructive; see Edward D. Snyder, *The Celtic Revival in English Literature, 1760–1800* (Cambridge, Mass., 1923), chap. 2.

118. Hearne in Leland, *Collectanea*, VI, 60.

119. See Joseph M. Levine, *Dr. Woodward's Shield: History, Science, and Satire in Augustan England* (Berkeley, Calif., 1977), pp. 133ff.

120. Thus Thomas Gale's *Antonini iter Britannicarum commentarius* (London, 1709), edited by his son Roger Gale. The latter's discourse on the four Roman ways was printed by Hearne in Leland's *Itineraries*, VI. For the Gales, with much correspondence on Roman antiquities, see *Bibliotheca topographica Britannica* (London, 1781), II; *Stukeley Family Memoirs*, Surtees Society, 73 (Durham, 1882).

121. For the following, see R. G. Collingwood, "John Horsley and Hadrian's Wall," *Archaeologia Aeliana*, 4th ser., 15 (1938), 1–42; John Bosanquet, "John Horsley and His Times," ibid., 10 (1933), 58–81; Sir George Macdonald, "John Horsley, Scholar and Gentleman," ibid., pp. 1–33; Eric Birley, "John Horsley and John Hodgson," ibid., 26 (1958), 1–46.

122. John Horsley, *Britannia Romana* (London, 1732), p. iii.

123. See the account on May 23, 1754, Society of Antiquaries Minute Book, VII, 129; other reports are in Evans, *History of the Society*, pp. 119–20, 153, 158–59. Hamilton's museum was illustrated by P. F. Hugues [d'Hancarville], *Collection of Etruscan, Greek and Roman Antiquities from the Cabinet of the Hon. Wm.*

Hamilton, 4 vols. (Naples, 1766–67). There is a life of Hamilton by Brian Fotheringill (New York, 1969).

124. Horace Walpole to Richard West, April 16, 1740 N. S., *Walpole Correspondence*, ed. W. S. Lewis (New Haven, Conn., 1937), 1, 222–24.

125. Some of that story is recounted in chap. 4 of this book. Most digging before 1800, like Gavin Hamilton's at Hadrian's Villa in 1769–71, was still treasure-hunting; see David Irwin, "Gavin Hamilton: Archaeologist, Painter, and Dealer," *Art Bulletin*, 44 (1962), 87–102.

126. Jacob Spon, *Voyage d'Italie, de Dalmatie, de Grèce* (Lyons, 1678); George Wheler, *A Journey into Greece* (London, 1682).

127. Edmund Chishull, *Inscriptio sigea antiquissima* (London, 1721); Edmund Chishull, *Antiquitates Asiaticae* (London, 1728). For earlier visitors, see Warner G. Rice, "Early English Travellers to Greece and the Levant," *University of Michigan Essays and Studies in English and Comparative Literature*, 10 (1933), 205–60. A later visitor who wrote a popular account was Richard Pococke, *Description of the East* (London, 1743–48).

128. Proposals (1748) in James Stuart and Nicholas Revett, *The Antiquities of Athens* (London, 1762), 1, v. For the Greek revival in general, see M. L. Clarke, *Greek Studies in England, 1700–1830* (Cambridge, 1945); John Buxton, *The Grecian Taste* (New York, 1978); Dora Wiebenson, *Sources of Greek Revival Architecture* (London, 1969); J. M. Crook, *The Greek Revival* (London, 1972).

129. See Lionel Cust and Sidney Colvin, *History of the Society of Dilettanti* (London, 1898).

130. James Stuart in A. M. Bandini, *De obelisco Caesaris Augusti* (1750). See Leslie Lawrence, "Stuart and Revett: Their Literary and Architectural Careers," *Journal of the Warburg and Courtauld Institutes*, 2 (1938–39), 128–46; David Watkin, *Athenian Stuart: Pioneer of the Greek Revival* (London, 1982).

131. Inevitably, they made mistakes anyway: see Jacob Landy, "Stuart and Revett: Pioneer Archaeologists," *Archaeology*, 9 (1956), 252–54. Their model may have been the Frenchman Antoine Desgodets, who measured the monuments in Rome (1676–77) and published his work, *Les édifices*, in 1682; it received an English translation in 1771. See W. Herrmann, "Antoine Desgodets and the Académie Royale d'Architecture," *Art Bulletin*, 40 (1950), 25–53.

132. Stuart and Revett were tardy getting into print and were preceded by J. D. Le Roy, *Les ruines de plus beaux monuments de la Grèce* (1758), translated (abridged) as the *Ruins of Athens* (London, 1759). See Marcus Whiffen, "An English Le Roy," *Architectural Review*, 126 (1959), 119–20.

133. Lady Montagu to Abbot Conti, July 31, 1718, in Lady Montagu, *Letters and Works*, ed. W. Moy Thomas (London, 1893), 1, 374–84. For the two controversies, see J. B. Spencer, "Robert Wood and the Problem of Troy in the Eighteenth Century," *Journal of the Warburg and Courtauld Institutes*, 20 (1957), 75–105. See also C. A. Hutton, "The Travels of 'Palmyra' Wood in 1750–51," *Journal of Hellenic Studies*, 47 (1927), 102–28.

134. One should not, I think, make too much of the undeniable differences that separated the adherents of ancient Rome (like the Palladians and, later, William Chambers) and ancient Greece. See Nicolaus Pevsner and S. Lang,

"Apollo or Baboon," *Architectural Review*, 104 (1948), 274; Rudolf Wittkower, "Piranesi's Parere sa Architettura," *Journal of the Warburg and Courtauld Institutes*, 2 (1938–39), 147ff.

135. Quoted in E. H. Gombrich, *The Heritage of Apelles* (Ithaca, 1976), p. 103.

136. See the complaint by F. Haverfield, *The Roman Occupation of Britain* (Oxford, 1924), pp. 86–87.

137. John Earle, *Microcosmography* (1628), ed. Harold Osborn (London, n.d.), pp. 20–21.

138. Shackerly Marmion's play was staged in 1641; for the perpetual joke about rust, see Levine, *Dr. Woodward's Shield*, pp. 246, 250; for a late repetition of the old satire, *Monthly Ledger*, 1 (1773), 138.

139. Camden, *Britannia*, preface.

140. Hearne, *Remarks*, x, 299. For Hearne's praise of Graves as an antiquary, see Nichols, *Literary Anecdotes*, II, 467–69.

141. Hearne, *Remarks*, VII, 371. For Hearne, see Levine, *Dr. Woodward's Shield*, chap. 10.

142. Baker to Ballard, Dec. 6, 1735, in Hearne, *Remarks*, XI, 463.

143. Quoted in Anthony Wood, *Life of Wood*, Ecclesiastical History Society, 3 (Oxford, 1848), p. 332.

144. See chap. 6 in this book.

145. See chap. 7 in this book.

146. For Bacon's view, see the section on "civil" history in the second book of his *Advancement of Learning*; for Bacon's practice, see Wilhelm Busch, *England under the Tudors*, trans. Alice M. Todd (London, 1895), I, 416–23. For the distinction between histories and antiquities, see Momigliano, "Ancient History"; Eric Cochrane, *History and Historiography in the Italian Renaissance* (Chicago, 1981), p. 444.

147. F. S. Fussner, *The Historical Revolution* (London, 1962), pp. 247–49. Camden's *Annales rerum Anglicarum Elizabethae* appeared in installments in 1615, 1625; it was edited by Hearne from the manuscript in 1717. For the composition, see H. R. Trevor-Roper, *Queen Elizabeth's First Historian*, Neale Lecture (London, 1971).

148. William Nicolson was one who remained hopeful, but his own antiquarian proclivities led him to censure most of the historians in his broad canvas; see his remarks on Temple in *Historical Libraries* (n. 110 above), pp. 28, 41.

149. Hume's deficiencies in research (i.e., his independence of antiquarian technique) were suspected by Gibbon and demonstrated by Petrie and Sharpe in the *Monumenta*, p. 6n. The complaints about previous histories run from Henry Savile's *Rerum Anglicarum Scriptores* (1596), dedicated to Elizabeth, through Selden's "Letter to Mr. Augustine Vincent," *Opera Omnia*, III, 1693–94, to the introduction to the *Complete History* (London, 1706), discussed above, chap. 6. For the chroniclers, see Douglas, *English Scholars*, pp. 134–35; J. G. A. Pocock, *The Ancient Constitution and the Feudal Law* (New York, 1967), pp. 182–228.

150. See Lawrence Echard's boast in the preface to his *Roman History*, 3d ed. (London, 1697): "There never was anything of this kind in our language before" (quoted in Momigliano, "Ancient History," p. 9).

151. Selden, "A Letter to Mr. Augustine Vincent," *Opera Omnia*, III, 1694.

152. See the modern appreciations by Harold D. Hazeltine, "Selden as Legal Historian," in *Festschrift Heinrich Brunner* (Weimar, 1910), pp. 579–630; W. S. Holdsworth, *Sources and Literature of English Law* (Oxford, 1925), pp. 148–49; Fussner, *Historical Revolution*, pp. 275–98.

153. H. Stuart Jones, "The Foundation and History of the Camden Chair," *Oxoniensia*, 8–9 (1943–44), 169–92.

154. Norman Farmer, Jr., "Fulke Greville and Sir John Coke: An Exchange of Letters on a History Lecture," *Huntington Library Quarterly*, 33 (1969–70), 217–36.

155. Degory Wheare, *De ratione et methodo legendi utrasque historias civilis et ecclesiasticas* (Oxford, 1623; Eng. trans. Edmund Bohun, 1694).

156. Levine, *Dr. Woodward's Shield*, pp. 200–215.

157. See Richard Gough, introduction, *Archaeologia*, 1 (London, 1770), ii.

158. Walpole to Lady Ossory, January 19, 1775, in Walpole, *Correspondence*, 32, 223–24; Walpole to William Cole, June 15, 1777, ibid., 2, 50 ff. See Joan Evans, *History of the Society*, p. 120; W. S. Lewis, "Horace Walpole, Antiquary," in *Essays to Sir Lewis Namier*, ed. Richard Pares and A. J. P. Taylor (London, 1956), pp. 178–203; W. S. Lewis *Horace Walpole* (New York, 1960), pp. 121ff.

159. Walpole to Cole, February 15, 1782, in Walpole, *Correspondence*, 2, 300–303. Cole had written earlier admitting that he, at least, retained "the vulgar prejudices of antiquarianism in wishing to see minutiae and things not worthy public notice, having been all my lifetime collecting such scraps" (ibid., 1, 359). His vast collections are now in the British Library. Walpole admired him and exempted him from criticism for not publishing anything (ibid., II, 115ff).

160. Walpole to Mason, July 10, 1775, ibid., 28, 210–14; Walpole to Cole, January 8, 1773, ibid., 1, 292–94.

161. Walpole to Lady Ossory, June 25, 1776, ibid., 32, 295–99. Walpole enjoyed the satire of the *Nabob* (Walpole to Cole, ibid., July 7, 1772, 1, 264–65). Walpole's *Historic Doubts on Richard III* appeared first in 1766.

162. Walpole to Cole, April 27, 1773, ibid., 1, 108–10; September 1, 1778, ibid., II, 115–18.

163. Walpole to Cole, April 25, 1775, ibid., 1, 366–69.

164. Walpole to Cole, March 13, 1780, ibid., II, 203–6. William Hutchinson's *View of Northumberland* was published in two volumes, 1776–78.

165. Edward Gibbon, *Essai sur l'étude de la littérature* (London, 1761).

166. On Gibbon's method, see Giuseppe Giarrizzo, *Gibbon e la cultura europea del settecento* (Naples, 1954); Arnaldo Momigliano, "Gibbon's Contribution to Historical Method," in *Studies in Historiography*, pp. 40–55; and chap. 7 in this book.

167. See the critical review of Gibbon in the *Göttingische gelehrte Anzeiger*, cited by Momigliano, "Gibbon's Contribution," p. 40; Herbert Butterfield, "The Rise of the German Historical School," in *Man on His Past* (Cambridge, 1955), pp. 32–61.

4. The Stonesfield Pavement

1. According to Glyn Daniel in the best recent book on the subject, "No authoritative and definitive history of archaeology has, as yet, been published"

(*A Hundred and Fifty Years of Archaeology* [Cambridge, Mass., 1976], p. 401). The only other general works appear to be, like his, limited to the recent period; see A. Michaelis, *A Century of Archaeological Discoveries*, trans. Bettina Kahnweiler (London, 1908); C. W. Ceram, *Gods, Graves and Scholars*, trans. E. B. Garside (New York, 1952); Glyn Daniel, *The Idea of Pre-history* (London, 1962); Robert F. Heizer, ed., *Man's Discovery of His Past* (Englewood Cliffs, N.J., 1962). The universal opinion remains that of O. G. S. Crawford: "All archaeology before the nineteenth century was pre-scientific" (*Archaeology in the Field* [London, 1953], p. 21). But the history of the discipline before 1900—when it belonged to the "antiquaries"—remains crucial to understanding the nineteenth-century achievement and is more significant than is usually appreciated, as I hope the Stonesfield example will show. For the English background there is hardly anything of use except T. D. Kendrick, *British Antiquity* (London, 1950), and Joan Evans, *History of the Society of Antiquaries* (London, 1956). There are some helpful treatments of particular antiquaries, like Stuart Piggott on William Camden in the *Proceedings of the British Academy*, 37 (1951), and on William Stukeley (Oxford, 1950), but the field remains largely *terra incognita*. I have set out my own views on the historiographical background in Chapter 6 of this book and *Dr. Woodward's Shield: History, Science, and Satire in Augustan England* (Berkeley, Calif., 1977).

2. The only modern accounts appear to be M. V. Taylor, "The Roman Tesselated Pavement at Stonesfield, Oxon.," *Oxoniensia*, 6 (1941), 3–8; Victoria County History, *Oxfordshire* (London, 1933), I, 315–16.

3. Thomas Hearne, *Remarks and Collections*, III, ed. C. E. Doble, Oxford Historical Society, 13 (Oxford, 1889), pp. 296, 297, 395–96.

4. Hearne, *Remarks*, III, 397. A thyrsus was a rod or staff associated with Dionysus, with the Bacchic celebrations, and with Bacchus himself. Ovid describes his thyrsus as "a spear enveloped in vine-leaves" (*Metamorphoses* III.667).

5. Bobart to Harley, February 11, 1712 (copy), British Museum Add. MS. 4253, ff. 54–54v; Urry to Harley, February 11, 1712, Historical Manuscript Commission Reports, *Portland MSS.*, V, 142.

6. Hearne, *Remarks*, III, 401.

7. Ibid., pp. 400–401, 402.

8. Urry to Harley, February 17, 1712, *Portland MSS.*, V, 144–45.

9. Bedford to Hearne, March 11, 1712, Bodleian Library MS. Rawl. Letter 13, f. 119.

10. Charlett to Lloyd, February 9, 1712, in Lloyd Letters, Hardwick Court MSS., Box 74, f. 27 (I am grateful to the present owner, Miss O. K. Lloyd-Baker, and to Col. A. B. Lloyd-Baker for permission to see and use this letter). Charlett had learned of the pavement on February 1 and swiftly sent word of it to Hans Sloane and others. See Charlett to the Rev. Thomas Isted, February 1, 1712, British Museum Sloane MS. 4065, ff. 18–19; William Bishop to Sloane, February 12, 1712, ibid., f. 21.

11. February 14, 1712, Royal Society MSS., Journal Book 10, p. 362.

12. Ibid.

13. Royal Society MSS., Classified Papers, 16 (1660–1740), no. 41.

14. Royal Society Journal Book 10, pp. 366–67.

15. Harwood had submitted some remarks on a newly discovered Roman hypocaust in 1701 (*Philosophical Transactions*, 25 [1701], 2228–30).

16. Royal Society Journal Book 10, pp. 369, 396.

17. Hearne, *Remarks*, III, 297. Elsewhere, Hearne wrote next to his denial of its Roman origin, "This I writ down hastily; but I soon after perceiv'd that the Pavement is Roman, and so I guess'd it at first sight and upon the first Account I receiv'd of it" (ibid., 395n). See also pp. 318–19, 397.

18. William Camden, *Britannia* (London, 1695), fig. 7, p. 697. The Monmouthshire pavement is described on p. 607; see also pp. 247, 451, 558, 607.

19. For the following, see the *Diary of Abraham De la Pryme*, ed. Charles De la Pryme, Surtees Society, 54 (Durham, 1870), pp. 209–10; *Philosophical Transactions*, 22 (1700), 561–67.

20. February 13, 1694, Bodleian MS. Ashmole 1817a, ff. 246–47.

21. Additions to Lancashire, Camden, *Britannia*, p. 451.

22. *Correspondence of Jonathan Swift*, ed. Harold Williams (Oxford, 1963), I, 139–41.

23. John Nichols, *The History and Antiquities of the County of Leicester* (London, 1795), I, pt. 1, 8; *Philosophical Transactions*, 27 (1710–12), 324–25; Royal Society Journal Book 10, p. 247.

24. Abraham De la Pryme and Thomas Hearne for example both cite Joannis Ciampini, *Vetera monumenta*, and everyone seems to have known the model discussion of a pavement at Lyons by Jacob Spon in his *Recherches curieuses d'antiquité* (1683). Arnaldo Momigliano complains that no one yet has described this literature ("Ancient History and the Antiquarian," in *Studies in Historiography* [New York, 1966], p. 17).

25. See Robert Plot, *Natural History of Oxfordshire* (Oxford, 1677), pp. 327–28; John Morton, *Natural History of Northamptonshire* (London, 1712), pp. 527–29. The British Museum copy has Morton's notes with additions about the pavements.

26. Hearne, *Remarks*, III, 297, 319, 321, 324, 326.

27. Ibid., pp. 403, 408, 369, 425.

28. *The Itinerary of John Leland*, ed. Thomas Hearne, 9 vols. (Oxford, 1710–17). VII (1711), ix–xxxix. It was also issued separately.

29. Ibid., p. xi. For the term *museum opus* [mosaic work], see R. P. Hinks, *Catalogue of the Greek, Etruscan, and Roman Paintings in the British Museum* (London, 1933), p. xlv.

30. Privately, Hearne noticed the influence of Plot on "abundance of People," in framing the military hypothesis (*Remarks*, III, 309, 311).

31. Leland, *Itinerary*, III, preface, p. lv.

32. "It was very well approv'd of and is by Order hung up over the spurious Cutt, or fiction shall I call it, which they had before. Your Itinerary was very much commended" (Rawlinson to Hearne, June 19, 1713, Bodleian MS. Rawl. Lett. 16, f.344). See also Royal Society Journal Book 10, p. 501.

33. Woodward to Hearne, August 19, 1712, Bodleian MS. Rawl. Lett. 18, f.146; Thoresby to Hearne, August 20, 1712, Rawl. Lett. 17, f. 7.

34. Hearne to Richard Richardson, August 12, 1712, J. Nichols, *Illustrations to the Literary History of the Eighteenth Century* (London, 1817–58), I, 302. See also

Hearne to Joas Tillard, October 23, 1712; January 18, 1713, *Remarks*, III, 473–74, and IV, 49–50; Hearne to a friend, February 15, 1713, *Remarks*, IV, 79–80. As early as February 8, Hearne had taken up the argument against Bacchus (who was then favored by the Christ Church men) and outlined his position: see *Remarks*, IV, 298.

35. Samuel Gale to Hearne, November 15, 1712, Bodleian MS. Rawl. Lett. 15, f.20. Gale's "Tour through Several Parts of England" contains a description of the Stonesfield pavement: see the "Reliquiae Galeana" in the *Bibliotheca Topographica Britannica* (London, 1790), III, 13. Roger Gale, the other son of Thomas, was also interested in the pavement; see his letter to Hearne of September 12, 1712, in *Letters from the Bodleian*, ed. J. Walker (London, 1913), I, 238–42.

36. For a catalogue of John Pointer's collections, see R. T. Gunther, *Early Science in Oxford* (Oxford, 1925), III, app. E.

37. Hearne to Woodward, August 25, 1712, *Remarks*, III, 435.

38. John Pointer, *An Account of a Roman Pavement Lately Found at Stonesfield* (Oxford, 1713), p. 24.

39. Ibid., p. 21.

40. Hearne, *Remarks*, IV, 212, 253–54, 388, 401; VI, 206–7.

41. *Joannis Lelandi Antiquarii de Rebus Britannicis Collectanea*, 6 vols. (Oxford, 1715), I, v; Browne Willis to Hearne, February 18, 1715, *Remarks*, V, 24–25.

42. Bodleian MS. Rawl. J, ff. 4, 224–27ᵛ. Pointer kept the relevant correspondence together with an eye toward publishing it; see Bodleian MS. Eng. Lett. d. 77. It contains flattering letters from Morton and Musgrave, John Kennett, and Austin Oldisworth.

43. See, e.g., John Waterman to Pointer, May 15, 1721, Bodleian MS. Eng. Lett. d. 77, f. 25.

44. Hearne, *Remarks*, XI, 133.

45. Taylor, "Roman Pavement," pp. 5–6. Samuel Pitiscus, *Lexicon antiquitatum Romanarum*, was published first in Leovardia (Leeuwarden, 1713) and several times thereafter. Bernard de Montfaucon's vast compilation appeared in Paris, 1719 and 1722–24; it was translated into English by David Humphries as *Antiquity Explain'd*, 15 vols. (London 1721–25). See I, 153, pl. 34.

46. When Roger Gale learned that Lord Hatton might become a patron for the newly discovered pavement at Weldon (1739), he wrote to William Stukeley that he would be "the first I believe England has produced and perhaps will be called a crazy one for his payns" (*The Family Memoirs of the Rev. William Stukeley*, ed. W. C. Lukis, 3 vols., Surtees Society [Durham, 1882–87], III, 41–42). In 1778, Mr. Lewis of Chepstow erected a stone building over a newly unearthed pavement to preserve it from sightseers and the elements, apparently with some success (Society of Antiquaries MSS., Minute Book 16, pp. 31–33).

47. March 1, 1713, in Nichols, *Illustrations*, I, 303, replying to Richardson's concern about frost, February 20, 1713, Bodleian MS. Rawl. Lett. 16, f. 360.

48. William Camden, *Britannia*, ed. Richard Gough, 3 vols. (London, 1789), II, 296n. Stukeley says, "This admirable curiosity deserved a better owner; for the landlord and tenant quarreling about sharing the profits of showing it, the latter maliciously tore it in pieces" (*Itinerarium Curiosum*, 2d ed. [London, 1776], p. 47).

49. Society of Antiquaries Minute Book 1, pp. 50, 133.

50. Brome to Rawlins, December 22, 1735, Bodleian MS. Ballard 19, ff. 61–62.

51. On November 3, 1737, it was agreed by the Society of Antiquaries that George Vertue should prepare as many drawings as he could of the most considerable pavements so that the members could choose the best to be engraved (Society of Antiquaries Minute Book 3, pp. 62, 63–64, 130).

52. Thus Hearne could not have known of the many other pavements with Bacchus on a tiger: see, e.g., Hinks, *Catalogue*, nos. 32a, 35; D. J. Smith, "The Mosaic Pavements," in *The Roman Villa in Britain*, ed. A. L. F. Rivet (London, 1969), pls. 3, 9, 15, 27. One of the earliest systematic efforts is Thomas Morgan, *Romano-British Mosaic Pavements* (London, 1886). But to see what systematic comparison can do to illuminate the pavements, see D. J. Smith, "Three Fourth-Century Schools of Mosaic in Roman Britain," in *Colloques internationaux du Centre national de la recherche scientifique: La mosaic greco-romaine* (Paris, 1963), pp. 95–115. Smith reports that there are about six hundred Roman mosaics now known in Britain alone.

53. Society of Antiquaries Minute Book 17, pp. 158, 163–68; ibid., 18, p. 11.

54. As early as 1737 a picture of a tesselated pavement from near Rome was shown to the Society of Antiquaries (ibid., 3, p. 13).

55. Tesselae may be seen today in the museum of the Society of Antiquaries. They are described in the catalog by Albert Way (London, 1847), p. 12.

56. Thomas Warton, *Specimen of a Parochial History of Oxfordshire*, n.d., pp. 41–42. There is a presentation copy in the library of the Society of Antiquaries dated January 28, 1782; a second edition appeared in 1783. For Warton, see chap. 8 below.

57. Society of Antiquaries Minute Book 18, pp. 397–99; 19, p. 193.

58. Red Portfolio, Oxfordshire, f. 38. There are six large drawings in all, one of which is reproduced in VCH, *Oxfordshire*, I, pl. 24, fig. 32.

59. December 12, 1782, Society of Antiquaries Minute Book 18, pp. 271–72.

60. June 9, 1783, ibid., pp. 295–99. (The pavement had been noticed before in 1766: ibid. 10, pp. 196–97.) See also Nichols, *County of Leicester*, pp. 9–11.

61. G. E. Fox, "Notes on Roman Architectural Fragments Found in Leicester and Now in the Town Museum," *Archaeological Journal*, 46 (1889), 46ff.; Victoria County History, *Leicestershire*, 1 (1907), 188–97.

62. Hearne, *Remarks*, VIII, 1–2; Society of Antiquaries Minute Book 1, pp. 111, 264. The drawing by R. Bradley was sent abroad to the famous Abbé Bignon; it was later printed by the Count de Caylus. The original is in B.M. Add. MS. 5238, f. 3. See Smith, "Three Fourth-Century Schools," p. 108n. In 1722, Sloane showed Stukeley a drawing of the pavement (Society of Antiquaries MS. 265, f. 13).

63. D. J. Smith, *The Great Pavement and Roman Villa at Woodchester* (Dursley, Glouc., 1973), p. 5; F. Haverfield, *The Roman Occupation of Britain* (Oxford, 1924), pp. 80–81. The story of this pavement in the eighteenth century is recounted fully by St. Clair Baddeley, "The Roman Pavement at Woodchester," *Transactions of the Bristol and Gloucestershire Archaeological Society*, 48 (1927), 75–96. Baddeley notices several errors in Lysons.

64. October 20, 1797, in Lindsay Fleming, *Memoir and Select Letters of Samuel Lysons, 1763–1819*, privately printed (Oxford, 1934), pp. 25–27.

65. Samuel Lysons, *An Account of Roman Antiquities Discovered at Woodchester* (London, 1797), p. 15.

66. Fleming, *Memoir and Letters*, pp. 17, 18–20, 21–22, 23–25, 25–27.

67. *New Description of Blenheim*, 7th ed. (1806), quoted in Taylor, "Roman Pavement," p. 7.

68. It was dated August 5, 1803. For the rivalry with Lysons, see Fleming, *Memoir and Letters*, p. 27. For Fowler, see W. H. Ball, *Notes on Mr. William Fowler* (Hull, 1869) and Joseph T. Fowler, ed., *The Correspondence of William Fowler*, privately printed (Durham, 1907).

69. Henry Hakewill, *An Account of the Roman Villa Discovered at Northleigh Oxfordshire in the Years 1813–16*, privately printed (London, 1826); his account was incorporated into Joseph Skelton. *Engraved Illustrations of the Principal Antiquities of Oxfordshire* (Oxford, 1823), pp. 9–15.

70. Hearne, *Remarks*, ix, 55; VCH, *Oxfordshire*, 1, 318.

71. VCH, *Oxfordshire*, 1, 306–7. See also M. V. Taylor, *The Roman Villa at North Leigh* (Oxford, 1923).

5. Natural History and the New Philosophy

Preliminary versions of this paper were read at the History of Science Association, 1982, and the Princeton Program in the History of Science, 1982.

1. Jean Le Rond d'Alembert, echoing Diderot, in the *Preliminary Discourse to the Encyclopedia* (1751), trans. Richard N. Schwab and Walter E. Rex (Indianapolis, 1963), pp. 74–76.

2. For a good example by a distinguished philosopher of science, see Morris R. Cohen, *Studies in Philosophy and Science* (New York, 1949), pp. 99–106; for a subtler and more recent example, Mary Hesse, "Francis Bacon's Philosophy of Science" (1964), in *Essential Articles for the Study of Francis Bacon*, ed. Brian Vickers (Hamden, Conn., 1968), p. 138. Macaulay's essay appeared originally in the *Edinburgh Review*, 1837; James Spedding's rejoinder as *Evenings with a Reviewer, or a Free and Particular Examination of Mr. Macaulay's Article on Lord Bacon*, ed. G. S. Venables, 2 vols. (London, 1881).

3. The most useful general work is Paolo Rossi, *Francis Bacon: From Magic to Science* (London, 1968). I have tried to indicate my indebtedness to specialized studies in the notes below.

4. *Ludovico Ariosto's Orlando Furioso*, trans. Sir John Harington (1591), ed. Robert McNulty (Oxford, 1972), Bk. XIV, p. 163n. Harington applauds its "harmless mirth" in his well-known preface (p. 9).

5. The text of *Pedantius* had been edited with commentary by G. C. Moore Smith, *Materialen zur Kunde des älteren Englischen Dramas*, VIII (Louvain, 1905). It was printed first in 1631. A picture of Pedantius shows him beneath a shelf of humanist texts: Cicero, Nizolius, etc. See Frederick Boas, *University Drama in the Tudor Age* (1914; reprinted, New York, 1971), pp. 148–56, and his review of the Smith edition in *Modern Language Review*, 1 (1905), 235–38.

6. The literature by now is very large. I have found useful James Bass Mullinger, *The University of Cambridge*, 3 vols. (Cambridge, 1873–1911); Mark

Curtis, *Oxford and Cambridge in Transition, 1558–1642* (Oxford, 1959); H. C. Porter, *Reformation and Reaction in Tudor Cambridge* (Cambridge, 1958); Joan Simon, "The Social Origins of Cambridge Students, 1603–40," *Past and Present*, 26 (1963), 58–67; Joan Simon, *Education and Society in Tudor England* (Cambridge, 1966); J. H. Hexter, "The Education of the Aristocracy in the Renaissance," *Journal of Modern History*, 22 (1950), 1–20; Lawrence Stone, "The Educational Revolution in England, 1540–1640," *Past and Present*, 28 (1964), 41–80; Lawrence Stone, *The Crisis of the Aristocracy, 1558–1641* (Oxford, 1965), chap. 12; Hugh Kearney, *Scholars and Gentlemen* (Ithaca, 1970).

7. Erasmus to Henry Bullock, August 1516, *Opus epistolarum*, ed. P. S. Allen, (Oxford, 1910), I, 43–54; *The Correspondence of Erasmus*, trans. R. A. B. Mynors and D. F. S. Thomson (Toronto, 1977), IV, 43–54. Erasmus began to teach Greek at Cambridge in 1511, Croke probably in 1518.

8. Thomas Fowler, *The History of Corpus Christi College*, Oxford Historical Society (Oxford, 1893), p. 39n; for Richard Foxe's statutes, see pp. 37–59.

9. Charles Edward Malet, *A History of the University of Oxford*, 3 vols. (1924; reprinted, New York, 1968), II, 62.

10. *The Correspondence of Thomas More*, ed. Elizabeth Rogers (Princeton, N.J., 1947), no. 60, pp. 112–20.

11. Erasmus' attack on scholasticism begins with his *Antibarbari*, begun in 1488, printed in 1520 and nine times more during his lifetime; see the edition by Craig Thompson in the *Collected Works*, XXIII (Toronto, 1978). For Richard Croke against the scholastics, see J. T. Sheppard, *Richard Croke* (Cambridge, 1919), p. 17; Mullinger, *Cambridge*, I, pp. 530ff. Another contemporary attack, very welcome in England, was by Juan Luis Vives, *Adversos Pseudo-Dialecticos* (1520), which Thomas More praised highly in a letter to Erasmus, noticing that there were "certain matters treated with almost the same arguments that I once put together myself" (Allen, *Opus epistolarum*, IV, no. 1106, pp. 266–69). See Rita Guerlac, ed. and trans., *Juan Luis Vives against the Pseudo-Dialecticians* (Dordrecht, 1979); Vives, *In Pseudo-Dialecticos: A Critical Edition*, ed. Charles Fantazzi (Leiden, 1979).

12. See Paul O. Kristeller, "Erasmus from an Italian Perspective," *Renaissance Quarterly*, 23 (1970), 5.

13. Werner Jaeger, *Paideia: The Ideals of Greek Culture*, trans. Gilbert Highet, 3 vols. (Oxford, 1944); Henri Marrou, *A History of Education in Antiquity*, trans. George Lamb (London, 1956), and *Saint Augustin et la fin de la culture antique*, Bibliothèque des écoles françaises d'Athènes et Rome, fasc. 145 (1938–49); Everett Lee Hunt, "Plato and Aristotle on Rhetoric and Rhetoricians," in *Studies in Rhetoric and Public Speaking in Honor of James Albert Winans* (New York, 1925), pp. 3–60. For the Renaissance, see John Monfasani, *George of Trebizond* (Leiden, 1976), pp. 242–99; and the essays of Quirinus Breen: "Giovanni Pico della Mirandola on the Conflict of Philosophy and Rhetoric," *Journal of the History of Ideas*, 13 (1952), 384–426; "The Subordination of Philosophy to Rhetoric in Melanchthon," *Archiv für Reformations Geschichte*, 43 (1952), 13–28; *Christianity and Humanism*, ed. N. P. Ross (Grand Rapids, Mich., 1968). See also James H. Overfield, "Scholastic Opposition to Humanism in Pre-Reformation Germany," *Viator*, 7 (1976), 391–420.

14. Samuel Eliot Morison, *The Founding of Harvard College* (Cambridge, Mass., 1935), pp. 56–57. C. P. Snow's "The Two Cultures" appeared first in the *New Statesman*, October 6, 1956, and was reprinted in *The Two Cultures and the Scientific Revolution* (New York, 1961). F. R. Leavis replied in *Two Cultures? The Significance of C. P. Snow* (London, 1962). It was followed by an enormous controversy which, as far as I know, still continues.

15. "In our fathers tyme nothing was red, but bookes of fayned chevalrie, wherein a man by redinge, should be led to none other ende, but onely to manslaughter and bawdye" (Roger Ascham, *Toxophilus* (1545), in *English Works*, ed. William A. Wright [Cambridge, 1904], p. xiv). Cf. Ascham's *Scholemaster* (1570), where the sentiment is repeated (*English Works*, p. 231).

16. There is the famous story of Richard Pace about a nobleman at a banquet who blurted out, "God damn it, I'd rather see my son hanged than be a student. Sons of the nobility ought to blow the horn properly, hunt like experts, and train and carry a hawk gracefully." To which Pace replied, "I don't think you're right, my good man. For if some foreigner came to the king, a royal ambassador, for example, and he had to be given an answer, your son, brought up as you suggest, would only blow on his horn" (*De fructu qui ex doctrina percipitur* [1517], ed. and trans. Frank Manley and Richard Sylvester, Renaissance Society of America: Text Series, 2 [New York, 1967], pp. 23–25).

17. See, for example, Charles Beard, "The Rise of Protestant Scholasticism," in *The Reformation of the Sixteenth Century* (London, 1883), chap. 8.

18. William T. Costello, *The Scholastic Curriculum at Early Seventeenth-Century Cambridge* (Cambridge, Mass., 1958).

19. Mullinger, *Cambridge*, I, 566ff. See too Arthur Tilley, "Greek Studies in England in the Early Sixteenth Century," *English Historical Review*, 53 (1938), 221–39; 438–56.

20. Mullinger, *Cambridge*, I, 624; II, 90–95.

21. Ascham to Brandesby (Cambridge, 1542–43), in *The Whole Works of Roger Ascham*, ed. J. A. Giles, 2 vols. (London, 1865), I, 1, 25–27. For an early performance of Plautus at Cambridge by a group of future politicians, see Samuel R. Gammon, *Statesman and Schemer: William First Lord Paget* (Hamden, Conn., 1973), p. 17.

22. Ascham to Sturm, April 4, 1550, *Whole Works*, I, 1, 181–93; December 24, 1550, ibid., I, 2, 224–29.

23. Ascham, *Scholemaster* in *English Works*, p. 219; Thomas Nashe, "To the Gentlemen Scholars," prefixed to Robert Greene's *Menaphon* (1589), Nashe, *Works*, ed. R. B. McKerrow, 5 vols. (Oxford, 1958), III, 317; John Strype, *Life of the Learned Sir John Cheke* (Oxford, 1705).

24. Thomas Wilson, trans., *The Three Orations of Demosthenes* (London, 1570), dedication to Cecil.

25. "To the Reader," quoted in full in James Shedd, "Beret's *Alvearie*: An Elizabethan Reference Book," *Studies in Philology*, 43 (1946), 147–49.

26. John Strype, *The Life of the Learned Sir Thomas Smith* (Oxford, 1820), pp. 6–7. Mary Dewar, Smith's latest biographer, is less appreciative; see *Sir Thomas Smith: A Tudor Intellectual in Office* (London, 1964).

27. Ascham to Smith (1561), *Whole Works*, I, 2, 306–7.

28. See Winthrop Hudson, *The Cambridge Connection and the Elizabethan Settlement of 1559* (Durham, N.C., 1980), pp. 38–39.

29. For a typical complaint, by Walter Haddon, about lack of attendance at lectures, see Mullinger, *Cambridge*, II, 96; for efforts to enforce the statutes under James I, Costello, *Curriculum*, pp. 8, 12.

30. E.g., Grindal, Lever, Pilkington, Parker, Ridley, Sandys, Cox, Ponet, Aylmer. Ascham praises the students of St. John's College, "which either for divinitie, on the one side, or for civill service to their Prince and contrie, have bene and are to this day, notable ornaments to this whole Realme" (*Scholemaster, English Works*, p. 280).

31. Costello, *Curriculum*, pp. 7–8, but challenged by Lisa Jardine, "The Place of Dialectical Teaching in Sixteenth-Century Cambridge," *Studies in the Renaissance*, 21 (1974), 35n. For the statutes and their continuity, see George Peacock, *Observations on the Statutes of the University* (London, 1841), app. A; Mullinger, *Cambridge*, II, 427.

32. Victoria County History, *Cambridge*, III, ed. J. P. C. Roach (London, 1959), p. 190.

33. Eugene E. White, "Master Holdsworth and a Knowledge Very Useful and Necessary," *Quarterly Journal of Speech*, 53 (1967), 1–16; Christopher Hill, *Intellectual Origins of the English Revolution* (Oxford, 1965), p. 307; Kearney, *Scholars*, pp. 103–4.

34. The text of Richard Holdsworth's *Directions* is given in Harris F. Fletcher, *The Intellectual Development of John Milton*, 2 vols. (Urbana, Ill., 1961), II, 623–64; see p. 624.

35. Ibid., p. 637.

36. Simonds D'Ewes, *The Autobiography and Correspondence*, ed. J. O. Halliwell, 2 vols. (London, 1845), I, 121–22. For the years 1622–24, see *The Diary of Sir Simonds D'Ewes*, ed. Elisabeth Bourcier, Publications de la Sorbonne, Litt. 5, (Paris, n.d.). For Andrew Downes's Greek teaching, see the "Life of Mr. John Bois" by Francis Peck, in *Desiderata curiosa* (London, 1732), p. 41.

37. Edward G. Harman, *Gabriel Harvey and Thomas Nashe* (London, 1923).

38. Nashe, *Works*, III, 80; Harman, *Harvey and Nashe*, p. 185.

39. Nashe, *Works*, V, 68ff. Some of Harvey's scribblings were collected in his *Marginalia*, ed. G. C. Moore Smith (Stratford, 1913). Others have since appeared in Smith, "Printed Books with Gabriel Harvey's Autograph or Marginal Notes," *Modern Language Review*, 28 (1933), 78–81; 29 (1934), 68–70, 321–22; and 30 (1935), 209. See also Samuel A. Tannenbaum, "Some Unpublished Harvey Marginalia," *Modern Language Review*, 25 (1930), 327–31; Caroll Camden, Jr., "Some Unnoticed Harvey Marginalia," *Philological Quarterly*, 13 (1934), 214–18; Harold J. Wilson, "Gabriel Harvey's Method of Annotating His Books," *Harvard Library Bulletin*, 2 (1948), 344–61; Eleanor Rolle, "Some New Marginalia and Poems of Gabriel Harvey," *Review of English Studies*, n.s., 23 (1972), 401–16; Virginia Stern, *Gabriel Harvey: His Life, Marginalia and Library* (Oxford, 1979).

40. For Walter Mildmay, see Stanford E. Lehmberg, *Sir Walter Mildmay and Tudor Government* (Austin, Tex., 1964); for Thomas Smith, see Harvey's verses in

Smithus vel musarum lachrymae, in *The Works of Gabriel Harvey*, ed. Alexander Grosart, 2 vols., privately printed (London, 1884), I, p. xxv; *Four Letters* (1592), ibid., I, 182.

41. Nashe, *Works*, III, 79; Stern, *Harvey*, pp. 45–46; Eleanor Rosenberg, *Leicester Patron of Letters* (New York, 1955), pp. 323–33.

42. Harvey to John Young, March 21, 1573, in *The Letter-Book of Gabriel Harvey, 1573–80*, Camden Society, n.s. 33 (London, 1884), pp. 1–20.

43. Ibid., p. 10.

44. Ibid., p. 11.

45. Nashe, *Works*, III, 61. For the Harvey–Spenser relationship, see "Gabriel Harvey as Hobbinol," in Paul McClane, *Spenser's Shepheardes Calendar* (Notre Dame, Ind., 1961), pp. 237–61.

46. Gabriel Harvey, *De discenda Graeca lingua*, two orations appended to Jean Crespin's Greek-Latin dictionary (1581); see T. W. Baldwin, *William Shakespeare's Small Latine and Lesse Greeke*, 2 vols. (Urbana, Ill., 1944), I, 436–37.

47. Gabriel Harvey, *Rhetor*, ed. and trans. Robert M. Chandler, *Allegorica*, 4 (1979), 146–290; and *Ciceronianus*, ed. Harold S. Wilson and trans. Clarence A. Forbes, University of Nebraska Studies, 4 (Lincoln, Neb., 1945); H. S. Wilson, "Gabriel Harvey's Orations on Rhetoric," *ELH*, 12 (1945), 167–82.

48. Harvey, *Ciceronianus*, pp. 58ff.

49. Ibid., p. 69. For the Nashe recollection, see his *Works*, II, 246; III, 66.

50. See Remigio Sabbadini, *Storia della Ciceronianismo* (Turin, 1885); Izora Scott, *Controversies over the Imitation of Cicero* (New York, 1910); M. L. Clarke, "Non hominis nomen, sed eloquentiae," in *Cicero*, ed. T. A. Dorey (London, 1965), pp. 81–107.

51. "I redd over this Ciceronianus twise in twoo dayes, being then a Sophister in Christes College" (Harvey, quoted in Smith, "Printed Books," p. 79). It is possible that Harvey encountered Ramus by way of Thomas Smith, who seems to have known Ramus in Paris; see Harold S. Wilson, "The Humanism of Gabriel Harvey," in *Joseph Quincy Adams Memorial Studies*, ed. James G. McManaway (Washington, D.C., 1948), p. 313.

52. Harvey, *Ciceronianus*, p. 18.

53. Harvey's own lectures were in Ciceronian style with *clausulae*, and each was followed by a close reading of one of the master's orations; see P. Albert Duhamel, "The *Ciceronianus* of Gabriel Harvey," *Studies in Philology*, 49 (1952), 155–70.

54. According to Ascham, Erasmus and Longolius differed only a little about Cicero, the one under- and the other over-dependent on the great orator (*Scholemaster, English Works*, p. 271). Father Ong calls Ramus a "moderate Ciceronian" (Walter J. Ong, *Ramus: Method and the Decay of Dialogue* [1958; reprinted, Boston, 1968], p. 49).

55. Harvey, *Ciceronianus*, p. 75.

56. Ramus was Regius Professor of Philosophy and Eloquence, a title quite without precedent; his 1546 address was entitled "Oratio de studiis philosophiae et eloquentiae conjugendis." See Ong, *Ramus*, p. 26; Frank R. Graves, *Peter Ramus and the Educational Reformation of the 16th Century* (New York, 1912), pp. 40–47. Peter Sharatt finds the attempt at reconciliation a failure; see "Peter

Ramus and the Reform of the University: The Divorce of Philosophy and Eloquence," in *French Studies, 1540–70*, ed. Peter Sharatt (Edinburgh, 1976), pp. 4–20. More sympathetic is Craig Walton, "Ramus and Socrates," *Proceedings of the American Philosophical Society*, 114 (1970), 119–39. I have also found useful Perry Miller, *The New England Mind: The Seventeenth Century* (1939; reprinted, Boston, 1968), pp. 111–53, 493–501; P. Albert Duhamel, "The Logic and Rhetoric of Peter Ramus," *Modern Philology*, 46 (1948), 163–71; P. Albert Duhamel, "Milton's Alleged Ramism," *PMLA*, 67 (1952), 1035–53.

57. So Ramus's early Cambridge interpreter, Abraham Fraunce, *The Lawiers Logike* (London, 1588), p. 2. Fraunce took a B.A. and M.A. at Cambridge, 1579–83, and went to Gray's Inn afterward, where he must have met Francis Bacon. See G. C. Moore Smith, introduction to *Victoria* (Louvain, 1906), p. xvi; Katherine Koller, "Abraham Fraunce and Edmund Spenser," *ELH*, 7 (1940), 108–20.

58. Ascham to Sturm, January 29, 1552, *Whole Works*, I, 2, 318–22; Lawrence V. Ryan, *Roger Ascham* (Stanford, 1963), p. 148.

59. Ascham, *Scholemaster, English Works*, p. 277.

60. The usual contrast is with an "orthodox" rhetorician like Thomas Wilson, whose *Arte of Rhetorique* went through eight editions between 1553 and 1585 and successfully revived the classical Ciceronian doctrine. There are modern editions by G. H. Mair (Oxford, 1909) and Robert H. Bowers (Gainesville, Fla., 1962). Wilson was a Cambridge friend of Cheke, Smith, Ascham, et al., and much respected by Harvey. See Russell Wagner, "Thomas Wilson's *Arte of Rhetorique*," *Speech Monographs*, 27 (1960), 1–32; Albert J. Schmidt, "Thomas Wilson, Tudor Scholar-Statesman," *Huntington Library Quarterly*, 20 (1957), 205–18; Schmidt, "Thomas Wilson and the Tudor Commonwealth," ibid., 23 (1959–60), 49–60.

61. See Lisa Jardine: "Lorenzo Valla and the Intellectual Origins of Humanist Dialectic," *Journal of the History of Philosophy*, 15 (1977), 146–64; "Humanism and Dialectic in Sixteenth-Century Cambridge," in *Classical Influence on European Culture, 1500–1700*, ed. R. R. Bolgar (Cambridge, 1976), pp. 141–54; "The Place of Dialectic Teaching in Sixteenth-Century Cambridge," *Studies in the Renaissance*, 21 (1974), 31–62. See also Guerlac, *Vives*, introduction, pp. 1–43.

62. Miller, *New England Mind*, p. 494; Ong, *Ramus*, p. ix.

63. For this distinction, see Fraunce, *Lawiers Logike*, f. 5^v.

64. Miller, *New England Mind*, pp. 134, 138–39, 143, 148–49; Ong, *Ramus*, p. 5; Duhamel, "Milton's Ramism," p. 1044. For a good contemporary definition of the commonplaces, see the passage from Agricola translated in Ong, *Ramus*, pp. 118–19.

65. Ascham, *English Works*, pp. 243–44, 292–94. Marlowe's *Massacre at Paris*, scene 7, commemorates Ramus' Protestant martyrdom in the St. Bartholemew's Day event: "Was it thou that scoftes the *Organon* and said it was a heap of vanities?" Ramus replies, "I knew the *Organon* to be confused and I reduc'd it into better forme" (Christopher Marlowe, *Complete Works*, ed. Fredson Bowers, 2d ed. (Cambridge, 1981), I, 375–76.

66. Sturm to Ascham, September 1550, in Ascham, *Whole Works*, I, 2, 195–207, replying to Ascham, who also urges the spirit before the letter (ibid., I, 1, 187);

Johannes Sturm's opposition to a narrow Ciceronianism is expressed in a work that appeared in England almost simultaneously with the *Scholemaster*; see his *Ritch Storehouse or Treasurie for Nobilitye* (London, 1570), pp. 32ff., 39ᵛ. Ascham's view of Ciceronian imitation appears in the *Scholemaster, English Works*, pp. 243–44, 292–94, and in a letter to Sturm, c. 1568, *Whole Works*, II, 174–91.

67. Harvey's first published work was a tribute to Ramus (1575); see Warren B. Austin, "Gabriel Harvey's 'Lost' Ode on Ramus," *Modern Language Notes*, 6 (1946), 242–47. Lawrence Chaderton also lectured on Ramus at Cambridge between 1571 and 1575: see W. S. Howell, *Logic and Rhetoric in England 1500–1700* (New York, 1961), p. 179.

68. Harvey, *Marginalia*, p. 117.

69. Ibid., p. 127.

70. Quoted in Harvey, *Ciceronianus*, pp. 34–43.

71. Lisa Jardine, *Francis Bacon: Discovery and the Art of Discourse* (Cambridge, 1974), chap. 2; Howell, *Logic and Rhetoric*, chaps. 3–4. Temple became Sidney's secretary and was very likely known to Bacon. Father Ong characterizes Temple as a Latin Gabriel Harvey and his rival Everard Digby as a Latin Tom Nashe; see Walter Ong, *Ramus and Talon Inventory* (Cambridge, Mass., 1965), pp. 506–10. For the very different Oxford situation and the reaction to Ramus there, see James McConica, "Humanism and Aristotle in Tudor Oxford," *English Historical Review*, 94 (1979), 291–317.

72. Harvey, *Marginalia*, pp. 94, 96, 147, 156, 195, etc. Harvey to Spenser in Harvey, *Works*, I, 69; Harvey to Young, *Letter-Book*, pp. 78–79; Harvey to Wood, ibid., p. 182. See T. H. Jameson, "The Machiavellianism of Gabriel Harvey," *PMLA*, 56 (1941), 645–46. For Harvey and Castiglione, see George L. Barnett, "Gabriel Harvey's *Castilio sive Aulicus* and *De Aulica*," *Studies in Philology*, 42 (1945), 146–63; Caroline Rautz-Rees, "Some Notes of Gabriel Harvey's in Hoby's Translation of Castiglione's *Courtier* (1561)," *PMLA*, 25 (1910), 608–39.

73. Harvey, *Marginalia*, pp. 223–24.

74. Nashe, *Works*, III, 73–77. For satires directed against Harvey within the university, see ibid., III, 80, and Warren B. Austin, "William Withie's Notebook: Lampoons on John Lily and Gabriel Harvey," *Review of English Studies*, 23 (1947), 297–309.

75. In Harvey's third letter to Spenser (or more likely to Smith's secretary, John Wood), Harvey compares his allegiance to civil law with Spenser's to common law: "We grant you the superioritye in some speciall particularityes concerning owre owne cuntrye, so as you must needes acknowledge as your masters in all generall poyntes of government"; see Josephine Waters Bennett, "Spenser and Gabriel Harvey's *Letter-Book*," *Modern Philology*, 29 (1931–32), 175–77.

76. Harvey, *Marginalia*, pp. 151, 156.

77. Ibid., pp. 157, 192, 107, 196, 91, 122, 141, 202.

78. Ibid., pp. 223–24.

79. Ibid., pp. 96–97.

80. Ibid., p. 113. The proverb was popular in England at least from the time of Chaucer; it was employed by Queen Elizabeth on at least one occasion (Mandell Creighton, *Queen Elizabeth* [London, 1899], p. 284).

81. Harvey, *Works*, I, 40–66. See also Gerald Snare, "Satire, Logic, and Rhetoric in Harvey's Letter to Spenser," *Tulane Studies in English*, 18 (1970), 17–33.

82. Harvey, *Marginalia*, pp. 212–13.

83. Ibid., pp. 160–61, 162–63.

84. Stern, *Harvey*, pp. 143, 167–68; F. R. Johnson, *Astronomical Thought in Renaissance England* (Baltimore, Md., 1937), pp. 191–92.

85. Harvey, *Marginalia*, pp. 211–12.

86. Ibid., p. 161.

87. In 1564, Ascham advised the Earl of Leicester against mathematics for fear of "injury in charging Tully's wisdom with Euclid's pricks and lines; the one doctrine is better of itself, apter for your nature, fitter for your place than the other" (*Whole Works*, II, 101–4).

88. Robert Recorde, *Grounde of Artes* (1542), quoted from the 1610 edition by F. R. Johnson and Sanford V. Larkey, "Robert Recorde's Mathematical Teaching and the Anti-Aristotelian Movement," *Huntington Library Record*, 7 (1935), 83.

89. Thomas Digges, *A Geometrical Practical Treatise Named Pantometria*, 2d ed. (London, 1591), dedication.

90. Johnson, *Astronomical Thought*, pp. 170, 173.

91. Harvey, *Works*, II, 289–90.

92. J. L. E. Dreyer, *A History of Astronomy from Thales to Kepler*, 2d ed. (New York, 1953), pp. 358–59, 401.

93. Harvey, *Marginalia*, p. 195.

94. Ibid., introduction, pp. 75–76.

95. Nashe, *Works*, I, 195; nevertheless, Richard Harvey was appointed praelector in philosophy, 1583–84.

96. Bacon's future patron studied Ramus at Cambridge in 1577; see Harvey, *Marginalia*, p. 43.

97. They published together *An Astrological Discourse* by Richard Harvey and *An Astrological Addition* by John Harvey (1583): "My brother Gabriel beeing of him selfe otherwise affected, hath not disliked either of my brother Richard's or of my exercise of this kind" (Harvey, *Marginalia*, p. 44).

98. Harvey to Spenser (1580), *Works*, I, 66. But see Harvey's note to Sacrobosco's *De sphaera*: "He is ignorant and unjust who spurns astrological judgments in so far as they prove artfully from natural causes to natural effects, from moral causes to moral effects, and finally from political causes to political effects" (quoted in Stern, *Harvey*, pp. 169–70).

99. Harvey, *Marginalia*, p. 131.

100. Ibid., pp. 72–73.

101. *The Letters and Life of Francis Bacon*, ed. James Spedding, 7 vols. (London, 1861–74), I, 108–9.

102. Rawley's life of Bacon is included in the *Works*, ed. James Spedding, R. L. Ellis, and D. D. Heath, 7 vols. (London, 1857–74). I have used the American edition in 15 vols. (1864; reprinted, St. Clair Shores, Mich., n.d.), I, 13.

103. Virgil B. Heltzel, "Young Francis Bacon's Tutor," *Modern Language Notes*, 63 (1948), 483–85.

104. See Paul H. Kocher, "Francis Bacon and His Father," *Huntington Library*

Quarterly, 21 (1957–58), 133–58; Alan Simpson, *The Wealth of the Gentry, 1540–1640* (Chicago, 1961), chaps. 2–3; Robert Tittler, *Nicholas Bacon* (Athens, Ohio, 1976). Contemporary testimonies to Nicholas are collected in Basil Montagu, *The Life of Francis Bacon* (London, 1834), note C.

105. Puttenham, *The Arte of English Poesie* (1589), ed. Edward Arber (London, 1869), p. 152.

106. Rawley in Bacon, *Works*, I, 36.

107. Nicholas Bacon, *Great House Sententiae*, ed. Elizabeth McCutchen, English Lit. Ren., supplement 3 (Storrs, Conn., 1972), p. 36; *Aubrey's Brief Lives*, ed. Oliver Lawson Dick (London, 1949), p. 14.

108. The text is given in *English Historical Documents, 1485–1548*, ed. C. H. Williams (New York, 1967), pp. 563–67. See H. E. Bell, *An Introduction to the History and Records of the Court of Wards and Liveries* (Cambridge, 1953), pp. 120–21.

109. *The Journals of all the Parliaments during the Reign of Queen Elizabeth*, ed. Sir Simonds D'Ewes (London, 1682), p. 12. For other educational activities by Nicholas, see Tittler, *Nicholas Bacon*, pp. 60–61; Baldwin, *Small Latine*, I, 393–94; Nicholas Carlisle, *A Concise Description of the Endowed Grammar Schools in England and Wales*, 2 vols. (London, 1818), I, 514–18.

110. Marjorie K. McIntosh, "Sir Anthony Cooke: Tudor Humanist, Educator and Religious Reformer," *Proceedings of the American Philosophical Society*, 119 (1975), 233–50.

111. McCutchen in N. Bacon, *Sententiae*, p. 42; Tittler, *Nicolas Bacon*, p. 57. See Ruth Hughey, "Lady Anne Bacon's Translations," *Review of English Studies*, 10 (1934), 211.

112. Montagu, *Bacon*, pp. xx–xxi.

113. Simpson, *Wealth*, pp. 103–5.

114. Joel Epstein, *Francis Bacon, A Political Biography* (Athens, Ohio, 1977), p. 32, n. 11.

115. Kocher, "Bacon and His Father," pp. 139–40, 149–50. For other significant recollections of his father, see Montagu, *Bacon*, notes XX, LL; Spedding, *Letters and Life*, I, 14, 361–63; II, 60–62; V, 241–44.

116. Sir George Paule, *The Life of the Most Reverend and Religious Prelate John Whitgift* (London, 1612), p. 17. See also John Strype, *Life and Acts of John Whitgift*, 3 vols. (Oxford, 1822), I, 156–57; Powel Mills Dawley, *John Whitgift and the English Reformation* (New York, 1954).

117. So Boas, *University Drama*, p. 149, and McKerrow in Nashe, *Works*, I, 303; Wingfield was a successful rival of Harvey for public orator in 1581.

118. S. R. Maitland, "Archbishop Whitgift's College Pupils," *British Magazine*, 32 (1847), 361–79, 508–28, 650–56; 33 (1848), 17–31, 185–96, 444–63. The Bacons' expenses (pp. 444–63) were for the period April 5, 1573 to Christmas of 1575.

119. At one point (1594) Bacon even thought of returning to Cambridge to spend his life "in studies and contemplations without looking back" (Bacon to Essex, *Letters and Life*, I, 297). For other contacts with Cambridge, see Mullinger, *Cambridge*, II, 465; for his career at Gray's Inn, Brian Vickers, *Francis Bacon and Renaissance Prose* (Cambridge, 1968), p. 271n. For the influence of Bacon's legal

career on his philosophical outlook, see the suggestions of Paul Kocher, "Francis Bacon on the Science of Jurisprudence," *Journal of the History of Ideas*, 18 (1957), 3–26; W. S. Holdsworth, *A History of English Law* (London, 1945), V, 238–54, 485–89.

120. Bacon, *Tempus partus masculus*, in *Works*, III, 523ff. There is a translation in Benjamin Farrington, *The Philosophy of Francis Bacon* (1964; reprinted Chicago, 1966), pp. 59–73. See Fulton Anderson, *The Philosophy of Francis Bacon* (Chicago, 1948), pp. 44–47.

121. *Letters and Life*, III, 82–83, 87.

122. In 1604, Bacon became learned counsel with a pension; in 1607, solicitor (*Letters and Life*, III, 217, 362). His reputation as an orator is attested by Archbishop Thomas Tenison: "'Twas well for Cicero, and the Honor of his Orations, that the Lord Bacon compos'd his in another Language" (*Baconiana* [London, 1679], pp. 62, 97). For other contemporary compliments, see Robert Hannah, "Francis Bacon the Political Orator," in *Studies in Rhetoric and Public Speaking to James A. Winans* (New York, 1925), pp. 91–132.

123. Bacon, *Advancement of Learning*, bk. I, in *Works*, VI, p. 181.

124. "To make doubtful things certain . . . not certain things doubtful" (ibid., VI, 232–33). For the English interest in Agrippa, see Charles G. Nauert, *Agrippa and the Crisis of Renaissance Thought* (Urbana, Ill., 1965), p. 376n.

125. *Advancement of Learning*, *Works*, VI, 99.

126. Ibid., VI, 105. Roger Ascham had chosen Varro, Sallust, Caesar, and Cicero, though Livy was a special favorite (*Scholemaster*, *English Works*, pp. 294, 285).

127. *Advancement of Learning*, *Works*, VI, 99–100.

128. *Letters and Life*, II, 6–15; cf. Francis Walsingham to his nephew, about the same time, in Conyers Read, *Mr. Secretary Walsingham and the Policy of Queen Elizabeth*, 3 vols. (Cambridge, 1925), I, 18–20.

129. Vernon Snow, "Francis Bacon's Advice to Fulke Greville on Research Techniques," *Huntington Library Quarterly*, 23 (1959–60), 369–78. Cf. the statutes of the Rivington School: "The Master and the Usher must see diligently that . . . the elder sort must be taught how to refer every thing they read to some common place, as to virtue, vice, learning, patience, adversity, war, peace, etc., for which purpose they must have paper books ready to write them in" (Baldwin, *Small Latine*, I, 351). See also Sister Joan Marie Lehner, *The Concepts of the Commonplaces* (New York, 1962); Jacob Zeitlin, "Commonplaces in Elizabethan Life and Letters," *Journal of English and Germanic Philology*, 19 (1920), 47–65.

130. Bacon, *Advancement of Learning*, *Works*, VI, 269–71. For Bacon's own commonplace book, see Mrs. Henry Pott, ed. *The Promus of Formularies and Elegancies* (London, 1883); *Letters and Life*, I, 297. On the vexed question of the relation of Bacon to Ramus (besides Rossi, *Bacon: From Magic to Science*, and Jardine, *Bacon: Discovery*), see Virgil K. Whitaker, "Francis Bacon's Intellectual Milieu," in *Essential Articles for the Study of Francis Bacon*, ed. Brian Vickers (Hamden, Conn., 1968), p. 40.

131. As in Bacon's letter to the Earl of Rutland, *Letters and Life*, II, 12.

132. "It is eloquence that prevaileth in an active life" (*Advancement of Learning*, *Works*, VI, 296ff).

133. But Ascham, who had once admired Osorio, criticized him in the *Schole-master* as "over-rank" (*English Works*, pp. 261–62; Lawrence V. Ryan, *Roger Ascham* [Stanford, 1963], p. 208). See also Ryan, "The Haddon-Osorio Controversy," *Church History*, 22 (1953), 142–54.

134. Bacon, *Advancement of Learning*, Works, VI, 120.

135. Ibid., pp. 121–24.

136. In the *Tempus partus masculus*, Bacon dismisses Ramus contemptuously, despite his criticism of Aristotle, as "a pestilent bookworm begotten of handy manuals" (Farrington, *Philosophy*, pp. 63–64).

137. Bacon, *Advancement of Learning*, Works, VI, 125–28; *Novum organum*, bk. 1, aph. 85, in *Works*, VIII, 121–22.

138. See the *Novum organum*, bk. 1, aph. 5, 7–8, 99–100, in *Works*, VIII, 68, 135–36.

139. Bacon, *Advancement of Learning*, Works, VI, 134–35; *Valerius terminus*, ibid., pp. 34–35; "Of Great Place," *A Harmony of the Essays of Francis Bacon*, ed. Edward Arber (London, 1871), p. 282.

140. Harvey, *Letter-Book*, pp. 166–67.

141. Bacon, *Valerius terminus*, Works, VI, 76.

142. Bacon, *Advancement of Learning*, Works, VI, 171–82; *Valerius terminus*, ibid., pp. 43–44; "Of Praise," *Essays*, p. 357.

143. Bacon, *Cogitationes de natura rerum* (c. 1604), Farrington, *Philosophy*, p. 93; *Letters and Life*, III, 82–85.

144. See the second speech in the anonymous *Gesta Grayorum* (1594), usually attributed to Bacon, which anticipates Solomon's House in the *New Atlantis* in its use of zoo, garden, instruments, etc., for acquiring a true natural history (*Letters and Life*, I, 334). Cf. "Mr. Bacon in Praise of Knowledge" (probably 1592; ibid., 124–25).

145. There is a plea for the unity of the sciences and their interconnection in the *Valerius terminus* (written probably 1603 but revised afterward), *Works*, VI, 42–44.

146. *Letters and Life*, III, 89–99.

147. Edward Forsett, *A Comparative Discourse of the Bodies Natural and Politique* (London, 1606). Forsett, like Wingfield, seems to have been known to Bacon. All sciences, Bacon was to write later, use the same method (*Novum organum*, bk. 1, aph. cxxvii, in *Works*, VIII, 159.

148. Bacon, *Advancement of Learning*, Works, VI, 191–92.

149. "Is not the ground, which Machiavel wisely and largely discourseth concerning government, that the way to establish and preserve them is to reduce them *ad principia*, a rule in religion and nature as well as civil administration?" (*Advancement of Learning*, Works, VI, 210). Bacon praises Machiavelli for writing about "what men do and not what they ought to do," and he particularly commends his "discourse upon histories or examples" (ibid., pp. 327, 359). For other references, see Vincent Luciani, "Bacon and Machiavelli," *Italica*, 24 (1947), 26–40. Suggestive is Herbert Butterfield, "The Rise of the Inductive Method," in *The Statecraft of Machiavelli* (New York, 1956), pp. 59–86.

150. Ascham to Sturm, April 4, 1550, *Whole Works*, I, 99.

151. Costello, *Curriculum*, p. 49.

152. Bacon, *Advancement of Learning, Works*, VI, 265.

153. Bacon to Egerton (1597), *Letters and Life*, II, 63.

154. Rawley, "To the Reader," preface to Bacon's *Sylva Sylvarum, Works*, IV, 155–56. See also Bacon's letters to James I (bearing the *Novum organum*), October 12, 1620, and to Father Baranzar, June 1622, *Letters and Life*, VII, 119–20, 375–77.

155. Bacon, *Advancement of Learning, Works*, VI, 221–22.

156. Bacon, *Cogitata de scientia humana* (1604), *Works*, III, 187–92; Farrington, *Philosophy*, p. 42. Cf. Ramus, whose complaint is similar (Graves, *Ramus*, pp. 168–69). The schoolmen, Bacon says, "were utterly ignorant of history" (*Filum labyrinthi, Works*, VI, 427).

157. Bacon, *Parasceve, Works*, VIII, 353–55; cf. *Valerius terminus*, ibid., VI, 69. In the *New Atlantis*, Solomon, the wisest of men, is credited with a natural history (now lost), and Solomon's House with a massive effort to renew the undertaking. *Works*, V, 355–413.

158. *Aubrey's Brief Lives*, 130.

159. A "Ciceronian structure" has been detected in Bacon's prose by Vickers, *Bacon and Renaissance Prose*, p. 132. His rhetoric has been studied by K. R. Wallace, *Francis Bacon on Communication and Rhetoric* (Chapel Hill, N.C., 1943).

160. Neal Gilbert, *The Renaissance Concept of Method* (New York, 1960), p. 224. Rossi argues that Bacon "substituted the collection of natural places for that of rhetorical places" (*Bacon: From Magic to Science*, p. 219).

161. Poetry is for Bacon "feigned history," and he finds no deficiencies (*Advancement of Learning, Works*, VI, 202–6). Poetry deals not with knowledge but with pleasure, a dissent from Aristotle and Philip Sidney; see chap. 1 in this book.

162. For the pre-Socratics, see Bacon's *Cogitationes de natura rerum*, Farrington, *Philosophy*, p. 84; for the history of "nature wrought," see *Advancement of Learning, Works*, VI, 183–84 (much enlarged in the *De augmentis*).

163. See "The Felicity of Queen Elizabeth and Her Times" (c. 1584); "Advertisement Touching the Controversies of the Church in England" (probably 1589); "Certain Considerations Touching the Better Pacification and Edification of the Church of England" (1603), in *Letters and Life*, I, 44–56, 73–95; III, 101–27.

6. Ancients, Moderns, and History

1. See, however, F. S. Fussner, *The Historical Revolution 1580–1640* (London, 1962); Christopher Hill, *Intellectual Origins of the English Revolution* (Oxford, 1965); J. G. A. Pocock, *The Ancient Constitution and the Feudal Law* (Cambridge, 1957). These very different works are all weakened, it seems to me, by their failure to appreciate the sixteenth-century achievement in England and abroad and therefore to credit the seventeenth century, one way or another, with too radical an innovation. For some very recent works on the earlier period, see, e.g., Fred J. Levy, *Tudor Historical Thought* (San Marino, Calif., 1967); May McKisack, *Medieval History in the Tudor Age* (Oxford, 1971); and Donald R. Kelley, *Foundations of Modern Historical Scholarship* (New York, 1970). For the later seventeenth

century, the standard work is still David Douglas, *English Scholars, 1660–1730*, 2d ed. (London, 1951). Unfortunately, we still lack particular studies of some of the major figures like Leland and Camden, and much remains obscure about the relationship between English historiography and the larger intellectual climate at home and abroad.

2. The last view was advanced in the influential works of R. F. Jones, "The Background of the Battle of the Books," *Washington University Studies*, 7 (1920), 99–162, and *Ancients and Moderns*, 2d ed. (St. Louis, 1961). Macaulay's views may be found in the essay "Francis Atterbury," *Miscellaneous Writings*, 2 vols. (London, 1860), II, 209–26. See now my article "Ancients and Moderns Reconsidered," *Eighteenth Century Studies*, 15 (1981), 72–89.

3. The most ambitious works remain in French: Hippolyte Rigault, *Histoire de la querelle des anciens et des modernes* (Paris, 1856); and Hubert Gillot, *La querelle des anciens et des modernes en France* (Paris, 1914). See also Arthur Tilley, *The Decline of the Age of Louis XIV* (Cambridge, 1929), pp. 317–56; J. B. Bury, *The Idea of Progress* (London, 1920), pp. 78ff. For background to the English episode, see (besides Jones), Ernest Lee Tuveson, *Millennium and Utopia* (Berkeley, Calif., 1949); Ronald S. Crane, "Anglican Apologetics and the Idea of Progress," *Modern Philology*, 31 (1933–34), 273–306, 349–82; "Shifting Definitions of the Humanities from the Renaissance to the Present," *The Idea of the Humanities*, 2 vols. (Chicago, 1967), I, 72–89; and Hans Baron, "The Querelle of the Ancients and the Moderns as a Problem for Renaissance Scholarship," *Journal of the History of Ideas*, 20 (1959), 3–22.

4. William Wotton, *Reflections upon Ancient and Modern Learning* (London, 1694). Apart from the entry in the *Dictionary of National Biography*, Wotton has not had a biography. There is a sketch in British Museum Add. MS. 4224, ff. 148–67, written by or employed by Thomas Birch in his *Life of Dr. John Tillotson* (London, 1752), pp. 332–33, and another in John Nichols, *Literary Anecdotes of the Eighteenth Century* (London, 1812), IV, 253–63. Henry Wotton's description of his son's education appeared in *An Essay on the Education of Children in the First Rudiments of Learning Together with a Narrative of What Knowledge, William Wotton, a Child of Six Years of Age, Had Attained unto* . . . (London, 1753). Further testimonies to Wotton's precocity are given by John Evelyn, *The Diary*, ed. E. S. de Beer (Oxford, 1953), IV, 172–73, and in a letter to Pepys, *Letters and a Second Diary of Samuel Pepys*, ed. R. G. Howarth (London, 1932), pp. 242–43, with Pepys' reply, pp. 246–48.

5. *Sir William Temple's Essays on Ancient and Modern Learning and on Poetry*, ed. J. E. Spingarn (Oxford, 1909), pp. 22–24, 34–36. Erasmus was generally taken as heralding the beginning of the revival of letters in the North; cf. Thomas Baker, *Reflections upon Learning* (London, 1699), p. 194; and Thomas Pope Blount, *Essays on Several Subjects* (London, 1691), p. 134.

6. Wotton, *Reflections*, pp. 317–18.

7. Temple, *Essays*, pp. 32–33.

8. "Of Heroic Virtue," in *The Works of Sir William Temple*, 4 vols. (London, 1814), III, 321–22.

9. All of these works were popular in English translations. *The History of Philip de Commines* (1489–98) was translated first in 1596 by Thomas Dannett and has

been edited by Charles Whibley, 2 vols. (London, 1897). It was reprinted often in the seventeenth century, revised and corrected in 1674, and newly translated in 1712. Paolo Sarpi's *Historia del Concilio Tridentino* was first published in London in 1619 and was translated almost at once by Nathaniel Brent (London, 1620), again appearing in several seventeenth-century editions. Enrico Davila's *Historia delle guerre civile di Francia* (1630) was translated into English in 1647 and 1678 by William Aylesbury and Charles Cotterel, and in the eighteenth century by Ellis Farnsworth (1758). Famiano Strada's *De bello Belgico* (1632) was translated by Sir R. Stapylton (London, 1650 and 1667).

10. Wotton, *Reflections*, pp. 310–12.

11. Ibid., p. 318.

12. Temple, "Some Thoughts upon Reviewing the Essay of Ancient and Modern Learning," *Works*, III, 487–518.

13. Wotton, *A Defense of the Reflections upon Ancient and Modern Learning* (London, 1705), pp. 23–26.

14. Ibid., pp. 32–33. Clarendon's work was widely acknowledged, on its appearance, to be the best of modern histories; cf. Edmund Gibson to Arthur Charlett, 18 August 1702, "It is the most instructive and entertaining Book that I ever read" Bodleian MS. Ballard VI, f. 78. Swift read it over four times with admiration (*Miscellaneous and Autobiographical Pieces, Fragments and Marginalia*, ed. Herbert Davis [Oxford, 1962], pp. xxxviii–xxxix, 295–320). See also Thomas Hearne's praise in his preface to the second volume of John Leland's *Collectanea*, 6 vols. (London, 1710–12), II, 56–57.

15. The systematic study of classical antiquities had advanced by Temple's day to the point where whole treatises were devoted both to special aspects of ancient culture—e.g., monographs on the ancient calendar, theater, or games—and to synthetic treatments of the entire culture of Greece or Rome. Two immensely popular and learned works date from this period and show the state of classical antiquarian study in England at this time: Basil Kennett, *Romae antiquae notitia; or, the Antiquities of Rome* (London, 1696); and John Potter, *Archaeologiae Graecae; or, the Antiquities of Greece*, 2 vols. (Oxford, 1697–99).

16. Temple, *Essays*, p. 34.

17. Richard Bentley's *Dissertations upon Phalaris* may be consulted in the edition by Wilhelm Wagner (London, 1883), or in the *Works*, ed. Alexander Dyce, 2 vols. (London, 1836). Charles Boyle's original edition of Phalaris was printed in 1695, *Phalarides agrigentinorum tyranni epistolae*; the reply to Bentley, in *Dr. Bentley's Dissertations on the Epistles of Phalaris and the Fables of Aesop, Examined* (London, 1698). The "examiner" was Francis Atterbury, with the assistance of various Christ Church confederates; cf. (besides Macaulay, "Atterbury") Atterbury's letter to Boyle in *The Epistolary Correspondence*, ed. J. Nichols, 5 vols. (London, 1783–90), II, 21–22; Folkestone Williams, *Memoirs and Correspondence of Francis Atterbury*, 2 vols. (London, 1869), I, 41ff.; Colin J. Horne, "The Phalaris Controversy: King vs. Bentley," *Review of English Studies*, 22 (1946), 289–303; and H. W. Garrod, "Phalaris and Phalarism," *Seventeenth-Century Studies Presented to Sir Herbert Grierson* (Oxford, 1938), pp. 360–71. There is an interesting series of letters by Wotton reporting on the Phalaris controversy to Jean Le Clerc in Abr. des Amorie van der Hoeven, *De Joanne Clerico et Philippo Limborch dissertationes duae*

(Amsterdam, 1843), pp. 81–90; extracts in J. E. B. Mayor, *Cambridge under Queen Anne* (Cambridge, 1911), pp. 428ff.

18. An extensive bibliography of the controversy is given by Dyce in the introduction to Bentley's *Works*, pp. xi–xix, reprinted in Wagner's edition of the *Dissertations*, pp. xii–xviii. The *Epistles* continued to appear and be defended as genuine. See, e.g., J. S. [Solomon Whately], ed., *The Epistles of Phalaris* (London, 1699); John Savage, *A Select Collection of Letters of the Ancients* (London, 1703), sig. A2ᵛ; and Thomas Francklin, ed., *The Epistles of Phalaris* (London, 1749), pp. iii–xvi. For other testimony in favor of Phalaris, see Eustace Budgell, *Memoirs of the Life and Character of the late Earl of Orrey* [i.e., Boyle] (London, 1732), pp. 161–66, 193; Hist. MSS. Com., Portland MSS., VII (1901), 437.

19. It may be traced in the letter of Thomas Swift to the publisher Richard Bentley, February 14, 1694–95, in *Letters by Several Eminent Persons . . . including John Hughes*, 2 vols. (London, 1772), I, 1–8. For Thomas Swift, see Robert M. Adams, "Jonathan Swift, Thomas Swift, and the Authorship of *A Tale of a Tub*," *Modern Philology*, 64 (1967), 198–232.

20. John Dunton, *The Life and Errors*, ed. John Nichols, 2 vols. (London, 1818).

21. These works appeared originally as follows: Thomas More, *History of Richard III* (c. 1513) in the *Chronicle* of John Hardyng, ed. Richard Grafton (London, 1543), in More's *Works* (London, 1557), and in More's own Latin version in 1566; Francis Bacon, *History of Henry the Seventh* (London, 1622); Herbert of Cherbury, *The Life of Henry VIII* (London, 1649); Sir John Hayward, *The Life and Raigne of King Edward The Sixt* (posth.; London, 1630); William Camden, *Annales rerum Anglicarum et Hibernicarum regnante Elizabetha* (London, 1615; 2d part, Leyden, 1625), trans. Abraham Darcie (London, 1625), and trans. R. Norton (London, 1635).

22. For Temple's use of Samuel Daniel, see Homer E. Woodbridge, *Sir William Temple* (New York, 1940), pp. 254–61. The fifth edition of *The Collection of the History of England* (London, 1685), was continued by John Trussel. Even Daniel's preface may have influenced Temple. "It is more than the work of one man," he wrote, "to compose a passable Contexture of the whole History of England. . . . I had rather be Master of a small piece handsomely contrived, than of vast rooms ill proportioned and furnished."

23. François Eudes de Mézeray, *Histoire de France* (1643–51), abridged (1667–68), trans. I. Bulteel, *A General Chronological History of France* (London, 1683). Cf. Wilfred H. Evans, *L'Historien Mézeray* (Paris, 1930).

24. William Temple, *An Introduction to the History of England* (London, 1695), sig. A2ff., pp. 299–300.

25. Abel Boyer, *Memoirs of the Life and Negotiations of Sir William Temple* (London, 1714), p. 413.

26. See Emile Pons, *Swift: Les années de jeunesse* (Strasbourg, 1925), pp. 204–19; Robert J. Allen, "Swift's Earliest Political Tract and Sir William Temple's *Essays*," *Harvard Studies and Notes in Philology and Literature*, 19 (1937), 3–12; Ricardo Quintana, *The Mind and Art of Jonathan Swift* (London, 1936), chap. 2; Irwin Ehrenpreis, *Swift*, 2 vols. (London, 1962–67), I, chap. 6, and II, 339; Woodbridge, *Temple*, chaps. 16–17.

27. In fact there are two fragments; here we are concerned with the more ambitious: see Swift, *Miscellaneous Pieces*. Swift had hoped to become Royal Historiographer; see Ehrenpreis, *Swift*, II, 746.

28. See Ehrenpreis, *Swift*, II, chap. 8; Ehrenpreis, "Swift's *History of England*," *Journal of English and Germanic Philology*, 51 (1952), 177–85; John R. Moore, "Swift as Historian," *Studies in Philology*, 49 (1952), 583–604; and James William Johnson, "Swift's Historical Outlook," *Journal of British Studies*, 4 (1965), 52–77.

29. "There's hardly a Bookseller in London that is not trumping up a New History of England, of one sort or another. Even John Dunton thinks he has still soe much reputation left as to give him leave to advance his project among the rest. And happy's the man that can get first out" (Edmund Gibson to Arthur Charlett, November 13, 1694, Bodl. MS. Ballard v, f. 70).

30. It was thought by many that Kennett was the editor of *A Complete History of England*, 3 vols. (London, 1706), and the work is still sometimes attributed to him; cf. Thomas Hearne, *Remarks and Collections*, 11 vols. (Oxford, 1885–1921), I, 280, 286, 332; III, 269–70, 339, 392, 424. But see Kennett's reply to Hearne denying that role, in Hearne, *Leland's Itinerary*, 9 vols. (Oxford, 1710–12), VII, xv–xvi. An article in *Notes and Queries*, 2d ser., 8 (1859), 343–44, assembles most of the evidence in favor of Hughes.

31. There is a life of Hughes by John Duncombe in the *Letters of John Hughes*, 2d ed., 3 vols. (London, 1773), and by Samuel Johnson in *Lives of the English Poets*, ed. G. B. Hill, 3 vols. (Oxford, 1905), II, 159–66.

32. John Hughes, "Of Style," in *Poems on Several Occasions*, ed. John Duncombe, 2 vols. (London, 1735), I, 247–55.

33. The antiquary John Bagford also thought that Mariana and Livy were the best of the ancients and moderns; cf. his letter to Hearne, September 19, 1714, in Hearne, *Remarks*, IV, 405–6. Juan de Mariana, *Historiae de rebus Hispaniae libri*, XXV (1592–1605), trans. John Stevens, *The General History of Spain* (London, 1699).

34. William Habington, *The Historie of Edward the Fourth* (London, 1648); Arthur Wilson, *The Five Yeares of King James* (London, 1643); Francis Godwin, *Annals of England* (London, 1675). None of these works was up to the original list, but the gaps had to be furnished somehow.

35. See White Kennett's note, *Complete History*, I, preface, *ad fin.*

36. Thus for the moderns, William Nicolson in *The English Historical Library* (London, 1696); for the ancients, Henry Felton, *A Dissertation on Reading the Classics and Forming a Just Style* (London, 1709; 2d ed., 1715).

37. Wotton, *A Defense*, p. 18. Temple's second edition (1699), however, had already been "corrected and amended"; cf. p. 67.

38. Wotton, *The History of Rome . . .* (London, 1701), dedication to Burnet, sig. A2ᵛ.

39. He recounts his intentions in the preface. Cf. Lawrence Echard's popular work, *The Roman History* (1695–99) in which he complains of an earlier writer, "his often mixing of Critical Learning, makes him far less pleasant than otherwise he might be" (sig. A2ᵛ). But the rhetorician was countered by the antiquarian, Thomas Hearne: "Eachard hath a good Pen, but he does not look into,

much less follow, Original Authors," *Remarks*, VI, 170; VII, 247–48. Here is the issue between the alternative historiographies in a nutshell.

40. Wotton, *A History of Rome*, VII, 377–78, note L; 453. The literature on coins is too large to cite fully, especially since many foreign works were read eagerly. Among the more popular English treatises were Obadiah Walker, *The Greek and Roman History Illustrated by Coins and Medals* (London, 1692); John Evelyn, *Numismata, a Discourse of Medals* (London, 1697); and Joseph Addison, *Dialogues upon the Usefulness of Ancient Medals*, written in 1702 (London, 1726).

41. See Rosemond Tuve, "Ancients, Moderns, and Saxons," *ELH*, 6 (1939), 165–90; Eleanor Adams, *Old English Scholarship in England from 1566–1800* (New Haven, Conn., 1917); K. Sisam, *Studies in the History of Old English Literature* (Oxford, 1953); N. R. Ker, introduction to *Catalogue of Manuscripts Containing Anglo-Saxon* (Oxford, 1957). There is a useful thesis at Oxford by J. A. W. Bennett, "The History of Old English and Old Norse Studies in England from the Time of Francis Junius till the End of the 18th Century" (1938), parts of which have appeared in the Viking Society for Northern Research, *Saga Book*, XIII, pt. 4 (1950–51), 269–83, and in *English Studies*, ed. F. P. Wilson (London, 1948).

42. Wotton, *Linguarum vett. septentrionalium thesauri . . . conspectus brevis* (London, 1708). It was translated by Maurice Shelton as *Wotton's Short View of George Hickes's Grammatico-Critical and Archaeological Treasure of the Ancient Northern-Languages* (London, 1735). The work was written apparently under the supervision of Hickes himself, who wrote the notes; cf. Hickes to R. Harley, February 10, 1708, Hist. MSS. Com., Portland MSS., IV, 477; Hearne, *Remarks*, II, 92–94, 96.

43. See Shelton, *Wotton's Short View*, pp. 36 ff; Hickes, *Linguarum veterum septentrionalis thesaurus* (Oxford, 1705), preface to Ottley, pp. xxviiiff.: "Dissertatio epistolaris," pp. 66ff. On the Ingulf problem, see Henry Thomas Riley, "The History and Charters of Ingulfus Considered," *Archaeological Journal*, 19 (1862), 32–49, 114–33; W. G. Searle, *Ingulf and the Historia Croylandensis* (Cambridge, 1894).

44. See British Museum MS. Harleian 7055, f. 4ff.; and Joan Evans, *A History of The Society of Antiquaries* (Oxford, 1956), pp. 41–44. Leland's plans were outlined in a New Year's Gift to Henry VIII, published by John Bale, *The Laboryouse Journey and Serche of Johan Leylande* (London, 1549), printed by Hearne in *Leland's Itinerary*, I.

45. Hearne's editions of Leland's *Itinerary* and *Collectanea* were accompanied by a first printing of Leland's *Commentarii de scriptoribus Britannicis* by Anthony Hall, 2 vols. (Oxford, 1709). Hall anticipated Thomas Tanner, who had been working on an edition for many years, and finally used it as the basis of his *Bibliotheca Britannica Hibernica* (1748). See his letters to Charlett, Bodl. MS. Ballard IV.

46. Camden's *Britannia* had appeared last in Latin in 1607 and in an English translation in 1610. It was newly translated (and enlarged) under the supervision of Edmund Gibson in 1695 and again in 1722; see Stuart Piggott, "William Camden and the *Britannia*," *Proceedings of the British Academy*, 38 (1951), 199–217. For an appreciation of Lhwyd, see Glyn E. Daniels, "Who Are the Welsh?" *Proceedings of the British Academy*, 40 (1954), 145–68; and Richard Ellis, *Life and*

Letters of Edward Lhwyd, in R. T. Gunther, ed., *Early Science in Oxford*, XIV (Oxford, 1945).

7. Edward Gibbon and the Quarrel between the Ancients and the Moderns

1. I have attempted to revise the traditional view of the quarrel in "Ancients and Moderns Reconsidered," *Eighteenth-Century Studies*, 15 (1981), 72–89.

2. The quarrel is generally overlooked by Gibbon's biographers and commentators, the most useful of which I have found to be D. M. Low, *Gibbon* (London, 1937); Patricia Craddock, *Young Edward Gibbon* (Baltimore, Md., 1982); Giuseppi Giarrizzo, *Edward Gibbon e la cultura Europea del settecento* (Naples, 1954); G. M. Young, *Gibbon* (London, 1932). It is briefly noticed in Michel Baridon, *Edward Gibbon et le mythe de Rome*, 2 vols. (Lille, 1975), I, 275–81.

3. Gibbon called Voltaire "the most extraordinary man of the age" (Memoir B, *The Autobiographies of Edward Gibbon*, ed. John Murray, 2d ed. [London, 1897], pp. 148–49); critical remarks can be found in the "Index Expurgatorius" (c. 1768–69), in *The English Essays of Edward Gibbon*, ed. Patricia Craddock (Oxford, 1972), pp. 116–17, 122; *Gibbon's Journal*, ed. D. M. Low (London, 1929), p. 129; *Le Journal de Gibbon à Lausanne*, ed. Georges Bonnard (Lausanne, 1945), pp. 238–40. *The Decline and Fall* is peppered with comments like the following: "M. de Voltaire, unsupported by either fact or probability, has generously bestowed the Canary Islands on the Roman Empire." See the edition by J. B. Bury, 7 vols. (London, 1897–1900), I, 26n. See also II, 252n.; V, 367n.; VI, 6, 39n.; VII, 139n., 188n.

4. See Noémi Hepp, *Homère en France au xviie siècle* (Paris, 1968).

5. Voltaire, "An Essay on Epick Poetry," in *An Essay upon the Civil Wars of France* (London, 1727), pp. 48–53. For the French version published later, Voltaire made changes: see Florence D. White, *Voltaire's Essay on Epic Poetry* (Albany, N.Y., 1915), pp. 66; *La Henriade*, ed. O. R. Taylor (Geneva, 1965), app. 1. Rolli replied in *Remarks upon M. Voltaire's Essay* (London, 1728), pp. 4–5, 9. See George E. Dorris, *Paolo Rolli and the Italian Circle in London 1715–44* (The Hague, 1967), pp. 195–204. For Fontenelle, see his *Entretiens sur la pluralité des mondes*, ed. Robert Shackleton (Oxford, 1955), with the text of the digression on the ancients and moderns (1688), pp. 159–76.

6. Voltaire, *Dictionnaire philosophique*, 8 vols. (Amsterdam, 1789), I, 329–52. The essay seems to have appeared first in the *Questions sur l' Encyclopédie* (1770). It is translated in the *Philosophical Dictionary*, 6 vols. (London, 1824), I, 112–28. It does not appear in any of the early versions (1764–69).

7. Gibbon, *Decline and Fall*, VII, 324.

8. *Dictionnaire philosophique*, I, 334–36. Voltaire's moral: "On conclut enfin, qu'heureux est celui qui, dégagé de tous les préjugés, est sensible au mérite des anciens et des modernes, apprécie leur beautés, connait leur fauts, et les pardonne" (I, 352). For the French *querelle*, see Hyppolyte Rigault, *Historie de la querelle des anciens et des modernes* (Paris, 1856); Hubert Gillot, *La querelle des*

anciens et des modernes en France (Paris, 1914); Antoine Adam, *Histoire de la littérature française au XVIIIe siècle*, 5 vols. (Paris, 1954–57), III, 125ff.

9. "Les anciens et les modernes," in Voltaire, *Oeuvres* (Paris, 1869), VI, 642–45. The dialogue appeared first in the *Nouveau mélanges* (1765).

10. Gibbon, *Decline and Fall*, III, 294–95, borrowed from Dr. Arbuthnot's *Tables of Coins* (1727).

11. For Gibbon's use of Voltaire's *Essai sur les moeurs* in the *Decline and Fall*, see Baridon, *Gibbon et le mythe*, I, 438–39.

12. See the introduction to Voltaire's *Siècle de Louis XIV* and chaps. 31–34, where Voltaire takes stock of the cultural life of the age and concludes: "Il suffit ici d'avoir fait voir que, dans le siècle passé, les hommes ont acquis plus de lumières, d'un bout de l'Europe à l'autre, que dans tous les âges précédents." For Voltaire's ambivalent idea of progress, see J. H. Brumfitt, *Voltaire Historian* (Oxford, 1958), pp. 125–27.

13. There are many other references in Voltaire to the *querelle*, David Williams has run some of them down and shown their importance in "Voltaire's Literary Criticism," *Studies on Voltaire and the Eighteenth Century*, 48 (1966), chap. 3.

14. Gibbon, Memoir B, *Autobiographies*, p. 164.

15. "Si les Anciens ont été plus savants que les Modernes et comment on peut apprécier le mérite des uns et des autres" (Gedoyn, quoted in *Histoire de l'Académie des Inscriptions*, 12 [1736], 105–6). Gibbon refers to Gedoyn in his Journal, pp. 108–9.

16. For some further argument in the academy, see W. J. Lorimer, "A Neglected Aspect of the *Querelle des anciens et des modernes*," *Modern Language Review*, 51 (1956), 179–85.

17. *Adventurer*, no. 127 (January 22, 1754), See also no. 133 (February 12, 1754): "In What Arts the Moderns Excel the Ancients"; and no. 44 (April 7, 1753): "Parallel between Ancient and Modern Learning."

18. Gibbon, "Index Expurgatorius," in *English Essays*, pp. 119–20.

19. "Indeed I inherit a respect for the ancient writers, having heard my father, a very steady reader of the Greek and Roman authors, recommend as the best plan of study, to read chronologically so as not to give one's time to the moderns till after having finished the ancients" (James Boswell, "On Parents and Children and Education," in *Hypochondriack*, ed. Margery Bailey, 2 vols. [Palo Alto, Calif., 1928], II, 96–101).

20. Gibbon, Memoir F, *Autobiographies*, p. 52. In the *Decline and Fall*, the two classical languages are referred to as a "painful though necessary attainment" (VI, 107).

21. For the *Ciceronianus* of Erasmus, see Gibbon, *Miscellaneous Works*, ed. Earl of Sheffield, 5 vols. (London, 1814), V, 259, 262.

22. Richard Hurd, "Poetical Imitation," *Works*, 8 vols. (London, 1811), II, 107–241; cf. "Paucity of Original Writers," *Adventurer*, no. 63 (1753).

23. Gibbon, *English Essays*, p. 49 (signed March 18, 1762).

24. Thus even a plea for originality which urges emulation rather than imitation pays deference to ancient authority; see Edward Young, *Conjectures on Original Composition* (London, 1759), pp. 18–20. Young testifies to the prevailing

ancienneté of the time in a letter to Tickell, March 1728, in *Correspondence*, ed. Henry Pettit (Oxford, 1971), pp. 63–64.

25. "Il n'y a jamais eu un combat aussi inégal. La Logique exacte de Terrasson; la Philosophie déliée de Fontenelle; le stile élégant et heureux de la Motte; le badinage léger de St. Hyacinte; travailloient de concert à réduire Homère au neveu de Chapelain. Leurs adversaires ne leur opposoient qu'un attachement aux minuties, je ne sais quelles prétentions à une supériorité naturelle des anciens des préjugés, des injurés et des citations. Tout le ridicules leur demeura. Il en rejaillit une partie sur ces anciens, dont ils soutenoient la querelle" (Gibbon, *Essai sur l'étude de la littérature* [London, 1761], pp. 9–10; I have consulted the Dublin translation of 1777).

26. *Essai*, pp. 11n., 15.

27. *Essai*, pp. 22–23.

28. *Decline and Fall*, I, 29n.; V, 58; VI, 158. Gibbon began reading the *Iliad* in Greek with Pope's translation in November 1761, resumed in March 1762, and finished on August 16. See *Journal*, pp. 42, 115–16; he seems to refer to the controversy on pp. 107, 113, 116. It has even been suggested that Gibbon modeled the *Decline and Fall* on the ancient epic. See Harold L. Bond, *The Literary Art of Edward Gibbon* (Oxford, 1960).

29. *Essai*, p. 85.

30. *Essai*, p. 85; *Decline and Fall*, I, 213, 319–22; II, 87.

31. J. Whitaker to Gibbon, May 11, 1776, in Gibbon, *Miscellaneous Works*, II, 151; Mme Necker to Gibbon, September 30, 1776, ibid., p. 177. See G. W. Bowersock, "Gibbon on Civil War and Rebellion in the Decline of the Roman Empire," in *Edward Gibbon and the Decline and Fall of the Roman Empire*, ed. G. W. Bowersock, John Clive, and S. L. Grabard (Cambridge, Mass., 1977), p. 34.

32. Arnaldo Momigliano, "Ancient History and the Antiquarian" (1950), in his *Studies in Historiography* (New York, 1966), pp. 6–9; "Am I worthy of pursuing a walk of literature, which Tacitus thought worthy of him, and of which Pliny doubted whether he was himself worthy?" (Gibbon, "Hints on Some Subjects for History" [1761], in *Miscellaneous Works*, V, 487–88; cf. *Decline and Fall*, IV, 98).

33. On this point Giarrizzo, *Gibbon*, is the best guide; see also Arnaldo Momigliano, "Gibbon's Contribution to Historical Method," in *Studies*, pp. 40–55.

34. The following discussion is based on my "Ancients, Moderns, and History," chap. 6 in this book.

35. "Index Expurgatorius," in *English Essays*, pp. 112–13; *Decline and Fall*, I, 223n.; VI, 22n., 128; VII, 90n., 150n.

36. William Wotton, *Reflections upon Ancient and Modern Learning* (London, 1694), pp. 317–18; *A Defense of the Reflections* (London, 1705), pp. 23–26, 32–34.

37. Gibbon, *Le Journal*, September 4, 1763, p. 23; *Decline and Fall*, VII, 99n.

38. William Temple, "Some Thoughts upon Reviewing the Essay of Ancient and Modern Learning," in *Works*, 4 vols. (London, 1814), III, 487–518; Wotton, *Reflections*, pp. 310–12.

39. See Gibbon's comment on Burman's variorum, *Poeti Latini minores* (1731), "in which the text peeps out amidst a heavy mass of commentary. The 700 verses

of Rutilius are spread over 200 quarto pages crowded with remarks. . . . Yet Rutilius is not a difficult author" (*Le Journal*, p. 177).

40. Gibbon refers to Bentley's "pénétration hardie" in the *Essai*, p. 14, and to the "tremendous Bentley" in his "Critical Observations on the Sixth Book of the Aeneid" (1770), in *English Essays*, p. 135n. See the *Decline and Fall*, IV, 445n.; VII, 129.

41. Gibbon cites d'Alembert's *Preliminary Discourse* and the article "Erudition" in the *Encyclopédie* in his *Essai*, p. 13. Voltaire was still trying to obtain a copy of Wotton's reply to Temple in 1741 (*Voltaire Correspondence*, ed. Theodore Bestermann [Geneva, 1955], XI, 157).

42. So even the apostle of progress, A. R. J. Turgot: "Time constantly brings to light new discoveries in the sciences; but poetry, painting and music have a fixed limit which the genius of languages, the imitation of nature, and the limited sensibility of an organ determine, which they obtain by slow steps, and which they cannot surpass. The great men of the Augustan Age reached it, and are still our models" ("A Philosophical Review of the Successive Advances of the Human Mind" [1750], in *Turgot on Progress, Sociology and Economics*, ed. and trans. Ronald L. Meek [Cambridge, 1973], p. 52; cf. pp. 103, 105, 114).

43. Gibbon, Memoir B, *Autobiographies*, p. 209. Gibbon's learned correspondence is in *The Letters of Edward Gibbon*, ed. J. E. Norton, 3 vols. (London, 1956), I, 1–2, 14–19, 25–58, 287–90; *Miscellaneous Works*, I, 433–86, 502–15. His very first essay was an exercise in chronology: "The Age of Sesostris" (see *Autobiographies*, pp. 79–81).

44. Gibbon, *Decline and Fall*, III, 296n. "The transcendent merit of Mr. Gibbon was, that his mind always rose superior to his erudition, which often suppresses the mortal energies but invigorated his. . . . The stomach was so strong, that all food became salutary" (Pinkerton to Sheffield [1814], in *Miscellaneous Works*, III, 579). For estimates of Gibbon's "rough and ready" scholarship, see Low in *Gibbon*, p. 64, and *Letters*, I, 387–90; Young, *Gibbon*, pp. 15–16; Craddock, *Young Gibbon*, p. 44.

45. Gibbon, *Decline and Fall*, V, 455.

46. "Wotton's reputation has been unworthily depreciated by the wits in the controversy of Boyle and Bentley" (*Decline and Fall*, VI, 32n). Gibbon criticized Terrasson in *Le Journal*, p. 44.

47. *Decline and Fall*, V, 144; Wotton, *Reflections*, pp. 23–24.

48. *Decline and Fall*, VI, 32–33.

49. Ibid., III, 144n.

50. Ibid., IV, 245–46.

51. Memoir B, *Autobiographies*, p. 105; *Miscellaneous Works*, V, 534–35; *Decline and Fall*, I, 59; IV, 104n.

52. *Decline and Fall*, VI, 35.

53. *Miscellaneous Works*, V, 534–35; *Decline and Fall*, I, 30n., 59; IV, 104n.

54. *Decline and Fall*, I, 78.

55. *Le Journal*, p. 115; *Decline and Fall*, I, 227. Gibbon may well have been recalling that formidable ancient, whose works he knew, Mme Dacier; see her *Des causes de la corruption du goust* (Paris, 1714).

56. Jerome Rosenthal, "Voltaire's Philosophy of History," *Journal of the History*

of Ideas, 16 (1955), 151–78; Baridon, *Gibbon et le mythe*, II, 666–85; David Hume, "Of the Populousness of Ancient Nations," in *Essays: Moral, Political, and Literary*, ed. T. H. Green and T. H. Grose, 2 vols. (London, 1875), I, 381–82; J. B. Bury, *The Idea of Progress* (1932; reprinted, New York, 1955), pp. 219–24.

57. *Decline and Fall*, III, 94; VII, 196.

58. Ibid., V, 275.

59. Ibid., VII, 130–31. This passage is anticipated in Gibbon's "Outlines of the History of the World" (c. 1771), in *English Essays*, p. 185.

60. *Decline and Fall*, VII, 130–31; cf. *Journal* (1762), p. 148.

61. *Decline and Fall*, IV, 160–69.

62. Ibid., I, 86n., 91n., 140n., 144n., 285n.

63. Memoir E, *Autobiographies*, p. 339n. For the circumstances of Wotton's work, see chap. 6 in this book.

64. In his preface, Wotton says he aimed at a plain style. His work was praised, however, in the *Ductor Historicus* (London, 1714), as "excellently written . . . a most exact History of that Time justified with Critical Notes, and written in a manly Polite Style" (p. 158). Gibbon recalls being introduced to the ancient historians by the *Ductor* (Memoir F, *Autobiographies*, pp. 56–57), calling it "an useful treatise" (Memoir B, ibid., p. 120).

65. See Geoffrey Keynes, *The Library of Edward Gibbon*, 2d ed. (n.p., 1980); *English Essays*, pp. 279, 281.

66. In the *Göttingische gelehrte Anzeigen* (1788), cited in Momigliano, "Gibbon's Contribution," p. 40. See also *Decline and Fall*, I, xlv–xlviii.

8. Eighteenth-Century Historicism and the First Gothic Revival

A preliminary version of this paper was presented at the American Historical Association annual meeting, December 1983.

1. Edward Gibbon, *Memoirs of My Life*, ed. Georges Bonnard (London, 1966), pp. 133–34; *The History of the Decline and Fall of the Roman Empire*, ed. J. B. Bury, 7 vols. (London, 1897–1900), chap. 71. In general, see chap. 7 in this book.

2. See Melvyn New, "Gibbon, Middleton and the Barefooted Friars," *Notes and Queries*, 223 (1978), 51–52. The *Ruins of Rome* was reprinted in *The Poems of John Dyer* by Edward Thomas (London, 1903), pp. 30–46; it is discussed by Ralph M. Williams in *Poet, Painter and Parson: The Life of John Dyer* (New York, 1956), pp. 53ff.

3. For some typical comments, see David Hume, "Of the Standard of Taste" (1757); Samuel Johnson, *Rasselas* (1759), chap. 10; Joshua Reynolds, *Discourses*, III (1770); and Gibbon, *Decline and Fall*, III, 112. In general, see Walter Jackson Bate, *From Classic to Romantic* (1946; reprinted, New York, 1961), chaps. 1–3; Carl Becker, *The Heavenly City of the Eighteenth-Century Philosophers* (New Haven, Conn., 1932), pp. 95, 109–18. According to A. O. Lovejoy, "Uniformitarianism is the first and fundamental principle of the . . . Enlightenment" ("The Parallel of Deism and Classicism," *Essays in the History of Ideas* [Baltimore, Md., 1948], pp. 79–80).

4. See, most recently, Isaiah Berlin, "Note on Alleged Relativism in Eigh-

teenth-Century European Thought," *Substance and Form in History: Essays to W. H. Walsh*, ed. L. Pompa and W. H. Dray (Edinburgh, 1981), pp. 1–14. In the vast literature on the subject, I have found the following helpful: Frederick Engel-Janosi, *The Growth of German Historicism* (Baltimore, Md., 1944); Dwight E. Lee and Robert N. Beck, "The Meaning of Historicism," *American Historical Review*, 39 (1953–54), 568–77; George Iggers, *The German Conception of History* (Middletown, Conn., 1968), pp. 287–90; George Nadel, "Philosophy of History before Historicism," in *Studies in Philosophy and History* (New York, 1965), pp. 49–73. The works of Ernst Troeltsch and Friedrich Meinecke remain fundamental; see Calvin C. Rand, "Two Meanings of Historicism in the Writings of Dilthey, Troeltsch and Meinecke," *Journal of the History of Ideas*, 25 (1964), 503–18. There are useful essays and further bibliography in Maurice Mandelbaum, *The Encyclopedia of Philosophy*, IV, 22–25; and George Iggers, *The Dictionary of the History of Ideas*, II, 456–64.

5. Jonathan Richardson, *Richardsoniana* (London, 1776), p. 2.

6. Ibid., p. 35; Carl Becker, "The New History," in *The Heavenly City*, pp. 71–118.

7. The modern tradition seems to begin with William Lyon Phelps, *The Beginnings of the Romantic Movement* (Boston, 1893), p. 92 et passim. See also Henry A. Beers, *A History of English Romanticism in the Eighteenth Century* (New York, 1916), pp. 186–220; Edmund Gosse, "Two Pioneers of Romanticism," *Proc. Brit. Acad.*, 7 (1915–16), 146–47.

8. See Arthur Fenner, Jr., "The Wartons Romanticize Their Verse," *Studies in Philology*, 53 (1956), 501–8; David Fairer, "The Poems of Thomas Warton the Elder?" *Review of English Studies*, n.s., 26 (1975), 287–300, 395–406. I have not been able to make as much use of Fairer's unpublished dissertation as I would have liked: "The Correspondence of Thomas Warton" (Ph.D. diss., Oxford University, 1974).

9. The first idea has been suggested by Erwin Panofsky, *Meaning in the Visual Arts* (New York, 1955), p. 188; and E. S. de Beer, "Gothic: Origin and Diffusion of the Term: The Idea of Style in Architecture," *Journal of the Warburg and Courtauld Institutes*, 11 (1948), 157. The second was also suggested by Panofsky: see *Meaning in the Visual Arts* (New York, 1955), pp. 186–88; *Renaissance and Renascences in Western Art* (1960; reprinted, New York, 1969), pp. 208–10. The argument about continuity as opposed to revival of Gothic is an old one and haunts the literature. The bibliography is too extensive to be treated here, but see Kenneth Clark, *The Gothic Revival* (1928; revised, London, 1950), pp. 9–35; H. M. Colvin, "Gothic Survival and Gothick Revival," *Architectural Review*, 103 (1948), 91–98; Nicolaus Pevsner, "Good King James's Gothic," *Architectural Review*, 109 (1950), 117–22; S. Lang, "The Principles of the Gothic Revival in England," *Journal of the Society for Architectural Historians*, 25 (1966), 240–67; Paul Frankl, *The Gothic: Literary Sources and Interpretations through Eight Centuries* (Princeton, N.J., 1960); Robert A. Aubin, "Some Augustan Gothicists," *Harvard Studies and Notes in Philology and Literature*, 17 (1935), 15–25; James Macaulay, *The Gothic Revival, 1745–1845* (Glasgow, 1975), pp. 32–35, 66.

10. The two poems may be consulted in James Wooll, *Biographical Memoirs of the Late Revd Joseph Warton* (London, 1806), pp. 111–24, 125–31.

11. *Odes on Various Subjects* (1746), intro. Richard Wendorf, Augustan Reprint Society, 197 (Berkeley, Calif., 1979).

12. Robert Dodsley to Joseph Warton, June 18, 1755; British Museum MS. Add. 42560, f. 32.

13. Wooll, *Warton*, pp. 133–36. It seems in fact to have been written by Thomas Warton; See Joseph to Thomas Warton, applauding the sentiment (ibid., pp. 214–15). For the ensuing controversy about Warton's designation as classic or romantic, see Julia Hysham, "Joseph Warton's Reputation as a Poet," *Studies in Romanticism*, 1 (1961), 220–29.

14. *Adventurer*, nos. 127, 133 (January 22; February 12, 1754).

15. *The Works of Virgil in Latin and English*, trans. Christopher Pitt and Joseph Warton, 2 vols. (London, 1753), with observations by Holdsworth and Spence and dissertations by Warburton, Whitehead, Atterbury, and Warton.

16. Joseph Warton, *An Essay on the Writings and Genius of Pope* (1756; reprinted, New York, 1974), I, 161, 187, 196; II, 8. The first volume appeared in 1756 and was revised in 1762; the second volume appeared after a twenty-six-year delay, in 1782. See J. Kinsley, "The Publication of Warton's *Essay on Pope*," *Modern Language Review*, 44 (1949), 91–93.

17. Samuel Johnson, in the *Literary Magazine* (1756); see William D. MacClintock, *Joseph Warton's Essay on Pope* (Chapel Hill, N.C., 1933), pp. 25–26.

18. See *The Works of Alexander Pope*, ed. Joseph Warton, 9 vols. (London, 1797), I, 199n., 7–8n.; Hoyt Trowbridge, "Joseph Warton on the Imagination," *Modern Philology*, 35 (1937–38), 80. In fact, Warton tried to steer a middle way; see the *Works of Pope*, I, 188–92n., 199n. The *Essay*, incidentally, had been dedicated to Edward Young.

19. MacClintock, *Warton's Essay*, p. 11. In a note to his version of Pope's *Dunciad*, Warton defends the traditional teaching of the classics: i.e., imitation and translation (Wooll, *Warton*, p. 49n.). In the second volume of the *Essay*, he criticized Locke for "depreciating" the ancients and applauded Shaftesbury for upholding them (II, 278–79). In 1797, he still found much to criticize in Pope, however; see *Works of Pope*, I, xxxi, lxviii.

20. Wooll, *Warton*, p. 29; Trowbridge, "Joseph Warton," p. 76. Aristotle remained for Joseph Warton "the first and best of critics" (*Works of Pope*, I, 251–53n.).

21. Printed in Richard Mant, ed., *The Poetical Works of Thomas Warton*, 2 vols. (Oxford, 1802), I, 68–95, with commentary and a valuable biography.

22. But see Warton's complaint about the burdens of teaching and administration in Warton to Hurd, June 17, 1772, "Correspondence of Thomas Warton," *Bodleian Quarterly Record*, 6 (1929–31), 306–7.

23. Thomas Warton, *Observations on the Faerie Queene of Spenser* (London, 1754), 2d ed., 2 vols. (London, 1762), II, 87, 264.

24. Samuel Johnson, *Letters*, ed. R. W. Chapman (Oxford, 1952), pp. 53–54. Johnson had already urged in his *Miscellaneous Observations on the Tragedy of Macbeth* (1754) the importance of examining the "genius of his age, and the opinions of his contemporaries" (*Works*, [London, 1825], V, 55); see René Wellek, *The Rise of English Literary History* (1941; reprinted, New York, 1966), p. 53.

25. "Of this method, Hughes and Men much greater than Hughes, never

seem to have thought" (Johnson, *Letters*, pp. 56–57). Spenser's editor, John Upton, had also advocated (in 1751) interpreting the poet in the light of his learning, though he too failed to appreciate or employ the medieval romances. Nevertheless, Warton learned much from his predecessors; see Jewel Wurtsburgh, *Two Centuries of Spenserian Scholarship, 1609–1805* (1936; reprinted, New York, 1970). John Hughes' remarks were printed as an introduction to his edition of Spenser's works in 1715 (2d ed., London, 1750), I, xliiff; there is an excerpt in *Critical Essays of the Eighteenth Century, 1700–25*, ed. W. H. Durham (1915; reprinted, New York, 1961), pp. 105–10.

26. Lewis Theobald, preface to *The Works of Shakespeare* (1734; 2d ed., 1740), in *Eighteenth Century Essays on Shakespeare*, ed. Nichol Smith (Oxford, 1963), pp. 58–84. Theobald's *Shakespeare Restor'd* had already appeared in 1726; see T. R. Lounsbury, *The Text of Shakespeare* (New York, 1906); R. F. Jones, *Lewis Theobald: His Contribution to English Scholarship* (New York, 1919). For Bentley, see the fine old biographies by J. H. Monk (1833) and R. C. Jebb (1882), and chap. 6 in this book: "Ancients, Moderns, and History."

27. T. Warton, *Observations* (1762), II, 265. (This passage does not appear in the first edition.) Joseph Warton also defended Theobald and Bentley in his *Essay on Pope*, II, 133–34, 235–37, 382.

28. *Observations* (1762), I, 15–16; (1754), p. 13.

29. *Observations* (1754 and 1762), p. 2.

30. Quoted by Clarissa Rinaker, *Thomas Warton: A Biographical and Critical Study*, University of Illinois Studies in Language and Literature, II, no. 1 (Urbana, Ill., 1916), p. 53. The idea of rejuvenating modern (i.e., neoclassical) poetry with medieval inspiration was one that Warton shared with his new friend Thomas Percy; see their correspondence (1762) in *The Percy Letters*, ed. M. G. Robinson and Leah Dennis (Baton Rouge, La., 1951), pp. 38–48. Percy's *Reliques of Ancient English Poetry* began to appear in 1765, Warton assisting. Gibbon too recognized the problem, though he did not endorse the Gothic remedy: "Among a polished people, a taste for poetry is rather an amusement than a passion of the soul" (*Decline and Fall*, I, 265–66).

31. *Observations* (1762), II, 184–98. The nearest thing is John Aubrey's "Chronologia Architectonica," which, however, remained in manuscript (Bodleian MS. Top. Gen. C 25, ff. 152–79); it was written in the 1670s and was without influence. See H. M. Colvin, "Aubrey's *Chronologia Architectonica*," in his edition of essays presented to Sir John Summerson, *Concerning Architecture* (London, 1968), pp. 184–98.

32. See Christopher Wren, *Parentalia*, ed. Stephen Wren (London, 1750), pp. 297, 306–8. Warton quotes Wren directly in a manuscript note on Salisbury Cathedral at Winchester College, MS. 111/4 (I am grateful to the Warden and Fellows of the College for permission to use these manuscripts and to the Librarian, Paul Yeats-Edwards, for his help).

33. *Observations* (1762), II, 188.

34. Walpole to Warton, August 21, 1762, Wooll, *Warton*, p. 281. Horace Walpole's *Anecdotes of Painting in England* appeared in the same year as Warton's work, with a discussion of Gothic architecture; see the edition by Ralph N. Wornum, 3 vols. (London, 1888), I, 114–30. There is an excellent example of

Warton's method, combining the evidence of style and documents, in a letter describing the Salisbury Cathedral spire: Bodleian MS. Dep. c. 640, ff. 29–30. Typical of contemporary interest and ignorance about Gothic is the article in the *Gentleman's Magazine*, 28 (1758), pp. 517–19; and the letters of Thomas Barker to William Stukeley, April 20, 1759, in the Stukeley *Family Memoirs*, I, Surtees Society, 73 (Durham, 1882), pp. 443–46; Richard Pococke to Andrew Ducarel, August 27, 1753, in Pococke's *Tours in Scotland*, ed. Daniel W. Kemp, Scottish Historical Society, 1 (Edinburgh, 1889), pp. xlv–xlvi.

35. Rinaker, *Thomas Warton*, p. 146. Notebooks and Itineraries are at Winchester College, MSS. 107–12; the Bodleian Library, MS. Dep. e. 287; and British Museum MS. Add. 11395. They appear to begin about 1760.

36. Cf. William Stukeley's *Itinerarium curiosum* (London, 1724), discussed below.

37. Thomas Balguy regretted that Warton had never seen York Minster (Wooll, *Warton*, pp. 287–88).

38. See Mant, *Poetical Works*, I, xxxi–xxxiii; *Illustrations of the Literary History of the Eighteenth Century*, ed. John Nichols (London, 1828), V, 528–29, 634–36. The digression was reprinted in *Essays on Gothic Architecture* (London, 1800, 1802, 1808).

39. Dated June 1742, Bodleian MS. Don. d. 602. Warton later found Cicero's arguments superficial; see his *History of English Poetry*, 4 vols. (London, 1775–1806), III (1781), 431 (hereafter cited as *HEP*).

40. Many of the lectures may be found among the Winchester Manuscripts, no. 108; and in Bodleian MS. Dep. d. 586–95.

41. Warton to Toup, February 7, 1767, British Museum MS. Add. 42560, f. 156.

42. James Harris to Warton, September 7, 1767, Wooll, *Warton*, pp. 323–34; William Warburton to Warton, May 9, 1767, British Museum MS. Add. 42560, ff. 159–60; Warburton to Hurd, February 24, 1764, and July 8, 1766, *Letters from a Late Eminent Prelate* (New York, 1809), pp. 359–61, 281–82. Some Warton-Toup correspondence may also be found in British Museum MS. Add. 42560.

43. Andrew Dalziel to Warton, September 19, 1777, British Museum MS. Add. 42561, ff. 68–69.

44. Wooll, *Warton*, p. 29.

45. Thomas Warton, *Life of Sir Thomas Pope* (London, 1772), pp. 134–35. There is a sketch of the decline of classical culture and its revival in England under Henry VIII in Bodleian MS. Dep. d. 619. A much more ambitious account appears in the *History of English Poetry*, I, diss. ii, "On the Introduction of Learning into England," and II, secs. xvii–xviii, where the tale embraces the Italian Renaissance.

46. For the *Linguarum veterum septentrionalium thesaurus*, see above chap. 6 and J. A. W. Bennett, "Hickes's *Thesaurus*: A Study in Oxford Book Production," *English Studies*, 1 (1948), 28–45; David Douglas, *English Scholars*, 2d ed. (London, 1951), pp. 77–97. Warton proclaims his knowledge of the *Thesaurus* in a letter to George Steevens in the Osborn Collection, Yale University, f.c. 76/2.

47. When Warton received Hurd's *Letters on Chivalry*, he wrote, "I have the vanity to say, that I was always of your Opinion in this Subject. But it was

reserved for you to *display the System*. . . . I have long been laying up materials for this work; and with regard to the influences of Chivalry and Romance on modern poetry, I may now enlarge with freedom and confidence" (Warton to Hurd, October 22, 1762, "Correspondence," pp. 303–4). An important source for both men was La Curne de Ste. Palaye, *Mémoires sur l'ancienne chevalrie* (1759), a work that Gibbon knew: see Lionel Gossman, *Medievalism and the Ideologies of the Enlightenment* (Baltimore, Md., 1968), p. 330; Gibbon, *Decline and Fall*, VI, 282–84.

48. The *Observations* developed out of a commentary on the author; there is a copy of Spenser's works with notes in Warton's hands in the British Library, C.28.47.

49. It was a commonplace that the *classical* authors could be understood only in the context of the whole of antique culture; see the remarks of John Dennis (1693), Samuel Johnson (1745), and Gibbon (1761), quoted by Wellek, *Rise*, pp. 29, 53. For Warton's generation, Bentley's *Dissertations upon the Epistles of Phalaris* (1699) remained exemplary.

50. See E. H. Gombrich, "Vasari's *Lives* and Cicero's *Brutus*," *Journal of the Warburg and Courtauld Institutes*, 23 (1960), 309–11; E. H. Gombrich, "The Renaissance Conception of Artistic Progress and its Consequences," in *Norm and Form*, 2d ed. (London, 1971), pp. 1–10. For simultaneously relative *and* absolute standards, see Panofsky, *Meaning*, pp. 208–9. Vasari was accessible in England in the adaptation by William Aglionby, *Painting Illustrated in Three Dialogues* (London, 1685). Warton, like many others, believed in the "necessary connection between literary composition and the arts of design" (*HEP*, II, 412).

51. Richard Hurd, *Letters on Chivalry and Romance*, ed. Edith Morley (London, 1911), p. 118.

52. *HEP*, I, 252. Cf. Robert Lowth, *De sacra poesi Hebraeorum praelectiones* (1753), trans. G. Gregory (1787); I cite the edition of 1847 (London), pp. 65–66.

53. So Raymond D. Havens, "Thomas Warton and the Eighteenth Century Dilemma," *Studies in Philology*, 25 (1928), 36–50; Frances S. Miller, "The Historic Sense of Thomas Warton, Jr.," *ELH*, 5 (1938), 71–92; Audley L. Smith, "Bishop Hurd's *Letters on Chivalry and Romance*," *ELH*, 6 (1939), 58–82; Hoyt Trowbridge, "Bishop Hurd: A Reinterpretation," *PMLA*, 58 (1943), 450–65, esp. 458n.

54. This transference of sentiment from classical to Gothic is discussed in Reinhard Haferkorn, *Gotik und Ruine in der englischen Dichtung des Achzehnten Jahrhunderts* (Leipzig, 1924), pp. 32ff.

55. *Observations* (1762), II, 189–90.

56. Ibid., p. 194.

57. See n. 23 above.

58. Wellek, *Rise*, pp. 166–201; Arthur Johnson, *Enchanted Ground* (London, 1964), pp. 100–119.

59. *Observations* (1762), II, 267–68.

60. Typically, even Warton continued to put the historical value of Gothic before its aesthetic appeal: "Even the dullest and inelegant productions of a remote period which have not life for their theme, become valuable and important by preserving authentic pictures of antient manners" (Winchester College MS. 111/8, ff. 88–89).

61. *Observations* (1754), pp. 101ff. In the second edition (1762), Warton promised to treat the subject "more at large in a regular history" (II, 101n.).

62. Hurd to Warton, October 14, 1762, British Museum MS. Add. 42560, f. 98. Pope's scheme had been promoted by Warburton, who sent a copy of it to William Mason in 1752; Mason and Gray had thought of developing it together, and Gray had collected materials actively from 1755 to 1758. Gray dropped his own scheme eventually in favor of Warton, "a person well qualified to do it, both by his taste and researches into antiquity"; see his advertisement to the *Fatal Sisters* (1768), in *The Correspondence of Richard Hurd and William Mason*, ed. Ernest H. Pearce and Leonard Whibley (Cambridge, 1932), pp. 36–38. As early as 1754 there is mention of Warton's "essay on the rise and progress of English poetry" (John Payne to Warton, British Museum MS. Add. 42560, ff. 30–31). Warton eventually obtained the designs of Pope and Gray and the encouragement of Warburton and Hurd. See also Nichol Smith, "Warton's *History of English Poetry*," *Proceedings of the British Academy*, 15 (1929), 73–99.

63. *HEP*, I, 209.

64. I have developed this theme at length in *Dr. Woodward's Shield* (Berkeley, Calif., 1977), pp. 114–32, 238–54.

65. In the *HEP*, Warton writes of "Hearne to whose diligence even the poetical antiquarian is much obliged, but whose conjectures are invariably wrong" (I, 87); Rinaker says that the *HEP* cites Hearne one hundred and thirteen times (*Thomas Warton*, p. 122n.). Warton satirized Hearne in *A Companion to the Guide and a Guide to the Companion* (Oxford, n.d.), p. 21; *The Oxford Sausage* (Oxford, 1764), pp. 27–28; and "Thomas Hearne Jr. to Thomas Warton," Bodleian MS. Dep. C. 638, ff. 34–35. Joseph Warton also poked fun at him (Wooll, *Warton*, pp. 347–48) but generally favored the antiquaries (*Essay on Pope*, II, 208). Gibbon defended learning, especially as an aid to understanding the classical authors, in his *Essai sur l'étude de la littérature* (London, 1761), secs. 14, 17. Of Hearne he writes elsewhere, "His minute and obscure diligence, his voracious and undistinguishing appetite, and the coarse vulgarity of his taste and style, have exposed him to the ridicule of idle wits. Yet . . . his editions will be always recommended for their accuracy and use" (*Miscellaneous Works* [London, 1814], p. 567). Several of Warton's minor works were strict antiquarian exercises: e.g., the lives of Thomas Pope (1772, but written earlier) and Ralph Bathurst (1761), and the *Specimen of a Parochial History of Oxfordshire* (1783), with a preface defending antiquarian studies. See also the correspondence with Richard Gough, Bodleian MS. Montagu, d. 2, ff. 39, 44.

66. See Hume's letter to Gibbon, April 1, 1776, *The Letters of David Hume*, ed. J. Y. T. Greig (Oxford, 1932), II, p. 311.

67. A parallel effort, but without influence on either Warton or Gibbon, was J. J. Winckelmann's *History of Ancient Art* (1764). See Arnaldo Momigliano, "Gibbon's Contribution to Historical Method," *Studies in Historiography* (New York, 1966), p. 67, and my essay on Gibbon in chap. 7.

68. *Gentleman's Magazine*, 44 (1774), 370, and *Monthly Review*, 66 (1782), 162, cited in Rinaker, *Thomas Warton*, p. 118.

69. Warburton to Warton, March 24, 1774, British Museum MS. Add. 42561, f. 22. Warburton claimed to have been the first to treat the medieval romances

seriously as a source of information about past life and manners; see his letters to Warton of November 25, 1770, and December 5, 1770, in British Museum MS. Add. 42560, ff. 231–33, and Johnson, *Enchanted Ground*, p. 18.

70. Mason to Walpole, March 29, 1781, in the Yale Edition of *Horace Walpole's Correspondence*, 29 (New Haven, Conn., 1955), pp. 119–21.

71. Walpole to Mason, April 7 and 18, 1774, ibid., 28, pp. 143–47, 382–86. The *Monthly Review Enlarged* (1793) regretted that Warton had shown "more solicitude in collecting than perspicuity and accuracy in arranging" his materials; see Mant, *Poetical Works* p. cxxvi; Mant defends Warton, however (p. cxxix). Wellek agrees for the most part, though he quotes Egerton Brydges (1822) that Warton had been able to unite the two opposite qualities of style and research (*Rise*, pp. 176–77).

72. "The Grecian Temple," writes Walpole in 1753 on a visit to Stowe, "is glorious, this I openly worship; in the heretical corner of my heart I adore the Gothic building" (*Letters*, ed. Mrs. Paget Toynbee [Oxford, 1903], III, 181). For an outright aversion to Gothic, more typical of the period, see Vicessimus Knox, "On the Prevailing Taste for the Old English Poets," and "Cursory Considerations on Architecture," *Moral and Literary Essays* (London, 1782), I, 214–18; I, 340–51. See also Beers, *English Romanticism*, pp. 211–12; Clark, *Gothic Revival*, pp. 56ff., 76. Unhappily, not all the antiquaries were satisfied with Warton either; he was attacked with great personal animus by Joseph Ritson, *Observations on the First Three Volumes of the History of English Poetry* (London, 1782); see Bertrand H. Bronson, *Joseph Ritson: Scholar at Arms* (Berkeley, Calif., 1938), I, 315–70.

73. Contracts for the first two volumes (1773) and the third (1777) are in Bodleian MS. d. 617, ff. 46, 49; a fourth fragmentary volume was issued in 1789 and an index in 1806. The work was reedited several times in the nineteenth century.

74. Warton to Gray, April 20, 1770, *Correspondence of Thomas Gray*, ed. Paget Toynbee and Leonard Whibley (Oxford, 1971), III, 1128–30.

75. Preface, *HEP*, I, i.

76. *HEP*, II, 407–8.

77. Gibbon, *Decline and Fall*, IV, 152; *HEP*, II, 407–8.

78. *HEP*, II, 462–63; I, 434; Hurd, *Letters on Chivalry*, pp. 71, 150.

79. Cf. Gibbon: "However laudable, the spirit of imitation is of a servile cast and the first disciples of the Greeks and Romans were a colony of strangers in the midst of their age and country" (*Decline and Fall*, VII, 147–49).

80. *HEP*, III, sec. xliii, pp. 490–501. See Earl Wasserman, *Elizabethan Poetry in the Eighteenth Century* (Urbana, Ill., 1947), pp. 192–252.

81. Warton to the Warden, the Rev. John Oglander, June 27, 1777, in Christopher Woodforde, *The Stained Glass of New College Oxford* (Oxford, 1951), p. 41.

82. Joshua Reynolds to Joseph Warton, July 5, 1777, ibid., p. 41.

83. Reynolds to Oglander, December 27, 1777, and January 9, 1778, *The Letters of Sir Joshua Reynolds*, ed. Frederick W. Hilles (Cambridge, 1929), pp. 58, 59–60; Woodforde, *Stained Glass*, pp. 44–45. There were two copies of Correggio's *Notte* in Oxford according to Mant, *Poetical Works*, p. 59n. For other circumstances of the composition, see James Northcote, *Memoirs of Sir Joshua Reynolds*,

ed. Henry W. Beechey (London, 1852), I, 239–41; Charles R. Leslie and Tom Taylor, *Life and Times of Joshua Reynolds* (London, 1865), I, 261–66; Algernon Graves and William V. Coffin, *A History of the Works of Sir Joshua Reynolds* (London, 1899), III, 1177–88.

84. Walpole, *Correspondence*, 12, 447; 13, 336; "Horace Walpole's Journals of Visits to Country Seats," ed. Paget Toynbee, Walpole Society, 16 (Oxford, 1937–38), p. 25; Leslie and Taylor, *Reynolds*, I, 265. Two sketches by Reynolds are reproduced in Gervaise Jackson-Stops, "Restoration and Expansion: Buildings since 1750," *New College Oxford*, ed. John Buxton and Penry Williams (Oxford, 1979), pls. 29–30, pp. 233–36; and an engraved version by Richard Earlom in Ellis Waterhouse, *Reynolds* (London, 1973), fig. 8, pp. 30–31.

85. Thomas Warton, *Verses on Sir Joshua Reynolds's Painted Window at New College Oxford* (London, 1782); reprinted in Mant, *Poetical Works*, pp. 54–62.

86. Reynolds' first theoretical pronouncements appeared in the *Idler*, nos. 75, 79, 82 (1759). The *Discourses* were delivered and printed almost annually between 1769 and 1791; see the edition by Robert R. Wark (1959; reprinted, New Haven, Conn., 1981). Joseph Warton praised them extravagantly in the *Essay on Pope*, II (1782), 394–95. "It requires an uncommon share of boldness," Reynolds wrote once, "to stand against the rising tide of Gothicism" (Northcote, *Memoirs*, II, xx). See also Walter Hipple, Jr., "General and Particular in the *Discourses* of Sir Joshua Reynolds," *Journal of Aesthetics and Art Criticism*, 2 (1952), 231–47; E. N. S. Thompson, "The *Discourses* of Joshua Reynolds," *PMLA*, 32 (1917), 339–66; E. H. Gombrich, "Reynolds's Theory and Practice of Imitation," in *Norm and Form* (London, 1971), pp. 129–34; Bate, *From Classic to Romantic*, pp. 79–92.

87. Reynolds to Warton, May 13, 1782, Mant, *Poetical Works*, I, lxxx–lxxxi.

88. Wellek too finds "no insincerity or later conversion" in these verses (*Rise*, p. 185).

89. Joseph to Thomas Warton, British Museum MS. Add. 42560, ff. 177–78. Pope had already compared Shakespeare to Gothic architecture in the preface to his edition of the Bard (1725).

90. See Stuart Piggott, *William Stukeley: An Eighteenth-Century Antiquary* (Oxford, 1950); Joan Evans, *A History of the Society of Antiquaries* (Oxford, 1956), pp. 52ff.

91. Stukeley, *Family Memoirs*, III, 379–81; I, 222–23, 324–26, 328–29, 331, 339; II, 19, 69. Stukeley designed a Gothic bridge and temple in the 1740s, neither of which seems to have been built; see ibid., I, 367–68, 370–92.

92. See Stukeley's remarks on Chertsey Abbey, ibid., III, 205–6.

93. Stukeley, *Iterarium*, I, 44–46.

94. Ibid., I, 76, 124.

95. Walpole, *Anecdotes*, I, 120–21.

96. Thomas Warton, *Life and Letters of Ralph Bathurst* (London, 1761), p. 87.

97. These are, of course, the Vitruvian virtues; see "T. Hearne to Mr. Jackson" (November 1766), meant presumably for Jackson's *Oxford Journal*, Bodleian MS. Dep. c. 638, ff. 34–35. This curious piece (by Warton?) appears to be a spoof on Hearne, who is himself being satirized for satirizing the "prevailing spirit of Improvement which of late years has been so happily deployed in adorning the venerable Gothic buildings of this ancient university." For another expression of

disapproval of the mixture of Gothic and classical at Oxford, see John Gwynn, *London and Westminster Improved* (1766), quoted by Aubin, "Augustan Gothicists," p. 24.

98. For example, at Westminster Abbey and the bell tower at Christ Church, Oxford. See Wren, *Parentalia*, pp. 302, 342; W. Douglas Caroe, *Tom Tower: Some Letters of Christopher Wren to John Fell* (Oxford, 1923), pp. 23–24, 31–32.

99. *HEP*, II, 20–22, 97, etc.

100. *HEP*, I, 396. Chaucer was for Warton a true poet, yet (he concedes) "of an age which compelled him to struggle with a barbarous language, and a national want of taste" (I, 457). Modernizing was not the answer, however.

101. *HEP*, III, xxii. Warton's interest extended inevitably to the forms of Gothic windows and their development; see his remarks on Nottley Abbey, August 17, 1767, Bodleian MS. Dep. e. 287, ff. 3ff.

102. There is a preliminary outline of "the grand Periods in which the State of Poetry received Improvement," from Chaucer to Dryden, among the Swann Papers, Bodleian MS. Dep. e. 282. Warton was here repeating the conventional opinion of Pope, Gray, and the rest of the Augustans; see Wasserman, *Elizabethan Poetry*, pp. 49–83.

103. Thomas Warton, *An Enquiry into the Authenticity of the Poems Attributed to Thomas Rowley* (London, 1782), pp. 7–8, 17. The subject had been broached first in *HEP*, II, 139–64. See Warton to Percy, July 29, 1774 and January 25, 1776, in *Percy Correspondence*, pp. 142–43, 144–45.

104. Needless to say, Warton made errors and omissions of his own; see Walter W. Skeat, "Essay on the Rowley Poems," in Thomas Chatterton, *Poetical Works* (London, 1875), II, ix. For Chatterton, see Edward H. W. Meyerstein, *A Life of Thomas Chatterton* (New York, 1930).

105. Reynolds, *Discourses*, p. 242.

106. Warton says of the twelfth-century humanists that their revival of the ancients was imperfect and premature; "their writings show that they did not know how to imitate the beauties of the antient classics" (*HEP*, II, 432). See also his excursus on Dante (III, 236–55, esp. 254–55).

107. Warton, *Enquiry*, p. 32.

108. So too we are informed that the "strictest classicist" in Vienna at this time was also the "strictest Gothicist," Hans Tietze (quoted in Panofsky, *Meaning*, p. 184). Gibbon's artistic taste, according to Francis Haskell, was "strictly conventional." He admired Correggio and the Venus de' Medici at Florence and was not at all interested in Gothic; see "Gibbon and the History of Art," in *Edward Gibbon and the Decline and Fall of the Roman Empire*, ed. G. W. Bowersock, John Clive, and Stephen Graubard (Cambridge, Mass., 1977), pp. 193–205.

Index

Index

Index

Index

Index

Index

Library of Congress Cataloging-in-Publication Data

Levine, Joseph M.
  Humanism and history.

  Includes index.
  1. Great Britain—Historiography. 2. Historiography—Great Britain—History. 3. Humanism—Great Britain. I. Title.
DA1.L47   1987   941'.0072   86-16776
ISBN 0-8014-1885-2 (alk. paper)